OBJECT ORIENTED PROGRAMMING WITH SMALLTALK/V

ELLIS HORWOOD SERIES IN COMPUTERS AND THEIR APPLICATIONS

Series Editor: IAN CHIVERS, Senior Analyst, The Computer Centre, King's College, London, and formerly Senior Programmer and Analyst, Imperial College of Science and Technology, University of London

Abramsky, S. & Hankin, C.J.	ABSTRACT INTERPRETATION OF DECLARATIVE LANGUAGES
Alexander, H.	FORMALLY-BASED TOOLS AND TECHNIQUES FOR HUMAN–COMPUTER DIALOGUES
Atherton, R.	STRUCTURED PROGRAMMING WITH BBC BASIC
Atherton, R.	STRUCTURED PROGRAMMING WITH COMAL
Baeza-Yates, R.A.	TEXT SEARCHING ALGORITHMS
Bailey, R.	FUNCTIONAL PROGRAMMING WITH HOPE
Barrett, R., Ramsay, A. & Sloman, A.	POP-11
Berztiss, A.	PROGRAMMING WITH GENERATORS
Bharath, R.	COMPUTERS AND GRAPH THEORY
Bishop, P.	FIFTH GENERATION COMPUTERS
Bullinger, H.-J. & Gunzenhauser, H.	SOFTWARE ERGONOMICS
Burns, A.	NEW INFORMATION TECHNOLOGY
Carberry, J.C.	COBOL
Carlini, U. & Villano, U.	TRANSPUTERS AND PARALLEL ARCHITECTURES
Chivers, I.D.	AN INTRODUCTION TO STANDARD PASCAL
Chivers, I.D.	MODULA 2
Chivers, I.D. & Sleighthome, J.	INTERACTIVE FORTRAN 77
Clark, M.W.	PC-PORTABLE FORTRAN
Clark, M.W.	TEX
Cockshott, W. P.	A COMPILER WRITER'S TOOLBOX: How to Implement Interactive Compilers for PCs with Turbo Pascal
Cockshott, W. P.	PS-ALGOL IMPLEMENTATIONS: Applications in Persistent Object-Oriented Programming
Colomb, R.	IMPLEMENTING PERSISTENT PROLOG
Cope, T.	COMPUTING USING BASIC
Curth, M.A. & Edelmann, H.	APL
Dahlstrand, I.	SOFTWARE PORTABILITY AND STANDARDS
Dongarra, J., Duff, I., Gaffney, P., & McKee, S.	VECTOR AND PARALLEL COMPUTING
Dunne, P.E.	COMPUTABILITY THEORY
Eastlake, J.J.	A STRUCTURED APPROACH TO COMPUTER STRATEGY
Eisenbach, S.	FUNCTIONAL PROGRAMMING
Ellis, D.	MEDICAL COMPUTING AND APPLICATIONS
Ennals, J.R.	ARTIFICIAL INTELLIGENCE
Ennals, J.R.	BEGINNING MICRO-PROLOG
Ennals, J.R., *et al.*	INFORMATION TECHNOLOGY AND EDUCATION
Filipič, B.	PROLOG USER'S HANDBOOK
Ford, N.	COMPUTER PROGRAMMING LANGUAGES
Grill, E.	RELATIONAL DATABASES
Grune, D. & Jacobs, C.J.H.	PARSING TECHNIQUES: A Practical Guide
Guariso, G. & Werthner, H.	ENVIRONMENTAL DECISION SUPPORT SYSTEMS
Harland, D.M.	CONCURRENCY AND PROGRAMMING LANGUAGES
Harland, D.M.	POLYMORPHIC PROGRAMMING LANGUAGES
Harland, D.M.	REKURSIV
Harris, D.J.	DEVELOPING DEDICATED DBASE SYSTEMS
Henshall, J. & Shaw, S.	OSI EXPLAINED, 2nd Edition
Hepburn, P.H.	FURTHER PROGRAMMING IN PROLOG
Hepburn, P.H.	PROGRAMMING IN MICRO-PROLOG MADE SIMPLE
Hill, I.D. & Meek, B.L.	PROGRAMMING LANGUAGE STANDARDISATION
Hirschheim, R., Smithson, S. & Whitehouse, D.	MICROCOMPUTERS AND THE HUMANITIES: Survey and Recommendations
Hutchins, W.J.	MACHINE TRANSLATION
Hutchison, D.	FUNDAMENTALS OF COMPUTER LOGIC
Hutchison, D. & Silvester, P.	COMPUTER LOGIC
Koopman, P.	STACK COMPUTERS
Kenning, M.-M. & Kenning, M.J.	COMPUTERS AND LANGUAGE LEARNING: Current Theory and Practice
Koskimies, K. & Paaki, J.	AUTOMATING LANGUAGE IMPLEMENTATION
Koster, C.H.A.	TOP-DOWN PROGRAMMING WITH ELAN
Last, R.	ARTIFICIAL INTELLIGENCE TECHNIQUES IN LANGUAGE LEARNING
Lester, C.	A PRACTICAL APPROACH TO DATA STRUCTURES
Lucas, R.	DATABASE APPLICATIONS USING PROLOG
Lucas, A.	DESKTOP PUBLISHING
Maddix, F.	HUMAN–COMPUTER INTERACTION: Theory and Practice
Maddix, F. & Morgan, G.	SYSTEMS SOFTWARE
Matthews, J.J.	FORTH
Millington, D.	SYSTEMS ANALYSIS AND DESIGN FOR COMPUTER APPLICATIONS
Moseley, L.G., Sharp, J.A. & Salenieks, P.	PASCAL IN PRACTICE
Moylan, P.	ASSEMBLY LANGUAGE FOR ENGINEERS

Series continued at back of book

OBJECT ORIENTED PROGRAMMING WITH SMALLTALK/V

DUŠKO SAVIĆ
Belgrade, Yugoslavia

Editorial Consultant
DON GOODSELL
Faversham Publishing Consultants, Faversham, Kent

ELLIS HORWOOD
NEW YORK LONDON TORONTO SYDNEY TOKYO SINGAPORE

First published in 1990 by
ELLIS HORWOOD LIMITED
Market Cross House, Cooper Street,
Chichester, West Sussex, PO19 1EB, England
A division of
Simon & Schuster International Group
A Paramount Communications Company

Typeset by Ellis Horwood Limited
Printed and bound in Great Britain by
Redwood Press Limited, Melksham, Wiltshire

British Library Cataloguing in Publication Data

Savić, Duško
Object oriented programming with Smalltalk/V. —
(Ellis Horwood series in computers and their applications).
1. Computers systems. Programming languages. Smalltalk/V
I. Title
ISBN 0–13–040692–9

Library of Congress Cataloging-in-Publication Data

Savić, Duško.
Object oriented programming with Smalltalk/V / Duško Savić :
editorial consultant, D. Goodsell
p. c. — (Ellis Horwood series in computers and their applications)
Includes bibliographical references and index.
ISBN 0–13–040692–9
1. Object oriented programming (Computer science) 2. Smalltalk/V (Computer program language. I. Title. II. Series: Computers and their applications.
QA76.64.S28 1990
005.13'3–dc20 90–39407
CIP

Contents

Preface

This book is about applications programming and how object-oriented programming can make programming easier and more enjoyable. It explains why object-oriented programming is the best way to program, and gives you a start with one of the most versatile and approachable languages, Smalltalk/V.

An application program is a program that somebody needs, but is not commercially available. Most such projects never actually get written. Either there is insufficient incentive or the individual is not skilful enough to program in traditional languages devised more to the computer's mentality than for the way humans think. If this has been your problem, object-oriented languages may be the answer for you, for they have evolved beyond the traditional hardware-oriented problem-solving ways to human-oriented thinking.

Smalltalk is a general-purpose programming language and is equally well at home with any programming task. An object-oriented language like Smalltalk gives the less experienced operator the chance to write programs that he or she needs.

In applications programming, no overriding theory prevails because everything is too dependent on the object of programming. This book, consequently, presents a selection of applications in the hope that one of them might be just one of those programs you always wanted, but never had the time or courage to write.

Chapter 1 gives an overall view of the need for object-oriented languages, their basic characteristics, some history, and a comparison of Smalltalk/V against traditional languages.

Chapter 2 introduces to this particular implementation of Smalltalk, Smalltalk/V, which comes with more than 100 classes and 2000 methods (procedures) not all of which are needed for mundane tasks. This chapter familiarizes you with a comfortable minimum of classes and methods (data types and procedures) to enable you to start creative program writing.

Chapter 3 presents several profound mathematical objects in object-oriented terms: matrices and elementary matrix operations, square, column and row matrices, elementary geometric transformations, three-dimensional points, linear transformations in space, central and perspective projection, two- and three-dimensional lines and curves.

Chapter 4 deals with other mathematical notions as seen from an object-oriented point of view: large integers, the power method for eigenvalues of a matrix, descriptive statistics, the least squares method of regression and interactive data exploration, shaded histograms for business presentations, the chi-square test, the

Runge-Kutta method for numerical solving of differential equations, heat transfer partial differential equation, and — finally — enhanced matrices.

The first language with object-oriented features was Simula 67. It was an Algol-like language with twists towards simulations, so it is quite normal that a pure object-oriented language such as Smalltalk/V can be used for simulations of all kinds. Chapter 5 is devoted to discrete simulations.

Finally, Smalltalk/V can be used in business environments. Life-like programs can never be given in a book, therefore Chapter 6 gives elements and ideas for further work. The application program is for Billing Schedules. It encompasses many self-contained classes — data base window, programmable HP-like calculator, font designer, graphical printing and the like. Particular care in this chapter is paid to integration of all these objects into one homogeneous whole: results from the calculator can be transferred to data base columns, new fonts can be generated and used throughout all the windows and so on.

The topics are intentionally taken from classical but diverse areas of science. One never knows where the next flash of inspiration will come from so this book will fulfil its purpose if you recognize a familiar background and understand how to express it in an object-oriented manner.

Duško Savić February 18, 1990

1

Introduction to object-oriented programming

Everybody has heard of computer-generated mistakes: pensions that come late because a computer program had to be modified, requests to pay a bill of 0.00 dollars, explosion of a space rocket because a full-stop was inserted instead of a comma.... In all these cases the programmers were to blame: their programs caused the trouble.

People have come to realize that programming is difficult but it wasn't always so. When computing began in the fifties, only mathematicians and electrical engineers were involved in programming. Nobody could have foreseen that some day everybody would use computers. Computers started out as tools for computing Bessel integrals but it was soon discovered that any information can be coded and processed as a series of bits. That led to the wider acceptance of computers in many walks of life. However, the art of programming was a mystery and remained so into the sixties. A phrase such as 'art of programming' was common because no programming rules existed. Programming was strictly an individual activity. Computers were proliferating, and more and more felt the need to come to terms with programming. But what kind of educational background was best suited to the task? The art cannot be taught, but the craft can, so programming methodologies came into focus. The question of what is the best way to program gave rise to heated discussions in papers, symposia and books. The situation was getting worse and in 1969 NATO held a conference on the 'software crisis'. All the biggest names in professional and educational computing attended and, luckily, all of them were so high in positions within their organizations that nobody was afraid to admit the existence of software crisis and that nobody knew the basic ingredients of programming and how to teach them to others. It was estimated that the programming community consisted of about one million programmers (all professional — there were no home or personal computers and even time-sharing systems weren't common). The sad fact was that most programmers of the time were totally unprepared for the business they voluntarily joined.

The need for more and more programs was simultaneously changing the psychology and sociology of programming. Programming was done by strictly hierarchical teams. Systems analysts were on the top: they analysed the problem and suggested computer-oriented solutions. Below them were systems programmers, applications programmers, programmer novices, administrators, secretaries, and so on. Eventually the main task shifted from writing new programs to maintaining the old ones. More often than not the original author of the program would be unavailable, which forced the management to start prescribing standards of programming. Programs now had to be readable, understandable, accompanied by good documentation, sufficiently tested, and so on. Assessing programs became impossible without the notion of program quality.

1.1 PROGRAM QUALITIES

Program qualities can be divided into *external* and *internal*. External are those that can be detected by program end-users, while internal are those that only programmers (and their management) see. For example, ease of use is an external quality, and program readability is an internal quality. In practice, users and programmers take disparate views on the matter. End-users do not care for internal program qualities, while programmers often tend to neglect their users. It is obvious that internal qualities are born before external and it is the task of programming methodology to relate the two facets of the program: the dynamic behaviour (external) and the static (internal) look of the program.

There are five most important external program qualities:

correctness — the software is correct if it does what it is supposed to do,
robustness — the software is robust if it can function in abnormal conditions,
extensibility — the ease with which the program can be adapted to changes in specification,
reusability — the ability of a program as a whole or of its parts to be reused for new or other applications,
compatibility — the ease of combining various programs to accomplish some goal.

Other external qualities might be:

expandability — a program is expandable if it can use additional computer resources without fuss,
efficiency — the maximal use of the environment in which the program runs — both hardware and software resources,
portability — the ease with which a program can be transferred to other computers and/or operating systems,
verifiability — the ease of ascertaining that the program works correctly,
integrity — the program's ability to protect the components it needs for work,
ease of use — which includes the ease of learning how to use the program,
reliability — some sensible measure of absence of errors in the program,
usefulness — a program is useful if it serves practical applications.

Internal program factors are, among others:

readability — the ease of reading the source code,
being natural — a program is natural if its structure follows the logic of the problem being solved through computer programming (that is what object-oriented programming is all about),
generality — to use an algorithm that works slower but encompasses a greater number of possible cases, or to program exactly what is required, no matter how?

the length of program text — if it is possible to choose between two similar, optimally coded algorithms, the longer one should contain more information and is probably better,
excessive parts of the program should not exist and, conversely,
the program must be complete — it must contain all parts necessary for functioning,
structural integrity — all parts of a program must be connected into one whole,
accessibility — the program is accessible if the programmer can selectively approach certain parts of the program,
openness — the program is open if its functions and the meaning of certain statements can easily be seen from the program text,
ease of modification — a program is easy to modify if its structure permits easy correction,
comprehensiveness — a program is comprehensive if the reader can start at his/her own set of premisses and reach the meaning of the text via some logical reasoning.

Program qualities must be considered during program writing. Attention must be focussed on programming methodology, which is the series of physical and mental steps taken to write a good program, i.e. a program that complies with certain standards.

1.2 PROGRAMMING METHODOLOGIES

Programming methodology is similar to ideology. There must be a general framework, a coherent way of thinking, and the tools for writing computer programs. Some methodologies have been quite influential: bottom-up, top-down, declarative programming, object-oriented program design. There were others, of course: Warnier–Orr methodology (derives programs from end-user data), Jackson Structured Programming (similar, but a bit more formal), data flow analysis, etc.

1.3 DECLARATIVE PROGRAMMING

Declarative programming is a prime example of a dream called 'just tell it to the computer and wait for the results'. The name 'declarative' comes from declarations of goals that the programmer wants to achieve. However, the exact way, the algorithm for achieving it, is left to the computer to decide upon. Ideally, there would be no such activity as programming. It would be enough just to state the goals . . . .

Too bad this dream can't come true. The existence of such languages would presuppose that computers perceive and understand as we do — only better, and more wisely. Such goals are also those of artificial intelligence (AI), so declarative languages are often primarily regarded as AI tools.

Some declarative languages have become popular, such as PROLOG. Since declarations take the form of logic assertions (which PROLOG evaluates to false or true), this style of programming is also known as logic programming (PROgramming in LOGic, hence the name). But the order of logic evaluations does matter, so the programmer must be familiar with underlying control mechanisms in order to submit proper logic assertions to the language processor. This defeats the very essence of declarative programming and is an inherent problem of all declarative languages.

1.4 BOTTOM-UP APPROACH

The idea of the bottom-up approach is to build low-level functions first and then combine them into a working whole. This technique has been effectively used for operating systems. The object-oriented approach is a special kind of bottom-up methodology.

1.5 TOP-DOWN APPROACH

Top-down approach is — in spite of the difficulties it invariably brings — considered to be the most popular and well-known strategy for program writing. It is the main result of the debates of the sixties and the seventies. The emphasis is on the functional decomposition of the problem. The programmer starts out by asking a question: 'What will the program do for me?' Actual writing is usually done as a main loop containing some 'unexecutable' parts. They are refined (an official term in this methodology) in the same way, recursively, until all refinements can be expressed in the target programming language. If the chosen main loop were correct and all the refinements were also correct, the programmer would be in control of the translation of the original problem into executable code and should end up with a correct program. This approach (usually known as structured programming) is logically flawless: start out correct, don't make mechanical mistakes, and you're guaranteed to finish correct. Structured programming can easily be taught, is akin to a mathematician's mind, and also inspired a hope of program proving — proving mathematically that a given program works as it should.

The term 'structured' is used to denote that the programmer structures the program from the very start. The structure is expressed through control statements of the target language. It was proved in 1965 (the famous Bohm–Jacopini theorem) that any program can be written with only three control structures: sequential statement(s), IF and WHILE. Ever since, language designers tended to include only a bare minimum of control statements, with the idea 'that everything can be programmed that way, anyway'. In practice, that led to a minimalistic view of control structures and lowered the general level of services the languages provided to users. For example, Pascal cannot raise to the power because students are supposed to learn more through coding that manually!

Quite a lot of time has been spent educating, re-educating and convincing programmers and students that this is 'the' programming methodology. Its proponents invented languages 'better suited to structured programming', out of which Pascal is the best-known example.

Granted, structured programming has many qualities: it is a systematic way of developing programs, it can be taught in lectures and books, and — most important — it is applicable to any problem. It was a big leap in programming methodologies and certainly increased productivity by an order of magnitude. Its drawbacks are uniformity of thought imposed on programmers, lack of continuity and premature temporal decisions that the method encourages.

Continuity is the program's ability to change as the program specifications change. It is the most important program quality in commercial terms. A working program is too precious to be discarded. Continuity is a precondition of program maintenance.

The second inherent error in structured programming is prematurely deciding on temporal relations. Structured programming results in a hard-coded picture of the problem being solved. But when the problem changes, the whole construction collapses. A program derived in this way heads for a problematic maintenance phase afterwards.

1.6 OBJECT-ORIENTED APPROACH

The argument against a top-down approach is continuity. Data structures remain more stable through time than algorithms. Each program 'revolves' around one or several data structures (objects), on which various operations are applied. Operations (functions, procedures) depend on a particular situation but data structures persist. The better way of programming follows this scheme:

(1) identify data structures,
(2) write small programs (procedures, methods) for all relevant basic operations,
(3) only then combine them into a working program.

This is heresy to most modern programmers who grew up with structured programming — but this is exactly the starting point of object-oriented design and programming.

Designing systems bottom-up with real-life objects in view gives the programmer something to manipulate, something to work with, and concrete operations to think about, whereas, in the top-down approach the programmer is supposed to orchestrate visions of future operations — not existing procedures. Top-down design is for adventurers: the programmer is constantly surprised. One notebook on Pascal even suggests that the next refinement need not be correct: if you make a mistake, you can always start again! This tends to conveniently forget about decreased productivity of the approach.

Data structure with corresponding operations is called a **class**. It is a set of properties of an **object**, while objects are concretizations of a class. Class is actually a new data type. The heart of object-oriented programming is writing new types with tightly coupled operations. A typical main program is assembled only after enough classes and their concretizations (objects) are brought into existence. The next change of program specification will easily be catered for since only the main loop (the top of the program) has to be changed. This requires a smaller effort compared to the top-down approach, where a change in external specifications means negating most of the internal program components and relations.

Objects are members of classes: a class of clerks and one specific clerk as an instance of that class, a class of programming languages and Smalltalk/V as an instance of that class; a class of computers and a personal computer as an instance of that class . . . . In logic, such definitions are known as operational definitions and they are the most economical way of introducing new concepts.

The essence of programming is a series of translations. The human brain recognizes a problem in the material world, processes it (almost always mathematically), organizes a computer program, codes it, feeds it into the computer and gets results. Each translation is also a restrictive mapping, but key elements of the original system ought to be preserved throughout. The program should be internally organized like the objects of programming in the real world — that's the basic idea of the object-oriented (OO) approach. Interaction between objects is handled just as in real life — through messages. An object can change its state only while answering a message. This leads to safer programs, with eventual errors localized. Mistakes are possible in object-oriented programming just as in any form of human endeavour. Nonetheless, the higher the level of abstraction that one puts into the program, the shorter the actual code is, the harder the computer works, and the more productive the programmer is.

Structured programming introduces foreign elements into this series of translations. The world is bigger and richer than seen through glasses of IFs and WHILEs. Everything *can* be programmed through them — but *need not* be if there are better ways. Object-oriented programming in general, and Smalltalk/V in particular, offer one better way. But a top-down approach is still essential for development of algorithms (procedures, subroutines, methods). It has its uses even in OO programming, but not as a design methodology. Object-oriented design is the way to go for 'programming-at-large', but top-down does away with small program units. Object-oriented programming really starts where the top-down approach ends — in the world of reusable software components.

1.7 SMALLTALK HISTORY

The paradigm of messages and objects is quite a general one. Object-oriented thinking originated within programs that were not based on that paradigm. The famous Sketchpad drawing program (one of the first interactive programs in history) essentially worked with graphical objects. The first programming language to contain elements of OO programming was Simula 67. It was invented in Sweden as a general-purpose language with special additions for simulations. The notion of class and garbage collection as a required part of the language, etc., were some of the ideas this language pioneered. The first person to realize that behind Sketchpad and Simula was an identical type of thinking was Alan Kay. His idea was to use objects in the computer as representations of objects in real life. His was also an epochal decision to introduce messages through which objects communicate. This was a radical departure from FORTRAN, Algol, and all other known languages. Kay proceeded with development along these lines to find out that a complete, new, powerful programming language could be built upon these ideas. (This later came to be known as Smalltalk — the first purely object-oriented language.) Soon after Kay's initial efforts, essential ingredients of OO programming were identified and many languages sprouted: Actor, Director, Pygmalion, EOM, Tinker . . . . Not all of them survived — or even emerged from the researcher's laboratory — but their very existence shows how fruitful the whole concept was. For a while, those languages were known as actor languages because an object is just what it acts like.

After taking his PhD at the University of Utah, Alan Kay went to Xerox Palo Alto Research Center (PARC). The place was something of a miracle. Xerox was paying dozens of the finest programmers in the world for almost ten years just to develop and invent new computer software, hardware and languages. Alan Kay teamed up with Adele Goldberg to produce Dynabook, an idea that must have looked like something out of this world at the time. Dynabook was intended to be a cheap but powerful computer with large storage capacity, a flat touch-sensitive screen, bit-mapped graphics display, all bundled with audio and communications facilities. The main users would be children and Smalltalk was to be the main programming vehicle for the Dynabook.

The development took almost ten years. Kay and Goldberg first concentrated on Smalltalk. The major revisions were named Smalltalk-72, Smalltalk-76, Smalltalk-78 and, finally, Smalltalk-80 (the number relates to the year in which the standard was published). The earlier versions could be described as 'normal' imperative languages coupled with objects and messages. Smalltalk-80 eliminated everything except the object-oriented metaphor: even characters and integers became objects. And it did not stop there. Smalltalk bred totally new concepts: menus, mice, bit-mapped graphics, windows, icons .... Today they are the toolkit of the computer world. The creation of Smalltalk and its environment turned out to be one of the milestones of computing history. Smalltalk environment made computers less fearsome and easier to use, preparing grounds for the computer as a mass-market commodity.

Smalltalk addressed the crucial question of the computing industry, namely, how to make computers easier to use? How to approach — those billions that still do not use computers! The problem is aggravated by the fact that every new program returns the user to infancy. But, aren't children beginners by definition? Surely if there were a kind of computer that children could use and like, then the adults might fare even better? Unfortunately, Smalltalk ideas were not available to the masses for a long time. One of the reasons was that Smalltalk required strong hardware platforms. The first Smalltalk implementations ran on the Xerox Star personal workstation, with a bit-mapped screen of resolution so high (780×992) that a page of text appeared on screen almost exactly as on paper. The prices, however, were as high as the resolution. About the same time, IBM introduced its PC, and Star workstations fell into oblivion. Smalltalk was subsequently implemented on DEC VAXes and 2020s, and a Tektronix 68000-based computer, but Smalltalk and WIMP environments had to wait for Steve Jobs, the co-founder of Apple. On a visit to PARC he noticed the Star workstations, their bit-mapped screens, mice, menus, icons, Smalltalk. He immediately decided to import all he saw to his new computer, Lisa. But Lisa was too expensive, so Apple stripped it down and produced Macintosh. Although in its first incarnation the Mac wasn't very powerful, it had the WIMP environment from day one. People liked it. Alan Kay's vision of an easy-to-use computer finally came true, although still not in a proper, Dynabook sense. Mac was a far cry from the hand-held children's computer but most other Dynabook features were there, allowing Mac to survive exclusively on the grounds of 'user-friendly' interface. Not surprisingly, there were versions of Smalltalk for both Lisa and Mac.

Users of other computers saw what Mac offered and started looking for the same on machines they already had, — IBM PC/XT/AT and compatibles. Indeed, many graphics programs on the PC were heavily influenced by Mac graphics, and through them the ideas once developed for Smalltalk started to serve millions of users. But the language itself was not readily available on the PC. The reason was simple: it takes a powerful computer to execute Smalltalk, which the original PC with meagre 64K certainly was not. The objects and messages metaphor is natural for humans and is, therefore, far from the machine level. Smalltalk requires a fast processor and lots of memory if it is to run at acceptable speeds. In time the PC standard acquired both: megabytes of RAM and fast processors such as Intel 80286, 80386, 80486. At the lower end, a simple 8088 processor and 640K memory could have been sufficient — were Smalltalk coded in an optimal way. And then such a product finally appeared — Smalltalk/V by a Los Angeles company, Digitalk (Digitalk Inc. 9841 Airport Blvd., Los Angeles, CA 90045, USA). It was cheap (under 100 dollars), powerful, and beautiful. Within two years more than 25 000 copies were sold, amounting to one half of all object-oriented installations in the world. For 80286, 80386, and 80486 processors there is a version called Smalltalk/V286. It directly addresses all available RAM in protected mode. A megaboard AT computer is the minimal configuration to run this program.

The latest release of Smalltalk/V is under the Presentation Manager of the OS/2 operating system. It is called Smalltalk/V PM (priced around 500 dollars). It is also source compatible with earlier releases.

There is an implementation of Smalltalk/V on the Mac, also by Digitalk. Smalltalk has always inspired the building of special hardware platforms. For Smalltalk/V there is one transputer board called Max2. It runs at some 40 MIPS.

All releases are source compatible across hardware platforms so the same program should work on XTs, ATs, 386s, Mac's, under OS/2 Presentation Managers, and others. This must be a boon to software developers, individuals and companies alike.

There are Smalltalk implementations other than Smalltalk/V, for instance, on Macintosh and Atari ST. And Smalltalk is by no means the only object-oriented language on the PC. Actor merges the syntax of Pascal and C with OOP but runs only under MS Windows. There is an extension of C, called C++. A company called Zortech even offers a true native 80×86 C++ compiler for MS DOS. Other C compilers have object-oriented pre-processors for the C++ language. Such preprocessors are PforC and AT&T C++, among others. There is also a non-C++-based preprocessor called C_talk, which successfully merges Smalltalk concepts and environment into C. Pascal is also no exception. Borland's Turbo Pascal 5.5 and Microsoft's QuickPascal 1.0 both feature (mutually incompatible, though) enhancements to Turbo Pascal 5.0. And there is even an object-oriented assembly language for the PC, called risC. By the time you read this book, there will certainly be many more object-oriented languages.

1.8 BASIC OBJECT-ORIENTED CONCEPTS

Computer programs have been described as 'data plus algorithms'. This is true, but much is left out of this definition. Standard programming languages view data as passive substances on which algorithms operate. Similar data might come in different versions, meaning that the language must support several slightly different statements to produce similar effects. Take a square root function, SQRT(X). X can normally be integer or real, or in some kind of extended precision, depending on the language. The result should be a floating-point number regardless of the type of argument. Most languages would require several similar procedures for this computation. In FORTRAN, for example, you would have to use SQRT for REALs and DSQRT for DOUBLEs. Suppose, now, you asked another person to perform the same calculation manually. He/she would first take a look at the number submitted, and would then apply the correct procedure. From the programmer's standpoint, the job would be accomplished simply by asking somebody else to do it. And that is the essence of object-oriented programming: you, the programmer, ask objects to perform operations. If the object is already there, then all you have to do is wait for the answer; if the object doesn't exist, you write it first — then ask for the favour once again. Object-oriented programming is nothing more than creating objects and making them behave consistently.

The objects–persons analogy can be taken further. There is no way of knowing the internal state of mind of any person you communicate with. All you are allowed is to observe how the person behaves. A person is what he or she does and so are objects in Smalltalk. Using a more formal vocabulary, objects hide information. Any programmer who had the chance of debugging a 1000-lines-long program will tell you that information hiding is a fundamental property of a computer language. Larger programs should always be divided into smaller units (modules) and it is imperative that events and computations in them cannot disturb other parts of the program. Most languages respond to this requirement through local variables — variables which are visible only in the scope of one module or procedure. Modules make it possible to restrict access to certain classes of data to just a few syntactical units. This approach becomes important during program maintenance. Most modern languages support information hiding (except standard Pascal).

Information hiding extends to data abstraction. No programming language can predict data structures the programmer will need in a particular situation. If the language is to be useful, it must be able to systematically define new data structures together with operations that are to be performed on them. Data abstraction is a powerful mental tool and can lead to re-usable code — which could, in turn, significantly improve a programmer's productivity.

Information hiding can be simulated to some extent but other desirable language features cannot. Two of the most important are **operator overloading** and **casting** (changing types during program execution). In traditional languages, they are performed too early to be useful — much before program execution. This prevents objects changing when needed. Only **dynamic binding** resolves those problems.

Every variable name is allocated a place in memory and type, which tells the run-time system what can be — or cannot be — done with the variable. The process of attaching the type is known as **binding**. There are two kinds: **early** and **late** (also called **dynamic**) **binding**. Early binding is used in all traditional languages, while late binding is a hallmark of OO languages. The former allows programs to run faster; the latter makes them significantly flexible in execution.

Flexibility costs. Dynamic binding is slower then static binding, and is performed with every method (i.e. Smalltalk procedure). According to one measurement, pure procedures are some 1.75 times faster than methods. Fortunately, total execution speed of a Smalltalk/V program compares well with imperative languages. For larger projects, with several programmers involved simultaneously, a Smalltalk solution can even run faster since novices can be as clever in their code as old hands. Smalltalk/V and Smalltalk/V286 run on Intel 80286 and 80386 AT compatible computers, making the lack of speed less important anyway.

Run-time problems should be resolved during program execution. However logical this approach might seem, most problems in programming arise from the presupposed discrepancy between the static structure of a program and its run-time behaviour. Late binding enables one essential advantage: **operator overloading**. This is the ability of a language to apply the same syntactical operator to different data types. Most programming languages support this feature to a limited extent and then only through type conversions. For example, the addition operator of Pascal, +, can be used with INTEGERs and REALs because the language standard prescribes how to convert types in such situations. Such conversions do not exist for, say, enumeration types or user-defined RECORDs so it is impossible in standard Pascal to use the + operator to add RECORDs — although their fields may all be INTEGERs and REALs.

Early binding forces variable type to be declared once and outlaws change of types during program execution. One of the consequences of this is that all array elements are of only one type. Dynamic binding resolves problems where problems occur: during program execution. This is extremely useful. Suppose the program puts several types of data into elements of an array. Those values should be, say, printed. In normal languages the programmer would have to use a CASE statement to ensure correct printing at run-time. Any time a new type is added to the array, the CASE would have to be updated, demanding new compilation as well. This is illogical: additions are supposed to be only additions, not partial or complete program modifications. Besides this, more and more parts of the program would acquire intimate knowledge of basic data structures.

Object-oriented languages turn this inside out. The programmer sends a message to an object and it becomes the receiver's responsibility to respond correctly. The same message can evoke different answers from different objects. This is known as **polymorphism**. For instance, the same message, **print**, would cause INTEGERs, REALs, strings, and all other objects that implement **print**, to be printed. Should the receiver not know what to do with the message, the programming system (i.e. Smalltalk) would return 'nil' as an answer. The programmer, of course, has to write actual **print** methods for every object. This is a rather dull job, because many such procedures are similar. Introduction of new objects would require entirely new procedures for essentially identical programming tasks (I/O operations, arithmetics, graphics, etc.). Modula-2 is an extreme example: there are separate procedures for reading and writing REALs, INTEGERs and CARDINALs: ReadReal, Write Real, ReadInt, ReadCard, WriteInt, WriteCard, and so on: new type — new procedures. The burden of rewriting similar code diminishes the programmer's eagerness for new, useful data types and this is exactly why all object-oriented languages provide classes and inheritance.

A class is a family of objects of a particular kind. Objects that belong to a class are named **instances**. A class may have several instances, but each instance has exactly one class (this is called **single inheritance**). Besides these relationships, a class has methods and variables. **Methods** are just procedures invoked when receiving a message from the outer world. (A method roughly corresponds to procedures of Pascal, functions of C, procedures of Modula-2, and subroutines or procedures of BBC BASIC; methods are the main building blocks of Smalltalk/V.) All **instances** of one class have identical methods and this class–methods–instances business is merely an analogy to modules–procedures–local variables in Modula-2, or units–procedures– local variables in Pascal. A class can have **temporary variables** (which lose their values when you leave the method) and **instance variables** (which maintain individual states across different methods).

Everything in Smalltalk is an object and so are classes. Therefore, two kinds of methods exist: **object methods** and **class methods**. The former are for class instances; the latter are for the classes themselves: creating a new class, terminating it and, in general, providing any other operation that the programmer finds useful. Class methods are similar to declarations of new types. Actually, the Smalltalk programmer is free to introduce as many new data types as needed, with the added bonus that all of them can permanently become a part of the language.

Classes can have **subclasses**. The class which contains a subclass is called a **superclass**. There is just one class that has no superclass — and that is called an **Object**. A subclass inherits everything from its superclass: instance variables, class variables, methods and, of course, adds its unique array of variables and methods. This is quite similar to classifications in biology, logic and everyday life. The programmer creates new objects by specifying the differences between the existing classes and the new class. Inheritance cuts down program development time since the programmer continually and deliberately borrows methods and properties of objects that already exist in the language. Inheritance is really no more than enriched cloning.

1.9 THE PROGRAMMER'S VIEW

How does all this affect the programmer? There are two major differences between Smalltalk and traditional languages. The first is philosophical; the second is practical.

Smalltalk requires the programmer to think in terms of classes and messages. The solution of any problem can be discovered by inventing classes that work together. The design of a Smalltalk application starts with asking the following question: 'Where in the universe of already existing classes do my new classes, objects, and methods fit best?' Or, similarly: 'Where should I put my new class in order to write as little new code as possible?' Or: 'From where can I borrow already existing code?' These are quite different questions to the usual approach characterized by questions like: 'What control and data structures can I combine until my program works?' The difference is one of attitude and — productivity.

Standard languages give you the tools — the programmer must use them to solve the problem at hand. The programmer is the only active entity around: procedures and data structures are passive. They are the building materials for the programmer to use. The programmer is the architect, the builder, the constructor; the tools are there, waiting to be used. No matter how long it takes, the tools will always be sufficient for the job, provided the builder is patient enough to arrange them in the right order.

Smalltalk offers a different perspective. Each time a new class is created, the programmer brings to life an 'expert' that will 'do it for you'. You simply ask your experts to solve your problem. After a while, they become old friends, ready to help at any time. The classes certainly do not come that way by themselves — the programmer creates a new universe in Smalltalk as well as in any procedural language. Care is still needed in object-oriented programming. Practice shows that classes should have many little features (i.e. methods) separately available. This coding style is known as factoring. Classes are usually lightly coupled, meaning that useful methods will probably continue to be useful in future applications.

So we come to the second, practical advantage of Smalltalk/V: factoring encourages *incremental program development*. Smalltalk is both an interpreter and a compiler. Almost all other languages are either interpreters or compilers. Neither is, in a broad perspective, satisfactory: interpreters are good for program development but lack speed, while compilers are boring to work with but are fast in execution. Smalltalk/V allows you to test a method interactively, then 'hammer it down' into the system, where it takes up residence as a new object. There is no way to distinguish user-defined classes and objects from the manufacturer's code. You can finish your application, that is, inject new classes into the body of Smalltalk/V, and then send (or sell) them to somebody else. (In order to distribute Smalltalk/V commercially, you must first reach a royalty agreement with the manufacturer, i.e. Digitalk. At the time of writing, this means paying 500 US$ for the right to distribute an unlimited number of copies of an unlimited number of programs for one year.)

The main attraction of interactive program development is the ability to stop execution of a program and immediately examine and/or alter values of one or several variables. The program usually continues execution after the break. All these features are present in Smalltalk/V. It is possible to inspect or debug any piece of code — at any time you like. The result of a method can be obtained interactively and can remain on the screen in its own, separate window. After changing the code, you can compare the results from the new and previous program run. In this highly interactive way you can fine-tune any code in very little time. The essence of success is the ability of Smalltalk/V to isolate a piece of code and have it tested and verified to work properly. This approach leads to more reliable code and less time spent in debugging, while greatly enhancing the programmer's confidence in the emerging program. Mistakes are easier to catch and debug.

The 'V' in the name stands for 'virtual' (not five). Smalltalk/V is virtual in the sense that if the code and data together need more than 640K, the implementation will swap unused parts to disk, making room for new objects. This traces a path to **persistent programming**. Objects in real life do not disappear of their own will but variables in traditional languages seem to do exactly that. As soon as the computer is shut down, everything vanishes and is brought back to life at the next program loading. It is only natural that once an object is created in the computer it persists as long as the program (the process that is being modelled) needs it. Virtuality of Smalltalk/V thus serves two purposes simultaneously: it skips over the artificial memory boundary of 640K imposed by DOS, and thus makes persistent programming possible. The syntactical rule is quite simple: variables whose names begin in upper case are persistent and remain intact across sessions of work in Smalltalk/V. (Technically, persistence is achieved by saving the complete memory image on disk.)

Smalltalk/V is a highly productive programming environment. Everything you need is there: compiler, text editor, file system, DOS functions, class browser, debugging facilities, bit-mapped WIMP environment, mouse support, PROLOG, even a two-dimensional graphics editor from which named figures can be imported into programs. And all these tools are objects, belonging to classes of their own, ready to be inherited or directly modified if the programmer so wishes.

Traditional languages, on the other hand, leave most of these services to the operating system, forcing the programmer to work in different modes: edit mode, compile mode, link mode, execute mode, then all over again until program development ends. This cycle wastes time and necessitates attention to a myriad of unnecessary details. Smalltalk/V offers modeless programming, allowing the programmer to concentrate exclusively on program writing. However, you — the programmer — still have to know what you're doing. Smalltalk/V makes your job easier — perhaps much easier — but it is still the programmer who has to know what to do and why. The nature of Smalltalk/V and its environment will certainly make the mechanics of program writing more tolerable, for no one other than you will write your programs!

1.10 GENERAL CHARACTERISTICS OF OBJECT-ORIENTED LANGUAGES

Here are the key requirements that a language must fulfil in order to be called an object-oriented language:

(1) MODULARITY: Programs are modular, with modules closely following data structures inherent in the problem.
(2) DATA ABSTRACTION: Objects are implemented as abstract data types.
(3) GARBAGE COLLECTION: Unused objects should be automatically disposed of without the programmer's explicit intervention.
(4) CLASSES: All data types (except the very basic ones) are modules, and every module is a type.
(5) INHERITANCE: A class can be defined as an extension or restriction of other classes.
(6) POLYMORPHISM AND DYNAMIC BINDING: An object can refer at run-time to instances of various classes (polymorphism) and instances of a class can at run-time recognize different objects (dynamic binding).
(7) MULTIPLE AND REPEATED INHERITANCE: A class can inherit properties of several classes at the same time (multiple inheritance), or a class can inherit more than once from the same superclass.

The first six properties distinguish OO languages from other kinds of language. The last requirement is convenient but not essential. It can (more or less) easily be emulated through single inheritance. Smalltalk/V fulfils the first six requirements, while the seventh is not readily available.

Some of these notions require some explanation. A module is a small piece of code. Practically all languages incorporate such a concept because modularity is an essential facility for creation of lengthy programs. Well written modular programs are easier to understand, read, and debug. A module is not an end in itself. It must be autonomous, coherent and robust. A set of modules is (in an ideal case) a toolkit for program building, much as bricks are building blocks for real houses.

A language is defined with modularity in mind if it supports modules on the syntactic level. Modula-2 and Ada are such languages. Furthermore, the best effects are achieved if all information is private to the module unless it is specifically declared public. This is the **information-hiding principle**. It is a prime extension of applied continuity. If a module changes internally, nobody else needs to know about it as long as only the private data are altered. Neither of the **client** modules (those that use services provided by other modules) will have to change in that case. And that is very important for implementation of any large project: a change in one (small) program part does not affect anything else.

The most important requirement for modules is to satisfy the **open-closed** principle. A module is **open** if it can still be extended, i.e. if at any time new operations and functions can be added to it. But a module is **closed** if it is available for use by other modules and programs. Practically no traditional language can claim this feature. And yet, this is exactly why software development in traditional languages is so painful and difficult to control. Moreover, it is outright impossible to write modules that are both open and closed with classical approaches to design and programming. The paradox can be resolved only through **inheritance**.

Distinction between public and private data also helps encapsulate abstractions. Such modules can represent new types. A **data type** is a set of values that a specific variable can take on. Every programming language defines several elementary data types and also declares operations applicable to them. The programmer must make all other data types. An **abstract data type** includes not only the permissible set of values but also a specification of the operations that are valid for the new type. An abstract data type can be defined regardless of the language, but has to rely on a specific **data structure** as a way of representing or implementing it in a program. A data structure is a concrete way of implementing an abstract data type. The key point is that in OO languages **module is data type and data type is module**.

Object-oriented languages have much to offer. **Data abstraction** is an integral part of Smalltalk, in contrast to traditional languages where it is left to the programmer's discretion to achieve it. Dynamic binding eliminates unnecessary modifications and inheritance permits building of re-usable program units. The programmer has to write less new code so programs can be finished in less time. Finally, data abstraction encapsulated in modules makes program maintenance much easier because program logic is concentrated in just one class or method.

1.11 WHY TRADITONAL LANGUAGES DO NOT SUFFICE

Could OO programming be achieved through traditional languages? The answer varies in detail and depth, but generally the answer is no! A very short look at the history of computer languages might reveal why.

The first non-machine language ever devised was FORTRAN (about 1954).

Syntactically speaking, it was just a DO loop ahead of machine language. Semantically, the main goal was achieving FORmula TRANslation — hence the name. FORTRAN broke the ice, gained popularity, and set many people thinking. New languages sprung up within several years. On one side, computers continued to compute. New versions of FORTRAN regularly appeared and the language spread over practically all available machines. But its algorithmic facilities could best be described as weak, and its static organization of memory was too simple-minded.

Meanwhile, it becomes evident that designing a computer language was too serious a thing to be left to gifted individuals or hardware manufacturers. So in 1960 Algol was born, through a joint effort of an international committee. It improved on all aspects of language organization, description, definition, etc. Only one thing was lacking: support from a major backer, publisher and manufacturer. The industry just did not push it. Algol 60 created a foundation for almost all programming languages developed ever since, but too few were actually using it as a production tool. Algol 60 failed in spite of being a very good language for the time.

It was not alone in Nowhereland. Almost all computer languages perished, except COBOL, FORTRAN, BASIC, Pascal, C, Ada, LISP, Modula-2, Smalltalk, FORTH, Actor, PL/I . . . the list of survivors is pitifully short. This triggers certain questions: What is it that makes a language succeed? How do we recognize a better language? Better for whom and better for what? It all depends on so many things, and firm answers cannot be given. It is easy to see that all computer languages are equally powerful in the sense that all of them take some string of characters as input and produce some other string as output. The computer processes symbols, no more–no less; all programming languages would be equal if execution speed and memory were infinite. In Utopia, programmers would choose languages according to personal preferences, but in the real world there is more to selecting languages than personal taste. For one thing, it is difficult to write in a language to which you do not have access. Fortunately, all surviving languages have been implemented on personal computers. They differ greatly amongst themselves. Some live because they are problem oriented — LISP and PROLOG for artificial intelligence, COBOL for business problems, FORTRAN for numerical and engineering work, BASIC and Pascal as introductions to programming, FORTH and Ada for real-time control and embedded systems. . . . Only a handful of general-purpose languages survived because most programmers liked them for their own qualities: C, Modula-2, Smalltalk.

Every language offers its own paradigm and a set of facilities as a basis for problem solving on a computer. The situation reminds one of the foundations of geometry: several competing systems of axioms exist and upon each a completely valid geometry can be built. The final facts are always the same although their proofs may vary within each particular system. Analogously, programming languages are theoretically equal but the styles of program writing — and the effort involved — might be quite different. It is easy to recognize the values of an OO approach but using it would be almost impossible if there were no explicit support at a syntactical level. Some languages make one or two steps towards these new ideals but this is not enough. Modula-2, for instance, is a successful imperative language because data hiding can be implemented through modules — which are a regular part of the language. Ada makes it possible to use parametrized types, and thus comes closer to using dynamic binding than any other language. It also gives the programmer the option of using a garbage collection mechanism. Also most languages allow procedures and subroutines to be used as modules for encapsulation of specific data structures and corresponding operations, but the very elements of OO programming that enable the programmer to increase productivity — classes, inheritance, polymorphism, late binding — are all absent. Although you might have invested considerable time and money in learning conventional languages, you still have to learn at least one object-oriented language in order to become a really productive program writer.

1.12 CONCLUSION

Most programmers like programming. There is a sense of god-like power — the power of creation, the immediate feedback from the product of one's mind and thinking. The feeling when the program finally starts working is what most programmers crave for. It confirms that one is right where it matters — in the mind. The computer screen is a mirror — not unlike that magic mirror that can say who is 'the most beautiful in the world'. Whenever the program works, the programmer is the one.

The electronic mirror works both ways, revealing the surroundings — the environment. But it is also a window to the world inhabited by the programmer's creations (and creatures). And a small window it is, for sure. Only a tiny part of the 'world beyond' can be observed at a time. One solution to this problem is, paradoxically, to create even smaller windows within the screen and enlarge or shrink them as the need arises. This is where Smalltalk/V excels. Windows are, however, of little use if we can't control the objects (the creations, the creatures) that we glimpse through them. The lowest level is a strict, deterministic, gramophone-record-like rigid type of control. The programmer has to foresee literally everything and has to spell out and write with his own hand every minute detail of the program. This is a machine-oriented approach to programming and is the metaphor on which most programming languages have grown. Computing has been infected by a wrong approach: instead of solving the problems in human terms, everything used to be expressed in computer-like terminology. Why think in terms of bits and bytes just because they are the actual hardware ingredients of modern computers? Why abuse the human mind to deal with the internal organization of a computer in order to program it? Obviously, such thinking and practice were inescapable when computers were toys by today's standards. But today's hardware is much stronger, and OO languages can finally turn computers into what they were meant to be from the very start: extensions of the human mind.

Writing a program in classical languages has been compared to writing an essay. Writing an object-oriented program is then comparable to writing a drama. Every object has its own behaviour and acts in accord with it. So every object-oriented program becomes a simulation of the real world, an executable logical system that imitates and reflects real-life objects. Object-oriented programming is the best way to program because the gap between reality and object-oriented programs is the least possible.

PROBLEMS

1.1 Find at least one occasion on which some damage was made by a computer program.
1.2 Would you agree that computing is 80 per cent craft and 20 per cent art?
1.3 Add at least two program qualities that have not been mentioned here.
1.4 Do you adhere to one of the publicly known programming methodologies or do you use one of your own? Would the latter work for other people as well?
1.5 Can any programming methodology be practised in its pure form? And if it were, would programmers like it that way?
1.6 Discuss the commercial value of program continuity.
1.7 Would human talk intermingled with a series of IFs and WHILEs be considered as normal?
1.8 What is the difference between coding and design of a computer program?
1.9 Can you imagine a language with unique operators for adding different types of numbers? Would anybody want to use such a language?
1.10 Dynamic binding brings freedom to the programmer but early binding uses the machine better. Which do you prefer? Whose time is more important? Is it always so? How about a language that could use late binding during program development and then switch to early binding for speed?
1.11 Take your favourite language and invent schemes for turning it into an object-oriented language. Use those seven key characteristics of object-oriented languages.
1.12 Do those seven features guarantee the writing of programs with all desirable external qualities?
1.13 Are you afraid that OO programming will shorten the time you spend with the computer? Which do you prefer: spending time at the keyboard or producing more programs faster and better?

2

Elements of the Smalltalk/V language and environment

We assume that Smalltalk/V is successfully installed for your particular hardware configuration, according to the instructions in the manual. After the very first loading of Smalltalk/V, a screen like the one in Fig. 2.1 appears. What you will actually see

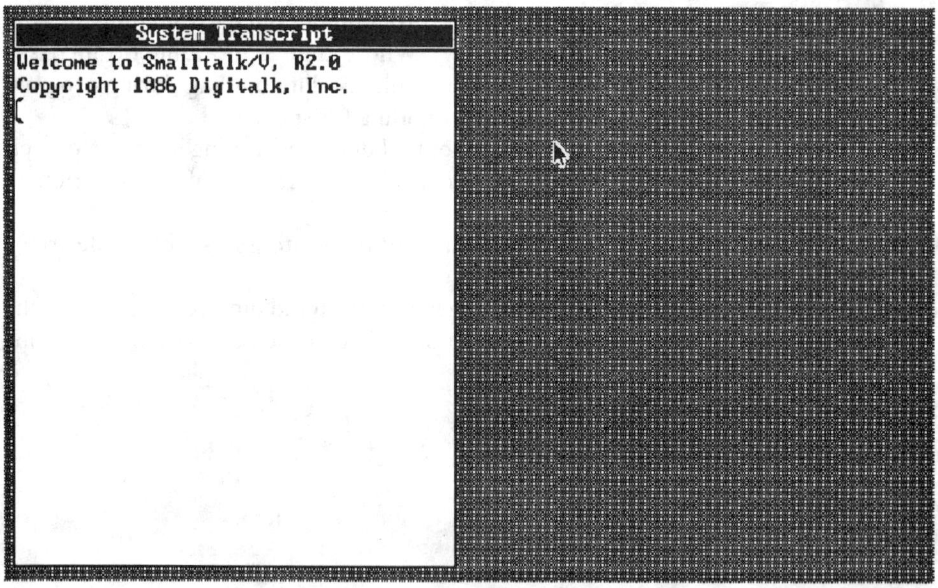

Fig. 2.1 — The start-up screen.

depends on the release and version of Smalltalk/V that you have. There ought to be a bright window on the left and a grey background on the right. The window is labelled **System Transcript**. The programs usually output their results to this window. You can **collapse** it so that it doesn't get in the way. It is possible to run Smalltalk/V without it, and we shall later actually create such an application (the Billing Schedules program).

System Transcript is the main window in Smalltalk/V. From this window the programs are run. The screen might show entirely different settings the next time you load Smalltalk/V. You will get used to this because you yourself will create them by writing and running Smalltalk/V programs.

Windows have common properties: size, label, menus, and different kinds of panes. Only one window can be active at any time. It is recognized by its label (the uppermost line which contains the window name) written in white letters on a black background. The user communicates only through an active window. A window is activated by bringing in the cursor and pressing either the **Grey Plus** key or the left mouse button. Non-active windows have grey labels.

A pane is an unlabelled 'subwindow'. A window has at least one pane (as in Fig. 2.1 but usually there are more). Otherwise, distinguishing panes from windows would not make sense.

The easiest way of communicating with Smalltalk/V is through menus. You can attach one to each pane and window so what will be invoked will depend on the current cursor position. The cursor is easily moved around by the mouse, but numeric cursor keys can be effective too. They move the cursor in larger steps if one of the **Shift** keys is pressed simultaneously. The cursor is normally a left-and-up-pointing black arrow, but it could take many other shapes; eleven are predefined by Smalltalk/V; others can be added easily.

The mouse must be Microsoft compatible. The original Smalltalk mouse had three buttons, but the Microsoft standard recognizes only two; hence two buttons are all you have in Smalltalk/V. There are two ways of using them: pressing and releasing one of them quickly (clicking) or driving the mouse around while holding one button pressed. Conventionally, the left button starts a selection, moves windows, changes the cursor position, etc., while the right button summons a menu. Smalltalk grew as a mouse–windows–menus system and using a mouse is strongly recommended.

2.1 MENUS

At least one menu must be within the user's reach at any time. That main menu (System Menu) is summoned by placing the cursor somewhere on the grey surface and clicking. Regardless of how many windows are opened, at least one part of the grey surface will be visible. Fig. 2.2 shows a typical Smalltalk/V display with the main menu placed in the upper right part of the screen. All menus are vertical. A full menu will always present itself regardless of the cursor position near screen borders. The cursor position within a menu is shown by inverting the menu item. Vertical cursor keys move the menu selection until the desired choice is reached, which is then selected by pressing the Grey Plus key. Moving the mouse also moves the inverted cursor within the menu, and clicking on the left mouse button selects the option. Leaving a menu is quite simple: steer the cursor away from the menu and it will disappear after a click.

2.2 SYSTEM MENU

This menu offers nine options divided into two groups. The upper group defines how Smalltalk/V interfaces with the environment. Through **dos shell** you can exit to DOS.

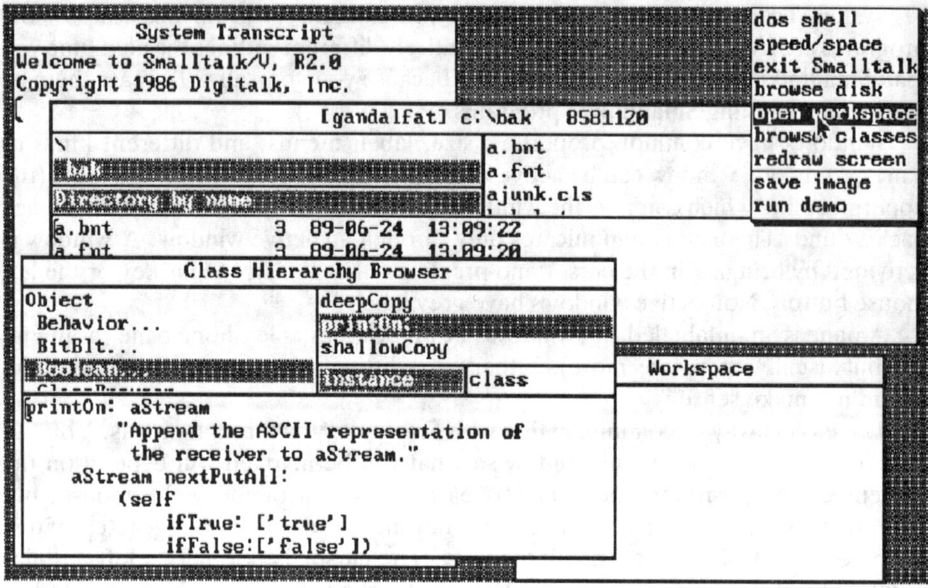

Fig. 2.2 — The System Menu.

Smalltalk/V then acts as a 'Terminate, Stay Resident' utility, leaving 128 kilobytes of central memory free for some other program (for example to format diskettes or to run some utility program).

Every window can be held in memory as a bit-image of its screen appearance. The **space/speed** option tells Smalltalk/V to actually represent them that way (the gain is in speed) or to create them anew (in which case the gain is in memory resources).

exit Smalltalk leads into another, smaller menu, with three suboptions. The middle one, **continue**, brings you back into the situation from which you issued the **exit Smalltalk** option; you may then continue using Smalltalk/V as if nothing had happened. The other two options take you to DOS, but with a difference:

— **save image** saves the exact memory image on the disk for future use. As noted in Chapter 1, this enables **persistent programming** in Smalltalk/V.
— **forget image** does not save recent additions to the environment. It is used to discard some unwanted work.

The lower, larger part of the System Menu contains heterogeneous functions. The **save image** option is a shortcut to saving an image and is otherwise identical to the **save image** option from the **exit Smalltalk** submenu. The **run demo** option does what it says: it offers you another menu with several demonstration programs. You will probably not want to use this option after learning elementary facts about the system, at least not until you decide to enhance it and offer some applications of your own to the user.

Redraw screen resolves the problem of screen cluttering as a result of drawing and re-drawing several different windows or forms.

2.3 WINDOWS

The other three options relate to different windows. **Open workspace** lets you create a completely new text window. You must specify the upper left and the lower right part of the window, together with the label (the window name). The process is entirely graphical: the cursor turns first into a small 'upper left' rectangle edge, and then into the inverted 'lower left' symbol. You immediately see what the final window borders would look like. Pressing the left mouse button confirms the positions of window edges. Smalltalk/V then prompts you for a label, using a special window. (This particular window is a Prompter. It just sits there and awaits your answer, which must be terminated by **Enter**. The newly created window is immediately active — everything you type from now on will appear in it. Windows may overlap on screen but only one is active at any time).

This process is a bit simpler with Smalltalk/V286: some special windows have predefined sizes and positions.

You can practise creating new windows by selecting options **browse disk** and **browse classes** from the System Menu. Both activate a special window (for browsing through the disk and classes contents, respectively). For both you have to undergo the same procedure for window creation but you are not asked for a window label. Selecting the **browse disk** options will eventually lead you to a window like the one in Fig. 2.3. The **Disk Browser** window has several panes. Each pane may have its own

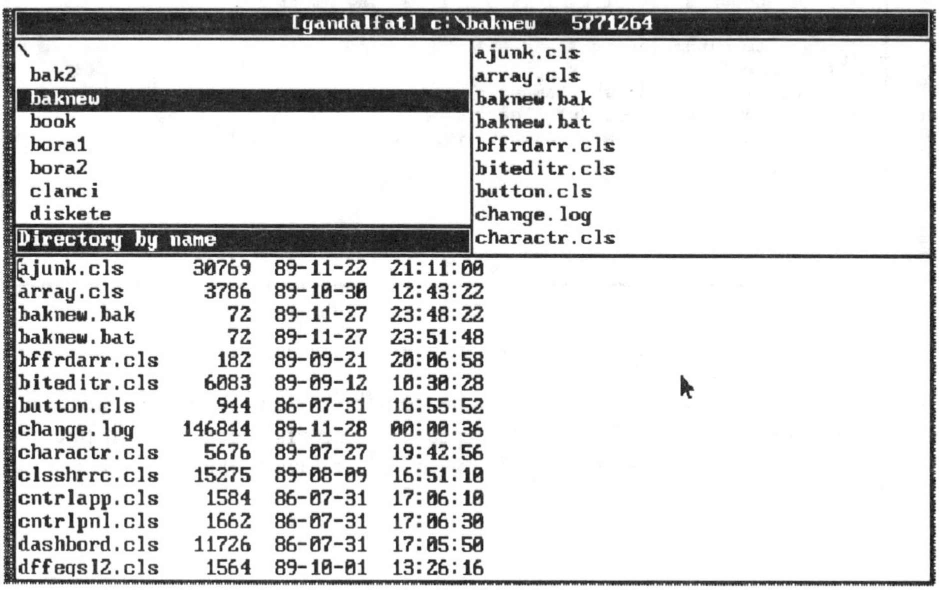

Fig. 2.3 — **Disk Browser** window.

menu and submenus. For instance, placing the cursor somewhere in the upper left pane (called the **directory pane**) and clicking on the right mouse button will pop up the menu with three selections: **remove** (eliminate a subdirectory and all related files from disk), **update** (change drive or repeat reading a directory of files from the same drive), and **create** (make a new subdirectory). The **files pane menu** (the upper right pane) offers **remove** (delete the selected file), **print** (print it), **mode** (change system file mode — hidden, read only, etc.), **rename** (rename the selected file), **copy** (copy the selected file), and **create** (generate a new file). Finally, the lower pane shows the contents of the file selected in the file pane. There you have standard options of a normal text editor.

The last option available from the System Menu is **browse classes**. It prompts you for a new window — the **Class Hierarchy Browser** window with its own panes and corresponding menus. From this option you enter Smalltalk/V program code. A typical **Class Hierarchy Browser** window might look like the one in Fig. 2.4. These

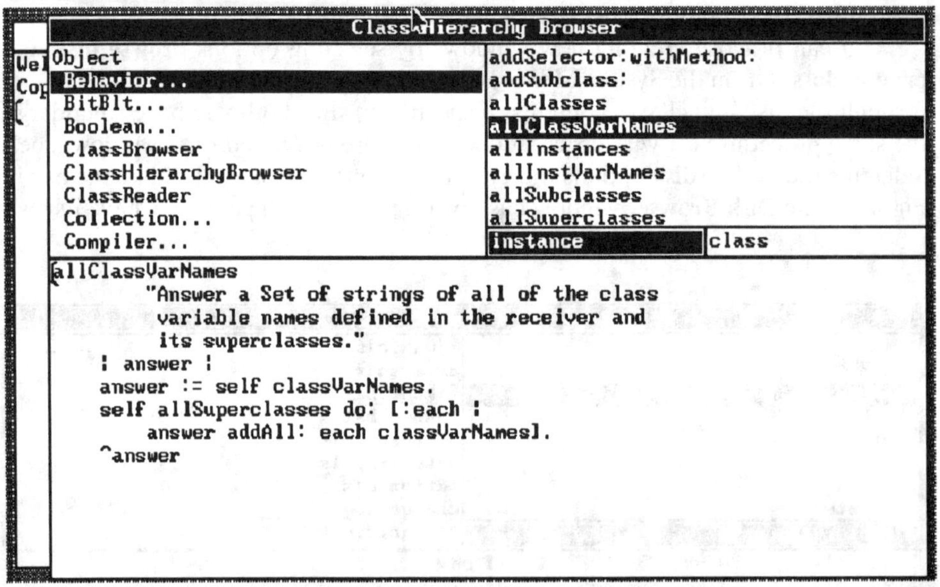

Fig. 2.4 — **Class Hierarchy Browser** window.

were all the windows immediately accessible from the System Menu. The Smalltalk/V programmer uses many other window types — Prompters, Debuggers, Inspectors, Walkback windows and the like, together with the windows that he himself creates.

2.4 WINDOWS AND MENUS

The **window menu** applies to the window as a whole. Usually, its options are: **label** (change window name), **collapse** (remove panes and leave only window label visible on screen), **cycle** (activate another window), **frame** (resize the window in the same way as you have created it), **move** (move the complete window to somewhere else on the screen), **close** (shut down the window; throw its contents away). The **System Transcript** window cannot be **closed**.

Most windows have one Text Editor pane in which you can edit program text or data. Editing is possible only if the cursor is inside the pane. Text is always entered in insert mode. Place the cursor where you want to insert something and click on the left mouse button. The cursor will change to an I-beam, marking the place of the next insert. The **Backspace** key is the only immediate way of deleting text. Not many other keys are alive within text panes. **Tab** inserts four white spaces into the pane; **Enter** moves the insertion point to the beginning of a new line. It also splits the line if the insertion point is in the middle of the previous line.

The concept of selection is the main means of letting Smalltalk/V learn what you intend to do. All operations from the text editing menu operate on the selected text. To select a text, you move the cursor to its beginning and press the **Grey Plus** key, then place the cursor to the end of selection and press the **Grey Minus** key. Text can also be selected by mouse. Anyway, the selection is painted black. Pop up the text menu and you'll see something similar to Fig. 2.5. This is the most frequent menu

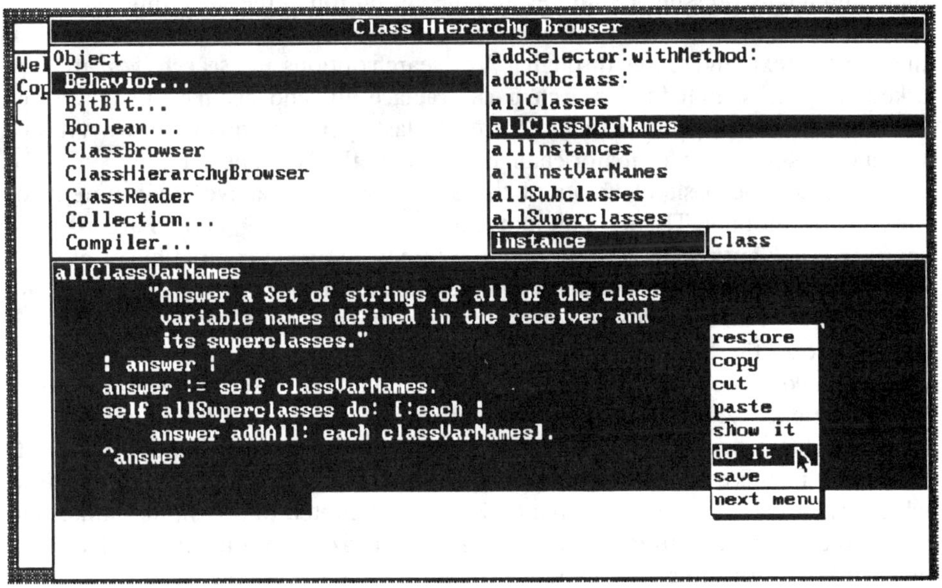

Fig. 2.5 — The selection mechanism with a text editor menu.

you'll encounter. It is divided into four parts. The **show it** and **do it** are by far the most important. Activating one of them will execute the selected text as a Smalltalk program — equivalent to a RUN statement in BASIC, for example. Every Smalltalk program returns a value and the only difference between **show it** and **do it** is that the computed value will be shown on screen if **show it** were carried out. We might say that **show it** is a **do it** with the last result printed on screen.

The selected text is actually a copy of an object that Smalltalk/V is maintaining behind the scene. If you change your mind about the selected text, you can choose the **restore** option to effectively erase text in the whole window. It is particularly handy for deleting warnings and errors from the compiler. On the other hand, if you are satisfied with the selected text, the option **save** will update (and effectively alter) the object whose 'picture' you have been editing.

The remaining four options from the text pane menu relate to text editing. The text editor has a buffer for transfers of text from place to place. The **cut** option erases the selection from the text pane, and puts it into the buffer. The **copy** option is similar, except that it doesn't erase the selection. The buffer contents can be inserted through the **paste** option. There is only one buffer for all text editors, regardless of how many windows you have on screen, so **cut**, **copy** and **paste** can move and copy text to and from different windows.

Sometimes, you'll need to select a piece of text which will not fit the screen. You can mark it in the usual way, starting and ending with the **Grey Plus** and **Minus** keys. A better way is to mark the beginning of the block with a click of the left mouse button, then scroll through the text pane by pressing the right button, moving the cursor simultaneously towards one of the window boundaries, releasing the button then, and finally pressing a **Shift** key and the left button at the same time.

The lowest option, **next menu**, displays another menu, from which you can **print** the selected text, and search through it. The search options are: **search** (you are then asked what to search for), **search back**, **replace all**, and **again** (repeat the last operation). This last option exactly repeats the last operation, no matter what it was, which comes in handy for major changes within methods of one class.

These are the basic elements of the Smalltalk/V interactive environment for program developing. There's a bit more, though. Keys **F2**, **F9**, and **F0** are assigned special roles. **F2** prints the contents of the screen to an Epson-compatible printer; **F9** takes you to the next window; and **F0** moves the cursor to the next pane if there are more panes within a window. (Note that in Smalltalk/V286, **F2** does not print — it merely freezes the computer!)

Smalltalk/V does everything graphically, so on the slowest (4.77 MHz) PCs you may experience some delay between depressing the keys and the appearance of letters on the screen. Also, Smalltalk/V manages virtual memory if more than 640K is needed. To this end, it will swap (sometimes quite large) parts of itself to the disk, which might take a while. Be patient. Do not be tempted to press random keys to attract the computer's attention! All keys are memorized, so you might end up in an awkward situation after a few minutes. However, if you do want to stop Smalltalk/V from doing what it's doing, press **Ctrl–Break:** it always does the job, halts everything and shows you the special window, which you can **close** and continue as if nothing had happened.

2.5 OBJECTS AND MESSAGES

Everything in Smalltalk is an object. This axiom is consistently applied to all aspects of Smalltalk/V. The control structures, compiler, debugger, code inspector, integers, booleans, reals, strings, rectangles, points, lines, forms, screens and windows are all objects which react to messages. A *message* has three parts: the *receiver*, the *selector*, and (optionally) the *argument(s)*. The message is evaluated and the result is sent to the receiver.

According to the number of arguments, there are three types of message: *unary*, *binary*, and *keyword*. Unary messages have no arguments, only a receiver and a selector. For example:

5 factorial

means that message **factorial** is sent to object 5. The statements

| alpha |
alpha := 40. alpha sin

mean that the selector **sin** is sent to the number to which identifier **alpha** points. **Selector** is a synonym for message, while **alpha** and **5** are receivers.

Binary messages have a single argument. Examples of such messages are:

1 + 3

in which **1** is the receiving object, + is the message, and **3** is the argument. This is all very much like standard programming languages such as BASIC and Pascal. But let us have a look at the following example:

(10 @ 20) + 50.

The same message, +, is directed to quite another receiver, a point **(10 @ 20)** in this case. The result will be another point, **(60 @ 70)**, because message + for points is defined as a simultaneous addition of the argument to both coordinates. What we have here is *operator overloading*. In both expressions the same message, +, has been used, but with quite different results. The receivers reacted to the same message differently, according to the nature of the particular object they represented.

Arithmetic messages are the main representatives of binary messages, which are always computed from left to right. This can lead to surprises. Messages like

1 + 2 * 3

evaluate incorrectly: the result would be 9 instead of 7. Parentheses must be used to denote the precise order of arithmetical evaluations:

1 + (2 * 3)

The messages we have seen so far are comparable to, say, Pascal statements and functions. We can mentally translate unary messages from Smalltalk/V to function calls with one argument in Pascal, like this:

y := sin(alpha).

And vice versa: just as Pascal functions may have several arguments, so Smalltalk messages may use several parameters. A message with more than one argument is called the *keyword* message. (Binary messages are probably the most common example of this group.) The following is an example of string accessing in several languages. In BASIC:

MID$("This is a Smalltalk string",2,1)

or in Pascal:

```
VAR A : ARRAY [1..26] OF CHAR;
    Y : CHAR;
....
A := 'This is a Smalltalk string';
Y := A[2];
....
```

Finally, in Smalltalk/V we use a binary message:

'This is a Smalltalk string' at: 2

which yields the character **$h** as the result. The message **at:** is defined for class **Object** (into which all other classes are embedded), so literally all objects in Smalltalk/V can respond to it. In other words, all classes can use this message, since all are subclasses of **Object**.

Now let's have a look at the message with two arguments:

#(1 2 2 3 4 5 6) at: 2 put: 3

which changes the receiver to

#(1 3 2 3 4 5 6).

The message **at:** is again determining the position within the receiver, while **put:** substitutes the value of its argument into the receiver object. To denote a *keyword message*, just leave out the arguments — **at:put:**, for instance. Smalltalk names are thus quite informative. Analogously, the message **copyFrom:to:** has two arguments, and copies elements of the receiver to make a new object:

#(1 2 3 4 5 6 7 8 9) copyFrom: 3 to: 7

The result is

#(3 4 5 6 7).

The results of all these examples can be seen in Fig. 2.6. For example:

#(1 2 3 4 5 6 7) size + 2

is executed like this. Unary messages are always evaluated before anything else; since the size of array **#(1 2 3 4 5 6 7)** is 7, the unary message **size** applied to that array yields 7. The total result is, therefore, 7 + 2 = 9. Similarly, 11 results from the following expression:

'asdfgh' size + #(12 56) size + 3

Binary messages are also evaluated before keyword messages. The following expression gives #**(2 3 4 5 6)** as a result:

#(1 2 3 4 5 6 7) copyFrom: 1 + 1 to: 2 + 4

Cascaded messages are a series of messages to the same receiver. Each message

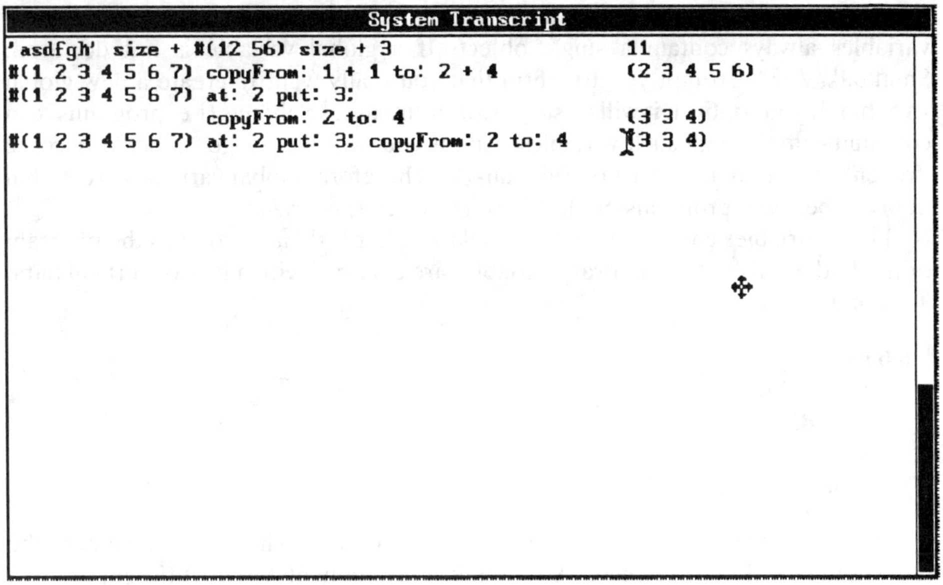

Fig. 2.6 — Messages and results can be freely combined.

after the first is preceded by a semicolon. This is just a shorthand. Consider this sequence of statements:

#(1 2 3 4 5 6 7) at: 2 put: 3.
#(1 2 3 4 5 6 7) copyFrom: 2 to: 4

The first statement finishes with a full-stop. It is much like a semicolon in Pascal — a statement separator. But the receiver is the same, so a cascaded message would serve better. Here it is:

```
#(1 2 3 4 5 6 7) at: 2 put: 3;
                 copyFrom: 2 to: 4
```

Tabs and spaces are not significant. This same message could have been written like this:

#(1 2 3 4 5 6 7) at: 2 put: 3; copyFrom: 2 to: 4

or like this:

#(1 2 3 4 5 6 7) at: 2 put:3; copyFrom: 2 to:4

and the result would still be the same. However, indenting enhances readability — one of the prime internal program qualities.

2.6 VARIABLES

A variable name can be any combination of upper and lower case letters and digits. There are two kinds of variables — *shared* (global) and *private* (local). The names of the former begin in upper case, while those of the latter begin in lower case. Global variables always contain a single object. If a global variable is not declared, Smalltalk/V will prompt you to affirm that you really want to create a new global variable. If you confirm, it will be stored for future use, so objects (i.e. programs) can communicate through such variables. And if you save the image, the data become 'frozen' as a permanent part of Smalltalk/V. Therefore, global variables are global not only between programs but last in time as well (*persistency*).

Local variables come and go; Smalltalk/V discards them as soon as the program or method is finished. Temporary variables are declared with a pair of vertical bars, | |. For example:

```
| a b c d |
a := #(1 3 5 7).
b := (1 @ 45).
c := 4.
d := 'Another string am I . . . '.
```

Variables are useless without values attached to them. The symbol := means the same as in Pascal—*assignment*. A Smalltalk/V assignment is quite different though, because a Pascal variable is the address of a memory location that contains the value, while a Smalltalk variable *points* to an object. This has far-reaching consequences: Pascal requires you to decide on the variable type once and for all, while a Smalltalk variable can change type as many times in a program as is needed (*late binding*).

Here is another example with variables and expressions:

```
| sum add1 add2 |
add1 := 20.
add2 := 30.
 ^add1 + add2.
sum := 40
```

The caret symbol indicates that the value after it is to return the result of the series expression. A statement beginning with a caret is called a *return expression*. There may be other statements after it but they will not be executed, like the assignment of 40 to **sum** in the above example.

Fig. 2.7 shows global variables as circles 'floating' in a Smalltalk/V ellipse that encompasses all objects (rectangles) and elements of the same class (shaded polygon). Rectangles in the shaded polygon represent instances of one and the same class while circles in the polygon are class variables. They are not accessible from other objects, just from the elements of the same class. Class variables are mostly used as the means of transferring data from one window to another. For example, you can **cut** a text in one window and **paste** it to another because the text is held in class variables for text editors.

Class variables also begin with a capital but are a bit 'more' private than global Smalltalk/V variables. But there is another layer of privacy — *pool dictionaries*, which contain global constants. An object is allowed to use them only if declared in advance. There are just three pool dictionaries, **CharacterConstants**, **Cursors** and **FunctionKeys**, though you can easily build others if you want to. (However,

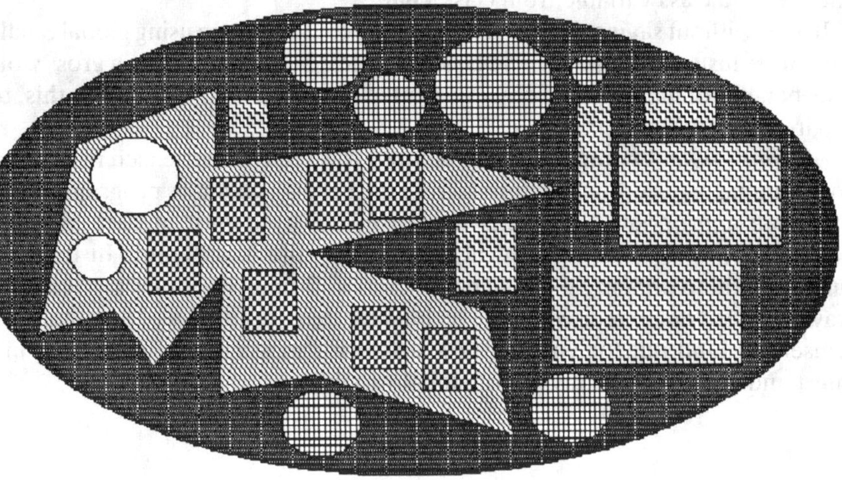

Fig. 2.7 — Global and local variables.

throughout two and a half years of intensive programming with Smalltalk/V I have never felt the need for new pool dictionaries.)

All these variables can be seen in the definition of a class as it appears after clicking on the class name in the **ClassHierarchyBrowser** window. For example, class **CursorManager** uses all three types of variables:

```
Object subclass: #CursorManager
    instanceVariableNames:
        'hotSpot image '
    classVariableNames:
        'NoMouse Position '
    poolDictionaries:
        'CharacterConstants Cursors FunctionKeys '
```

Beware of the term 'instance variable name'. Such variables are global for the class, just like global variables in Modula-2 modules or in Turbo Pascal units. They apply to one instance of a class, i.e. to one particular object. They are both global in the sense that all methods from that class have access to them, and non-global in the sense of class variables. In other words, objects maintain the privacy of these values. Instance variable names are known within the class but are not known outside of it. Their values can be set or read only through special methods that must exist in the class. This is true information hiding, and Smalltalk not only offers this facility but actually enforces it.

Class variables can be exported from the class. It is important to note that they survive periods in which no instance of their class exists in the system. They are true global variables in this respect. For example, you can always ask for the time with the class message

Time now

which reads a class variable from class **Time**.

It goes without saying that all programming could be done using global Smalltalk/V variables instead of instance and class variables. but this would be a gross violation of the benefits of modular and object-oriented programming. You can do this, but be prepared for problems.

(*Author's note*. I wrote the above before I was really experienced in Smalltalk/V programming, and certainly before I wrote the Billing Schedules program. It seemed more than appropriate then. It is written in the true spirit of data hiding, data encapsulation and other theoretical goodies, but life is different. In the event, I found it useful to organize printing parameters in Billing Schedules as several global arrays. This led me to rediscover the techniques that the authors of Smalltalk/V used themselves. Find out for yourself how disk error messages are organized in class **Object** and compare it to my use of global variables.)

2.7 LOGICAL OPERATORS AND BLOCKS

Logical operators are fairly similar to those in Pascal. Familiar relational operators (<, <=, =, >=, >,>=) are implemented as binary messages. Comparisons return either **false** or **true**. For example:

3 < 4

returns **true**, and

4 >= 5

returns **false**. All objects understand equality, =, and the majority of objects understand all other comparisons. Standard Smalltalk rules apply: ordering messages do not enjoy any special precedence over other messages, so use of parentheses in expressions is recommended.

Smalltalk/V comes with many predefined messages which test some state of an object. For example, the expression

7 odd

returns **true**, and the expression

4 strictlyPositive

answers **true** since the receiver is positive.

Most classes contain a couple of such interrogative methods. For example, a line

^(NumberValues at: 8) = 'YES'

accesses a global variable **NumberValues**. If several classes need to ask for the same thing, then it is best that the data are in a global variable.

Much of the power of Smalltalk comes from blocks. A block is an analogue of the **BEGIN...END** construct in Pascal. A Smalltalk block is a sequence of actions to be performed at a later time. Block syntax is simple: a sequence of expressions enclosed by square brackets. Within a block, statements are separated by full-stops. Any of the above expressions could have been a block. For example:

```
[ 7 even. x strictlyPositive ]
```

A block is evaluated after receiving the message **value**. There can be exactly one or two arguments. Here is a block with one argument:

```
[ :i | i := i + 1 ]
```

Variable **i** is a block argument because it is preceded by a colon. The vertical bar denotes the end of the argument's declaration and the start of executable block code. Such a block cannot exist alone; something must direct the argument's value to it. And here's an example of a block with two arguments:

```
| y |
...
4 7 [ :temp :x | temp = x + y ]
```

The value of **temp** will not be known outside the block.

Class **DiffEqSolver** will later use blocks to read and compile user-defined differential equations.

2.8 CONDITIONALS AND BOOLEAN EXPRESSIONS

Blocks are quite handy for conditional and iterative execution. Smalltalk/V has four predefined messages for conditional execution: **ifTrue:**, **ifFalse:**, **ifTrue:ifFalse:**, **ifFalse:ifTrue:**. These have the effect of **IF**, **IF . . . THEN**, and **IF . . . THEN . . . ELSE** statements of Pascal. For example, the following Pascal code:

```
IF aa<bb THEN cc := aa+bb;
```

would be written like this:

```
aa < bb ifTrue: [ cc := aa + bb ]
```

where **aa**, **bb**, and **cc** are local variables, declared before this statement has been executed. In a similar way, the Smalltalk/V piece of code

```
aa >= bb
      ifFalse: [ cc := aa − bb. cc := cc * cc ]
      ifTrue: [ cc := aa + bb. cc := cc − 1 ]
```

in Pascal might look like this:

```
IF aa>=bb THEN
      BEGIN cc := aa+bb; cc:=cc−1 END
ELSE BEGIN cc := aa-bb; cc:=cc*cc END;
```

Note that in the Smalltalk/V version the 'false' part may come before the 'true' part, contrary to Pascal in which the ordering **IF . . . THEN . . . ELSE** is mandatory. Smalltalk/V is more flexible here — consider the simplicity of this:

```
aa < bb ifFalse: [ aa := bb ]
```

versus the corresponding Pascal code:

```
aa < bb IF THEN
        BEGIN
        END
    ELSE
      aa := bb
    END;
```

Smalltalk/V has two pairs of predefined boolean operators. The first pair is **&** and |; the second pair is **and: aBlock i or: aBlock**. Both are quite similar to the AND/OR pair of Pascal but differ in one important aspect. The **&** and | always take both the receiver and the argument into account and never end prematurely. The **and:** and **or:** cause the boolean evaluation to stop as soon as possible. The technical term is that the 'boolean evaluation short circuits'. If the receiver of **and:** is false, the complete message will be assigned the value of **false**, and the block behind it may never be executed. The case with **or:** and the boolean value of **true** is similar. Boolean evaluation will never short circuit in standard Pascal (and it is an option in Turbo Pascal), but always will in Modula-2 and C.

I have never found use for **&** or |.

Examples of **and:** and **or:** messages could be:

```
| number tempNum |
number >9 and: [ tempNum <= 2 ]
```

The second part must be a block. The same goes for more extensive conditions; the following line tries to ascertain that **posChar** is a special character (neither digit nor letter):

```
| aVal |
aVal := posChar asciiValue.
(aVal >= 32 and: [ aVal < $0 asciiValue ])
or:
(aVal >= $z asciiValue and: [ aVal < 129 ])
```

This, of course, assumes characters to be in ASCII order. Message **asciiValue** returns character position within ASCII sequence. A dollar sign, **$**, in front of a character means the character itself.

2.9 ITERATORS

Smalltalk/V has several iteration statements. The most basic is the iteration message **to:do:**. It has two arguments. The receiver object is the lower limit of the iteration, the first argument is the upper limit, and the second argument is a block of code that is to be repeated. The block can be an arbitrary Smalltalk/V block, but usually it uses the block argument as a loop counter. The following statement computes the sum of the first 7 integers:

```
| sum |
```

```
sum := 0.
1 to: 7 do: [ :i | sum := sum + i ].
 ^sum
```

There is also a keyword message **to:by:do:**, which uses the second argument as an increment. The following method evaluates the product of all odd numbers between 1 and 10:

```
| product |
product := 1.
1 to: 10 by: 2 do: [ :p | product := product * p ].
 ^product
```

Both variations of **to:do:** messages are quite similar to Pascal's **FOR... TO...BY...DO** construct. However, Pascal limits you to integer loop counters, while here they can be any object. Blocks as arguments provide for several other types of loop. Smalltalk/V offers four such generalized iterators: **do:**, **select:**, **reject:**, and **collect:**. The **do:** message is the simplest. It can iterate over collections, not only arrays. Here's a typical example:

```
| stringLen |
stringLen := 0.
'this is the string' do: [ :i |
    stringLen := stringLen + 1 ].
 ^stringLen
```

This code finds the string length. The **do:** message takes a string as its argument, iterates it character by character, and performs the block. The block itself is very simple; it only counts how many times it is executed, producing a string length as the result. Here a **do:** message iterates over a classical array:

```
    | gt10 |
gt10 := 0.
#( 1 23 24 111 3 66 ) do: [ :arrayElement |
    arrayElement > 10 ifTrue: [ gt10 := gt10 + 1 ] ]
 ^gt10
```

This time the **do:** iterates over an array. The block variable is **arrayElement**; the **do:** message takes array elements one by one, passes the value of each to the block variable **arrayElement**, then compares it with **10**. Should **arrayElement** be greater than **10**, the counter **gt10** is updated.

Three other iterators are similar to the **do:** message, but are quite powerful in their own right. The first is the **select:** message. The following piece of code also counts how many members of the receiver array are greater than **10**.

```
#( 1 23 24 111 3 66 ) select: [ :arrayElement |
        arrayElement > 10 ]) size
```

The **select:** message iterates across the receiver and returns all of the elements for which the argument block evaluates to **true**. The resultant array would look like this:

```
#( 23 24 111 66 ).
```

size then yields only the dimension of that intermediate array. The **select:** message returns the result which is of the same type as its receiver.

The **reject:** message is quite similar to **select:**, except that it answers all elements of the receiver for which the argument block evaluates to **false**, instead of **true**. The statement

```
#( 1 23 24 111 3 66 ) reject: [ :arrayElement |
    arrayElement > 10 ]) size
```

returns the value of 2, since there are only two elements smaller than **10**. Finally, the **collect:** message iterates across all of the elements of the receiver, evaluates the argument block for each element one at a time, and answers the collection of all the results returned by the block. For example:

```
#( 1 23 24 111 3 66 ) collect: [ :arrayElement |
    arrayElement := arrayElement + 1 ])
```

This increases all array elements by one.

Smalltalk/V has two **while** statements: **whileTrue:** and **whileFalse:**. Both act only on non-argument blocks. The **whileTrue:** message repeatedly executes the block until it evaluates to **false** for the first time. **whileFalse:** stops the first time the block evaluates to **true**. The **whileTrue:** and **whileFalse:** correspond to **REPEAT... UNTIL** and **WHILE... DO** loops of Pascal. The **while** loop is very general and can replace all other loops. The following **to:do:** message

```
| counter |
counter := 0.
1 to: 10 do: [ :i | counter := counter + 1 ].
 ^counter
```

might be expressed like this:

```
| counter |
counter := 0.
[ counter <= 10 ] whileTrue: [ counter := counter + 1 ].
 ^counter
```

There is yet another type of loop — the **timesRepeat:** message. It repeats the argument block for a predefined number of times:

```
| counter |
counter := 0.
10 timesRepeat: [ counter := counter + 1 ].
```

A theoretical note. One thing might bother you, especially if you previously programmed in BASIC or FORTRAN: is there a GOTO statement? It is well known that in at least two situations GOTO is useful:

— as a premature exit from the middle of a loop, and
— to exit from deep down in several nested loops at once.

An emergency exit like this does exist in Smalltalk/V, in the form of the caret symbol,

^. It returns the result of a computation, halting the computation as a whole — both in the block in which it is executed and in the method in which the block appears.

The structure of Smalltalk forbids the existence of an explicit GOTO, but it exists in another guise. There is a set of **perform:** methods in class **Object** which enables execution of any method of any class provided the model of the class is known. The **model** is a variable inherent in any class and practically contains a means of identifying a class.

The existence of this *incognito* GOTO is necessary to make useful programs. The class hierarchy of Smalltalk/V forces you to separate the keyboard/screen interaction into one group of classes, Dispatchers, while the routines that have to be triggered when a certain key is depressed are in your new class, the one you are writing and that is your program. Without **perform:** it would be impossible to connect events on the keyboard and to execute methods already existing in the system.

Maybe it is not yet quite clear to you; but it should be when you see the Billings Schedule program excerpts in the last chapter. It cost me dearly (several months of development time) to understand this relationship, how to use **perform:** and how not to forget to fill in the value of **model** in the new classes.

I wish I had been able to read about it somewhere else and not have been forced to discover it all alone.

But back to our example — linear search for a value within an array:

```
| value array index array |
array:= #( 1 3 4 5 6 7 8 9 0 33 ). "The array."
value := 7. "This is what we're looking for."
1 to: array size do: [ :i | value = (array at: i)
    ifTrue: [ ^index := i ] "Possible premature exit." ].
^index := 0
```

Text between double quotes contains comments, which Smalltalk/V ignores while interpreting and compiling the code. The third comment points to the place in which the caret may (and eventually will) terminate loop execution. **index** will remember the exact position of the first match, or will return a 0 to the receiver, signalling no match. Only one caret can be executed per loop or method.

It takes some time to get used to the new iterators that Smalltalk/V offers. Some of them offer very elegant solutions to mundane programming tasks. For example, instead of the following code for increasing each array element by one:

```
| array |
array := #(1 2 3 4 5 6 7 8 ).
1 to: array size do: [ :i |
    array at: i put: ((array at: i) + 1) ]
^array
```

you could use the **collect:** message:

```
#(1 2 3 4 5 6 7 8 ) collect: [ :i |
    i := i + 1 ]
```

The above linear search example could also be rewritten in the same manner. But don't get depressed if you do not pick up all these new ways of looping over data. You don't have to use them because **to:do:** does a marvellous job most of the time. Object-oriented programs do not contain that many loops anyway.

Also, we shall shortly meet *streams*. They usually control files, but are also a means of looping over the data.

In my first draft of this part I said something like this: 'People who have recently converted to Smalltalk/V usually use the **to:do:** message instead of **collect:**.' It seemed at the time that the new fabulous iterating operators were so much better than the old-fashioned integer-based iterations. I practised what I preached and consistently tried to replace the **to:do:** message with something else. Most of the time, I had to revert to **to:do:**, as only this gave me what I needed: both access to the index and access to the collection value. After a while I almost forgot that other looping constructs exist. You'll find only a handful of **collect:** iterations in my code.

2.10 CLASSES AND METHODS

Data and algorithms are essential parts of every program. Smalltalk organizes them both into *classes*. A *class* is a description of similar objects. An object described by a particular class is an instance of that class. A class contains data about objects as well as algorithms (methods) for their manipulation. Smalltalk/V variables keep track of objects' internal states. Classes are objects too, with the corresponding *class variables*. The internal state of an object is memorized in *instance variables*. The message **class** displays the class to which an object belongs. For example:

#(1 2 3 4 5 6) class

returns **Array**, which tells us that **#(1 2 3 4 5 6)** is an instance of class **Array**.

A class has a fixed internal representation. You must specify the following items in order to describe a class completely:

— from which class it inherits its behaviour,
— which classes inherit it (if any),
— named instance variables,
— class variables, pool dictionaries,
— class methods, and
— instance methods.

A comment on coding style. We shall denote classes in bold, their instances beginning with an upper case letter, but in normal type. We shall also use nouns in their usual sense. **Form** is a class and Form is an instance of **Form**. Putting indefinite articles **a** and **an** in front of the class name is usual practice for naming Smalltalk variables. (Capitals at the beginning of the word denote global variables.) A name of the class written as a comment frequently precedes the first line of the method. The method is easier to read and the reader knows for sure where the method should be inserted. Methods that are added to an already existing class usually have comments starting with label 'APS', which is a shorthand for '**A**pplications **P**rogramming with **S**malltalk/V'.

You can be pretty sure you will open at least one new class for every new application that you write. To create a new class, you have to perform several well-defined steps. First of all, you find its place within the existing hierarchy of classes. That's the creative part. Then, mechanically, you select the class to which your new class will be a subclass. For example, let us attach a class called **ComplexNumbers** directly to the class **Object**. To do this, invoke the System Menu, select the '**browse classes**' option, and interactively create the **Class Hierarchy Browser** window. The class **Object** will be on the top. Move the cursor to it, pop up the pane menu and select '**add subclass**'. The prompter will ask you for the name of the new class, and after you supply it, a menu will appear. You should get something like the window in Fig. 2.8.The menu offers you four ways of declaring a class in Smalltalk/V:

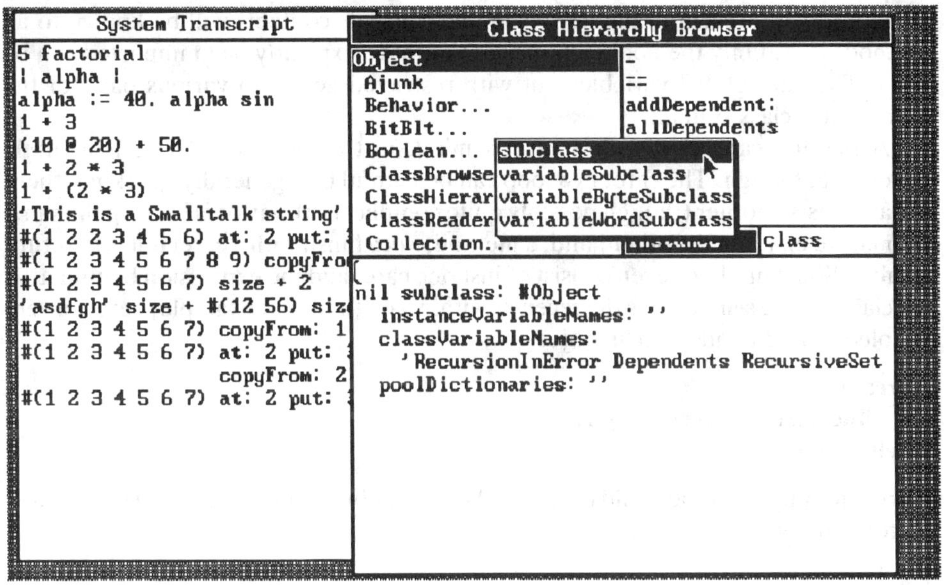

Fig. 2.8 — **Class Hierarchy Browser**.

— **subclass**,
— **variableSubclass**,
— **variableWordSubclass**, and
— **variableByteSubclass**.

The first two create classes whose member objects contain pointers. The third message defines a class whose member objects contain words, and the fourth defines a class whose member objects contain bytes. The first two options are more useful than the other two. Choose an option and Smalltalk/V will then update the classes, inserting your new class into the environment. If you do not see your new class in the list, choose **update** or close and re-open the **Class Hierarchy Browser** window.

Then you must do the actual programming. This means writing methods — the pieces of executable code. The **Class Hierarchy Browser** has several panes, and some of them will be updated by now. Edit the text pane until it looks like this:

```
Object variableSubclass: #ComplexNumbers
    instanceVariableNames: ''
    classVariableNames: ''
    PoolDictionaries: ''
```

You supply the names for pool dictionaries (if any), instance and class variables, inserting them in literals. When done, pop up the text pane menu and select the **save** option. This compiles and updates the class definition on disk.

Not all of these names need be present. For example, *pool dictionaries* are frequently left out. In Pascal terms, a pool dictionary plays the role of a **CONST** declaration. If present in the newly created class, its contents will be known to all methods in it. Only the pool dictionaries that have explicitly been imported can be used. They are global variables but with restricted access to various parts of the hierarchical class system.

A method can finish with a caret symbol, just as in loops. There is a subtle difference, though. The caret in a loop can be helpful but, generally speaking, there always exists another (though possibly quite complicated) way of achieving the same premature exit. On the other hand, a method, *must* finish with a caret if it is to return a value. Some methods even consist of just one caret and the expression behind it. A special variable **self** denotes the receiver within a method. For example, here is a very simple method to add 1 to an object:

```
increase
    "Increase the receiver by 1."
 ^self := self + 1
```

Here is how this method could be used. These three lines should be keyed in from any editor window.

```
| k |
k := 10.
k increase
```

k would become **11** after selecting them and choosing '**show it**'.

increase will also increase by one *any* object for which addition is defined.

self — if it exists — returns a value that is computed in the method. The caret is equivalent here to the RETURN in FORTRAN, C and Modula-2, or the last procedure END in Pascal. Of course, not all the methods need even contain the caret symbol. Methods that operate on instance variables usually end up assigning some values to them, not using the caret. Such methods cause so-called side-effects. They are often a topic for a heated debate but we need not bother with this here. Side-effects are useful, and many methods in this book will use them as a standard technique.

2.11 RECURSION

Recursion is a powerful idea in programming. It takes three steps to use it properly:

(1) Investigate which parts of an algorithm or data are defined in terms of themselves but with smaller dimensions than the original problem.
(2) Introduce a parameter (usually a counter) which must decrease in order to provide a break-out of the recursive process (a trivial case).
(3) Identify and provide the code for the trivial case. Usually, the condition is met when the parameter is equal to 0, 1, or 2.

The most often cited case is the factorial function. The second most cited recursive function is 'The Tower of Hanoi' game. The third prize goes to Fibonacci numbers, the fourth to Ackermann's function. We'll spare you of all of them. (The methods for factorial and Fibonacci numbers are in the manual anyway.) So here is McCarty's function. It is defined as

maccarty(n) = IF n > 100 THEN n − 10
ELSE maccarty (maccarty (n + 11)).

How do we compute it? The Smalltalk/V code is quite simple:

```
mac
    "MacCarty's function."
self > 100 ifTrue: [ ^self - 10 ].
 ^ (( self + 11) mac) mac
```

This should be inserted as a "**new method**" into class **Integer** (subclass of **Magnitude**). And it works: select **(3 mac)** in any text pane, "**show it**" and you'll get **91** as answer. This example shows that recursive coding in Smalltalk/V is quite easy.

By the way, it is not at all difficult to prove that McCarty's function boils down to

max (n − 10, 91).

2.12 CREATING CLASS METHODS

Classes are objects too, so messages to classes exist as well. There are only two types of message: to classes and to instances. To differentiate between the two, the **Class Hierarchy Browser** has a special 'toggle' pane — '**class**' and '**instance**'. If the class pane is selected, all the code that you input will be regarded as class methods, and if the instance pane is selected, the methods will relate to instances. The number of instance methods is usually far greater than the number of class methods; the most often used class messages create initialized instances of a class, and nothing else.

Regardless of the method type, a new method is inserted in the following way:

— place the cursor into the method list pane,
— pop up its menu, and
— select '**new method**'.

The text pane then changes into a method template — you edit this, one method at a time. Once you are satisfied with the method, pop up the text pane menu, select '**save**' to both compile and physically save code on the disk. The '**save**' option acts therefore as a 'compile' option of classical compilers. To run the new method, key in the statements you want to test, select them, pop up the text pane menu and choose either the '**show it**' or the '**do it**' option; the code will be executed immediately. And if you select the '**save image**' option when leaving the system, the test code will be saved too, and it'll be back the next time you load Smalltalk/V.

2.13 CLASS HIERARCHY BROWSER

The **Class Hierarchy Browser** has five panes:

— the class hierarchy list (the upper left pane),
— the method list (the upper right pane),
— the instance pane (left and below the method list pane),
— the class pane (to the right of the instance pane), and
— the text pane.

Three of these panes have menus. The text pane menu is identical to other text panes already described (it is also called the *contents pane*).

It is worth going into more detail about the class hierarchy list and the methods list pane menus. There are four functions available from the class hierarchy list pane. The **file out** option writes the class definition (both methods and various variables) as a file with the default extension **.CLS**. The **update** option recomputes the class hierarchy list and is used if you have removed or added a class using another window. The **hide/show** lets you hide or show the subclasses of the selected class. Finally, we have already seen what the **add** subclass option does.

The *method list pane* also has four options. **remove** does what it says — removes (erases) the selected method from the environment. Much as you would expect, the **new method** option adds a method to the class. A template appears in the text pane and you then edit it or key in a new method. The **senders** option searches all of the methods in the environment for methods that call the selected method. This option automatically creates a small window in the upper right screen corner and lists all senders there. Finally, the **implementors** option searches among all of the classes in the environment for implementors of the selected message selector. This will also open a window but in the right lower corner of the screen.

In practice, you'll mostly use the **new method** option — whenever you are creating a new method. Use the **remove** option sparingly — there is no way of retrieving a method you have never saved to the disk. Finally, the **senders** and **implementors** options take a lot of time to execute (they search through all existing classes) and on slower machines you may find the information they give not worth the wait.

In Smalltalk/V one capability is left out of the **Class Hierarchy Browser** — removing whole classes at once. There is, of course, a way of doing this. Evaluate the following expression from any text pane:

NameOfClass removeFromSystem

It is quite a long statement and you cannot decree it unintentionally. Smalltalk/V will complain if the class which is to be terminated has subclasses or if its instances are alive somewhere in the system. A particularly practical piece of information follows: to delete all instances of class, say, **ComplexNumbers** execute this expression from any window:

ComplexNumbers

This removes all references to instances of the prosecuted class. In Smalltalk/V286 **remove class** is a menu option too, so it's a bit easier to use.

Class Hierarchy Browser can be used for actual text input of new programming code, but it is not well suited for the task. Its contents pane is limited in height so Smalltalk/V supports a special type of window — **Class Browser**. It is evoked by typing the name of the class followed by message **edit**, and evaluating it by using '**do it**'. (Alternatively, you can activate it with option '**browse**' in the **Class Hierarchy Browser** window.) You are then prompted for a special **Class Browser** window. It has three panes:

— the dictionary list pane,
— the method list pane, and
— the contents pane.

Fig. 2.8. shows a typical **ClassBrowser**.

The dictionary list pane is the top-left pane. It has two choices: **class** and **instance**. Depending on your selection, the class or instance methods will be available for editing. The method list pane is below the dictionary pane list and contains the list of methods that you can choose from. Finally, the contents pane displays the actual code of the selected method. It is bigger and therefore better for editing purposes. Otherwise, it is a standard Smalltalk/V text pane.

2.14 INHERITANCE AND POLYMORPHISM

Smalltalk/V has about 100 classes as shipped (this number depends on the actual release and version that you have). Class **Object** serves as an abstract class — it contains the most general methods appropriate to all classes. We've already seen many of its messages: **at:**, **put:**, etc. All other classes (except one) are subclasses of **Object** and most of them contain further subclasses of their own. Let us take the class **Magnitude** as an example. **Magnitude** (classes always begin with an upper case letter) has only **Object** as its ancestor, and has many offsprings: **Association**, **Character**, **Date**, **Number**, and **Time**. It is an abstract class unifying objects that can be compared, measured, ordered, and counted. Instances of class **Magnitude** all respond to five usual comparisons (<, <=, =, >, >=) and to some others as well (**between:and:**, **hash**, **max:**, **min:**). These operations are common background for the subclasses, because both dates and, say, numbers can be compared. But the representations of instances of the subclasses are different, and each subclass has to provide its own implementation for each of the common operations. Besides this, each subclass may contribute additional methods, additional instance variables, override certain methods of the superclass, or restrict access to the instances of the superclass.

Before showing how you can actually add a method, another special variable deserves mentioning: **super**. It is needed because methods are inherited just like instance variables. Smalltalk/V obeys the following search mechanism: when a message is sent to an object, Smalltalk/V tries to find such a message within the object's class. If the search is successful, the method is performed. But if the method isn't there, Smalltalk/V repeats the procedure in the object's superclass. If the method isn't there either, the search goes on in one class above and so on, until messages in class **Object** are tried. If the message isn't even that high, you get a walkback window. The process is pictorially represented in Fig. 2.9. This works fine

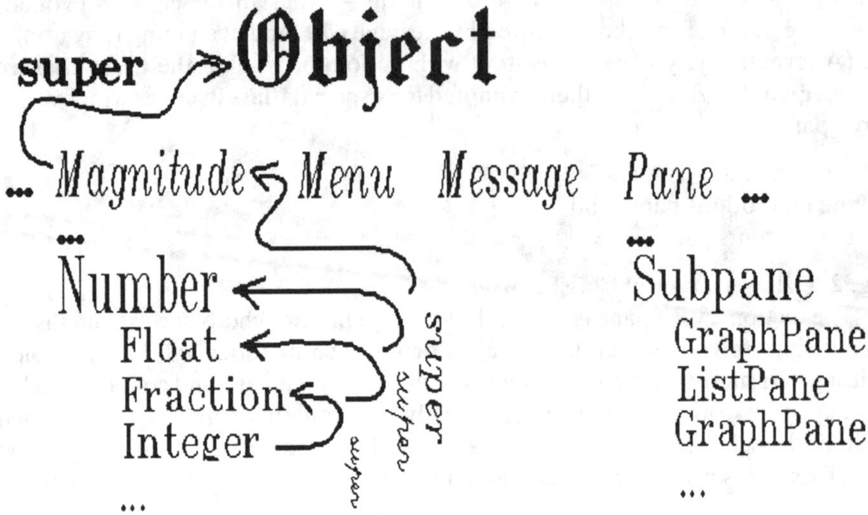

Fig. 2.9 — Inheritance and **super**.

in most situations. But occasionally you want to override this mechanism and use directly a method from the superclass, even though the method with the same name exists in a subclass. This is what **super** enables. It resembles **self** because it represents the receiver in the methods in which it appears. But **super** breaks the search mechanism just described, and forces an *immediate* transfer of search to the superclass. This happens regardless of the existence of that method in the class in which **super** is used. If such a method exists it will be circumvented. But there is more: even if it does not exist in a given class, the use of **super** will force the method from the class 'above' to be executed.

One important occasion for using **super** is when you want to add a new class to the system. Namely, all objects — instances and classes alike — are created by sending the message **new** to some name. So how will Smalltalk/V know that the new class inherits behaviour from the superclass? Of course, the very fact of creating a subclass within the **Class Hierarchy Browser** is enough to put inheritance into effect and most of the time you will not have to do anything else. However, as often as not, you must introduce a '**new**' method for the new class. The question arises: how to make a class method if the class itself is as yet undefined? Here **super** comes in handy. For example, the following code will ensure that the emerging class inherits everything from the class 'above':

new: anInteger

```
"Answer a new Polygon."
| answer |
answer := super new.
^answer
```

There is nothing to force you to identify this message as 'new'. You are free to use any other name — but this would be neither practical nor consistent with other Smalltalk conventions. The greatest benefit of polymorphism is mental ease while creating new method names.

2.15 STREAMS

Most languages support the concept of files as a means of permanent data storage on external media. Smalltalk/V views data as streams of characters. A stream would normally remind you of sequential media only, but each Smalltalk/V stream has an associated current position pointer. There are messages for changing that pointer, so random access to data is possible. The notion of stream encompasses files, devices, and internal objects. They are all sequences of characters (or other objects) as far as Smalltalk/V is concerned. The class hierarchy for streams is:

```
Stream
    ReadStream
    WriteStream
        ReadWriteStream
        FileStream
        TerminalStream
```

The messages from **Stream** are inherited in all its subclasses. It might seem illogical to put **ReadWriteStream** one level below **WriteStream** but in practice this particularity bears no ill fruits.

The most important message is **on:**; it creates a new stream. The following code converts a string into an Array of characters:

```
| stringStream arrayStream |
stringStream := ReadStream on: 'this string'.
arrayStream := WriteStream on: Array new.
[ stringStream atEnd ]
    whileFalse: – arrayStream nextPut: stringStream next ].
^arrayStream contents
(#t #h #i #s # #s #t #r #i #n #g)
```

The message **on:** has a class name as its receiver, while the argument can be anything you want the stream to contain. That is, you declare a variable to be a stream and assign it a type simultaneously. The actual stream type depends on the class you use as a receiver. The above example merely streams over a string and copies it to an array of characters. The last line is the result after **show it**. (Array elements start with a #.)

There are several typical stream messages in this example. The message **atEnd** stops reading the stream when its last element has been read. **next** fetches the next stream element and **nextPut:** writes it onto the receiving stream. Finally, the **contents** message reveals what is in the receiving stream, as shown in the last line of the example. It is necessary to explicitly use that message — without it the answer would be the class to which the stream belongs ('a **WriteStream**', in this case).

The above example converts a homogeneous string into an array of characters. Since we already know the **at:put:** message for arrays, this might be a roundabout way of changing a stream. There is a much more direct way — the position message answers an integer representing the stream's position. The message **position: anInteger** sets the stream position to **anInteger**. Combined with the **next** and the **nextPut: anObject** messages, the **position** enables you to do whatever you want with streams.

These are, of course, the basics. There are many other convenient messages:

— **reset**, reset the stream's position to zero, which effectively puts the stream pointer at the very beginning,
— **skip: anInteger**, move the current stream pointer position by *anInteger*,
— **peek**, fetch the next stream element but do not change the pointer — useful when scouting for the end of the record or file,
— **nextPutAll: aCollection**, write the elements of **aCollection** to the stream and answer **aCollection**,
— **cr**, write a line-terminating character to the stream,
— **printOn: aStream**, produce a character description of the receiver object on **aStream**, and so on.

Subclasses of **Stream** have all these, and some other messages as well.

2.16 FILE STREAMS

The major purpose of streams is to access files. There are two ways of creating a file stream:

— send a message to class **File** specifying a partial or complete path name, and
— send a message to an instance of class **Directory** specifying a particular file in that directory.

There's no need to use the complete path name when sending a message to an instance of class **Directory**. There is also a directory object **Disk**, which contains the current path name. Here are some examples of file creation:

File pathName: 'c:\smaltalk\myprog.lst'
File pathName: 'yourprog.prg'
File pathName: '\dos\link.exe'

The message **pathName:** is the primary means of creating arbitrarily placed disk files. Messages **file:** and **newFile:** also create files but path names are not permitted. Both will create a file if one does not exist. The difference between them is that **newFile:** will erase an already existing file of the same name. Examples of these two messages could be:

Disk file: 'oldprog.pgm'

Disk newFile: 'newprog.opt'

Besides **Disk**, Smalltalk/V also has variables **DiskA** and **DiskB**. They contain root directories for disks **A:** and **B:**. These variables act as real directories — but need not be physically written to the disk. A special message **create** must be sent to a directory object in order to create a 'real' directory.

2.17 FILE STREAMS EXAMPLE — SCREEN TO ASCII FILES TRANSFER

How do we output a piece of Smalltalk/V code onto the disk? Smalltalk/V itself has several ways of writing code to disk (**fileOut**, **save**), but these may not be suitable for your word processor. One possibility is to define a special new class, put all you want to record into one of its methods and save it all to the disk. The other way is to use streams. The following piece of code will output contents of variable **string** to a disk file named ASCII1.DOC.

```
| screenString asciiFile string |
string := ''.
screenString := ReadStream on: string.
asciiFile := Disk file: 'ascii1.doc'.
[ screenString atEnd ] whileFalse: [
  asciiFile nextPut: screenString next ].
asciiFile close
```

You can manually **copy** and **paste** any piece of code on the screen as the contents of the **string**, then select the complete code and '**do it**'. The result is the piece of screen code written to the file ASCII1.DOC. The only problem might arise from using single quotes within strings. Then you have to insert single quotes twice into a string in order to denote a single quote. For example, after the following assignment:

```
string := 'aa bb cc ''aa gg'
```

The contents of the **string** will actually be

```
aa bb cc 'aa gg
```

2.18 COLLECTIONS

A collection is a group of related objects. It is quite a general notion. The **Collection** class is defined as an abstract class in order to provide protocol for:

— iterating over the elements of a collection,
— searching a collection for a particular element,
— adding and removing elements, and
— accessing and changing elements.

Smalltalk/V collections are all characterized by the following four attributes:

— relation of order is imposed on collection elements,
— fixed or expandable collection size,

— whether duplicate elements are allowed, and
— whether collection elements are accessible by indices or lookup keys.

Here is the hierarchical subclass tree for **Collection:**

```
Collection
    Bag
    IndexedCollection
        FixedSizeCollection
            Array
            ByteArray
            Interval
            String
                Symbol
        OrderedCollection
    Set
        Dictionary
            IdentityDictionary
```

This hierarchy of subclasses is typical of the object-oriented way of thinking. At the top we find an abstract class **Collection**. It provides the most basic operations with collections, and all its subclasses inherit its methods. It is a common protocol for its subclasses and no instance of class **Collection** can exist. The most important general **Collection** methods are:

— **add:** (to add an object to the collection),
— **isEmpty** (are there any elements in the collection),
— **notEmpty** (opposite of **isEmpty**),
— **remove:** (remove an object from the collection).

Those messages can be sent to any collection. The immediate ancestors of **Collection** are **Bag**, **IndexedCollection**, and **Set**, as indicated by indentation. They are actually new data types, and so are their subclasses. Only **Array**, **ByteArray**, and **String** have direct counterparts in Pascal or BASIC.

2.19 BAGS

Some classes might come as a complete surprise to the Pascal programmer. Class **Bag**, for example. Duplicate elements are allowed and the ordering is arbitrary. There are no special external keys or indices by which one might gain direct access to an arbitrary element of **Bag**. Standard messages **at:** and **at:put:** are blocked and yield no answer. Bags are useful for containing arbitrary objects and for counting occurrences of equal objects. The following code streams over an array, adds its elements to a Bag, **bb**, then counts them.

```
| aa bb cc |
aa := ReadStream on: #(1 1 2 3 4 1 2 5 6 ).
bb := Bag new.
[ aa atEnd ] whileFalse: [ bb add: aa next ].
```

```
cc := bb occurrencesOf: 1.
cc. bb
Bag(6 5 4 3 2 2 1 1 1 )
```

The last line is the resulting Bag.

2.20 ARRAYS

Class **Array** has (or seems to have) only two methods. They are **printOn:** (appends the ASCII representation of the receiver to aStream), and **storeOn:** (the same, but the receiver can be brought back from a stream). This does not mean that no other messages can be sent to instances of class **Array**. Quite the contrary: all methods from **Collection** (32 of them), **IndexedCollection** (30) and **FixedSizeCollection** (11) can be sent to its elements. All in all, there are 75 methods to chose from when dealing with arrays!

Array elements can be anything you want — anything you assign to them. The following example is impossible in Pascal:

```
| arrayVariable setVariable bagVariable |
setVariable := Set new.
bagVariable := Bag new.
arrayVariable := Array new: 5.
arrayVariable at: 1 put: 2.
arrayVariable at: 2 put: setVariable.
arrayVariable at: 3 put: 'This is some string'.
arrayVariable at: 4 put: #(12 13 45).
arrayVariable at: 5 put: bagVariable.
arrayVariable := 55
```

The first line just denotes that three names will be used for variables. Although their names strongly suggest what will be contained in them, the actual contents can be almost anything. However, the first three lines define variables in an intuitive way. **arrayVariable** will contain five elements and will be an instance of class **Array**. In Pascal, the declaration

```
VAR   arrayVariable : ARRAY [1..5] OF CHAR;
```

would reserve memory for five characters with a collective name **arrayVariable**. Note that you have to declare in advance the type of array elements. Quite unlike that, the fifth statement in the above Smalltalk/V code assigns the number 2 to the first element of **arrayVariable**, the second statement assigns a set to the second element of **arrayVariable**, the third element is a constant string, the fourth becomes a constant numerical array, and the fifth is a Bag. At this point, the contents of **arrayVariable** look like this:

```
(2 Set() 'This is some string' (12 13 45) Bag())
```

and, finally, the sixth statement erases all those assignments and turns **arrayVariable** into 55, a simple number!

It is not possible to write something like this in Smalltalk/V:

```
arrayElement[1] := 2
```

You must use the **at:put:** message to access an array element. This sometimes forces you to write inelegant pieces of code, for instance:

```
| arrayVariable |
1 to: len do: [ :i |

    (arrayVariable at: i) := (arrayVariable at: i) + 8 ]
```

A better solution would be to use the **collect:** message in a proper manner.

A great deal of Smalltalk power comes from the fact that collections can contain any data type. This takes some time to get used to, but after a while your imagination starts to work. Arrays of windows, arrays of screens, arrays of arrays, arrays of sets and sets of arrays, bags of strings, dictionaries of arrays . . . you can have them all.

2.21 STRINGS

Strings are fixed-size indexable sequences of characters. Characters can have numerical codes from 0 to 255. The class **String** has conversions to classes **Date**, **Integer**, **Symbol** as well as to several others. All comparisons are rewritten specifically for strings.

The following string operations are quite common: concatenation, appending, insertion, deletion, comparison, searching, matching, and conversions to and from various other data types. Most of these operations are already included within Smalltalk/V. However, it might take some time to get used to using them, especially if the only programming language you already know is BASIC. String handling is one of BASIC's strongest points, so it would be interesting to see how Smalltalk/V compares. The three most important string functions in BASIC are LEFT$(A$,M), RIGHT$(A$,M), and MID$(A$,M,N).

Take LEFT$(A$,M), for example. It extracts the M leftmost characters from string A$ and assigns them to another string, say, B$. A typical call would be:

```
PRINT LEFT$("12345678',3)
```

and the result is string '123'. Since Smalltalk/V does not deliver by itself a message directly comparable to BASIC's LEFT$, we have to write it ourselves.

One of the proposed benefits of Smalltalk is that of reusing existing code. Class **String** does not contain any code that could be reused on this occasion. The related classes, within the larger class **FixedSizeCollection**, are also unsatisfactory. The class **OrderedCollection**, however, seemed to have the desired qualities (its elements can grow dynamically). **String** is not a subclass of **OrderedCollection**, so inheritance is not possible in a straightforward way. Finally, **IndexedCollection** is a superclass for both **OrderedCollection** and **FixedSizeCollection**. Indeed, there is a method **copyFrom:to:** which fits the bill just fine. So look for some free space in the **Transcript** window, and key in the following:

```
| s1 s2 leftMost |"Trial code for LEFT$"
leftMost := 3.
s1 := '123456'.
```

```
s2 := s1 copyFrom: 1 to: leftMost
```

This is the very first step — would-be variables are turned into constants, and in this phase you should only be interested in what **s2** would be. After evaluating this piece of code with **show it**, the result is: **123**. That is exactly what a LEFT$("123456",3) function in BASIC would have done, so this is promising.

The next step is turning this 'interactive' code into a method. The first question always is: into which class should a method be inserted? ***A new method goes into the class to whose objects it will be sent***. In this case, it is obvious that your new method belongs to **String**. So what name should we give to it? That's easy enough — let it be **left:**. Then sort out input parameters, internal variables and constants. To do this, you first have to envisage how you would like to use the code. Perhaps this syntax is satisfactory:

```
'123456' left: 3
```

or, in a general case:

```
| string1 string2 numberOfLeftmostChars |
string1 := String new.
string2 := String new.
numberOfLeftmostChars := Integer new.
...
string2 := string1 left: numberOfLeftmostChars
...
```

Now invoke the main menu, select **browse classes**, open the window for the **Class Hierarchy Browser**, select class **Collection** and its subclass **String**, move the cursor into the class list pane, invoke its menu and select **new method**. A method template appears in the text pane. Use the **copy** and **paste** editor functions to transfer trial code from the **Transcript** window into the **Class Hierarchy Browser** text pane window, and edit comments until you get something like this:

```
left: numberOfLeftmostChars
    "Answer the numberOfLeftmostChars in a string"
 ^string1 copyFrom: 1 to: numberOfLeftmostChars
```

You can use the **save** option from the text pane menu now in order to both save on disk and compile this text as a new method. The compilation passes without problems, but this does not mean that the new method will work as expected. We note that **string1** receives the message **left:**, which was all right for our trial code. However, we want a general method for string operations and not to be restricted to **string1** only. In other words, we want **left:** to be able to handle all possible strings as input parameters — not only the specific string named **string1**. This is a common problem in Smalltalk, so there is an efficient solution built into the language: use variable **self** to denote the receiver within a method. With this knowledge, we need only change **string1** into **self** and get the last line to read:

```
 ^self copyFrom: 1 to: numberOfLeftmostChars
```

One of the beauties of the Smalltalk/V environment is that after saving this altered method, you can immediately — at the very same window in which the method is shown — type something like

```
'1234567' left: 3
```

select and evaluate it with **show it**, then immediately see whether the new method works. (But beware! — if it does not work, you will have to erase the test code from the text pane window, otherwise the next **save** will report an error.)

After the method is **saved**, it becomes part of the Smalltalk/V system. You have enhanced the basic Smalltalk/V to imitate BASIC's LEFT$ function. It is quite easy now to write the code for the RIGHT$ and the MID$ functions. They are:

```
right: numberOfRightmostChars
   "The rightmost characters"
 ^self copyFrom: numberOfRightmostChars to: (self size)

mid: from to: to

   "Extract middle characters"
 ^self copyFrom: from to: to
```

The **mid:to:** message as written here takes absolute addresses of characters within the string. This may differ slightly from the version of BASIC you have previously used.

Strings can be given values by an ordinary := symbol, or through using the message **with:**. An example is:

```
| str1 str2 str3 |
str1 := String with: $M.
str2 := (String with: $I with: $a).
str3 := (String with: $Y with: $o with: $u).
```

The values will be **M**, **Ia**, and **You**, respectively.

Strings are sooner or later sent to the printer, via message **outputToPrinter**. The following example will underline a string on an Epson FX-compatible printer and produce a new line after that:

```
| eol text underlineStart underlineFinish |
underlineStart := (String with: Esc with: $- with: $1).
underlineFinish := (String with: Esc with: $- with: $0).
eol := (String with: Cr with: Lf).
text := 'This will be underlined.'.
(underlineStart, text, underlineFinish, eol) outputToPrinter.
```

This code is interesting for many reasons. First of all, it is compact. Second, it contains constants such as **Esc**, **Lf**, which begin with an upper case letter and are, therefore, shared variables. In fact, they belong to a pool dictionary named **CharacterConstants** — browsing the **String** class will reveal that it is 'imported' into that class. Then we see constants such as **eol**, which might also be shared variables if we wanted them to be. (We would just have to change their first letters into upper case.) Finally, in the last line, we see an unusual but effective string operator — the comma. It concatenates two strings, so the last line puts the printer in underline mode, prints text, cancels the underline mode, and issues a **Cr/Lf** pair. This signals to a PC-compatible printer to print the current line and start the next one.

The above code can be a starting point for other printer-related messages.

2.22 SETS

Smalltalk/V offers class **Set** to represent unordered collections of unique objects with no external keys. Exactly one object of a kind can exist within a set. The class **Set** is relatively high in the hierarchy — its parent classes are only **Collection** and **Object** itself. Messages **new** and **new:** create new sets, and you can (among other things) order a set to **grow** (expand an existing set to receive more elements), to **add:** some object into it, and to do other, similar, things. None of the usual set operations is included, so we shall add methods for set union, difference, intersection, and symmetric difference.

Set union creates a single set that combines all of the elements of two sets. **Set intersection** creates a set that contains all the elements that the two sets share. **Set difference** creates a set that contains all of the elements of the first set that do not belong to the second set. Finally, symmetric difference creates a set that contains all the elements that are members of either the first or the second set, but do not belong to both at the same time. For example, suppose that sets contain these elements: $A=\{a, b, c, d\}$ and $B=\{c, d, e, f\}$. Then we would like to issue the following Smalltalk/V-like statements (the results are shown in the rightmost column):

```
A setUnion: B                  abcdef
A setDifference: B             ab
A setIntersection: B           cd
A setSymmetricDiff: B          abef
```

The following four methods implement these set operations:

```
setDifference: set2
    "Difference between two sets."
 ^self reject: [ :set set2 includes: set ]

setIntersection: set2
    "Intersection of two sets"
 ^self select: [ :set | set2 includes: set ].

setSymmetricDiff: set2
    "Symmetric difference of two sets"
  | u1 u2 |
u2 := self setIntersection: set2.
u1 := self setUnion: set2.
 ^u1

setUnion: set2
    "Union of two sets"
  set2 do: [ :s | self add: s ].
 ^self
```

The first three are quite straightforward and are used without problems. **setUnion**, however, relies on the **add:** method of the **Set** class, which is the reason why the receiver is changed by the **setUnion** method. The first three methods are free from this.

2.23 DICTIONARIES

A dictionary is a set of pairs consisting of keys and corresponding values. A key can be found through its value and vice versa. (It is customary to use keys to find values, but Smalltalk/V dictionaries work both ways.) Each pair must be unique though, so class **Dictionary** is rightfully located as an immediate subclass of **Set**. Smalltalk/V sets are not such useful structures after all — they do not impose any specific structure on their elements. So dictionaries are widely used as a more usable kind of sets. A **Dictionary** is best understood as two parallel arrays, one holding the keys, the other holding the values.

There are two ways of describing the dictionary structure in Pascal terms. In the first, we would use this declaration:

```
VAR Keys [1..MaxDict]   OF INTEGER;
    Values [1..MaxDict] OF CHAR;
...
```

which uses two separate arrays for keys and values. There is nothing in this code to denote connection between arrays **Keys** and **Values**; however, the programmer must act as if there were such a connection.

The other type of declaration would use an array of records:

```
TYPE Pair = RECORD
              Key : INTEGER;
              Value : CHAR;
            END;
...
VAR Dictionary [1..MaxDict] of Pair;
```

Both types of coding have the same effect, except that Pascal programmers tend to use the first because it is much shorter to type. Also note that in both declarations, data types (INTEGER and CHAR) had to be defined in advance.

Smalltalk/V can address instances of class **Dictionary** both ways. Since class **Dictionary** already exists, we just create its instances, much as we would use the reserved word VAR in Pascal. For example:

```
| phoneBook |
phoneBook := Dictionary new.
```

Variable **phoneBook** is now of type **Dictionary**. We can use all the existing messages such as **add:** and **add:put:**, which closely correspond to the two kinds of Pascal declarations above. A dictionary can grow dynamically (the message **grow**), and it is easy to **inspect** a dictionary (i.e. open an inspector window), have a look at the **keys** (the message keys), remove a pair of data (**removeKey**), and so on.

Dictionaries are very useful for all data to which fast access must be provided. Just as with all other types of objects, dictionary data can be much more than simple pairs of numbers.

2.24 SCREEN HANDLING

The screen is the primary interface between a human and a computer. Regardless of the particular method of pixel creation (projected electrons hit a cathode ray tube and produce light, or by activation of light-emitting diodes (LEDs), etc.), the computer has to reserve a special part of RAM in which the generated picture will be held. This RAM is called VRAM (Visual RAM). It can be organized in several ways, but the simplest is to set aside a bit for every pixel. A pixel is then lit or extinguished when the corresponding bit is set to 1 or 0. Bit manipulation of VRAM directly changes the screen status. This is known as *bit-image display* or *raster*. All shapes can be built out of pixels, including such common symbols as letters and punctuation. *Everything* is high-resolution graphics in Smalltalk/V.

Most computer languages provide only the basic tools for drawing pixels and lines. Such operations are rarely a part of the language itself, and are usually implemented through add-on libraries (toolkits). Smalltalk/V, however, incorporates useful concepts and a large number of graphics operations from the very start. The biggest advance is the concept of *form*. A form is a rectangular bit map onto which something can be drawn. As you would expect, forms are instances of class **Form**. Technically speaking, **Form** is a subclass of other two classes, **DisplayMedium** and **DisplayObject**. Both are abstract classes, not being allowed to have instances. Actually, if you try out something like this:

| newVariable |
newVariable := DisplayMedium new.

you will get an error.

Methods in **DisplayObject** define a general framework for transferring rectangular blocks from an instance of **DisplayObject** to an instance of class **DisplayMedium**. The most important instance methods are:

— **boundingBox**, which returns a Rectangle which bounds the receiver;
— **displayAt: aPoint**, which actually draws or writes the receiver on the screen. The receiver is usually a Form.

Finally, there is a general keyword for displaying an instance of **DisplayObject** on the screen. It can be described as:

displayOn: aDisplayMedium
    at: aPoint
    clippingBox: aRectangle
    rule: anInteger
    mask: aForm

The intention should be clear: an instance of **DisplayObject**, called **aDisplayMedium**, is to be shown somewhere on the screen. **aDisplayMedium** has to be declared in advance; it will almost always be an instance of class **Form**. A picture in **aDisplayMedium** can be larger than the window (**aRectangle**) in which we want to display it, so one parameter of the **displayOn:** keyword has to set limits. It is named, quite appropriately, **clippingBox:**, with **aRectangle** as an argument. But where exactly on screen will the clipping rectangle be placed? Since rectangles are quite predictable figures, it suffices to name the upper left edge — and that is exactly what the **at: aPoint** part does. But this is not all. A Smalltalk/V screen can get quite cluttered at times — windows, forms, characters overlapping each other all of which we simply do not care to watch when issuing a **displayOn:** message. Two other parameters paint the rectangle (**mask: aForm**) and then control the interaction of **DisplayObject** with the masked form.

Now we have to spell out what values the parameters can take and how to write them down. The parameters belong to classes **Integer**, **Point**, **Rectangle**, **Form**, and **DisplayMedium**. Class **Integer** is a subclass of **Magnitude** and it behaves like integers in all other languages. Now let us study graphics classes.

2.25 POINTS

Elements of class **Point** usually denote geometrical points and are written as two numbers separated by @. For example:

0 @ 0

is the upper left point of the screen, and

100 @ 200

is another point, 100 pixels away from the left screen edge and 200 points down from the upper screen edge.

Just defining a point is not enough to see it; the notion of point in Smalltalk/V is wider than its pure geometrical representation. A point can also be used as an ordered pair of numbers, even without any visual significance on certain occasions! We bear this in mind for the future; for the time being we use Points as points, in their usual geometrical sense. You can add, subtract, multiply, compare and do other natural operations on points, just as in school mathematics. For instance:

(10 @ 20) + (100 @ 345)
(110 @ 365)

(10 @ 20) – (100 @ 345)
(–90 @ –325)

*(10 @ 20) * (100 @ 345)*
(1000 @ 6900)

There are special messages for accessing and changing elements of a point: **x** and **x:** for the first coordinate, and **y** and **y:** for the second coordinate. Message **x** sent to **aPoint** returns just the value of the x-coordinate:

(33 @ 45) x
33

while binary message **y:** alters the *y*-coordinate:

(33 @ 45) y: 67
(33 @ 67)

2.26 RECTANGLES

Class **Rectangle** is a pair of points which define a rectangular block of bits contained in a form. The first Point, called **origin**, is the upper left vertex, and the second Point (called **corner**) is the lower right vertex of the Rectangle. There are several ways of defining a Rectangle: through **origin** and **corner**, through **origin**, **width** and **height** (these last two represent the sides), or through **origin** and **extent**. All three are equivalent and reduce to the **origin** and **corner** definitions. They differ in how **corner** is calculated. The following two definitions are equivalent:

1 @ 1 corner: 200 @ 200
1 @ 1 extent: 199 @ 199

Class **Rectangle** contains many messages, but they do not concern us right now. We shall explain them as the need arises.

2.27 FORMS

Class **Form** describes a bit matrix. It is the primary means of displaying graphics entities in Smalltalk/V. A Form is always rectangular in shape, so Rectangles are always used when defining a Form. By analogy with class **Rectangle**, class **Form** has named instance variables **width** and **height**, together with messages **width:** and **height:** for setting their values. A typical use would be defining a new form, perhaps like this:

| f |
f := Form new.
f width: 34 height: 89

Executing this code will not bring a visual representation of Form **f** to the screen — not until you send it a **displayOn:** message.

The principal exemplar of this class is the global variable **Display**. It is a Form that resides in VRAM. Therefore, anything you send to Display will immediately appear on the screen.

Message **fromDisplay: aRectangle** 'steals' contents of the screen that are bounded by **aRectangle**. You can also interactively create a Form, by sending messages **fromUser** and **fromUserSize: aPoint**. The former is the same moving rectangle as when creating windows from the main menu; the latter takes the present cursor position as the corner and asks the user to point to the bottom right corner.

Forms compete to be visible on the screen, so there are two other messages: **rule: anInteger**, for initial background colour, and **mask: aForm**, to specify the means of interaction with already existing graphics entities. Formally, both messages belong to a class called **BitBlt**. This is a highly technical class in its contents and contains messages for fast copying of bit maps from one Smalltalk/V object to another. Actually, it transfers source Rectangles to destination Rectangles, specifying the texture of the destination Rectangles and how to merge bits from source Rectangle with the bit map of the destination Rectangle. There are five choices of background masks: **white**, **black**, **grey**, **darkGrey**, and **lightGrey**, and they are denoted by sending messages of the same name to a Form. For example:

Form grey

will set the mask of the destination Form to grey.

Messages **over**, **orRule**, **andRule**, **under**, **erase**, **reverse**, and **orThru** specify how to resolve the collision of bits in the source and the destination Form. **over** merely copies the source form bit by bit to the destination Form — no boolean evaluation takes place. This is what you want most of the time: drawing on the screen, regardless of what is there already. Three logic operations are expressed as **orRule** (pairs of bits from source and destination are first logically ORed and the resultant bit is kept), **andRule** (logical AND), **reverse** (logical XOR). **under** is the same as **andRule**; **erase** does what it implies — changes every 1 bit into a 0, and finally, **orThru** is a sequence of unconditional erasing and ORing.

The following code can be used as a model. It simply declares a new Form, **f**, and brings it to the middle of the screen:

```
| f |
f := Form new.
f width: 200 height: 200.
f displayOn: Display
    at: 110 @ 91
    clippingBox: ((50 @ 50) extent: (300 @ 150))
    rule: Form orThru
    mask: Form black
```

The result is shown in Fig. 2.10. You are encouraged to experiment further with various combinations of **rule:** and **mask:** parameters. The above code transfers Form **f** to **Display**, making **f** visible. The upper left corner of **Display** is always at **(0@0)**. The Point specified for the **at:** keyword is added to the **Display** corner, so the **f**'s corner is scheduled to there. This still does not guarantee that it will be visible — it depends on the Rectangle from the **clippingBox:** keyword. In this particular case, the left corner will be visible, and the visible lower right corner will be at **(300 @ 150)**.

We started to explain **Points, Rectangles** and **Forms** in order to explain the **displayOn:** keyword from class **DisplayObject**. Incidentally, we meet the same message at the end of the story. This is one of many examples of inheritance in Smalltalk/V. In the above example we sent the **displayOn:** message to a Form, while using other Forms as parameters for the **rule:** and **mask:** keywords. This is perfectly legal in Smalltalk/V.

Let us sum it up. Now we can

— specify Points and Rectangles,
— create Forms in which drawings will reside,
— display them anywhere on the screen,

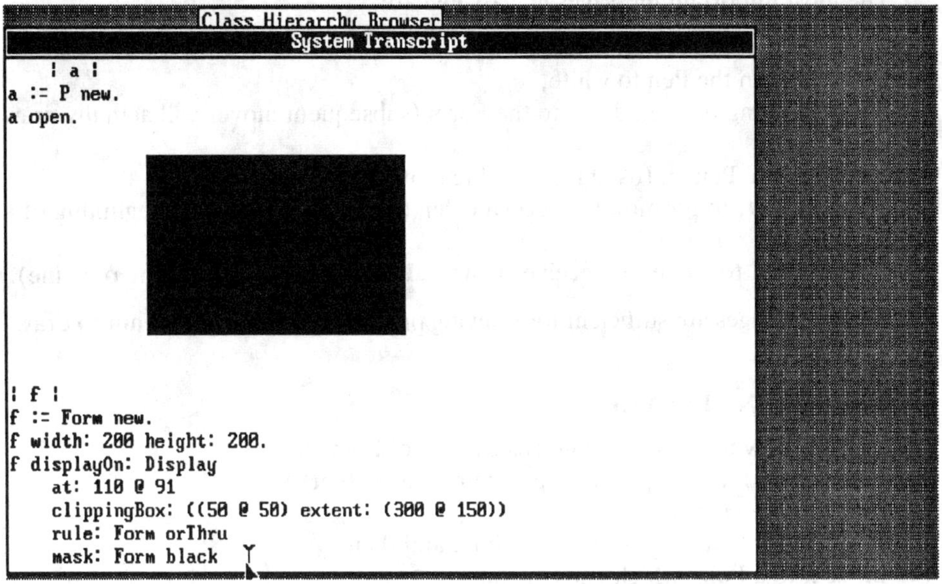

Fig. 2.10 — Creation of a new Form.

but we still haven't seen how to draw. Class **Pen** contains methods to draw points and specifies other related parameters.

2.28 CLASS PEN

Instances of class **Pen** actually draw points and lines. **Pen** is a subclass of **BitBlt**, so all messages valid for **BitBlt** are still valid for **Pen**. As usual, it makes sense to introduce a new subclass only if the behaviour of the parent class is going to be enriched in some way. **Pen** imitates a normal pen — you can move it, change its position and direction, hold it up or down, enlarge the thickness of the line, and so on. Pens cannot exist without target Forms, on and over which they would move. (This is a straightforward translation of material pens and forms of paper into useful programming entities.) The Form must already exist in the system, be it a global Form such as **Display**, or something else. The message

Pen new

binds a Pen to **Display**, specifying the colour black and a nib (line thickness) of size 1 by 1. Message **new:** is rather more general, with a typical usage such as:

| pen |

pen := Pen new: aForm

where **pen** is a new Pen, bound to **aForm**.

The most important messages in class **Pen** are:

— **black**, to turn the Pen to black,
— **white**, to turn the Pen to white,
— **down**, to bring the Pen down to the Form (subsequent moves will actually draw lines),
— **up**, to lift the Pen up (used for invisible movements of the Pen),
— **place: aPoint**, to position the receiver Pen at **aPoint** (useful as a beginning of a line),
— **goto: aPoint**, to move the receiver Pen to **aPoint** (useful as an ending of a line).

These messages are sufficient for drawing practically anything we want to draw.

2.29 LINES AND POLYGONS

Now we see how to draw a line given as a pair of Points:
(1) put the Pen into an appropriate colour (usually **black**),
(2) force the Pen **down**,
(3) place it to a Point which starts the line, and then
(4) move it to a Point which ends the line.

These messages are sent to the same Pen and are usually cascaded. Let us draw a line between points (**100@100**) and (**200@200**):

```
| pen |
pen := Pen new.
pen down;
    black;
    place: (100 @ 100);
    goto: (200 @ 200)
```

This is the basic algorithm for drawing particular lines. Polygons are just as easy:

```
| pen a |
pen := Pen new.
a := Array new: 10.
a := #( 10 10 10 100 99 300).
1 to: a size - 2 by: 2 do: [ :i |
   pen down;
         gray;
         place: (a at: i) @ (a at: i + 1);
         goto: (a at: i + 2) (a at: i + 3).
   ].
```

Elements of Array **a** are just amorphous numbers. There is no specific structure laid upon them. The above code treats them as pairs of coordinates (odd elements are *x*-coordinates), which act as parameters for the **place:** and **goto:** messages. However, it is possible to improve the code by opening a whole new class to deal with polygons exclusively. Quite reasonably, its name is **Polygon**.

2.30 POLYGONS

The primary reason for creating a new class in this case is to establish a new data structure, **Polygon**. Here we are presented with a typical task of borrowing as much code as possible from the existing classes. A polygon is just a series of vertices — points, that is. Evidently, we need some sort of Collection. Its elements will be Points. Smalltalk/V is particularly rich in Collections, and the candidates are Bags, FixedSizeCollections (Arrays in particular), OrderedCollections, Sets, and Dictionaries. Arrays would be the only choice in **imperative** languages, and indeed an Array would fit well as a data structure for class **Polygon**. But we prefer OrderedCollections because of their flexibility: elements can be freely added or deleted from an OrderedCollection, while instances of **Array** — as a subclass of **FixedSizeCollection** — cannot change size that easily.

Once a data structure is decided upon, it influences the choice of available methods. In particular, we have to use the **add:** method to put something into a Polygon, instead of the **at:put:** keyword used for Arrays.

We shall present the complete class **Polygon** in a so-called *chunk format*. It is what you get on disk after executing the fileout option from the **Class Hierarchy Browser** window. A file in chunk format is an ASCII file with exclamation marks denoting the ends of methods, and with two consecutive exclamation marks denoting the end(s) of class and instance methods. Here it is:

```
OrderedCollection variableSubclass: #Polygon
  instanceVariableNames: ''
  classVariableNames: ''
  poolDictionaries: '' !
! Polygon class methods !

new
        "Create Polygon class"
    | answer |
    answer := super new.
    ^answer! !

!Polygon methods !

drawPolygon
    | pen form |
form:= Form new width: Display width height: Display height.
pen := Pen new: form white.
1 to: self size - 1 do: [ :i |
pen place: ( self at: i);
    down;
    goto: ( self at: i + 1).].
form displayAt: 0 @ 0.
"Redraw screen."
Menu message: 'continue'.
Scheduler systemDispatcher redraw!

printPolygon          "Print vertices vertically, as pairs."
    | inputStream outputStream vertex |
```

```
    inputStream := ReadStream on: self.
    outputStream := WriteStream on: String new.
    outputStream cr.
    [ inputStream atEnd]
    whileFalse: [ vertex := inputStream next.
            vertex x printOn: outputStream.
            outputStream space.
            vertex y printOn: outputStream.
            outputStream space; cr. ].
  ^outputStream contents!
testPolygon
   "Initialize a polygon for testing purposes."
   self add: 100 @ 250; add: 100 @ 250;
      add: 100 @ 110; add: 124 @ 100;
      add: 154 @ 90; add: 180 @ 78;
      add: 201 @ 72; add: 213 @ 50;
      add: 300 @ 30; add: 330 @ 40;
      add: 331 @ 43; add: 358 @ 48.
      self addLast: (self at: 1).! !
```

How do we import this file into Smalltalk/V? We could key in the above lines just as they are, with any ASCII editor. After saving it to disk under the name of P.CLS, we would execute the following line:

```
(File pathName: 'P.CLS') fileIn
```

in order to compile this class into the Smalltalk/V programming system. Another way would be to activate the **Class Hierarchy Browser** window and to key in all the methods and class variables, this time *without* exclamation marks. Then we would also compile this class method by method, using the **save** option from the text editor pane.

Polygon is a simple and yet fully defined class. It has just one class method, **new**, the purpose of which is to inherit complete behaviour from parent classes such as **OrderedCollection** and **IndexedCollection**. Generally speaking, **new** could incorporate much more detail on **Polygon** data structures, but this is not needed now. All other methods are instance methods, the most important of which is **testPolygon**. It initializes the polygon through a series of **add:** messages, with Points as parameters. The last line is food for discussion: it binds the last vertex to the first, as is true for all polygons in geometry. Leaving it out transforms polygons into broken lines, which could also be useful on many occasions. The distinction depends only on **testPolygon**, since the **drawPolygon** method does not force any restrictions on the underlying data structure.

drawPolygon contains several interesting techniques. It creates a **form** equal in size to the **Display**, then binds **pen** to it and paints it white. The **do:** loop draws a series of points in the same manner as before, only using **self** directly as a source of adjacent points. Note that nothing can be seen of it until the **displayAt:** message sends it to the screen. This, of course, messes it up. Ideally, we would like to get rid of the picture and return to the usual **Transcript** window. To do this we include lines

Menu message: 'continue'.
Scheduler systemDispatcher redraw!

into the code. The first line produces a small window with the word 'continue', which disappears as soon as you press any key. In this way, you can see program results, then easily erase the screen. The second line returns you to the screen state before drawing the polygon. These two lines are quite useful, particularly when testing new code.

printPolygon is a fairly ordinary stream-oriented print routine. It can be used to examine actual coordinates of a given Polygon.

The following code initializes a test polygon and draws it on the screen. You should key it into the **Transcript** window, select it and **do it**.

```
| p |
  p := Polygon new.
  p testPolygon.
  p drawPolygon
```

The result can be seen in Fig. 2.11. Of course, there are many other uses for a

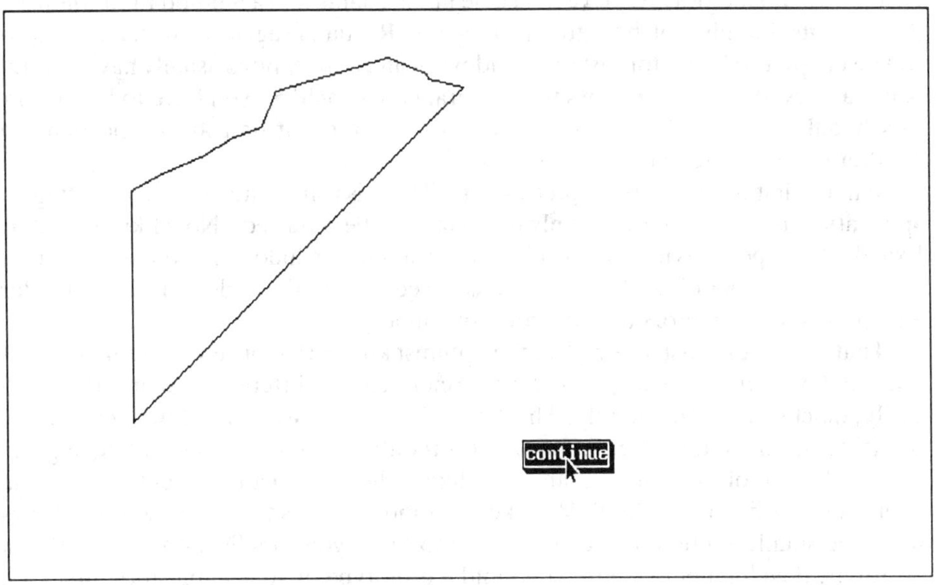

Fig. 2.11 — Drawing a polygon.

class such as **Polygon**. You could implement them simply by adding new methods to the skeleton given here.

2.31 INTRODUCTION TO WINDOWS

Class **Polygon** draws using the whole screen (see Fig. 2.11). In this respect its structure and final appearance differ little from Pascal. The data and the picture are hopelessly divorced; you either edit the data, or you look at the picture. A superior approach would be to handle both data and picture simultaneously. The windowing technology of Smalltalk/V makes that not only possible, but straightforward. Our aim is to create a window with two panes, one for data, the other for the picture.

The mechanism for window creation is not easy to grasp, because of the many parameters involved. Every window can contain several panes (subwindows). For each you must specify the means of user interaction. This boils down to two events:

— the left mouse button has been pressed, and
— the right mouse button has been pressed.

The right button is easier to take care of: by convention, it activates a menu, letting the user select an option and thus communicate with the program. The left button generally denotes that something should change in the pane. You have to supply the routine which will carry out the change and display it visually.

For every pane you also have to decide upon a name and a method for initializing the contents. Finally, you have to state the exact Rectangle against which the window will be clipped. All that for just one window — and applications usually have several panes and even several windows with several panes each! So you have to know how to schedule windows for execution and how to transmit data from one pane to another (or to several windows at once).

When I first drafted this chapter I wrote 'There is usually no point in directing an application as window-based if only one pane will be required.' Now I know better. Exactly the opposite is most convenient: open as many windows as you like, perhaps even a window per object! Most programs are editors for the underlying data. Under Smalltalk/V those editors take the form of windows.

That was a pessimist's view. But the optimist knows that once you create the first few windows on your own, you can routinely create different user interfaces — easily, quickly and competently. The main advantage in using windows' technology is letting the Smalltalk/V environment do the dirty work for you: organizing the screen, layout of the menus, and the like. Then you can concentrate on the application in hand. Smalltalk/V makes you more productive because you always write the smallest amount of code needed to bring your application to life. It is a prototype development system: you build a prototype of your application first (i.e. window, menus, etc.), then fine tune the methods needed for the program to start working. Incidentally, when all the details are taken care of, the program itself is finished. Each time you write a Smalltalk/V program, you experience a sensation of the problem melting away before your eyes into a group of precise little methods, each one sealed, individually testable, and refinable to perfection.

That vision (and reality!) presupposes that you have learned the necessary details of windowing technology. The art of commanding windows starts with menus and the two main types of pane: **ListPane** and **GraphPane**. A **ListPane** is a standard facility for all browsers in Smalltalk/V. Its presence gives the interactive 'feel' to the application. A **GraphPane** is a place for drawing. System windows do not contain it, but application programs are inconceivable without it.

2.32 BUILDING YOUR FIRST WINDOW WITH GraphPane

A window always consists of several elements: a label, a menu, and at least one pane. Here is a class (called **PK**) that will produce a window with just one GraphPane.

```
Object subclass: #PK
   instanceVariableNames:
     'demoPane '
   classVariableNames: ''
   poolDictionaries: ''

PK class methods

PK methods
demo "DS The GraphPane demo."
     | aRect pen |
CursorManager execute change.
aRect := Form new
         width: (demoPane frame width )
         height: (demoPane frame height);
         white.
pen := Pen new: aRect. pen black. pen down.
pen drawFrom: 30 @ 200 to: 200 @ 30.
aRect displayAt: demoPane frame origin.
CursorManager normal change.
 ^aRect

demoFunction: aPoint
     | aRect pen |
CursorManager execute change.
aRect := Form new
         width: (demoPane frame width )
         height: (demoPane frame height);
         white.
pen := Pen new: aRect. pen black. pen down.
pen drawFrom: 30 @ 30 to: 200 @ 200.
aRect displayAt: demoPane frame origin.
CursorManager normal change.
 ^aRect

demoMenu
      "Menu for original data."
 ^Menu
         labels: 'demo' withCrs
         lines: Array new
         selectors: #(demo)
```

```
openOn: aRectangle
  | aTopPane |
      aTopPane := TopPane new
      label: 'Demo function in a window'.
  aTopPane addSubpane:
  (demoPane := GraphPane new
          model: self;
          name: #demoFunction:;
          change: #demoFunction:;
          menu: #demoMenu;
          framingRatio: (0 @ 0 extent: 1 @ 1) ).
  aTopPane reframe: aRectangle.
  aTopPane dispatcher openWindow scheduleWindow
```

This is almost the same class format as the chunk format. All we have done is to delete unnecessary declarations and exclamation marks in order to improve readability. We shall use both formats of presenting Smalltalk/V code in this book.

To create a window which is an instance of class **PK**, key in the following code into the **Transcript** window :

```
  | aaa |
aaa := PK new.
aaa openOn: (10 @ 10 extent: 300 @ 300)
```

Select it and **do it**. You should see something like Fig. 2.12. A class by itself does

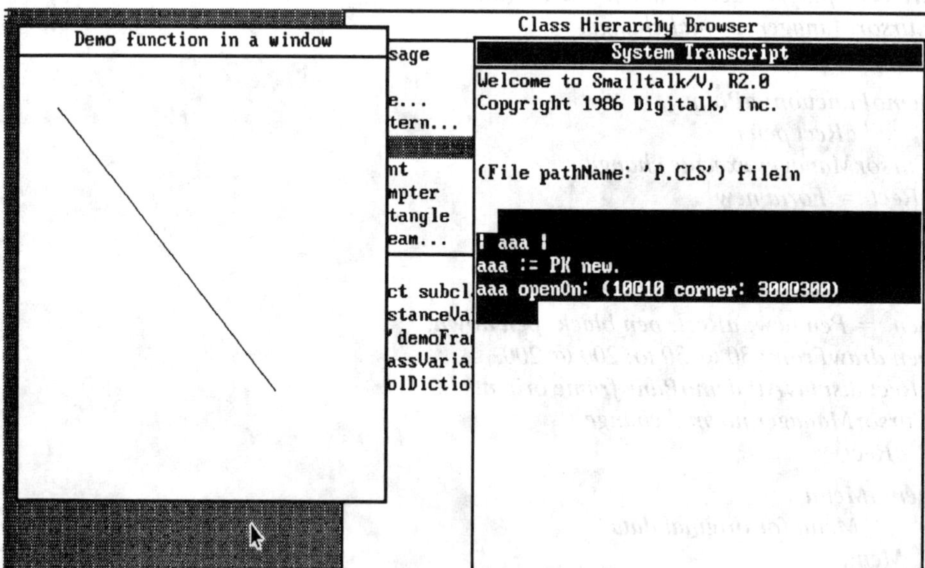

Fig. 2.12 — **GraphPane** — an instance of class **PK**.

nothing — you must create an instance of a class and then send one or several messages to initiate action. Instances are usually created from the **Transcript** window. **aaa** is an instance of class **PK**. The message **openOn:** creates a window — an instance of class **PK**. By convention, all methods for creation of new windows are named **openOn:** or **open**, depending on whether they have input parameters or not.

Let us analyse the code. There is just one instance variable, **demoPane**. An instance variable declared in the method header is both global and local at the same time. It is global for the class because all methods within it can access it. But it is also local since there is no way of exporting it across class boundaries. More precisely, objects from other classes can have access to **demoPane** only if class **PK** contains explicit methods for that. But within every method, variables can be declared that are local only for that one method. So, classes have two kinds of local variable: global for the class and local for the methods. Therefore, data hiding in Smalltalk/V is built right into the language and is not dependent on the programmer's good will or inclination to fail-safe program writing.

There are neither class variables nor pool dictionaries in **PK**. There are no class methods either. This is the least possible windowing class.

2.33 HOW PK WORKS

There are only four class methods. Browser sorts them alphabetically, but the main method is **openOn:** — everything branches from it. Its input parameter is a Rectangle needed to define a window pane. There can be as many panes as you need in a window but this introductory example has only one. The first three lines:

```
| aTopPane |
    aTopPane := TopPane new
    label: 'Demo function in a window'.
```

create a variable called **aTopPane** as an instance of class **TopPane**. The third line labels the window. Class **TopPane** takes care of operations related to entire windows. One of its most important messages is **addSubpane:**, which adds exactly one pane at a time to the instance of **TopPane**. (More panes can be attached to a window by sending a separate **addSubpane:** message for each pane.) However, the code listed in class **PK** above:

```
aTopPane addSubpane:
        (demoPane := GraphPane new
            ...
            framingRatio: (0 @ 0 extent: 1 @ 1) ).
```

can be quite confusing in the beginning. It would be much clearer if it were written as follows: first create a new instance of **GraphPane:**

```
| explicitPane |
explicitPane :=GraphPane new
```

then send it as many defining messages as you want:

```
explicitPane menu: #explicitFunctionMenu.
```

explicitPane model: self.
explicitPane name: #explicitFunction.
. . .

Next attach the pane to the window:

aTopPane addSubpane: demoPane.

and only then initialize other parts of the system, visualize the window, and so on. But all the code that you will see in the manual or elsewhere will be of the same shape as in the **openOn:** method above, so it is worthwhile getting used to it right now.

Pane creation boils down to sending the following messages to the pane instance: **menu:, model:, name:, change:, framingRatio:**, together with several others that we shall see later. These methods can be grouped according to the parameter type. The methods **model:, framingRatio:, returnIndex** take parameters directly, while **menu:, change:, name:** take input parameters indirectly, as symbols.

What is the meaning of **self** in the **open** method? It represents variable **aaa**. Therefore, the line

model: self;

actually executes as

demoPane model: aaa;

Model is another name for the application class that you are writing. In this case, the model class is **PK**. The message **model:** binds the pane to the application class. This enables the application class to send messages to the pane to read, write and process list data. If the **model:** message were missing, your program could not reach the pane. At this stage, you should always include **model: self** into your own **open** methods.

The last line in the **addSubpane:** message reads

framingRatio: (0 @ 0 extent: 1 @ 1)).

Message **framingRatio:** assigns one part of the window to the pane. Its argument is a Rectangle. In this example we have just one pane per window, so we equate them in size.

Now we come to the more exciting part — messages **menu:, name:**, and **change:**. All three methods take symbols as arguments (recognizable as such because they start with a #). The symbols are actually the names of the methods that will be executed on a specific occasion. So if you put a line such as

menu: #demoMenu;

the model class has to contain a method called **demoMenu** or else it will complain when the right mouse button is depressed.

Here are the concrete methods for class **PK:**

name: #demoFunction:;
change: #demoFunction:;
menu: #demoMenu;

Now we have to see how to build the methods called **demoFunction:** and **demoMenu**. The structure of the latter is always the same:

```
demoMenu
    "Menu for original data."
 ^Menu

        labels: 'demo' withCrs
        lines: Array new
        selectors: #(demo)
```

You merely change options' names from class to class (in message **label:**), and call the appropriate methods (in message **selectors:**). There is only one option here: **demo**. It draws a line from **30 @ 200** to **200 @ 30**. To see this line, press the right mouse button somewhere within the pane. A small menu will appear, with only one option — 'demo'. Clicking the left button will execute the **demo** method which, in turn, will erase the pane and draw the line.

demoFunction: is executed whenever the cursor is in the pane and the left mouse button is pressed. The pane is then redrawn, bringing the line from **30 @ 30** to **200 @ 200** to display. The parameter of the **change:** method is the method to be executed whenever the left button is pressed.

This completes the two standard ways of communicating with a windowing application. Note that both methods of drawing lines are identical. Both **demo** and **demoFunction:** use the same lines for this, save for the changed point coordinates. Both have one Point as the input parameter — that is the position of the cursor when the left button is pressed. It is of no use now, but it could be in games, for instance. The cursor changes while drawing so that the user knows something is happening (that's what the messages to the **CursorManager** do). Before using a **pen** for drawing, we must attach it to a Form. The Form here is **aRect**, declared as a local variable both in **demo** and in **demoFunction:**. This is why drawing from the menu erases the pane; there are two local and thus independent Forms at work here.

This technique for drawing within a window is important. Generally speaking, nothing forces us to use the whole pane, black lines on a white background, etc. It can all be changed. But remember that nothing of it will be seen until a **displayAt:** message is sent to the **aRect**.

But how has the initial state been set up? Well, this is the responsibility of the method that is stated as a parameter for the **name:** message to the **demoPane**. In class **PK**, both the greeting pane and the changed pane call the same method, **demoFunction:**, so the same line appears. This, of course, does not have to be so. The parameter of **name:** can be a true greetings screen, for example.

The window will not be visible until the last line of the **openOn:** method is executed:

```
aTopPane dispatcher open scheduleWindow
```

First comes the window name, **aTopPane**. Message **dispatcher** answers the dispatcher for this specific window. **Dispatcher** is an abstract class which processes input from both the keyboard and the mouse; every window has exactly one 'private' dispatcher and it must be 'awakened' otherwise we will not be able to communicate with the window. Having activated the right dispatcher, we send it the message **openOn:** to create a new window. Finally, the message **scheduleWindow** merges the newcomer with the already existing windows and activates it.

Creation of GraphPanes is easy if you bear in mind that arguments of argument methods are supplied for you automatically by Smalltalk/V.

2.34 BUILDING YOUR FIRST WINDOW WITH ListPane

ListPane lists an IndexedCollection of strings and is perfect for selecting an item to which the next menu operation will be applied. Class **P** builds a window with exactly one ListPane. Here is the code.

```
Object subclass: #P
   instanceVariableNames:
     'data pointList'
   classVariableNames: ''
   poolDictionaries: ''
add
     "Invoke a prompter to
      add a string to ListPane."
| prompt |
prompt := Prompter prompt: 'New element, please?'
            default: (String new).
data size == 0
     ifTrue:     [ data add: prompt]
     ifFalse:    [ data add: prompt
                    afterIndex: (pointList selection).].
self show: prompt.!
erase
    "Erase data in the ListPane,
     reverse the unexisting first element."
data := OrderedCollection new.
self show: 1.!
initElements
     "Initialize elements in the ListPane."
   ^data!
initializeData
    "Initialize data itself."
data := OrderedCollection new.
data add: 'self';
     add: '1 @ 3';
     add: '777777'.!
open
        "Create a ListPane window."
     | aTopPane |
```

```
    aTopPane := TopPane new.
    aTopPane label: 'Example List Pane'.
    aTopPane addSubpane:
        (pointList := ListPane new
            change: #show:; "left mouse button — action"
            menu: #pointsMenu; "right mouse button — menu"
            model: self;
            name: #initElements; "initialize pane"
            returnIndex: true; "specific to ListPanes"
            framingRatio: (0 @ 0 extent: 1 @ 1) ).
    self initializeData.
    aTopPane dispatcher open scheduleWindow!
pointsMenu
    "Select menu operation."
 ^Menu
      labels: 'add\remove\erase' withCrs
      lines: Array new
      selectors: #(add remove erase)!

remove
    "Remove an element from ListPane."
| where |
where := pointList selection.
(data size = 0 or: [ where = 1])
    ifFalse: [
        data removeIndex: where.
        self show: (data at: where - 1).
        ].
show: anInteger
    "Left mouse button pressed,
     change reversed item."
pointList changed: #initPoints.
pointList restoreSelected: anInteger.
```

To create a window which is an instance of class **P**, key in the following code into the **Transcript** window:

```
  | win |
win := P new.
win open
```

Select it and **do it**. You will be prompted for a window. After defining it interactively, you might see on screen something like Fig. 2.13.

As before, the **open** method coordinates all activities. The role of the **name:**, **change:** and **menu:** methods is exactly the same as before — they define how to initialize the ListPane (**name:**), what will happen when the left mouse button is pressed (**change:**), and what will happen when the right mouse button is pressed (**menu:**). For this particular ListPane, the arguments of these methods are:

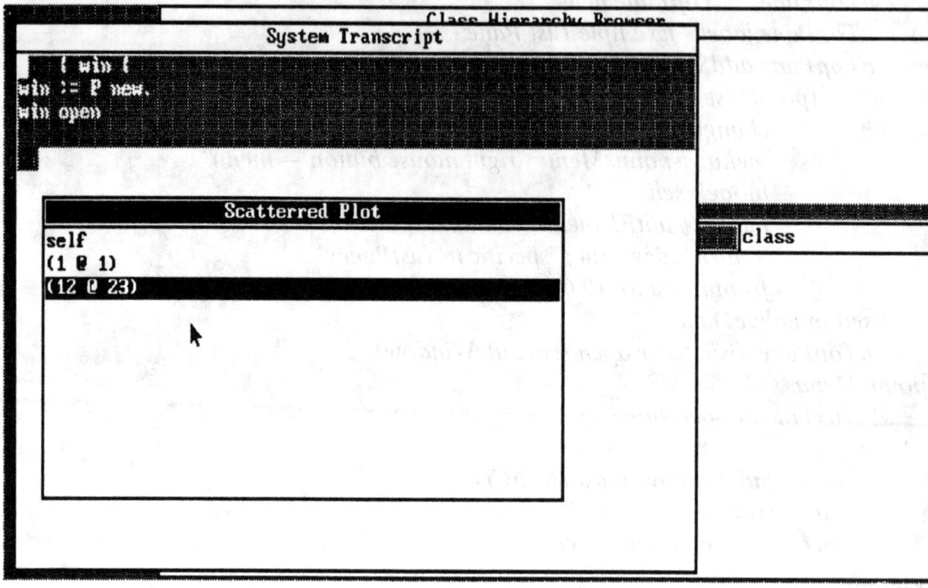

Fig. 2.13 — **ListPane** — an instance of class **P**.

```
change: #show:;               "left mouse button — action"
menu: #pointsMenu;            "right mouse button — menu"
name: #initElements;          "initialize pane"
```

Now we have to see how to build **pointsMenu**, **initElements**, and **show:**. **pointsMenu** is the easiest, since its structure remains the same regardless of the pane type. Since we are shortly going to merge this ListPane with graphics, we can consider the elements of the list to be points, therefore the name — **pointsMenu**. Currently, only three operations are implemented: *add* a point to the list, *remove* a point from the list, and *erase* the complete list.

Data structures make or break the program. The inner workings of the best programs strongly resemble their outward appearance (spreadsheets are a classic example). The outward appearance of a ListPane suggests a choice of some Collection for internal representation. Sets and Bags are notable for their lack of structure, so we are left with FixedSizeCollections and OrderedCollections. Which one should we choose? A look at the menu options rules out FixedSizeCollections, since **add** and **remove** require the internal program structure to dynamically grow and shrink at run-time. OrderedCollection is our choice.

The structure of **open** forces subservient methods to access data through global instance variables. In such methods, nothing has to be returned. So a message

self initializeData.

in **open** sets the initial value of **data** just as if it were a procedure in Pascal or a subroutine in FORTRAN — nothing is returned to the receiver.

You should feed a ListPane with strings for best results. This is the key to using

ListPanes: you can hold data within the model class in any type you like, but the interface to a ListPane is of a String. Therefore, **initElements** returns strings. Note that **initElements** has no parameters, while the corresponding **name:** method for GraphPanes has one. In this introductory example we have set **data** to hold actual strings, meaning that words, numbers, and points are deliberately mixed as ListPane elements.

initElements is a very small method:

initElements
"Initialize elements in the ListPane."
^data

It is also quite general (other methods can call it to communicate with an instance of ListPane). **data** has to be initialized somewhere else, and this is why a method **initializeData** has to be executed from the **open** method.

The essence of **add** is to prompt the user for a value of the list element, to add it into the list and to let **pointList** know about the change.

How do we add something to an OrderedCollection? One possibility is to use the **add:afterIndex:** message, but this requires knowledge of which ListPane element is reversed. Fortunately enough, the method **selection** from **ListPane** returns an index of the reversed element. So the line

ifFalse: [data add: prompt
afterIndex: (pointList selection).].

merges the new string (in **prompt**) into **data**, right after the reversed list element.

The last line in **add** is quite important:

self show: prompt.

The value of **self** is now **pointList**, and **show:** is our own method from class **P**. **show:** is called from **add**, **remove** and **erase** messages, as a post-processor. **add**, **remove** and **erase** alter **data** in some way but such changes would remain within **P**, without ever affecting the pane in which we can only see them. So **show:** has two tasks to accomplish:

— to effectively change the internal list of the **pointList** pane, and
— to change the corresponding visual display.

Quite fittingly, **show:** consists of just two lines, one per task.

show: anInteger
"Left mouse button pressed, change reversed item."
pointList changed: #initPoints.
pointList restoreSelected: anInteger.

The **changed:** method (taken directly from class **Object**) delivers **data** to **pointList**, updating the internal ListPane data structure. The **changed:** method will itself not cause any change on the screen. This is why we have to send **restoreSelected:** to **pointList**. It will change the display, reversing the item whose ordinal number is **anInteger**.

show: is also called from the **change:** method in open. As before, the argument of

change: is executed every time you press the left mouse button somewhere within the ListPane. A new method, equivalent to **show:** in **P**, has to be written for every new application class. Its function depends on the pane type. You can pretty well count on transferring the first line from **show:** to all other application classes, but the second line will differ according to the type of pane. For ListPanes, the default behaviour is reversing and displaying a list element. For GraphPanes, the equivalents of **show:** should probably copy some Form to the pane, and so on.

The line in **open** that reads

returnIndex: true;

is specific to ListPanes. You already know that the only thing you can do with an item in a ListPane is to select it (shown as reversed). The selected item should be somehow read by methods in class **P**. A ListPane has two ways of returning such information:

— as an item's index within a list (class instance variable **returnIndex** becomes **true**), or
— as a string value (**returnIndex** is then **false**).

The method **returnIndex:** sets variable **returnIndex** to one of these two values and thus decides how the application methods will receive data. This behaviour is very specific to the **ListPane** class; other panes will exhibit their own peculiarities.

When dealing with ListPanes, it is practical to hold only strings in **data**. Although you might be tempted to interpret a string such as '1 @ 3' to be a Point — this is not so. So you might consider introducing another array besides **data**, just to keep the data in the proper type. This, of course, demands routines for coding and encoding the real data type to and from strings. Smalltalk/V is quite well equipped for such conversions. If everything else fails, you can always read from and write to streams of strings.

The remaining two methods, **remove** and **erase**, work as a pair. **remove** will delete the selected item from the list, but will not operate on the very first list element. You can use it to delete all elements one by one — except the first. Therefore, we introduce the **erase** method. This immediately wipes out the whole list. You can build a new list adding an element through a series of selections of the **add** options from the pane menu. These two menu choices are merely an example of what is possible. They are not elegant. The same is true for the complete ListPane shown here: it is not very useful as it stands, but merely illustrates the techniques of window and pane building.

2.35 INSPECTORS

A true interactive programming system enables you to compile one method at a time and test it without delay, possibly accessing the values of certain variables, if needed. Smalltalk/V is precisely such a system. **Inspector** is a special kind of window which allows you to interactively view and alter an object's instance variables. A typical **Inspector** is shown in Fig. 2.14. Creation of an **inspector** window is as easy as typing the object's name followed by the message **inspect** from any text pane. There will only be two panes:

— the instance variable list pane on the left,

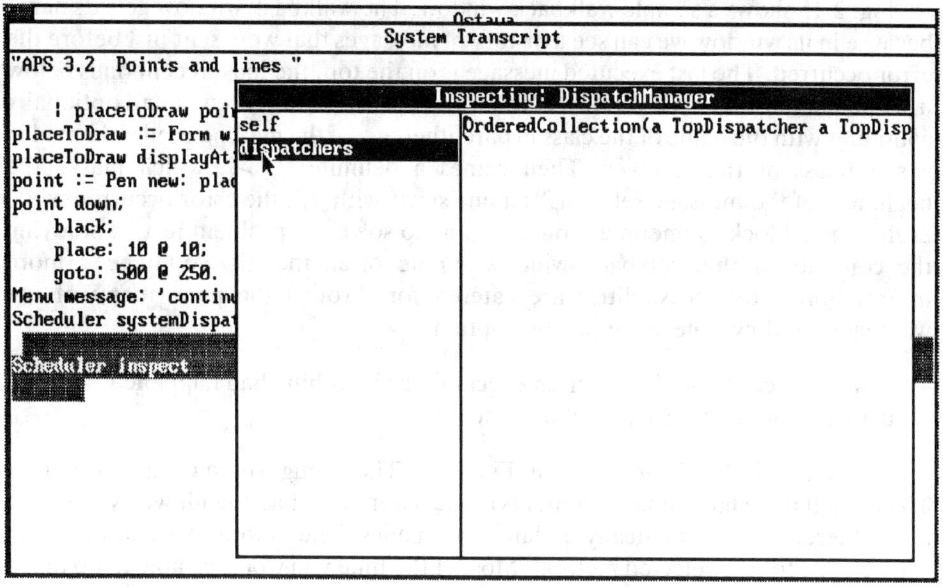

Fig. 2.14 — A typical **Inspector**.

— the instance variable contents pane on the right.

You select one of the variables from the list and its contents automatically appear on the right pane. You can move the cursor to it and change the values shown. If you then use the **save** option from the pane menu, Smalltalk/V will actually change the value, and from that moment on, the program runs with the new value.

You can insert the **inspect** message anywhere in the method, in case you want to debug it. However, the inspectors are low-level debugging aids and Smalltalk/V offers better facilities for this — special debugger windows. Inspectors are useful if you want to see what is in pool dictionaries such as **CharacterConstants.** You might also want to have a look at a complicated data structure that you yourself have not written. Inspectors come handy then, too.

2.36 DEBUGGER WINDOWS

These come in two flavours:

— walkback and
— debug windows.

You'll see the former ones quite often — they are the Smalltalk/V way of telling you what went wrong in run-time. And you can also explicitly require a walkback window by sending messages **error:** and **halt** to any object. The walkback window automatically appears after pressing the **Ctrl–Break** combination from the keyboard. Finally, a walkback window sometimes materializes because a stack overflow occurred somewhere deep within Smalltalk/V.

Fig. 2.15 shows a sample walkback window. The walkback window gets its name because in its window we can see a history of messages that were sent just before the error occurred. The last executed message is on the top, the most recent ones below it. A line in the walkback window starts with the class of the receiver and optionally continues with the name of the class in parentheses — if the method used is defined in a superclass of the receiver. Then comes a delimiter '>>', which marks the beginning of the message selector. If a line starts with '[]', the error occurred while evaluating a block. Sometimes you'll be able to solve the problem just by studying the contents of the walkback window. Quite often though, you'll need more information. Both possibilities are catered for through the pane menu of the walkback window. There are just two options:

— **resume** — continue the program execution as if nothing had happened, and
— **debug** — obtain a special, debug window.

One such window is presented in Fig. 2.16. The debug window has four panes. The top left pane has the same contents as the parent walkback window. By selecting a line there, you automatically update other panes. The bottom pane displays the source code for the selected method. Most of the time you won't be able to do much with it since errors generally invoke low-level Smalltalk/V methods and messages. However, one of the lines will contain precisely the method that caused the misbehaviour — you can then edit and save it just as in any other text pane. This is another shortcut to program debugging.

There are also two inspector panes, placed in the middle of the upper pane row and on the right. You can inspect the current values and change them just as from any ordinary inspector window. The walkback list pane menu has four options:
— **resume**,
— **restart**,
— **senders**, and
— **implementors**.

These last two are identical to the **senders** and **implementors** options of the **Class Hierarchy Browser**. The **resume** option continues the execution of the program. It will be disabled if you have changed the walkback list (i.e. changed a method there). The **restart** option continues the program execution from the selected method. Both options erase the walkback window.

All in all, Smalltalk/V offers an extensive and easy to use array of interactive debugging facilities. Such facilities enable even unskilled programmers to achieve greater productivity. Smalltalk/V286 is more capable still in this respect. It offers four more options: **hop**, **skip**, **jump**, and breakpoints. **hop** executes the next expression in the debugged process, **skip** executes the next expression in the selected method or up to the next breakpoint, whichever comes first, while **jump** executes up to the next breakpoint. The breakpoint is the line on which the cursor was when the pane labelled **breakpoint** was activated. These facilities are powerful in their own right and are at least equal to or even better than debugging facilities in other languages.

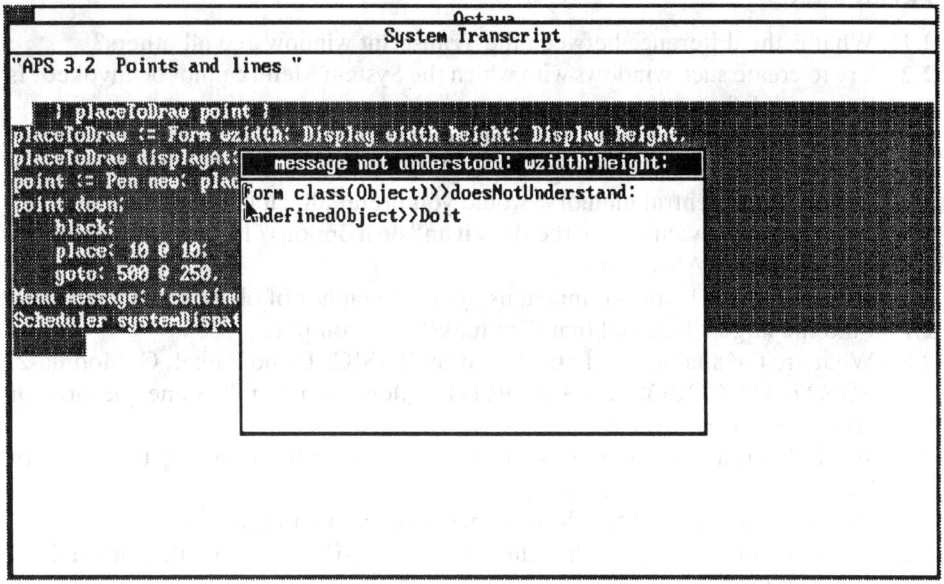

Fig. 2.15 — A sample walkback window.

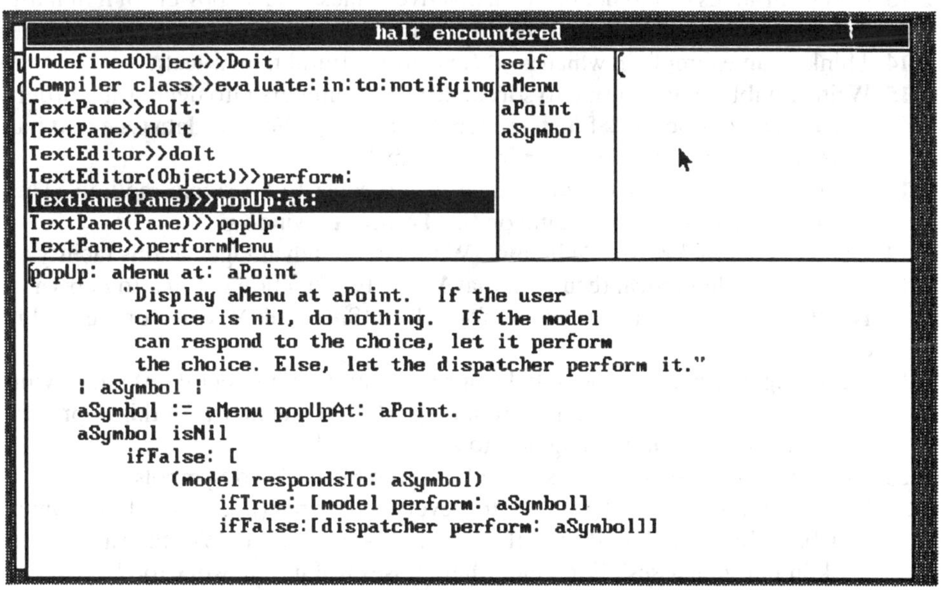

Fig. 2.16 — A sample debug window.

PROBLEMS

2.1 What is the difference between the **Transcript** window and all others?

2.2 Try to create such windows with which the System Menu cannot be invoked. Is this possible?

2.3 Measure the speed gained by the **space/speed** option. Is the gain worthwhile?

2.4 Discuss the merits of defining data as global variables. If the computer had ten megabytes of central memory, would you prefer all data to be persistent?

2.5 What are the advantages of the **show it** and **do it** options? How do they compare with RUN in BASIC?

2.6 Can everything be programmed using the metaphor of objects and messages?

2.7 Find the largest factorial that Smalltalk/V can compute.

2.8 What are the analogues of **at:** and **put:** in BASIC, Turbo Pascal, C, Modula-2, FORTRAN, COBOL, C++, FORTH, Trilogy? Answer the same question for arrays, matrices, strings... .

2.9 Write down a taxonomy of Smalltalk/V variables according to the scope of locality.

2.10 Find at least ten Smalltalk/V messages that act like Boolean tests.

2.11 Compare Smalltalk/V block to the BEGIN...END pair of Pascal, Modula-2, C, and Algol.

2.12 Which of the following Boolean expressions are correct:

number odd and: [tempNum <= 2]

eps = 0.00001 or: ('str fff' size 9)
a = 2 or: b=3 and: c>=5

2.13 Given variables **m** and **n**, both with positive values, find all powers of **n** that are less than **m**. Put all such numbers in an array.

2.14 Think of an example in which **reject:** is more natural than **select:**.

2.15 Write a bubble sort routine to sort an array of numbers into decreasing order. Will the same code work for characters? For strings? For any data type that has a predefined operation of comparison? Why?

2.16 Create a new class, **MyName**, which would consist of a single method. This method should print your name on the **Transcript** window.

2.17 Open two **Class Browser Windows**. What are the advantages of this facility?

2.18 Prove by mathematical recursion that McCarty's function is equal to **max (n – 10, 91)**. What is the largest **n** for which Smalltalk/V can compute this expression?

2.19 Declaring a variable to be global (those that start with upper case) and saving the image enable persistent programming. Discuss the merits of this approach to regular saving and reading files to and from disk.

2.20 How many messages can be sent to Bags? To Strings? To Symbols?

2.21 Write a method called **reverse** to reverse a string (i.e. 'abcdef' becomes 'fedcba'). In what class should this method be logged in? Will the same code work in parent classes? For what other classes will it then work too?

2.22 Implement page-defining messages for an Epson FX compatible printer (margins, line spacing, etc.). Do the same for a LaserJet printer.

2.23 Discuss the design of a database program based on dictionaries as the main data structure.

2.24 Can Rectangles be added or subtracted? Divided? How about Forms? Would set operations help?

2.25 Create four Forms of various shades, and place them one after the other in different parts of the screen. What other visual effects are possible?

2.26 Draw a hexagon using class **Pen** only. Do the same using Polygons.

2.27 Write a method called **open** for class **PK** that will have the same effect as **openOn: (10 @ 10 extent: 300 @300).**

2.28 Write **openOn:** for class **P**.

2.29 Rewrite **P** so that **erase** will work on all list elements. Add **recover**, an option for re-initializing the whole list. Write **undo**, an option to undo all deletions from the list.

3

Smalltalk/V for computer graphics

Knowledge begins with classification, said the ancient Chinese. Object-oriented programming methodology agrees. The first step in object-oriented design is to classify objects (i.e. define classes) whose behaviour you want to simulate. Finding objects is easy. For example, objects in computer graphics would be points, lines, graphs, shadings, drawings, solid bodies, etc. Geometry is rather specific because objects of programming (figures, solid bodies) coincide with material objects (edge of a table, the human body). Standard mathematical notions also make good candidates for program objects: matrices, functions, derivatives, integrals, and the like.

The main time saver is inheritance, which presupposes a hierarchy of notions. Classification in mathematics has been possible but wasn't useful for programming until the invention of object-oriented programming. Our goal is to show how to draw different objects in the plane and in space. First come matrices, which are not only the foundation of computer graphics but also turn up in unexpected places. Other classes reflect what we want to draw: functions, approximations, surfaces, etc.

3.1 MATRICES

Matrices are rectangular tables filled with numbers or variables. If a matrix has m rows and n columns we say that it is an 'm by n' matrix or 'm×n'. Matrix names are by convention capital letters, while names of matrix elements are in lower case with two subscripts. Matrix A is usually written like this:

$$A = \begin{bmatrix} a_{11} & a_{12} & \dots & a_{1n} \\ a_{21} & a_{22} & \dots & a_{2n} \\ \dots & \dots & \dots & \dots \\ a_{m1} & a_{m2} & \dots & a_{mn} \end{bmatrix}.$$

A general matrix element is denoted as (a_{ij}), $i = 1, \dots, m; j = 1, \dots, n$, where i and j are row and column numbers, respectively. Matrices are always rectangular. A special case of $m = n$ is the most important in practice, and is known as a *square* matrix. Other special cases are $m = 1$ and $n = 1$, when the matrix degenerates into a row or column, respectively. Row and column matrices are also called row and column *vectors*.

Matrices relieve us of technicalities; the above matrix A holds all the important facts (i.e. the coefficients) of a general linear system of equations of n rows and m unknowns, without spelling out the names of the unknowns. Matrices are also the most general kind of numbers. Many arithmetic operations transpose naturally from real numbers to matrices (with some important differences, though).

Here are some formal definitions.

3.2 MATRIX OPERATIONS

Let matrices A and B be of the same type, say $m \times n$. Their sum, $A + B$, is C, the third matrix of the same type, whose elements are computed as

$$c_{ij} = a_{ij} + b_{ij} , \qquad \text{where} \quad i = 1, \ldots, m; \quad j = 1, \ldots, n . \tag{3.1}$$

The difference $A - B$ is similar:

$$d_{ij} = a_{ij} - b_{ij} , \qquad \text{where} \quad i = 1, \ldots, m; \quad j = 1, \ldots, n . \tag{3.2}$$

Matrices A *and* B are equal, $A = B$, if

$$a_{ij} = b_{ij} \quad , \qquad \text{where} \quad i = 1, \ldots, m \ ; \quad j = 1, \ldots, n . \tag{3.3}$$

The zero matrix, Z, has all elements equal to 0:

$$z_{ij} = 0 \ , \qquad \text{where} \quad i = 1, \ldots, m \ ; \quad j = 1, \ldots, n . \tag{3.4}$$

There are many types of zero matrix, but for all possible combinations of m and n there exists only one such matrix. Two zero matrices of different type are *not* equal.

Matrix A is multiplied by scalar s, $B = sA$, if

$$b_{ij} = sa_{ij} \qquad \text{where} \quad i = 1, \ldots, m \ ; \quad j = 1, \ldots, n . \tag{3.5}$$

The multiplication of a matrix by a matrix is not so simple. The result is a third matrix C, $C = AB$, under the following conditions and rules:

— the number of columns in matrix A must be equal to the number of rows in matrix B, that is, if A is of order $m \times n$, then B must be of order $n \times p$;
— the resulting matrix C is of order $m \times p$, and
— the computation rule is:

$$c_{ij} = \sum_{k=1}^{n} a_{ik} b_{kj} \ , \qquad \text{where} \quad i = 1, \ldots, m \ ; \quad j = 1, \ldots, n . \tag{3.6}$$

The product of two square matrices of the same type is also a square matrix of the same type. If the number of rows in A does not match the number of columns in B, the product matrix does not exist. Matrix multiplication is *not* commutative.

Matrix Z is a neutral element for matrix summation. There is also a corresponding neutral element for matrix multiplication, denoted I_n. It is defined as a square n by n matrix, with diagonal elements equal to 1, and with all other elements equal to 0. More precisely:

$$I_n = \begin{cases} a_{1,j} = 0 & \text{if } i <> j \\ a_{i,j} = 1 & \text{if } i = j \end{cases} . \tag{3.7}$$

For example, a 3 × 3 identity matrix is

$$I_n = \begin{bmatrix} 1 & 0 & 0 \\ 0 & 1 & 0 \\ 0 & 0 & 1 \end{bmatrix} . \tag{3.8}$$

The identity matrix I_n plays the same role in square matrices of order n as the number 1 in real numbers.

The most problematic matrix operation is division. Actually, ordinary division cannot extend to matrices since matrix multiplication is not always commutative. The concept of division is replaced by the concept of inverse matrix. If A is known, then matrix B in the matrix equation

$$AB = I_n$$

is called the *inverse* matrix, and is denoted

$$B = A^{-1} \quad \text{and} \quad AA^{-1} = I_n \; .$$

This implies the following rule for finding the inverse of a matrix product:

$$(A \times B)^{-1} = B^{-1} \times A^{-1}$$

Matrices can be inverted, which means that elements that are symmetric according to the main diagonal are to swap places. A matrix is symmetric if its symmetric elements are equal.

3.3 MATRIX OPERATIONS IN Smalltalk/V

Smalltalk/V, as delivered, has no class **Matrix**. If we want matrix operations, we have to write such a class. There are several ways of doing so. As usual, the first question is: 'Where in the existing hierarchy of classes does this new class **Matrix** fit best?', or, 'From what class(es) will **Matrix** inherit most of its code?'. One possible parent class is **Magnitude**. There, matrices would fit as 'universal numbers', as a subclass of **Number**. Most operations (+, −, ∗, etc.) already exist, and should only be rewritten for matrices. On the other hand, there is no structure to inherit from anything in **Magnitude**. This is a serious objection. We found the best solution was to embed **Matrix** into class **Array**.

There are at least two ways for an array to act as a matrix. The first stems directly from one definition of matrices, which says that they are 'ordered m-tuples of ordered n-tuples'. In programming terms, a matrix would be an array whose every element is also an array. This is how such matrices are defined in Pascal:

```
TYPE
    rows   = ARRAY [1..10] OF REAL;
    matrix = ARRAY [2..34] OF rows;
```

The other possibility — and the one we implement here — is to reserve a long enough linear array and compute addresses of matrix elements as needed. This approach is of a lower level, resembling more the internal workings of traditional programming languages. In this concept, all operations will depend on the calculation of the element's address. We isolate it into the method **loc:with:**.

Class **Array** is not particularly rich in its own messages (if we ignore the fact that it inherits more than 70 methods and variables from the parent classes). Before showing you the new **Matrix** class, here are some enhancing methods for **Array**:

```
FixedSizeCollection variableSubclass: #Array
    instanceVariableNames: ''
    classVariableNames: ''
    poolDictionaries: ''

Array class methods

Array methods

* anArray
    "Multiply two arrays — scalar multiplication."
    | size sum |
size := anArray size.
self size = size ifFalse: [ ^nil ].
sum := 0.
1 to: size do: [ :i |
    sum := sum + ((self at: i) * (anArray at: i) ).].
^sum

+ anArray
    | s r |
s := anArray size.
r := Array new: s.
1 to: s do: [ :i | r at: i put: ((self at: i) + (anArray at: i)) ].
^r

- anArray
    | s r |
s := anArray size.
r := Array new: s.
1 to: s do: [ :i | r at: i put:
    ((self at: i) - (anArray at: i)) ].
^r

max
    "APS Find maximum elements in the array."
    | max |
max := self at: 1.
1 to: self size do: [:i |
    max <= (self at: i)
```

```
        ifTrue: [ max := (self at: i)]. ].
  ^max

min
    "APS Find minimum element in the array."
    | min |
min := self at: 1.
1 to: self size do: [ :i |
    min >= (self at: i) ifTrue: [ min := (self at: i)].].
  ^min

sum
    "Sum the whole array."
    | sum |
sum := 0.
1 to: self size do: [ :i |
    sum := sum + (self at: i).].
  ^sum

zero
    "Create a zero matrix of dimensions (rows,columns.)"
1 to: self size do: [ :i | self at: i put: 0 ].
  ^self
```

This class is now enhanced towards operations that act upon arrays as a whole. Note the last method, **zero**. Its comment is wrong. We first created that message in the **Matrix** subclass, but it immediately became obvious that it will do a fine job in **Array** as well. So we moved it up one class, leaving the comment as it was to show that good methods do not come out of the box.

Now here is **Matrix**:

```
Array variableSubclass: #Matrix
    instanceVariableNames:
        'rows columns pivotValue'
    classVariableNames: ''
    poolDictionaries:
        'CharacterConstants'

Matrix class methods

new: row with: column
    | answer |
answer := super new: row *column.
answer rows: row. answer columns: column.
  ^answer!

rows: row columns: column
    | answer |
answer := super new: row *column.
answer rows: row. answer columns: column.
```

```
 ^answer!

Matrix methods

* aMat
      "Classical matrix multiplication."
      | result v1 v2 td |
result := self class new: self rows with: self columns.
1 to: self rows do: [ :i |
      1 to: aMat columns do: [ :j |
            td := 0.
            1 to: self columns do: [ :k |
                  td := td + ((self at: i at: k) *(aMat at: k at: j)).
                  ].
            result at: i at: j put: td.
            ].
      ].
 ^result!

at: i at: j
      "Access matrix element in (i,j)."
      | value |
(i < 0 or: [ i > self rows]) ifTrue: [ ^ nil ].
(j < 0 or: [ j > self columns]) ifTrue: [ ^ nil ].
value := self loc: i with: j.
 ^(self at: value)!

at: i at: j put: k "Assignment for matrices."
      | value |
value := self loc: i with: j.
self at: value put: k.
 ^self

columns
      "Answer the number of columns in matrix."
 ^columns!

columns: anInt
      "Force new number of columns."
columns := anInt.!

initForTest " Test for solving simultaneous equations."
self at: 1 at: 1 put: 1.
self at: 1 at: 2 put: 2.
self at: 1 at: 3 put: 1.
self at: 1 at: 4 put: -1.
self at: 1 at: 5 put: 6.

self at: 2 at: 1 put: 3.
self at: 2 at: 2 put: 1.
self at: 2 at: 3 put: -1.
```

```
self at: 2 at: 4 put: 3.
self at: 2 at: 5 put: 12.

self at: 3 at: 1 put: 4.
self at: 3 at: 2 put: 2.
self at: 3 at: 3 put: 2.
self at: 3 at: 4 put: 1.
self at: 3 at: 5 put: 14.

self at: 4 at: 1 put: 1.
self at: 4 at: 2 put: -1.
self at: 4 at: 3 put: -1.
self at: 4 at: 4 put: 2.
self at: 4 at: 5 put: 2.
 ^self!

loc: i with: j
      " Locate the (i,j) matrix element in Matrix."
 ^((i - 1) * (self columns) + j)

pivotValue "The result of the pivot process in simulEq."
 ^pivotValue!

rows
      "Answer the number of rows in matrix."
 ^rows!

rows: anInt
      "Force new number of rows."
rows := anInt.!

show
      "Print matrix row by row."
      | sum |
sum := 0.
1 to: self rows do: [ :i |
      1 to: self columns do: [ :j |
            Transcript show:
                  (self at: i at: j) printString , '        '.].
      Transcript show: Lf printString.
      ].!

simulEq: a " a is the equation to be solved.
               self is the solution vector."
| pivot temp pivotRow size |
pivotValue := true.
size := a rows.
1 to: size do: [ :k |
      pivot := 0.
      k to: size do: [ :i |
      (a at: i at: k) abs > pivot abs
```

```
        ifTrue: [
            pivot := (a at: i at: k).
            pivotRow := i.
        ].
    ].
pivot = 0 ifTrue: [ ^pivotValue := false ].
" If necessary exchange rows."
    pivotRow ~= k
        ifTrue: [
            1 to: (size + 1) do: [ :j |
                temp := (a at: k at: j).
                a at: k at: j put: (a at: pivotRow at: j).
                a at: pivotRow at: j put: temp.
            ].
        ].
" Normalize pivot row."
    k to: (size + 1) do: [ :j |
        a at: k at: j put: ((a at: k at: j) / pivot).
    ].
" Reduce row      (k+1) . . . size."
        k ~= size ifTrue: [
            (k + 1) to: size do: [ :i |
                (size + 1) to: k by: -1 do: [ :j |
                    temp := (a at: i at: j).
                    a at: i at: j
                        put: (temp - ((a at: i at: k) *(a at: k at: j))).
                ].
            ].
        ].
    ].
" Back substitution."
    (size - 1) to: 1 by: -1 do: [ :k |
        size to: (k + 1) by: -1 do: [ :i |
            temp := (a at: k at: (size + 1)).
            a at: k at: (size + 1)
                put: (temp - ((a at: i at: (size + 1)) *(a at: k at: i))).
        ].
    ].
" Copy solution to the vector."
    1 to: size do: [ :i |
        self at: i put: (a at: i at: (size + 1)).
    ].
 ^self!
```

Matrix has two instance variables, **rows** and **columns**, and it also accesses the dictionary **CharacterConstants**. The class method **new:with:** creates an Array long enough to hold all matrix values, and places matrix dimensions into variables **rows**

and **columns**. They keep the corresponding values for every instance of class **Matrix**. Message **super** enables inheritance of all the features from **Collection** down to **Array**.

These are the central messages:

loc:with: — returns the position of matrix element (i,j) within Array that acts as an internal data structure for matrix emulation;

at:at: — returns the value of the element in position (i,j);

at:at:put: — assigns a value to element (i,j).

Other messages (+, *, **identity**) are similar to the corresponding mathematical definition (see equations (3.1), (3.6), and (3.8)).

Method **show** prints the matrix contents on the **Transcript** window, and is handy when testing new code. It imports **Lf** (line feed) and **Eol** (end of line) as global constants from dictionary **CharacterConstants**.

Finally, the method **simulEq:** solves a system of simultaneous equations. It is based on the well-known Gauss–Jordan elimination method.

Here is a piece of code to illustrate the usage:

```
" Test code for simultaneous equations."
| aaa |
aaa := Matrix rows: 4 columns: 5.
s := Matrix rows: 1 columns: aaa rows.
aaa initForTest.
s simulEq: aaa.
s show.
    3    2    -1    0    $
```

Two variables, **aaa** and **s**, are defined as matrices of dimensions 4 by 5 and 1 by 4. (The class message **rows:columns:** also defines a new matrix.) The method **initForTest** initializes matrix **aaa**, which then serves as an input parameter to **simulEq:**. The last line, **s show**, prints the result on the **Transcript** window. Vector **(3 2 −1 0)** is a solution of the following system of four linear equations in four unknowns, say x, y, z and t:

$$\begin{aligned} x+2y+z-t&=6\\ 3x+y-z+3t&=12\\ 4x+2y+2z+t&=14\\ x-y-z+2t&=2\ . \end{aligned}$$

Class **Matrix** is merely the first step towards a useful set of matrix operations. We can further enrich **Matrix** by defining its subclasses. How do we decide what will be a new subclass? One or more criteria are needed. In this particular case, the following two are useful:

— dimensions, and

— structure of rows, colums, and diagonals.

Taking matrix dimensions as a criterion, the subclasses could be **SquareMatrix**, **ColumnMatrix** and **RowMatrix**. Here they are:

```
Matrix variableSubclass: #SquareMatrix
    instanceVariableNames: ''
    classVariableNames: ''
    poolDictionaries: ''

SquareMatrix class methods

new: size
    | matrix |
matrix := super rows: size columns: size.
 ^matrix!

SquareMatrix methods
identity
    "Make a square matrix an identity matrix."
    | value |
self columns = self rows ifFalse: [ ^nil ].
1 to: self columns do: [ :i |
    1 to: self rows do: [ :j |
        self at: i at: j put: 0.
      i = j ifTrue: [ self at: i at: j put: 1.]
      ].
    ].
 ^ self!

initForTest " Test for matrix inversion."
self at: 1 at: 1 put: 2.
self at: 1 at: 2 put: 2. "
self at: 1 at: 3 put: 1.
self at: 1 at: 4 put: -1. "
self at: 2 at: 1 put: 3.
self at: 2 at: 2 put: 1. "
self at: 2 at: 3 put: -1.
self at: 2 at: 4 put: 3.
self at: 3 at: 1 put: 4.
self at: 3 at: 2 put: 2.
self at: 3 at: 3 put: 2.
self at: 3 at: 4 put: 1.
self at: 4 at: 1 put: 1.
self at: 4 at: 2 put: -1.
self at: 4 at: 3 put: -1.
self at: 4 at: 4 put: 2. "
 ^self!
```

```
inverse: aMatrix
| a det pivotRow pivotColumn pivot temp pivotUsed size a1|
" Initialize."
pivotValue := true.
size := self columns.
a := Matrix rows: size columns: (2 * size).
pivotRow := Array new: size. pivotRow at: 1 put: 1.
pivotColumn := Array new: size. pivotColumn at: 1 put: 1.

" Set-up augmented matrix."
1 to: size do: [ :i |
    1 to: size do: [ :j |
        a at: i at: j put: (aMatrix at: i at: j).
        i = j ifTrue: [ a at: i at: (size + j) put: 1 ]
            ifFalse:[ a at: i at: (size + j) put: 0 ]
    ].
].

" Initialize determinant."
det := 1.
" Begin Gauss-Jordan reduction."
1 to: size do: [ :k " |
" Selext maximum pivot."
    pivot := 0.
    1 to: size do: [ :i |
        1 to: size do: [ :j |
            pivotUsed := false.
            k ~= 1 ifTrue: [
                1 to: (k - 1) do: [ :l |
                    ((i = (pivotRow at: l)) or: [ j = (pivotColumn at: l)])
                        ifTrue: [ pivotUsed := true ]
                ].
            ].
            pivotUsed ifFalse: [ a1 := (a at: i at: j).
                (a1 abs) > pivot
                    ifTrue: [ pivot := (a at: i at: j).
                            pivotRow at: k put: i.
                            pivotColumn at: k put: j.
                    ].
            ].
        ].
    ].

" Check for singular matrix."
pivot = 0 ifTrue: [ Transcript show: ' exit by force'.
                ^pivotValue := false ].

" Update value of determinant."
```

```
        det := det *pivot.
" Normalize row."

        1 to: (2 * size) do: [ :j /
            a at: (pivotRow at: k) at: j
                put: ((a at: (pivotRow at: k) at: j) / pivot).
        ].

" Reduce remaining rows."
        1 to: size do: [ :i /;
            temp := a at: i at: (pivotColumn at: k).
            1 to: (2 * size) do: [ :j /
                i ~= (pivotRow at: k)
                    ifTrue: [ a at: i at: j
                        put: ((a at: i at: j) -
                            (temp * (a at: (pivotRow at: k) at: j))).
                    ].
                ].
            ].
        ].

" Order rows and correct sign of determinant."

        1 to: (size - 1) do: [ :k /
            (pivotRow at: k) ~= (pivotColumn at: k)
                ifTrue: [
                    det := 0 - det.
                    1 to: (2 * size) do: [ :j /
                        temp := a at: (pivotRow at: k) at: j.
                        a at: (pivotRow at: k) at: j put: (a at: (pivotColumn at: k) at:
j).
                        a at: (pivotColumn at: k) at: j put: temp.
                    ].

                    (k + 1) to: size do: [ :j /
                        (pivotRow at: j) = (pivotColumn at: k)
                            ifTrue: [
                                pivotRow at: j put: (pivotRow at: k)
                        ].
                    ].
                ].

" Move columns of inverse matrix."

        1 to: size do: [ :i /
            1 to: size do: [ :j /
                self at: i at: j put: (a at: i at: (size + j)).
            ].
        ].
].
```

```
 ^self

inverted "Invert matrix elements."
    | mat |
mat := SquareMatrix new: (self columns).
1 to: self rows do: [ :i |
    1 to: self columns do: [ :i |
        mat at: i at: j put: (self at: j at: i).
    ].
].
 ^mat!
```

There is only one class method for **SquareMatrix**, **new:**. The **identity** method produces an identity matrix. **initForTest** now returns a 4 by 4 matrix while **invert:** computes the inverse matrix. This is quite a long method as Smalltalk methods go. It is based on the well-known algorithm of Gauss–Jordan reduction of a square matrix to a semi-diagonal form. The following code illustrates the usage:

```
| aaa bbb ccc | "Test code for matrix inversion."
aaa := SquareMatrix new: 2.
bbb := SquareMatrix new: 2.
ccc := SquareMatrix new: 2.
aaa initForTest.
bbb inverse: aaa.
aaa show.
bbb show.
ccc := aaa * bbb. ccc show
```

Matrix **bbb** is the inverse of **aaa**. **ccc** is their product — the identity matrix. Method **inverted** inverts a matrix.

The other two classes are shorter and here are their class methods only:

```
ColumnMatrix class methods

new: rows
 ^super rows: rows columns: 1.!

RowMatrix class methods

new: columns
 ^super rows: 1 columns columns!
```

ColumnMatrices and RowMatrices are also known as vectors.

This rounds up the most elementary characteristics of type **Matrix**. We need some additional theory to obtain further subclasses. Enhancements will concentrate in **SquareMatrix**.

Matrices abound in all technical, mathematical, and statistical applications. We restrict ourselves to elements of computer graphics for the rest of the chapter.

3.4 LINEAR TRANSFORMATIONS

Matrices are an efficient way of representing and manipulating linear transformations. Their general form is

$$y = Ax \tag{3.9}$$

where x and y are vector variables. Geometrically, x and y are points in the plane. It is a useful custom in computer graphics to represent points with vectors of one dimension 'higher'. A two-dimensional point is therefore mapped into a 1 by 3 vector, and matrix A is of type 3 × 3. The most general form of A is

$$A = \begin{bmatrix} \mathrm{a} & \mathrm{b} & 0 \\ \mathrm{c} & \mathrm{d} & 0 \\ \mathrm{e} & \mathrm{f} & 1 \end{bmatrix}. \tag{3.10}$$

The third column is fixed and does not take part in the transformations. Its role is only to ensure that A is a square matrix, so that later we can compute its inverse.

Matrices that have the last column as in relation (3.10) are called homogeneous matrices. They are square matrices with the last column equal to a zero vector. Note that this last sentence is a natural way of expressing a new relationship, and that inheritance in Smalltalk/V is a perfect way of encapsulating it in a computer language. Therefore, we define a new subclass, **HomogeneousMatrix**. It will inherit everything from **SquareMatrix**, except that its only class method, **new:**, will 'hammer down' the structure of the last column:

```
new: size
    | matrix |
matrix := super new: size.
matrix zero.
1 to: (size - 1) do: [ :i |
    matrix at: size at: i put: 0. ].
matrix at: size at: size put: 1.
 ^matrix
```

Now we can specify constants in the first two columns. This directs the type of geometrical transformation. Translation is defined as the matrix

$$T = \begin{bmatrix} 1 & 0 & 0 \\ 0 & 1 & 0 \\ T_x & T_y & 1 \end{bmatrix}. \tag{3.11}$$

By direct computation we check that

$$X = x + T_x$$
$$Y = y + T_y$$
$$1 = 1$$

Rotation around the coordinate beginning for angle θ is defined as

$$R = \begin{bmatrix} \cos(\theta) & -\sin(\theta) & 0 \\ \sin(\theta) & \cos(\theta) & 0 \\ 0 & 0 & 1 \end{bmatrix}. \tag{3.12}$$

while scaling is defined as

$$S = \begin{bmatrix} S_x & 0 & 0 \\ 0 & S_y & 0 \\ 0 & 0 & 1 \end{bmatrix}. \tag{3.13}$$

These three matrices may be combined to describe any transformation of a point in the plane. Again, thanks to the inheritance, they are straightforward subclasses of the class **HomogeneousMatrix**. The translation matrix has a class called **Translation**.

Translation class methods

```
new: aPoint
    | matrix size t |
t := aPoint asArray.
size := t size + 1.
matrix := super new: size.
matrix identity.
1 to: (size - 1) do: [ :i |
    matrix at: size at: i put: (t at: i).].
^matrix!
```

Translation methods

```
inverse: tMat
    | t |
t := tMat rows.
self at: 1 at: t put: (tMat at: 1 at: t) negated.
self at: 2 at: t put: (tMat at: 2 at: t) negated.
t = 4 ifTrue: [
    self at: 3 at: t put: (tMat at: 3 at: t) negated. ].
^self!
```

This code is interesting both for what it shows and for what it does not show. The translation matrix is conveniently defined by a Point, so that a piece of code such as

```
| aaa |
aaa := Translation new: (2 @ 4)
```

or

```
| aaa |
aaa := Translation new: #(2  4)
```

will produce the matrix:

$$T = \begin{bmatrix} 1 & 0 & 0 \\ 0 & 1 & 0 \\ 2 & 4 & 1 \end{bmatrix}.$$

The line

```
matrix := super new: size.
```

calls upon inheritance to implicitly initialize the third row to all zeros except the diagonal element. The next line, **matrix identity**, produces a 3×3 identity matrix (once again assigning the same values to the third row). The **to:do:** message finally sets the second-to-last row to its values. Note that all data are derived from **aPoint**. This method will generate a 3×3 matrix for a plane point but will similarly produce a 4×4 homogeneous matrix for a point in space.

inverse: is the only new instance method in **Translation**. We have already seen this method in **SquareMatrix**. It is very general and, therefore, not very fast. Two levels lower, in **Translation**, we know better: a translated point has the same coordinates as the original one, only it is prefixed with a minus sign (the **negated** message in Smalltalk/V terms). It is quite natural to redefine the **inverse**: method—something that non-object-oriented languages are just not capable of doing.

Scaling from equation (3.13) is also easy to write as a subclass of **Homogeneous-Matrix**. Here it is:

```
Scaling class methods

new: aNewPoint "This is an array of scaling factors."
    | matrix size t |
t := aNewPoint.
aNewPoint class = Point ifTrue: [
    t := Array new: 2.
    t at: 1 put: (aNewPoint x).
    t at: 2 put: (aNewPoint y).
].
size := t size + 1.
```

```
matrix := super new: size.
1 to: (size - 1) do: [ :i |
    matrix at: i at: i put: (t at: i).].
 ^matrix!
```

Scaling methods

```
inverse: aPoint
    | m a b |
a := 1 / (aPoint x).
b := 1 / (aPoint y).
m := Scaling new: (a @ b).
 ^m!
```

Using it is a bit tricky:

```
| aaa bbb ccc |
aaa := Scaling new: 2 @ 3.
bbb := Scaling new: 4 @ 6.
ccc := bbb inverse: (2 @ 3). ccc show
```

Rotation is the most complicated transformation. It is completely different for 2D and 3D cases. We present two classes for rotation: **Rotation** for 2D points and **Axis3DRotation** for 3D points. Here we also touch on an unpleasant topic: class **Float**. Rotations require use of trigonometric functions, that is, the use of floating-point numbers (class REAL in Pascal and other languages). Smalltalk/V in its original form does not come with a floating-point package but is able to recognize and use the math co-processor 8087, 80287 or 80387 if one is present. This is not as bad as it seems because 8087 for XT is quite cheap. But its younger and more powerful cousins, 80287 and 80387, are much too dear for occasional use.

There are three solutions to this problem (except acquiring new hardware):

— let Smalltalk/V calculate with integers and fractions — this is cheap but not satisfactory,
— write your own set of floating-point operations — this is a doubtful enterprise in the least (unless you are excellent at numerical mathematics, PC assembler and inner workings of Smalltalk/V), and
— buy the software. Digitalk markets several add-on libraries of Smalltalk/V classes and one of these (Goodies #2) contains an excellent floating-point package.

In the rest of the book we shall assume that you have somehow resolved this difficulty so that you can follow the syntax of class **Float** as stated in the manual.

Back to rotation. The class **Rotation** implements matrix (3.12):

Rotation class methods

Rotation methods

inverse: anAngle

```
    | matrix |
matrix := Rotation new: self size.
 ^matrix setRotation: anAngle negated.
setRotation: anAngle
self at: 1 at: 1 put: anAngle cos.
self at: 1 at: 2 put: (anAngle sin) negated.
self at: 2 at: 1 put: anAngle sin.
self at: 2 at: 2 put: anAngle cos.
 ^self
```

Here is how we could try out that class from the **Transcript** window. The results are produced using the floating-point package from Goodies #2:

```
| aaa bbb |
aaa := Rotation new: 3.
aaa setRotation: 45 degreesToRadians. aaa show.
bbb := #(1 0 0 ) asRowMatrix.
(bbb * aaa) show

7.0710678e-1     -7.0710678e-1    0    $
7.0710678e-1    7.0710678e-1    0    $
0    0    1    $
7.0710678e-1     -7.0710678e-1    0    $
```

This rotates point (1 0) through an angle of 45 degrees. The rotation matrix is in the first three rows of numbers and the rotated point (7.0710678e – 1 – 7.0710678e – 1) is in the last row. The matrix is written out by the sentence **aaa show**. A 2D number has to be represented as a row matrix of size 3 in order to conform to the rules of matrix multiplication. The resulting point is ready to be transformed again, and again if need be. Successive application of transformations is called *concatenation*.

Concatenation of transformations boils down to successive multiplication of matrices that represent those transformations. The final result is just another (possibly more complicated) matrix. Nevertheless, if we have to apply one concatenated transformation frequently, it pays to compute it once at the beginning of the program, and then use it as if it were an elementary transformation itself. Here is a classical example:

Write down the transformation which rotates a point (x,y) about a given point (P_x,P_y) through a positive angle θ.

This seems quite similar to the rotation that has already been defined. The difference is that matrix R produces only rotations about the origin, not about some arbitrary point in the plane. The solution is easy to see: translate the point to the origin, apply the existing rotation there, then return the point back for the same amount. The concatenated transformations are:

$$[X \quad Y \quad 1] = [x \quad y \quad 1] \begin{bmatrix} 1 & 0 & 0 \\ 0 & 1 & 0 \\ -P_x & -P_y & 1 \end{bmatrix}$$

$$\times \begin{bmatrix} \cos(\theta) & -\sin(\theta) & 0 \\ \sin(\theta) & \cos(\theta) & 0 \\ 0 & 0 & 1 \end{bmatrix} \begin{bmatrix} 1 & 0 & 0 \\ 0 & 1 & 0 \\ P_x & P_y & 1 \end{bmatrix} \tag{3.14}$$

and it would be quite easy to actually multiply these matrices, obtain explicit equations and write a new class for general planar rotation around a point.

All geometrical objects consist of points, so any figure or body could be transformed point by point.

3.5 TWO-DIMENSIONAL EDITOR

Writing a two-dimensional graphics editor would be a formidable task in almost any other programming language. Smalltalk/V makes it easy, with its immediate mouse support, windows and panes, built-in classes for points, rectangles and other graphical objects. Everything is there, and indeed Smalltalk/V comes with a special graphics editor. Installation is straightforward, although a bit slow on XTs. Complete documentation is given in file FREDRWNG.DOC.

This editor is quite usable and we shall later, in the Billing Schedules program, write a subclass that will inherit drawing capabilities and merge them with the rest of the program.

3.6 THREE-DIMENSIONAL POINTS

A point in a three-dimensional space is an ordered triple of numbers:

$$A = A(x,y,z)$$

where x, y, and z are Cartesian coordinates in a three-dimensional coordinate system. Smalltalk/V has class **Point** so it was easy to write 2D routines around it. Now we need a class for 3D points. One suitable name is **Point3D**. As always when adding a subclass, we face the problem of inserting it in a proper place within the Smalltalk/V class hierarchy. The best way of deciding from which class to inherit comes from contemplating the structure of a 3D point. It obviously has three internal (instance) variables, and it is natural to call them **x**, **y**, and **z**. There are several candidates among existing classes. For example, **Point3** could be a subclass of **Array**. An array with three elements would then represent **x**, **y**, and **z**— this would be the easy part. There is a drawback, too: Arrays do not have all those operations that we would like to apply to points of any kind. We would have to build them ourselves and it is not in the spirit of object-oriented programming.

The alternative is making **Point3D** a subclass of **Point**. This saves a lot of labour since we can just redefine existing operations, i.e. just add the code for the third coordinate. A quick look at **Point** tells us that **x** and **y** are already global there. One especially fine point of inheritance is that the subclass inherits not only the methods but also the instance variable as well! That is to say, **Point3D** requires only the addition of **z** as its instance variable while **x** and **y** can be taken from **Point**. All in all, **Point3D** fits neatly into **Point** from the programmer's point of view.

On the other hand, it is unnatural for 3D points to inherit from 2D because space contains a plane and not vice versa. It would be ideal if Smalltalk/V from the start had **Point3D** as a base class (that is, subject only to **Object** itself), and **Point** as a subclass. It would not be practical to change Smalltalk/V that much now, so here is class **Point3D**:

```
Point variableSubclass: #Point3D
    instanceVariableNames:
        'z '
    classVariableNames: ''
    poolDictionaries: ''

Point3D class methods

Point3D methods

* scale
    | point |
point := Point3D new.
scale class == Point3D ifTrue: [
    point x: (self x) * (scale x).
    point y: (self y) * (scale y).
    point z: (self z) * (scale z). ].
scale class = Point ifTrue: [
    point x: (self x) * (scale x).
    point y: (self y) * (scale y).
    point z: (self z)              ].
(scale class == Number
    or: [ scale class == Integer
    or: [ scale class == SmallInteger
    or: [ scale class == Fraction] ]]) ifTrue: [
        point x: (self x) * scale.
        point y: (self y) * scale.
        point z: (self z) * scale.].
 ^point!

+ addend
    | point |
point := Point3D new.
addend class == Point3D ifTrue: [
    point x: (self x) + (addend x).
    point y: (self y) + (addend y).
    point z: (self z) + (addend z). ].
addend class = Point ifTrue: [
    point x: (self x) + (addend x).
    point y: (self y) + (addend y).
```

```
    point z: (self z)                    ].
(addend class == Number
    or: [ addend class == Integer
    or: [ addend class == SmallInteger
    or: – addend class == Fraction] ]]) ifTrue: [
        point x: (self x) + addend.
        point y: (self y) + addend.
        point z: (self z) + addend.].
 ^point!

" subtractor
    | point |
point := Point3D new.
subtractor class == Point3D ifTrue: [
    point x: (self x) - (subtractor x).
    point y: (self y) - (subtractor y).
    point z: (self z) - (subtractor z). ].
subtractor class = Point ifTrue: [
    point x: (self x) - (subtractor x).
    point y: (self y) - (subtractor y).
    point z: (self z)                    ].
(subtractor class == Number
    or: [ subtractor class == Integer
    or: [ subtractor class == SmallInteger
    or: [ subtractor class == Fraction] ]]) ifTrue: [
        point x: (self x) - subtractor.
        point y: (self y) - subtractor.
    point z: (self z) - subtractor.].
 ^point!

/ scale
    | point |
point := Point3D new.
scale class == Point3D ifTrue: [
    point x: (self x) / (scale x).
    point y: (self y) / (scale y).
    point z: (self z) / (scale z). ].
scale class = Point ifTrue: [
    point x: (self x) / (scale x).
    point y: (self y) / (scale y).
    point z: (self z)                    ].
(scale class == Number
    or: [ scale class == Integer
    or: [ scale class == SmallInteger
    or: [ scale class == Fraction] ]]) ifTrue: [
        point x: (self x) / scale.
        point y: (self y) / scale.
    point z: (self z) / scale.].
```

```
 ^point!

// scale
    | point |
point := Point3D new.
scale class == Point3D ifTrue: [
    point x: (self x) // (scale x).
    point y: (self y) // (scale y).
    point z: (self z) // (scale z). ].
scale class = Point ifTrue: [
    point x: (self x) // (scale x).
    point y: (self y) // (scale y).
    point z: (self z)                ].
(scale class == Number
    or: [ scale class == Integer
    or: [ scale class == SmallInteger
    or: [ scale class == Fraction] ]]) ifTrue: [
        point x: (self x) // scale.
        point y: (self y) // scale.
        point z: (self z) // scale.].
 ^point!

abs
    ^ x abs @ y abs @ z abs!

asArray
    | array |
array := Array new: 3.
array at: 1 put: self x.
array at: 2 put: self y.
array at: 3 put: self z.
 ^array!

asRowMatrix
    | rowMatrix |
rowMatrix := RowMatrix new: 3.
rowMatrix at: 1 put: self x.
rowMatrix at: 2 put: self y.
rowMatrix at: 3 put: self z.
 ^rowMatrix!

dotProduct: aPoint
    ^(x * aPoint) @ (y * aPoint y) @ (z * aPoint z)!

max: aPoint
 ^(x max: aPoint x) @ (y max: aPoint y) @ (z max: aPoint z)!

min: aPoint
    ^(x min: aPoint x) @ (y min: aPoint y) @ (z min: aPoint z)!

moveBy: aPoint3D
```

```
    x := x + aPoint3D x.
    y := y + aPoint3D y.
    z := z + aPoint3D z!

negated
    ^x negated @ y negated @ z negated!

printOn: aStream
    x printOn: aStream.
    aStream nextPutAll: ' @ '.
    y printOn: aStream.
    aStream nextPutAll: ' @ '.
    z printOn: aStream!

rounded
    ^x rounded @ y rounded @ z rounded!

show "Write it to the Transcript window."
self printOn: Transcript.!

sphericalCoordinates: wd psi: psi eps: eps
    "APS Express aPoint3D in spherical coordinates."
    | c s v q r |
c := psi cos.
s := eps sin.
v := psi sin.
q := eps cos.
r := Point3D new.
self x: c * s. self y: q. self z: v.
 ^self * wd!

truncated
    ^x truncated @ y truncated @ z truncated!

z "Answer the third coordinate of the point."
    ^ z!

z: aNumber "Put aNumber into the third coordinate."
    z := aNumber.!
```

There is a lot of code here but it was easy to produce. After adding a subclass **Point3D**, we selected it from the class pane in the **Class Hierarchy Browser**, inserted **z** as an argument for **instanceVariableNames:** and saved the text pane. So **z** became the third coordinate of a Point3D. The methods **z** and **z:** were obvious next steps. Together with methods **x**, **x:**, **y**, and **y:** from **Point** we could assign values to instances of **Point3D.**

What good are values if we cannot write them out? This triggers the question: 'How does Smalltalk/V write the values of variables in general?' The answer is the **printOn:** method. You will see it in practically all classes because it writes values of instances as strings, transferring them to a **Stream** or to the **Transcript** window. So, next we wrote the **printOn:** method. This was a simple matter of rewriting the same method from **Point**. After that, Smalltalk/V was able to write out any Point3D. For example:

```
| aaa |
aaa := Point3D new.
aaa := (1 @ 2 @ 3).
aaa show
1 @ 2 @ 3
```

This is just one side of a coin. The other is how to specify values of a Point3D? This is a brand new class so some innovative syntax is in order. It is entirely up to the designer to invent the syntax that is appropriate for the new data type. Here, we were guided by the syntax of Points — the @ sign separating two numbers. The new **printOn:** method produced the last line of the above example, but what made the third line

```
aaa := (1 @ 2 @ 3).
```

possible? Here is the corresponding method from class **Point**:

```
@ thirdCoord "APS -- This is for subclass Point3D.
                     A sly way of defining a 3D point naturally."
    | point |
point := Point3D new.
point x: (self x).
point y: (self y).
point z: thirdCoord.
 ^point
```

The idea is to regard the first three symbols, **1 @ 2**, as a Point.

This is an excellent example of Smalltalk/V capabilities. It lets you make up your own language(s), introduce new and meaningful notation ... thus fulfilling all the promises FORTH held but was never able to deliver.

Other methods in **Point3D** are self-documenting. The only surprise is called **sphericalCoordinates:psi:eps:**. We shall explain this shortly, after introducing transformations of 3D points.

3.7 LINEAR TRANSFORMATIONS IN SPACE

The same principles from the two-dimensional world apply in three dimensions, except that matrices of linear transformations are of type 4×4. Again, it suffices to learn how to transform just one point. The matrices for translation and scaling are just extended matrices that we have already studied. The translation is

$$T = \begin{bmatrix} 1 & 0 & 0 & 0 \\ 0 & 1 & 0 & 0 \\ 0 & 0 & 1 & 0 \\ T_x & T_y & T_z & 1 \end{bmatrix}. \tag{3.15}$$

while scaling is

$$S) = \begin{bmatrix} S_x & 0 & 0 & 0 \\ 0 & S_y & 0 & 0 \\ 0 & 0 & S_z & 0 \\ 0 & 0 & 0 & 1 \end{bmatrix}. \tag{3.16}$$

Rotation is more complicated. There are no less than three possible rotations, one per each axis. Another difference is that in the 2D world, rotation was defined about a point, while in 3D space, rotations are about lines (axes). There is a further complication in that a 3D coordinate system can have one of two possible orientations: right-handed and left-handed. It is not important which is used, as long as it is used consistently. Let us decide upon the left-handed system. Rotation about the x coordinate axis through point (0,0,0) is given by the matrix

$$R(\alpha) = \begin{bmatrix} 1 & 0 & 0 & 0 \\ 0 & \cos(\alpha) & -\sin(\alpha) & 0 \\ 0 & \sin(\alpha) & -\cos(\alpha) & 0 \\ 0 & 0 & 0 & 1 \end{bmatrix}. \tag{3.17}$$

The rotation angle is measured clockwise about the origin when looking from a point in the $+x$ axis.

Rotations about the y and z axes, through the point (0,0,0) are represented by these two matrices:

$$R(\beta) = \begin{bmatrix} \cos(\beta) & 0 & \sin(\beta) & 0 \\ 0 & 1 & 0 & 0 \\ -\sin(\beta) & 0 & \cos(\beta) & 0 \\ 0 & 0 & 0 & 1 \end{bmatrix} \tag{3.18}$$

$$R(\gamma) = \begin{bmatrix} \cos(\gamma) & -\sin(\gamma) & 0 & 0 \\ \sin(\gamma) & \cos(\gamma) & 0 & 0 \\ 0 & 0 & 1 & 0 \\ 0 & 0 & 0 & 1 \end{bmatrix} \tag{3.19}$$

respectively. The second matrix requests rotation about the z axis, and its 3×3 submatrix is identical to the rotation matrix in the plane (see the matrix in (3.12)).

Everything else is the same: concatenation is a matrix multiplication, inverse matrices for linear transformations do not need special algorithms, etc. It is enough to perform a transformation 'backwards' in order to obtain an inverse transformation. For example, an inverse rotation is simply a rotation with negative parameters:

$$R^{-1}(\alpha) = R(-\alpha) \ . \tag{3.20}$$

It is almost a trivial task to write methods for these space transformations. But before we do that, we might ask ourselves why are three separate rotation matrices needed? Would it be possible to have just one matrix per linear transformation as we did in the 2D world? It turns out that indeed such a matrix exists. More to the point, we are now going to expose a matrix which performs rotation about an axis defined by the origin and an arbitrary point W. Let the rotation angle about the w-axis be θ, and let α, β and γ be angles between the w axis and the x, y, z axes, respectively. Let point W be defined as

$$\mathrm{W} = \mathrm{W}(w_x, w_y, w_z) \ .$$

As we shall see, sines and cosines of these angles will be needed:

$$a = \cos(\alpha) = \frac{w_x}{\sqrt{(w_x^2 + w_y^2 + w_z^2)}} \tag{3.21}$$

$$b = \cos(\beta) = \frac{w_y}{\sqrt{(w_x^2 + w_y^2 + w_z^2)}} \tag{3.22}$$

$$c = \cos(\gamma) = \frac{w_z}{\sqrt{(w_x^2 + w_y^2 + w_z^2)}} \ . \tag{3.23}$$

We can now spell out matrix elements:

$$\begin{aligned}
r_{11} &= a*a \ + \ (1 - a*a)*cos(\theta) \\
r_{12} &= a*b*(1 - \cos(\theta)) + c*sin(\theta) \\
r_{13} &= a*c*(1 - \cos(\theta)) - b*sin(\theta) \\
r_{21} &= a*b*(1 - \cos(\theta)) - c*sin(\theta) \\
r_{22} &= b*b + (1 - b*b)*\cos(\theta) \\
r_{23} &= b*c*(1 - \cos(\theta)) + a*\sin(\theta) \\
r_{31} &= a*c*(1 - \cos(\theta)) + b*\sin(\theta) \\
r_{32} &= b*c*(1 - \cos(\theta)) - a*\sin(\theta) \\
r_{33} &= c*c + (1 - c*c)*\cos(\theta) \\
r_{44} &= 1 \\
r_{41} &= r_{42} = r_{43} = r_{14} = r_{24} = r_{34} = 0 \ .
\end{aligned} \tag{3.24}$$

This general transformation will be in class **Axis3DRotation**:

Axis3DRotation class methods

```
new: aPoint with: angle
    | matrix a b c d co si x y z t size |
    aPoint class = Array
        ifTrue: [ size := 4. "It's in 3D."
                x := aPoint at: 1. "This is an array of points."
                y := aPoint at: 2.
                z := aPoint at: 3.
        ].
    aPoint class == Point3D
        ifTrue: [ size := 4.
                x := Point3D x.
                y := Point3D y.
                z := Point3D z.
    ].
        aPoint class = Point
            ifTrue: [ size := 3. "A 2D case."
                    x := aPoint x. "Simple points now."
                    y := aPoint y.
                    z := 0.
            ].

matrix := super new: size.
d := ( (x * x) + (y * y) + (z * z) ) sqrt.
a := x / d. b := y / d. c := z / d.
si := angle sin.
co := angle cos.
t:= 1 - co.
matrix at: 1 at: 1 put: (a *a) + ((1 - (a *a)) *co).
matrix at: 1 at: 2 put: (a *b *t) + (c *si ).
matrix at: 1 at: 3 put: (a *c *t) - (b *si).
matrix at: 2 at: 1 put: (a *b *t) - (c *si).
matrix at: 2 at: 2 put: (b *b) + ((1 - (b *b)) *co).
matrix at: 2 at: 3 put: (b *c *t) + (a *si).
matrix at: 3 at: 1 put: (a *c *t) + (b *si).
matrix at: 3 at: 2 put: (b *c *t) - (a *si).
matrix at: 3 at: 3 put: (c *c) + ((1 - (c *c)) *co).
 ^matrix
```

Axis3DRotation methods
This class method has two parts. The former allows **aPoint** to be an Array, Point or Point3D; the latter fills a homogeneous matrix according to relations (3.24).

Matrix R is general as far as angles are concerned, but is still tied to the origin. Just as for plane rotation, it is possible to wrap matrix R with two translations and thus obtain a truly general space rotation around an arbitrary axis.

It would be nice to see the effects of space transformations. We have to devise a means of rendering three-dimensional points on the screen. Central projection is the most popular choice.

3.8 CENTRAL PROJECTION

The computer graphics are displayed on a two-dimensional screen, while the represented objects are three dimensional. The missing information can be compensated for by several techniques: perspective, elimination of hidden lines and/or surfaces, shading, intensity of light, kinetic depth effect, stereoscopic view .... We limit ourselves to the first two approaches.

The basic elements of central projection are:

— fixed point C, the centre of projection,
— the plane onto which something is projected (called the image plane),
— the point $P(x,y,z)$, which is projected,
— the line defined by C and P (called the *projector*), which intersects the image plane and thus creates the last important element, and
— point P′, called the *central projection of point P.*

All projectors contain a centre of projection (point C). The projectors become parallel when C moves to infinity, and this then is *parallel projection*. Parallel projectors are normal to the image plane, and that is why such a projection is often called *orthographic*.

Just as before, it suffices to study the central projection of only one point. Central projection of a straight line remains a straight line, but the angles may not be preserved.

So much for the theory. We apply it now to an observer (user) sitting in front of a computer screen and looking at a 2D representation of 3D objects. The observer's eye is the centre of projection; the screen is the image plane; 3D bodies are beyond the screen; the screen itself is like a window to the 'world beyond the mirror'. There are three different coordinate systems involved:

— Eye coordinate system. The system's origin is in the observer's eye with the x axis placed horizontally, the z axis vertically, and the y axis pointing to the screen and to the 'world beyond'.
— Screen coordinate system: the x axis is horizontal, the y axis is vertical, and the z axis does not exist.
— Object coordinate system, which is the coordinate system of the bodies that we want to look at. Its skeleton will appear on the screen, together with the objects themselves.

Generally speaking, the origins of all these systems are not coincident, but we shall first suppose that some of them are. Let the origins of the eye and object systems be identical. The y axis of the screen coordinate system is parallel to the z axis of the eye coordinate system. It is easy to put together formulae which connect these two coordinate systems:

$$x_s = (w_d x_e)/y_e$$
$$y_s = (w_d z_e)/y_e \quad . \tag{3.25}$$

w_d is the distance from the common origin of eye and the object coordinate system to the screen (i.e. image) plane. These two equations perform the projective transformation from a point with three coordinates to a point with only two coordinates. We can regard division here as the operation which lessens the dimension of a projected point.

These formulae are central (if you'll excuse the pun) to the whole procedure of rendering 3D solids on a 2D screen. All other transformations just prepare the ground for these two equations. For instance, we have presupposed that the screen and the eye coordinate systems are identical. In practice they are not, so we need a transformation which will make them such. How can those two systems differ in space? The best case would be when their origins are identical but their axes are not. Then only certain rotations are needed to align the axes. The arguments of this transformation are the three angles formed by the corresponding coordinate axes:

$$\begin{aligned} \psi &= \text{angle}\ (x_e, x_o) \\ \theta &= \text{angle}\ (y_e, y_o) \\ \varepsilon &= \text{angle}\ (z_e, z_o) \end{aligned} \tag{3.26}$$

Let D denote the matrix of this transformation. It is of type 3x3 and its elements are:

$$\begin{aligned} d_{11} &= \cos(\theta)\cos(\varepsilon) - \sin(\varepsilon)\sin(\psi)\sin(\theta) \\ d_{12} &= -\cos(\theta)\sin(\varepsilon) - \sin(\psi)\cos(\varepsilon)\sin(\theta) \\ d_{13} &= \cos(\psi)\sin(\theta) \\ d_{21} &= \sin(\varepsilon)\cos(\psi) \\ d_{22} &= \cos(\psi)\cos(\varepsilon) \\ d_{23} &= \sin(\psi) \\ d_{31} &= -\cos(\varepsilon)\sin(\psi) - \sin(\varepsilon)\sin(\psi)\sin(\theta) \\ d_{32} &= \sin(\varepsilon)\sin(\theta) - \sin(\psi)\cos(\varepsilon)\cos(\theta) \\ d_{33} &= \cos(\psi)\cos(\theta) \quad . \end{aligned} \tag{3.27}$$

There remains only one step now: suppose the origins are not identical, in which case we simply translate the object system to the eye coordinate system. To that end we need to express the origin of the object system as a point in the eye coordinate system. We can do this in a number of ways, but since we have just calculated the angles between the axes, we can use them in the following spherical coordinates formulae:

$$\begin{aligned} o_1 &= w_d * \cos(\psi) * \sin(\varepsilon) \\ o_2 &= w_d * \cos(\psi) * \cos(\varepsilon) \\ o_3 &= w_d * \sin(\psi) \end{aligned} \tag{3.28}$$

The point $O = O(o_1, o_2, o_3)$ is the origin of the object coordinate system in terms of the eye coordinate system.

Now we can give the following general algorithm:

Algorithm 3.1 Perspective projection to the screen
(i) Calculate matrix D using formulae (3.27).
(ii) Calculate the translation parameters using formulae (3.28).
(iii) Translate the point by multiplying it by the translation matrix.
(iv) Align the axes by multiplying the resulting point by matrix D.
(v) Project the point to the screen plane using formulae (3.25).

This algorithm is crucial. It enables us to stop thinking about the details and implementational techniques of representing 3D points on the screen. Algorithm 3.1 is a post-processor for all 3D calculations, and with it we can think in terms of 3D bodies exclusively. Here is how we can implement this algorithm.

Once again, we need several new types (classes). The obvious candidate is the matrix of perspective transformation from relations (3.27). It is a square, 3 by 3 matrix, so its natural place is as a subclass of **SquareMatrix**. Here is the code:

```
SquareMatrix variableSubclass: #PerspProj
    instanceVariableNames:
        'o distance '
    classVariableNames: ''
    poolDictionaries: ''

PerspProj class methods
new
 ^super new: 3!

PerspProj methods
new: wd psi: xa eps: ya theta: za
    | xc xs yc ys zc zs |
        "xa ya za are angles in radians;
        wd is radial distance"
distance := wd.
xc := xa cos. xs := xa sin.
yc := ya cos. ys := ya sin.
zc := za cos. zs := za sin.
"Now the matrix itself - see eq. (3.27)"
self at: 1 at: 1 put: ((yc *zc) - (zs *xs *ys)).
self at: 1 at: 2 put: ((0 - (yc *zs)) - (xs *zc *ys)).
self at: 1 at: 3 put: (xc *ys).
self at: 2 at: 1 put: (zs *xc).
self at: 2 at: 2 put: (xc *zc).
self at: 2 at: 3 put: (xs).
self at: 3 at: 1 put: ((0 - (zc *ys)) - (zs *xs *yc)).
self at: 3 at: 2 put: ((zs *ys) - (xs *zc *yc)).
```

```
self at: 3 at: 3 put: (xc *yc).
"Translation parameters are in point o."
o := (wd*xc*zs) @ (wd*xc*zc) @ (wd*xs).
 ^self!

o "Return the translation parameters."
 ^o!

wd
 ^distance!
```

The only class method, **new**, merely inherits from **SquareMatrix** and defines the matrix dimension. The actual calculation from equations (3.27) and (3.28) is left to instance method **new:psi:eps:theta:**. The first argument, **wd**, is the radial distance of the receiver (i.e. of the transformed point); the other three are the angles. Translation from relations (3.28) is kept in instance variable, **o** — hence the need to determine that result (see method **o**). Finally, method **wd** is purely technical and comes in handy later.

This class accomplished the first two steps from Algorithm 3.1. We need to apply its results to one or several 3D points. Since perspective transformation is essentially a mapping from three coordinates to two, we need a method with a 3D point as an input parameter and with a 2D point as an output. This determines the receiver of a perspective transformation — a Point. The test code in **Transcript Window** might look like this:

```
"Test code for perspective transformation."
| aaa p b c |
aaa := PerspProj new.
aaa new: 50
    psi: 30 degreesToRadians
    eps: 60 degreesToRadians
    theta: 90 degreesToRadians .
c := Point new.
c perspTrans: (1 @ 1 @ 1) perspMat: aaa.
    91.30127 @ 50.0
```

This perspectively transforms space point (**1 @ 1 @ 1**) into a planar point (**91.30127 @ 50.0**), as seen from a point that is radially distant for 50 units and with angles of 30, 60, and 90 degrees. Here is the method **perspTrans:perspMat:** from class **Point**:

```
perspTrans: point3D perspMat: aaa "APS"
    | p b d1 d2 d3 d4 d5 d6 d7 d8 d9 tx ty tz e1 e2 e3 |
tx := (point3D + (aaa o)) x.
ty := (point3D + (aaa o)) y.
tz := (point3D + (aaa o)) z.
d1 := aaa at: 1 at: 1.
d2 := aaa at: 1 at: 2.
```

```
d3 := aaa at: 1 at: 3.
d4 := aaa at: 2 at: 1.
d5 := aaa at: 2 at: 2.
d6 := aaa at: 2 at: 3.
d7 := aaa at: 3 at: 1.
d8 := aaa at: 3 at: 2.
d9 := aaa at: 3 at: 3.
e1 := (d1 * tx) + (d2 * ty) + (d3 * tz).
e2 := (d4 * tx) + (d5 * ty) + (d6 * tz).
e3 := (d7 * tx) + (d8 * ty) + (d9 * tz).
self x: (Factor * (aaa wd) * (e1 / e2)).
self y: (Factor * (aaa wd) * (e3 / e2)).
 ^self
```

The penultimate two lines are actually relations (3.25) — the perspective transformation itself. These could be coded in various ways, but the present method is simple, direct, and works.

Now we can represent 3D points on the computer screen, but one point is not completely meaningful. The smallest unit is the line, though. (Actually, it's only a segment on screen but the term 'line' is generally used.) To use Algorithm 3.1 we must invent two additional classes: **Line and Line3D**.

3.9 CLASSES Line AND Line3D

A line is defined by two points. What facilities does Smalltalk/V offer for pairs? A pair, for example, might be an array of two entities, as in all classical languages. But Points are pairs, too. We could even define a Line to be a Point that has other Points as its elements! But it's a bit controversial so we'll stick to the former definition — a two-element array. This means adding yet another subclass to **Array**, and here it is:

```
Array variableSubclass: #Line
    instanceVariableNames: ''
    classVariableNames: ''
    poolDictionaries: ''

Line class methods

new
    | line |
line := super new: 2.
line at: 1 put: Point.
line at: 2 put: Point.
 ^line!

Line methods

abs
self at: 1 put: ((self at: 1) abs).
```

```
self at: 2 put: ((self at: 2) abs).
 ^self!

drawOn: demoFrame
    | aRect pen width height |
width := demoFrame frame width.
height := demoFrame frame height.
CursorManager execute change.
aRect := Form new
    width: width
    height: height;
    white.
(self at: 1) x: ( (self at: 1) x + (width // 2) ) truncated.
(self at: 2) x: ( (self at: 2) x + (width // 2) ) truncated.
(self at: 1) y: ( (height // 2) -
                (Aspect * (self at: 1) y) ) truncated.
(self at: 2) y: ( (height // 2) -
                (Aspect * (self at: 2) y) ) truncated .
pen := Pen new: aRect. pen black. pen down.
pen drawFrom: (self at: 1) to: (self at: 2).
aRect displayAt: demoFrame frame origin rule: 1.
CursorManager normal change.
 ^aRect!

perspTrans: line3D perspMat: aaa "APS "
    | f3D s3D f s |
f3D := line3D at: 1. "This is a Point3D."
s3D := line3D at: 2.
f := Point new. s := Point new.
f perspTrans: f3D perspMat: aaa.
s perspTrans: s3D perspMat: aaa.
self at: 1 put: f.
self at: 2 put: s.
 ^self!

printOn: aStream
    (self at: 1) printOn: aStream.
    aStream nextPutAll: ' ∧ '.
    (self at: 2) printOn: aStream.!

truncated
self at: 1 put: ((self at: 1) truncated).
self at: 2 put: ((self at: 2) truncated).
 ^self!
```

Messages **abs** and **truncated** are natural enhancements of the same methods for Points, Numbers and everything else. The method **printOn:** defines the syntax for lines: two points with a ∧ symbol between. For example:

(1 @ 2) ∧ (34 @ 3)

The same syntax is valid for assigning values, thanks to the following method from **Point**:

```
∧ aPoint "APS -- Turn two 2D points as a Line."
    | line |
line := Line new.
line at: 1 put: self.
line at: 2 put: aPoint.
^line
```

so we can write like this:

```
| aaa |
aaa := (2 @ 3) ∧ (4 @ 3)
```

This syntax is pictorial but any other could have been adopted with equal effect.

The **perspTrans:perspMat:** method extends that transformation to Lines, only now the input parameter is Line3D and not Point3D. (We shall shortly see the definition of **Line3D**, as a pair of 3D points.) Finally, the **drawOn:** method draws a Line on a GraphPane. This presupposes some other method to already open a window with a graph pane in it. We use a method from class **PK** and alter it somewhat. All drawings should start from the centre of the window. To this end we translate coordinates of the input point from the upper left window corner to its middle. Then we draw a line sending messages to a Pen. We want many lines on the same pane, so the **displayAt:** message becomes **displayAt:rule:**. Rule is 1 so when sending **aRect** to the window it merges the new line with the already existing graphics.

Finally, here is class **Line3D**:

```
Array variableSubclass: #Line3D
    instanceVariableNames: ''
    classVariableNames: ''
    poolDictionaries: '' !

!Line3D class methods !

new "Create a brand new line."
    | line3D |
line3D := super new: 2.
line3D at: 1 put: Point3D new.
line3D at: 2 put: Point3D new.
 ^line3D

!Line3D methods !

printOn: aStream
    (self at: 1) printOn: aStream.
```

```
    aStream nextPutAll: ' ∧ '.
    (self at: 2) printOn: aStream.
```

Line3D is subclass directly to **Array** and not to **Line** as one might expect by analogy with **Point** and **Point3D**. A Line3D is written as:

```
(1 @ 2 @ 3) ∧ (3 @ 4 @ 5)
```

and for that to work completely we also have to add the following method to **Point3D**:

```
∧ aPoint3D "APS -- Make two points as a Line3D."
    | line3D |
line3D := Line3D new.
line3D at: 1 put: self.
line3D at: 2 put: aPoint3D.
 ^line3D
```

At long last, the method **line3DDemo** in class **PK** draws a coordinate system in the PK window:

```
 ^Menu
    labels: 'demo—lineDemo—line3DDemo' withCrs
    lines: Array new
    selectors: #(demo lineDemo line3DDemo)!

line3DDemo "Demo for drawing a 3D line."
    | aaa b c line2D |
aaa := PerspProj new.
aaa new: 50
    psi: 60 degreesToRadians
    eps: 0 degreesToRadians
    theta: 60 degreesToRadians.
c := Line new.
b := (0 @ 0 @ 0) ∧ (10 @ 0 @ 0).
line2D := (c perspTrans: b perspMat: aaa) truncated.
line2D drawOn: demoFrame.
b := (0 @ 0 @ 0) ∧ (0 @ 10 @ 0).
line2D := (c perspTrans: b perspMat: aaa) truncated.
line2D drawOn: demoFrame.
b := (0 @ 0 @ 0) ∧ (0 @ 0 @ 10).
line2D := (c perspTrans: b perspMat: aaa) truncated.
line2D drawOn: demoFrame.
b := (10 @ 0 @ 0) ∧ (10 @ 2 @ 0).
line2D := (c perspTrans: b perspMat: aaa) truncated.
line2D drawOn: demoFrame.
```

The z axis is upright (the **eps** parameter is zero), and the x axis has an additional segment so that we can tell it from the y axis.

Only now can we meaningfully draw 3D lines on the screen.

3.10 THREE-DIMENSIONAL CURVES

Curves in three dimensions are usually described by parametric equations:

$$x = x(t) \ , \qquad y = y(t) \ , \qquad z = z(t) \ . \tag{3.29}$$

Point can be directly expressed through parameter t:

$$A = A[x(t) \quad y(t) \quad z(t)] \ . \tag{3.30}$$

A helix is a simple example of a 3D curve which does not have a corresponding 2D curve:

$$\begin{aligned} x(t) &= a * \cos(t) \\ y(t) &= a * \sin(t) \\ z(t) &= \ b * t \ . \end{aligned} \tag{3.31}$$

How do we draw a 3D curve? According to relation (3.30), all we need to do is to compute points on the curve and then draw them. Algorithm 3.1 relieves us of all problems in the drawing of 3D lines. Therefore, it is natural to approximate curves through a series of lines. Taking advantage of class organization, we are free to invent another new class, **PolyLine3D**. It is merely a series of **Line3D** objects. And it is easy to compute them, as a series of lines, usually defined in an equidistant manner. Here is a method from class **PK** that will draw a helix. The result is seen in Fig. 3.1

```
helixDemo "Demo helix."
| a b c i bound arrayLength p aaa points |
    " Auxilliary variables. "
    arrayLength := 200.
    points := Array new: arrayLength.
    aaa := PerspProj new.      " Computes matrix od persp. trans."
    aaa new: 29
        psi: 52 degreesToRadians
        eps: 0 degreesToRadians
        theta: 48 degreesToRadians.

    c := PolyLine3D new: 4.
    c coordinateSystem: demoFrame with: aaa.
    a := 5. " Cylindar radius. "
    b := 0.2. " Multiplies rotation angle. "
    p := 0. " Counter."
    bound := 4 * 3.14159.

    bound negated
        to: bound
```

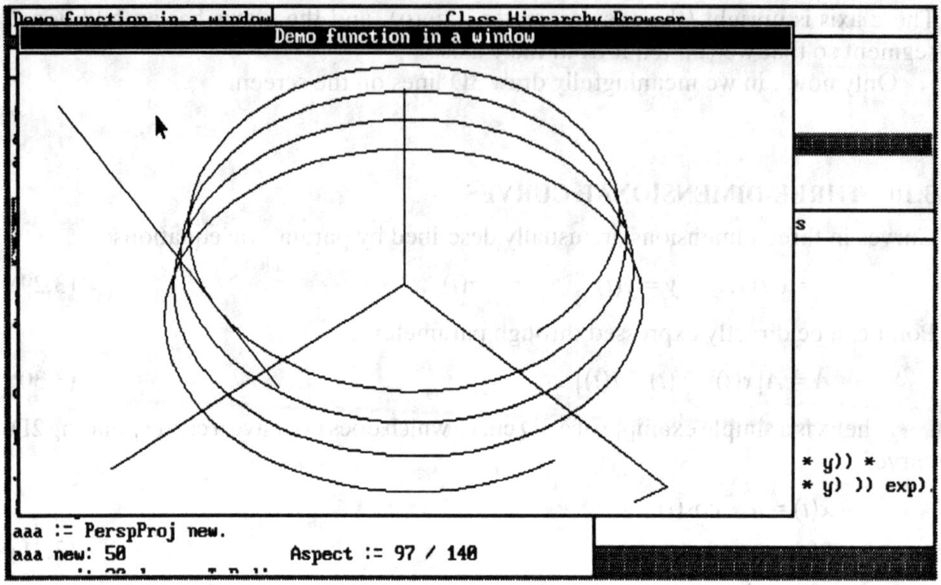

Fig. 3.1 — Helix.

```
            by: (2 * bound) / (arrayLength - 1) " Step. "
            do: [ :ta | points at: (p:= p + 1) put: Point3D new.
"Comment 1"
                    (points at: p) x: (a * (ta cos)).
                    (points at: p) y: (a * (ta sin)).
                    (points at: p) z: (b * ta).       ].
"Comment 1"

    c := PolyLine3D new: p.
    i := 0. b := 0.
    [i <= (p - 2) ] whileTrue: [
        i := i + 1.
        a := Line3D new.
        a at: 1 put: (points at: i).
        a at: 2 put: (points at: (i+1)).
        b := b + 1.
        c at: b put: a. ].
        a at: 1 put: (points at: (p - 1) ).
        a at: 2 put: (points at: p).
        b := b + 1.
        c at: b put: a.
        c drawOn: demoFrame with: aaa.
```

Lines surrounded by "**Comment 1**" correspond to equations (3.31).

PolyLine3D is a new type. It is an Array of Point3D. These points can be contiguous but this is not mandatory. The message **coordinateSystem:with:** draws a coordinate system in a standard manner. The main loop then computes 3D points along the helix. The result is in array **points**. The rest of the method puts it into a polyline and the last message draws it.

The drawing requested several adjustments in classes **Line3D** and **Line**. First, here is **PolyLine3D**:

```
Array variableSubclass: #PolyLine3D
    instanceVariableNames: ''
    classVariableNames: ''
    poolDictionaries: ''

PolyLine3D class methods

new: size
    | polyLine3D |
polyLine3D := super new: size.
polyLine3D do: [ :pl |
    pl := Line3D ].
 ^polyLine3D!

PolyLine3D methods

coordinateSystem: demoFrame with: perspTrans
self at: 1 put:  (0 @ 0 @ 0) ∧ (10 @ 0 @ 0).
self at: 2 put:  (0 @ 0 @ 0) ∧ (0 @ 10 @ 0).
self at: 3 put:  (0 @ 0 @ 0) ∧ (0 @ 0 @ 10).
self at: 4 put: (10 @ 0 @ 0) ∧ (10 @ 1 @ 0).
self drawOn: demoFrame with: perspTrans!

drawOn: demoFrame with: perspTrans
self do: [ :line3D |
    line3D drawOn: demoFrame with: perspTrans
    ].!
```

The **drawOn:with:** method calls the same method from class **Line3D**. Here it is:

```
drawOn: demoFrame with: perspTrans
    | line2D c |
c := Line new.
line2D := (c perspTrans: self perspMat: perspTrans) truncated.
line2D drawOn: demoFrame.
```

It finds the perspective transformation of the receiver and draws it by calling a **drawOn:** method for lines. And that is the last method in the chain:

```
drawOn: demoFrame
    | aRect pen width height |
width := demoFrame frame width.
```

```
height := demoFrame frame height.
CursorManager execute change.
aRect := Form new
    width: width
    height: height;
    white.

" Comment 1"
(self at: 1) x: ( (self at: 1) x + (width // 2) ) truncated.
(self at: 2) x: ( (self at: 2) x + (width // 2) ) truncated.
(self at: 1) y: ( (height // 2) - (Aspect *(self at: 1) y) ) truncated.
(self at: 2) y: ( (height // 2) - (Aspect *(self at: 2) y) ) truncated .
pen := Pen new: aRect. pen black. pen down.
" Comment 1"

pen drawFrom: (self at: 1) to: (self at: 2).
aRect displayAt: demoFrame frame origin rule: 1.
CursorManager normal change.
 ^aRect
```

Lines surrounded by "**Comment 1**" move the point to the middle of the graph pane. The x axis is translated by half a pane's width and is pushed down also by half a pane's depth. Smalltalk/V draws in the fourth quadrant ($x>0$ but $y<0$) and the **y** part of "**Comment 1**" reverses this.

3.11 THREE-DIMENSIONAL SURFACES

A surface is a function of two independent variables, say

$$z=f(x,y) \ . \tag{3.32}$$

A point on this surface has these coordinates:

$$A=A[x\ y\ f(x,y)] \ . \tag{3.33}$$

Variables x and y have domains D_x and D_y, respectively. The domain of function (3.33) is then a Cartesian product of these two domains:

$$D_z=D_x \times D_y \ . \tag{3.34}$$

In other words, a surface is defined over a rectangle D_z. The simplest way of drawing a surface is to compute the surface in as many points as is needed for a given screen resolution, and then let Algorithm 3.1 take care of the presentation technicalities. More precisely, the surface points will be computed in points

$$z_{ij}=f(x_i,y_j) \ , \qquad \text{where} \quad i=1,\ldots,m \ ; \quad j=1,\ldots,n \ ,$$

where m and n are the numbers of points along the x and y axes, respectively. The following method, **surfaceDemo**, implements the idea:

```
surfaceDemo
```

```
| a b c i arrayLength p aaa points tl th st |
"Auxiliary variables."
Factor := 35.
arrayLength := 30.
points := Array new: (arrayLength + 1).
aaa := PerspProj new.
" Computes matrix od persp. trans."
aaa new: 29
    psi: 52 degreesToRadians
    eps: 0 degreesToRadians
    theta: 48 degreesToRadians.
c := PolyLine3D new: 4.
c coordinateSystem: demoFrame with: aaa.
p := 0. " No. of points to draw. "
tl := -5. " lower bound"
th := 5. " upper bound "
st := (th - tl) abs / (arrayLength - 1). " step "
tl to: th by: st do: [ :x |
    tl to: (th + st) by: st do: [ :y |
        points at: (p:= p + 1) put: Point3D new.
            (points at: p) x: (x + 4).
            (points at: p) y: (y + 4).
            (points at: p) z: (5 * (1 - (x * x) - (y * y)) *
                              (0 - ((x * x) + (y * y) )) exp).
        ]. " end y loop "
        c := PolyLine3D new: p. "The same as in helixDemo."
        i := 0. b := 0.
        [i <= (p - 2) ] whileTrue: [
            i := i + 1.
            a := Line3D new.
            a at: 1 put: (points at: i).
            a at: 2 put: (points at: (i+1)).
            b := b + 1.
            c at: b put: a.
        ].
        a at: 1 put: (points at: (p - 1) ).
        a at: 2 put: (points at: p).
        b := b + 1.
        c at: b put: a.
        c drawOn: demoFrame with: aaa.
    p := 0. " Prepare for new slice."
    ]. " end x loop "
```

The drawbacks of this simple approach are literally visible in Fig. 3.2: the points that normally would not be seen are still there, marring the view. Even for the most elementary surfaces, this would be unacceptable. But what is easy for humans is

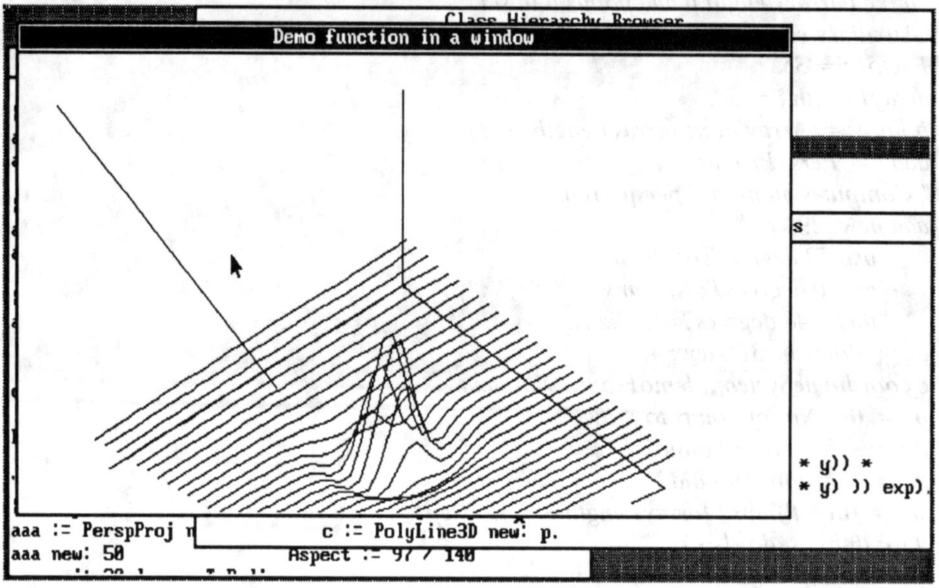

Fig. 3.2 — Surface with hidden lines.

difficult for computers: elimination of hidden lines and surfaces is tedious and costly in machine resources.

PROBLEMS

3.1 Given

$$A=\begin{bmatrix}3&0&2\\5&1&7\\7&9&1\end{bmatrix},\quad B=\begin{bmatrix}3&2\\5&7\\7&1\end{bmatrix},\quad C=\begin{bmatrix}3&0&2\\5&1&7\\7&9&1\end{bmatrix}$$

calculate A^*B, A^*C, $B+C^*A-(A^*C)$. Are all these operations possible?

3.2 Is there a full analogy in operations that can be performed on numbers and matrices? Draw a class hierarchy of classes of numbers, starting with the natural numbers up to vectors, quaternions and matrices. Could it be the same hierarchy as in Smalltalk/V?

3.3 Implement class **Matrix** using the "ordered *m*-tuples of ordered *n*-tuples" definition.

3.4 Implement class **Matrix** using OrderedCollections instead of arrays. What would be the benefits?

3.5 Enrich class **Array** with method **fill:** which will set all elements of the receiving Array to the value of the input argument. For example,

Array new fill: 45

would put number 45 into all elements of the new Array.

3.6 Eliminate instance variable **pivotValue** from class **Matrix**.

3.7 Discuss alternative names for methods in class **Matrix**. The chosen syntax, **at:at:** and **at:at:put:**, emulates messages **at:** and **at:put:** for Arrays. One other possibility is to use the same message **at:** but with a Point as an input argument. And how about messages such as **atColumn:atRow:**, or **column:row:** ?

3.8 Solve the following system of five linear equations in five unknowns:

$$\begin{aligned} x + 2y + z - t + 5u &= 6 \\ 3x + y - z + 3t - 3u &= 12 \\ x + 2y + 2z + t - 2u &= 14 \\ x - y - z + 2t + 8u &= 2 \\ x - y - z + 2t + 4u &= 5 \end{aligned}$$

3.9 Draw the hierarchy of classes after all the classes of this chapter are filed into the system.

3.10 Rewrite method **initForTest** from class **SquareMatrix** using streams or simple arrays to hold constants.

3.11 Rewrite method **initForTest** from class **SquareMatrix** so that the user inputs data interactively.

3.12 Compute the inverse matrices of the following:

$$A = \begin{bmatrix} 1 & 0 & 0 \\ 0 & 1 & 0 \\ 7 & 9 & 0 \end{bmatrix}, \quad B = \begin{bmatrix} \cos 30 & -\sin 30 & 0 \\ \sin 30 & \cos 30 & 0 \\ 0 & 0 & 1 \end{bmatrix},$$

$$C = \begin{bmatrix} 13 & 0 & 0 \\ 0 & 21 & 0 \\ 0 & 0 & 51 \end{bmatrix}.$$

3.13 Do you object to using $\wedge$ to signify a Line? These two characters are available on all keyboards. Suggest some alternative syntax for lines and segments.

3.14 In what order do the classes of this chapter have to be filed into Smalltalk/V?

3.15 Could method **line3DDemo** in class **PK** be written in a more elegant and shorter way? Modify method **perspTrans:perspMat:**.

3.16 Draw a curve defined as

$$\begin{aligned} x(t) &= a*\exp(t) \\ y(t) &= a/t \\ z(t) &= b*t \ . \end{aligned}$$

3.17 Write a method to perform elementary geometrical transformations upon a helix.

3.18 Write a GraphPane window to perform elementary geometrical transformations upon 3D surfaces.

4

Smalltalk/V for numerical mathematics

4.1 LARGE INTEGERS

Most languages support elementary data types identical to those found at hardware level: bytes, signed and unsigned integers, characters, real numbers and others. Such close correspondence is, generally speaking, useful. Only on rare occasions do things go wrong — consider a loop pointer that somehow exceeds the arbitrary bounds of the [−32768; 32767] margins for two-byte integers.

Smalltalk/V has various types of integer, all of them subclasses of class **Integer**:

— **LargeNegativeInteger**
— **LargePositiveInteger**, and
— **SmallInteger**.

Together they cover the complete range of integers. SmallIntegers are in the range [−16384; 16383] and are frequently used as counters or indices. Should a program require smaller or larger values, the instances of **LargeNegativeInteger** or **LargePositiveInteger** are automatically substituted. The precision of integer numbers is virtually infinite, but the integer bit representation must be less than 64K bytes.

The next example will demonstrate how many digits Smalltalk/V can use for integer calculations. Here is the **factorial** method with several arguments:

5 120
55 12696403353658275925965100847566516959580321051449436762275
840000000000000
305 78161436727006180268422178189219578307032983534637494772866
41396628167179239386921729943301041362095024220206171624257
00058797032565740466783753084597192037586704967802732965215
01067572077524899979717511037428293659582178693340334766424
99018904484546251288781096823882834465942173048496008989522
99902231063153132498207051036643662358797071920655905838970
55359515398355946774139563697824612784477249330709006355896
11997485643598647287035722731427765369893630467082264431683
43792230829254425088116175304088347716083363571475561008294
97816420479734592307200000000000000000000000000000000000000
0000000000000000000000000000000000000

306 factorial

306 is the first number whose **factorial** Smalltalk/V cannot compute directly because of stack overflow. It has some 627 digits! Smalltalk/V286 is even more powerful, computing **999 factorial** and **1500 factorial** without a problem. This means dealing with numbers with one or two or more thousand digits.

Commercial programs could benefit from this overextended precision, thus avoiding roundoff errors in, say, gross totals on sales and receipt figures. Usual single precision yields some 6–7 significant digits; double precision actually doubles the number of significant digits to 13–15. Some languages implement BCD arithmetics (Binary Coded Digits) to increase the total significant digits to 18. Smalltalk/V is clearly capable of even more significant digits. Its class **Fraction** and practically unlimited precision make it superior to other programming languages. Consider how much easier computing would be if there were devices that could calculate without roundoff errors!

4.2 LINEAR SYSTEM

Let us consider a classical example of a linear system with three unknowns. Its coefficients belong to a so-called Hilbert matrix, which is notorious for its numerical instability. We already have a general Gauss elimination method at our disposal (**simulEq:** in class **Matrix**) and can use it to illustrate the point. Let the system coefficients be:

```
 1  1/2 1/3 1
1/2 1/3 1/4 0
1/3 1/4 1/5 0
```

where the fourth column is the right-hand side of the system.

Eliminating it by hand and working only with fractions, we obtain $x_1=9$, $x_2=-36$, and $x_3=30$ as solutions. This is exactly what Smalltalk/V gives as an answer, after the following code is executed with **show it:**

```
| aaa s | "Test code for matrix inversion."
aaa := Matrix rows: 3 columns: 4.
aaa at: 1 at: 1 put: 1.          aaa at: 1 at: 2 put: (1/2).
aaa at: 1 at: 3 put: (1/3).      aaa at: 1 at: 4 put: 1.
aaa at: 2 at: 1 put: (1/2).      aaa at: 2 at: 2 put: (1/3).
aaa at: 2 at: 3 put: (1/4).      aaa at: 2 at: 4 put: 0.
aaa at: 3 at: 1 put: (1/3).      aaa at: 3 at: 2 put: (1/4).
aaa at: 3 at: 3 put: (1/5).      aaa at: 3 at: 4 put: 0.
s:=Matrix rows: 1 columns: aaa rows.
s simulEq: aaa.
s show.
9 -36 30 $
```

Suppose, now, that coefficients were given as floating-point numbers:

```
| aaa s three |
three := 0.33"333333333".
```

```
aaa := Matrix rows: 3 columns: 4.
aaa at: 1 at: 1 put: 1.          aaa at: 1 at: 2 put: 0.5.
aaa at: 1 at: 3 put: three.      aaa at: 1 at: 4 put: 1.
aaa at: 2 at: 1 put: 0.50.       aaa at: 2 at: 2 put: three.
aaa at: 2 at: 3 put: 0.25.       aaa at: 2 at: 4 put: 0.
aaa at: 3 at: 1 put: three.      aaa at: 3 at: 2 put: 0.25.
aaa at: 3 at: 3 put: 0.20.       aaa at: 3 at: 4 put: 0.
s := Matrix rows: 1 columns: aaa rows.
s simulEq: aaa.
s show.
```

The result

(55.555556 −277.77778 255.55556)

is an unbelievable error, which nicely illustrates the pitfalls of practical numerical mathematics. However, as the number of significant digits grows larger, the results once more become acceptable. For values of variable **three**=0.3333 the result is

(9.0617404 −36.323202 30.302612)

and for **three**=0.33333333333, we are back to (9.0 −36.0 30.0).

The moral is obvious: never lose significant digits if you do not have to — and with Smalltalk/V you do not have to if you do not want to!

4.3 THE POWER METHOD FOR EIGENVALUES OF A MATRIX

These features of Smalltalk/V can be put to good use in a variety of numerical methods. Consider the power method for computing the dominant eigenvalue of a matrix. (We take it for granted that you already know what matrix eigenvalues are and how important this problem is.)

Assume matrix A is of size $n \times n$, with n independent eigenvectors $V_1, V_2, \ldots, V_n$ and with a truly dominant eigenvalue, λ. The power method leads to its value through raising A to the $(p+1)$th and pth powers, multiplying them with an arbitrary vector V and dividing any of the corresponding components of $A^{(p+1)}V$ and A^pV. All of this is contained in the following method from class **SquareMatrix:**

```
"SquareMatrix" highestEigenValue
    "Power method for dominant
        eigen value of a matrix"
    | rrr bbb ccc up down |
rrr := RowMatrix new: self rows.
1 to: rrr size do: [ :i |
    rrr at: i put: (self at: i at: 1)].
bbb := self class new: self rows self: columns.
bbb := self * self * self * self * self * self.
ccc := self class new: self rows self: columns.
ccc := bbb * self.
up := (rrr * bbb) at: 1.
```

```
    down := (rrr * ccc) at: 1.
    ^up / down
```

Variable **rrr** is the arbitrary vector *V* and is initialized to be the same as the first row of the receiving matrix. Variables **bbb** and **ccc** contain the original matrix raised to the sixth and seventh powers. Parameter **p** has a fixed value of 6, which is a good practical compromise. Of course, it can be changed to other values by adding or deleting the word **self**, or you can rewrite the routine using a loop. Variables **up** and **down** contain the first elements of products of vector **rrr** and consecutive powers of the receiving matrix. Their quotient is the required dominant eigenvalue. Here is an example:

```
/ aaa result / "Power method for
         dominant eigenvalues."
aaa := SquareMatrix new: 4 .
aaa at: 1 at: 1 put: 1.      aaa at: 1 at: 2 put: (1/2).
aaa at: 1 at: 3 put: (1/3). aaa at: 1 at: 4 put: (1/4).
aaa at: 2 at: 1 put: (1/2). aaa at: 2 at: 2 put: (1/3).
aaa at: 2 at: 3 put: (1/4). aaa at: 2 at: 4 put: (1/5).
aaa at: 3 at: 1 put: (1/3). aaa at: 3 at: 2 put: (1/4).
aaa at: 3 at: 3 put: (1/5). aaa at: 3 at: 4 put: (1/6).
aaa at: 4 at: 1 put: (1/4). aaa at: 4 at: 2 put: (1/5).
aaa at: 4 at: 3 put: (1/6). aaa at: 4 at: 4 put: (1/7).
result := aaa highestEigenValue.
    849275461747590696/12740950342402097321
    6.6657152e-1
```

The resulting huge fraction shows that there were no roundoff errors. The number below is the fraction multiplied by 1.0, just to see its real value of 0.66657152.

This shows that routines without roundoff errors are possible. Of course, they take longer to compute. But that old dilemma — fast or precise — must be resolved in favour of precision: what good are incorrect results obtained with astonishing speed?

4.4 ELEMENTS OF STATISTICS

It is difficult to go through a day without hearing about, talking about, and using statistical data and notions. In a strict sense, a *statistic* is any measure of a set of data. The broad picture is this. There are some data obtained by standard techniques such as questionnaires, laboratory measurements, interviews and the like. Usually, there are thousands of numbers to deal with. Humans cannot think in more than seven notions at a time. Anything beyond that is not comprehensible, *ergo* we need a way of reducing data to a handful of derived numbers. Those representatives — the statistics — are what we call *information*. The information (in this context) is one or several numbers which catch the behaviour of data in some understandable manner.

This method of replacing an excess of numbers with several related numbers is not without danger. The complete information is contained only in the original data, everything else being less precise. Therefore, all statistical inference is done with a degree of uncertainty. We might even define statistics as a body of methods for making wise decisions in the presence of uncertainty. The key notions are samples, population, distributions.

A whole group that is under our attention is called a *population*. It is usually too large. You can measure all citizens of a city to see whether they have grown taller, but this would be impractical. It is outright impossible to measure all the stars in the universe to gain more knowledge about them. So the idea is to use *samples*, which are smaller parts of the complete population. We draw statistics and conclusions upon samples but extend them to the complete population, which is exactly the source of the mentioned uncertainty.

The process of obtaining samples is called *sampling*.

The word *population* in this context does not refer to the number of habitants of a particular area. Here, it means all the possible outcomes of a situation under study (counting, asking questions, casting a die, etc.). Only on rare occasions does a sample equal the whole population. Since we draw conclusions upon the sample and not upon the population, we should always use terms such as 'statistical inference' in order to stress the true nature of our work (see Fig. 4.1). The best sample should

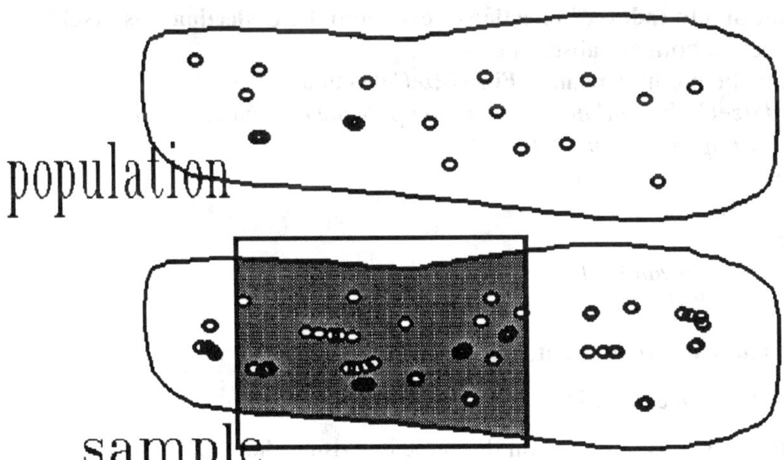

Fig. 4.1 — Population and sample.

ideally have all the properties of the population except that it is smaller in size. One way of choosing such a sample would be to make sure that each member of the population had the same chance of being included in the sample. This is called *random sampling*. And since it is random, we use the language of probability. For example, a population is defined by the probability distribution $f(x)$ of the associated random variable X. If X is normally distributed we say that the population itself is normally distributed. Then we also know the population parameters μ and σ. In contrast, the related parameters from the sample are called *sample statistics*. Population parameters are usually denoted by Greek letters while sample statistics are denoted by Roman letters.

The simplest statistics consist mainly of individual numbers. The three most popular and useful are the *mean*, the *median*, and the *mode*.

4.5 THE MEAN

The mean is also known as the arithmetic average. It is computed as the sum of all the members of the sample divided by its size:

$$M=\frac{D_1+D_2+D_3+\ldots+D_n}{n}. \tag{4.1}$$

D denotes the sample elements, and *n* the size.

Let us see how this is written in Smalltalk/V.

It is evident that computing the mean affects the whole array of sample values. We might be tempted to include our forthcoming method called **mean** into class **Array**. The same effect is possible if we put **mean** one class higher, into **FixedSizeCollection**. From there **mean** will be available to other **FixedSizeCollection** subclasses (whether they have some imminent use for it or not). The best of all would be to include **mean** into **IndexedCollection** or even into the **Collection** class itself, but, this is not possible: both are abstract classes.

Here is the method **mean** in **FixedSizeCollection:**

```
"FixedSizeCollection" mean "APS Compute the arithmetic mean
        Chapter , equation 4.1"
    | mean |
mean := 0.
self do: [ :i |
    mean := mean+i. ].
 ^mean / self size
```

This is how we could use it:

```
#(1.3 2 3 4 ) mean 2.575
```

This result, 2.575, is obtained on the same line using **show it.**

4.6 THE MODE

The mode of a sample is the value of the most frequently occurring element. It does not have to be unique. For example, the sample

1 2 3 4 3 4 5 6 6 7

has three modes — 3, 4 and 6 — because all of them occur twice. Ideally, we would like to put another method in class **FixedSizeCollection,** called **mode,** and use it like this:

```
#(1 2 3 4 3 4 5 6 6 7 ) mode (3 4 6)
```

The resulting array (3 4 6) appears after **show it.** Here is the method itself:

```
"FixedSizeCollection" mode    "APS Compute the mode
                                Chapter 4"
        | count maxcount modeArray j |
  count := Array new: self size.
  1 to: self size do: [ :t |
      count at: t put: 1.
      (t+1) to: self size do: [ :w |
          (self at: t)=(self at: w)
          ifTrue: [count at: t put: ((count at: t)+1) ]].
          ].
  maxcount := count max.
  modeArray := Array new: count size.
  j := 0.
  1 to: modeArray size do: [ :i |
          maxcount=(count at: i)
              ifTrue: [ modeArray at: (j := j+1) put: i ]
      ].
  count := Array new: j.
  1 to: j do: [ :i | count at: i put: (self at: (modeArray at: i))].
  ^count
```

Array **count** gathers frequencies from the receiver (usually an Array), variable **maxcount** finds its maximal value, **modeArray** contains indices of those maximal values and, finally, we use the name **count** again to return the original values with highest frequencies.

This code expects methods **max:** and **min:** to already exist in class **Array.**

4.7 THE MEDIAN

The median of a sample is the middle value, based on the order of magnitude. For example, in the set

1 2 3 4 5

3 would be the median, while in the set

1 2 3 4 5 6

both 3 and 4 could be taken as the median. The mean and the median are quite similar in data sets with a normal distribution.

Calculating the median is simple, as there are only two cases: the sample size is either odd or even. Sort the data first, then take the middle element, indexed as *N*/2. The method — also in class **FixedSizeCollection** — is called **median.** It takes advantage of Smalltalk/V's built-in sorting routines, such as **asSortedCollection.** The code is quite simple:

```
"FixedSizeCollection" median
```

```
    "APS Compute the median Chapter 4"
   | median array |
array := self asArray.
array asSortedCollection.
 ^ array at: (array size // 2+1)
```

And it works:

```
#(1 2 3 4 5 ) median 3
#(1 2 3 4 5 6) median 4
```

4.8 THE VARIANCE AND THE STANDARD DEVIATION

These three statistics are quite elementary. More insight can be obtained by using the variance and the standard deviation. The mean and the median do not convey any meaning of variations in data; they just point to where the 'points of gravity' lie in a sample. So more statistics are needed. The variance and standard deviation give the average distances from the data points to the mean of the sample. N is the number of elements in the sample, and M is the sample's mean. The squares make all the summands positive, but it is still not a proper definition of the distance between two numbers. To achieve it, we must find the square root of V:

$$V = \frac{1}{N} \sum_{i=1}^{N} (D_i - M)^2, \ \sigma = \sqrt{V}.$$

The standard deviation is more important than the variance. It tells us how representative the mean is of the entire sample. For a normal distribution, about 68% of the sample will be within one standard deviation of the mean, and about 95% will be within two standard deviations of the mean. For other distributions, similar rules apply.

Computing the standard deviation is as easy in Smalltalk/V as in any other computer language — provided you have access to floating-point hardware or software. The method **stDev** in class **FixedSizeCollection** is:

```
"FixedSizeCollection" stDev "APS Standard deviation"
stDev
   1st M |
M : = self mean.
ST: = self collect : [ : element |
   (element – M) *(element – M)].
↑ st mean sqrt
```

and is applied as:

```
#(1 2 3) stDev 8.1649658e – 1
```

All in all, it is quite easy to compute basic sample statistics using Smalltalk/V.

4.9 REGRESSION AND INTERACTIVE EXPLORATION OF DATA

Experiment is one of the main tools for exploring nature. The outcome is always a set of data. The explorer's job is to make sense out of them. The easiest way is to plot the data and to try to find out what mathematical curve best fits the data. Data always reflect the past whereas we are mostly interested in the future, so there is little sense in producing exact approximations in the numerical sense of the word. Qualitative data analysis is more important. It determines the relationships between measured data conditions under which the experiment was conducted. In data analysis we are content to learn what *type* of mathematical function makes the most sense in a given case.

The traditional approach is to approximate the data by means of some well-known mathematical curve. The straight line is almost always the first candidate in any investigation. It is relatively easy to do the required numerical work, and the interpretation of the resultant line is straightforward. The technique usually used is the method of least squares. We merely quote the main results.

Fig. 4.2 explains the idea: a set of points (x_i, y_i), $i = 1, \ldots, n$, is approximated by

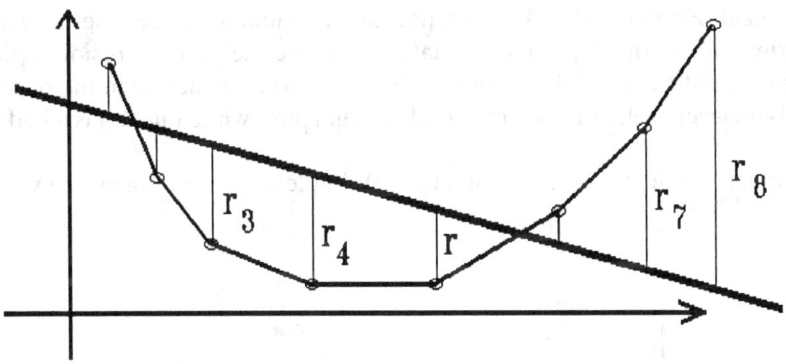

Fig. 4.2 — The idea of the least squares method.

means of the straight line

$$y = ax + b$$

where coefficients a and b are determined by

$$a = \frac{n\sum_{i=1}^{n} X_i Y_i - \sum_{i=1}^{n} X_i \sum_{i=1}^{n} Y_i}{n\sum_{i=1}^{n} X_i^2 - \left[\sum_{i=1}^{n} X_i\right]^2} \tag{4.4}$$

$$b = \frac{\sum_{i=1}^{n} Y_i - a\sum_{i=1}^{n} X_i}{n} \, . \tag{4.5}$$

Quite often a situation like that in Fig. 4.2 occurs. A different curve approximates the data better than a simple straight line. In such a case the investigator has to search for some other functional relationship. There are no specific rules as to how to choose possible candidate functions, and the investigator has to rely on his/her experience, erudition, special circumstances, and so on.

When is the proposed curve satisfactory? One statistical criterion is to calculate the residuals R_i, $i = 1, \ldots, n$,

defined as:

$$R_i = Y_i - f(X_i),\ i = 1, \ldots, n, \tag{4.6}$$

where Y_i are the measured values, and f is the proposed curve, computed in experimental points X_i. In Fig. 4.2, the residuals are drawn as vertical lines. The residuals themselves are a function of the experimental data, and it also makes sense to plot *them*. From the visual representation of residuals we see whether f is a good approximation to the experimental data. More precisely, if the residual plot looks random, f is satisfactory; if we can visually detect some structure in the residual plot then f is unacceptable. Fig. 4.3 is a good residual plot, while Fig. 4.4 is a bad residual plot.

So much for the theory. Our Smalltalk/V implementation is a window with *three*

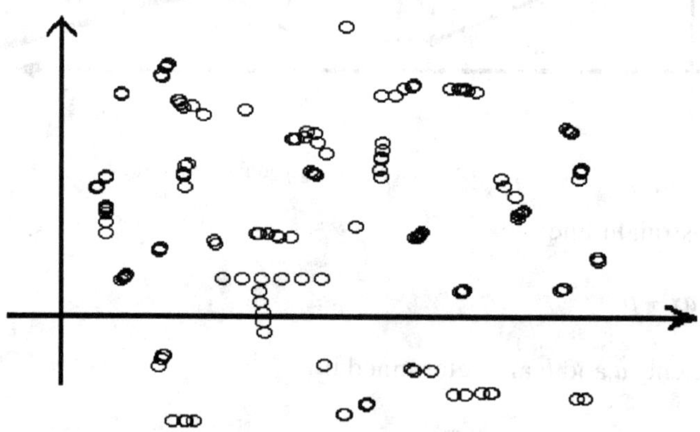

Fig. 4.3 — A good residual plot.

panes. One is a ListPane to hold the measured data (i.e. points); the other will be a picture of the data and the proposed function; and the third will be the residual plot. Fig. 4.5 makes all this clear.

Let us make a new class, called **P3**, to make a data analysis window from Fig. 4.5.

```
Object subclass: #P3
   instanceVariableNames:
      'data lPane originalData reducedData a b x y '
   classVariableNames: ''
```

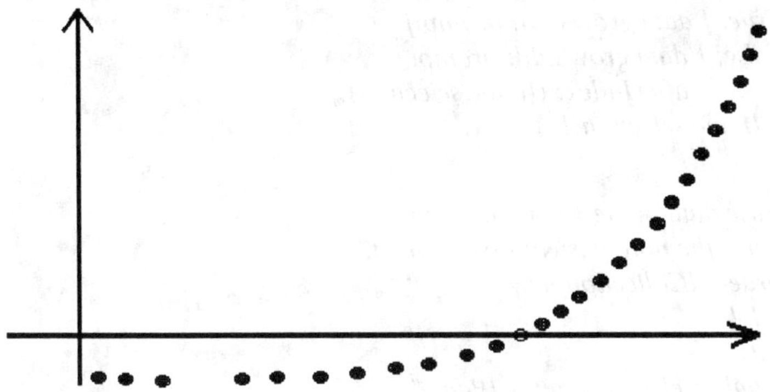

Fig. 4.4 — A residual plot with structure (*f* unacceptable).

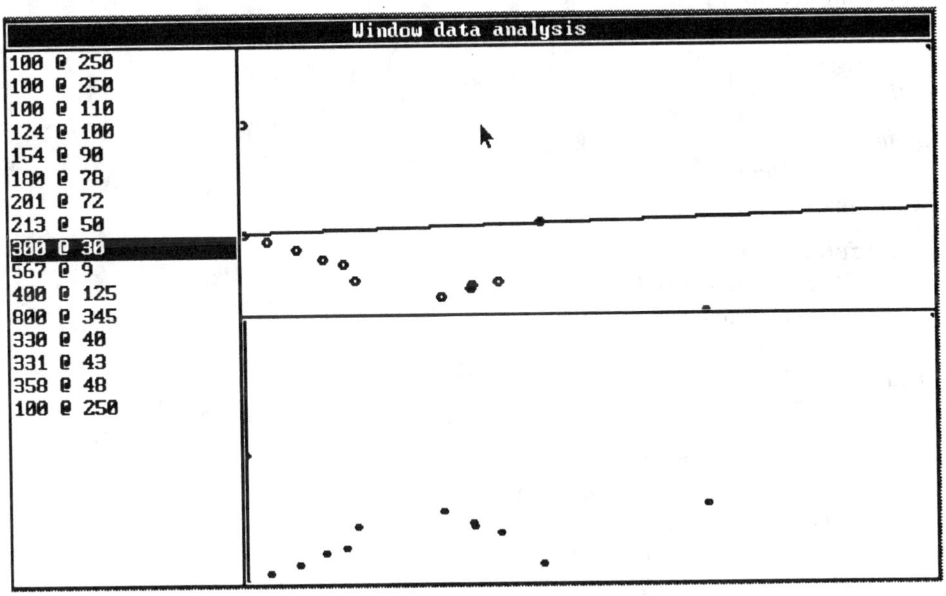

Fig. 4.5 — Data analysis window.

```
    poolDictionaries: ''

P3 methods

add
        "Invoke a prompter to
        add a string to ListPane."
| prompt |
prompt := Prompter prompt: 'New element, please?'
          defaultExpression: (String new).

data size == 0
```

```
        ifTrue: [ data grow add: prompt]
        ifFalse: [ data grow add: prompt
                  afterIndex: (lPane selection).].
self show: lPane selection.!

erase
        "Erase data in the ListPane,
        reverse the non-existent first element."
data := OrderedCollection new.
self show: 1.!
initElements
        "Initialize elements in the lPane."
        | t |
t := Array new: (data size).
1 to: data size do: [ :i |
        t at: i put: ((data at: i) printString)
        ].
 ^t!

initialize
self initializeData.
self show: 1.!

initializeData
        "Initialize data itself."
data := Polygon new.
data testPolygon.
data collect: [ :d |
        d+273 ].!

initOriginalGraph: aaRect
        | aRect xMin xMax yMin yMax
        c d e f g h n xx yy r
        pen c1 c2 c3 c4 x8 x9 y8 y9 |
CursorManager execute change.
aRect := Form new
            width: aaRect width
            height: aaRect height; white.

n := data size.
pen := Pen new: aRect. pen black. pen down.
x := Array new: n. y := Array new: n.

1 to: n do: [ :i |
        x at: i put: ((data at: i) x).
        y at: i put: ((data at: i) y).].

"Constants."
xMax := x max. xMin := x min.
yMax := y max. yMin := y min.
```

```
c3 := aRect width. c4 := aRect height.
c1 := c3 / (xMax−xMin). c2 := c4 / (yMax−yMin).

"Scale points into a pane."
1 to: n do: – :i /
        x at: i put: ((c1 * ( (x at: i)−xMin ))).
        y at: i put: (c4−(c2 * ((y at: i)−yMin) )). ].

"Draw points as small circles."
1 to: n do: [ :i /
        pen place: ((x at: i) @ (y at: i)) truncated.
        pen ellipse: 2 aspect: 1 . .].

"Axes."
pen "Vertical axis."
        drawFrom: ( (c1 * (0−xMin)) @ 0) truncated
                to: ( (c1 * (0−xMin)) @ (c4−1)) truncated.
pen "Horizontal axis."
        drawFrom: ( 0 @ (c4−(c2 * (0−yMin) ))) truncated
                to: ( (c3−1) @ (c4−(c2 * (0 − yMin) ))) truncated.

"Calculate the approximating straight line."
c := d := e := f := h := 0.
1 to: n do: [ :i /
        xx := (data at: i) x. yy := (data at: i) y.
        c := c+xx. d := d+yy. e := e+(xx * yy).
        f := f+(xx * xx). h := h+(yy * yy).].
g := c * c.
a := ( e−( (c * d) / n) ) / (f−(g / n)).
b := (d / n)−( (a * c) / n).

"Now draw the line."
x8 := xMin. y8 := (a * x8)+b.
x9 := xMax. y9 := (a * x9)+b.
pen drawFrom: ( (c1 * ( x8−xMin ))
                @ (c4−(c2 * ( y8−yMin) ))) truncated
        to: ( (c1 * ( x9−xMin ) )
                @ (c4−(c2 * ( y9−yMin) )) truncated).
aRect displayAt: originalData frame origin.
CursorManager normal change.
 ^aRect!

initReducedGraph: aRect
        "Initialize the form for the reduced data."
        / f pen r c1 c2 c3 c4 xMin xMax yMin yMax xx yy /
CursorManager execute change.
f := Form width: aRect width height: aRect height.
f white.

"Calculate residuals."
```

```
r := Array new: data size.
1 to: data size do: [ :i |
        r at: i put: ( (y at: i)-((a * (x at: i))+b)) abs.].
xMax := x max. xMin := x min.
yMax := r max. yMin := r min.
c3 := f width. c4 := f height.
c1 := c3 / (xMax-xMin). c2 := c4 / (yMax-yMin).

"Draw residuals in the lower window."
pen := Pen new: f. pen down. pen black.
1 to: data size do: [ :i |
        xx := ( c1 * ( (x at: i)-xMin)) truncated.
        yy := ( c4-(c2 * ( (r at: i)-yMin) )) truncated.
        pen place: xx @ yy.
        pen ellipse: 2 aspect: 1.].

"Axes."
pen "Vertical axis."
        drawFrom: ( (c1 * (0-xMin)) @ 0) truncated
                to: ( (c1 * (0-xMin)) @ (c4-1)) truncated.
pen "Horizontal axis."
        drawFrom: ( 0 @ (c4-(c2 * (0-yMin) ))) truncated
                to: ( (c3-1) @ (c4-(c2 * (0-yMin) ))) truncated.
f displayAt: reducedData frame origin.
CursorManager normal change.
 ^f!

openOn: aRectangle
    | aTopPane |use
                aTopPane := TopPane new
                label: 'Window data analysis'.
        aTopPane addSubpane:
        (lPane := ListPane new
                        change: #show:; "left mouse button — action"
                        menu: #pointsMenu; "right mouse button — menu"
                        model: self;
                        name: #initElements; "initialize pane"
                        returnIndex: true; "specific to ListPanes"
                        framingRatio: (0 @ 0 extent: 1/4 @ 1) ).

        aTopPane addSubpane:
        (originalData := GraphPane new
                        model: self;
                        name: #initOriginalGraph:;
                        change: #plotOriginalData:;
                        menu: #originalDataMenu;
                        framingRatio: (1/4 @ 0 extent: 3/4 (1/2)) ).

        aTopPane addSubpane:
```

```
        (reducedData := GraphPane new
                model: self;
                name: #initReducedGraph:;
                change: #plotReducedData:;
                menu: #reducedDataMenu;
                framingRatio: (1/4 @ (1/2) extent: 3/4 @ (1/2)) ).
        self initializeData.use
        aTopPane reframe: aRectangle.
        aTopPane dispatcher openWindow scheduleWindow!

originalDataMenu
 ^Menu
        labels: 'add\remove\scale //\erase\initialize' withCrs
        lines: Array new
        selectors: #(add remove scale erase initialize)!

plotOriginalData: aPoint
        "Plot the data in a XY-coordinate system."
CursorManager execute change.
self initOriginalGraph: originalData frame.
CursorManager normal change.

plotReducedData: aPoint
        "Plot the data in a XY-coordinate system."
CursorManager execute change.
self initReducedGraph: reducedData frame.
CursorManager normal change.!

pointsMenu
        "Select menu operation."
 ^Menu
        labels: 'add\remove\scale //\erase\initialize' withCrs
        lines: Array new
        selectors: #(add remove scale erase initialize).!

reducedDataMenu
 ^Menu
        labels: 'add\remove\scale //\erase\initialize' withCrs
        lines: Array new
        selectors: #(add remove scale erase initialize)!
remove
        "Remove an element from lPane."
| where |
where := lPane selection.
(data size=0 or: [ where=1 ] )
        ifFalse: [
                data removeIndex: where.
```

```
            self show: (data at: 1).
            ].

(data size > 0 and: [ where=1 ])
      ifTrue: [
            data removeIndex: where.
            self show: (data at: 1).
            ].!

scale
      "Divide data by input number."
      | d p |
p := Prompter prompt: 'A number, please?'
                  defaultExpression: (String new).
CursorManager execute change.

1 to: data size do: [ :e |
      d := (data at: e) // p.
      data at: e put: d.].
lPane update.
CursorManager normal change.!

show: anInteger
      "Left mouse button pressed,
      change reversed item."
lPane changed: #initPoints.
lPane restoreSelected: anInteger.!
```

Class **P3** lives up to its promise: both data and their graphical representations are visible simultaneously. The GraphPanes do not have any special menus — pressing the right mouse button on them returns the same menu as for the ListPane. There are five operations that you can perform on the data:

— **add,** add data to the list,
— **remove,** remove an element from the list,
— **scale,** divide all elements in the ListPane by a number,
— **erase,** erase all points,
— **initialize,** no matter what the current state in the ListPane is, initialize data again.

The changes are not immediately visible in either of the GraphPanes; you have to press the left mouse button in a GraphPane when you want to see the effect of changes made to the list of points. This way, several changes at once are possible. For example, you could decide to remove several distant points in order to obtain more sense from your data.

The most interesting possibility, however, is to transform data in any way you please, until some reasonable fit to a straight line is accomplished. Two methods are involved in data initialization: **testPolygon** from **Polygon** and **initializeData** from **P3.** The last line in **initializeData**

```
data collect: [ :d |
   d+273 ].
```

transforms data. This is the place to introduce your own function — enter it, **save** the method (both the **Data analysis window** and the **Class Hierarchy Browser** window have to be present on the screen at the same time), go back to the **Data analysis window,** initialize the ListPane and change the GraphPanes. All this goes quite smoothly with a mouse and is a good example of how the openness of the Smalltalk/V environment can make life easier. Of course, if this were a commercial application, it would be mandatory to let the user change the function directly from the ListPane menu. Catering for this requirement is one of the major problems solved in the Billing Schedules program.

I readily admit that this may be a crude attempt to do the job. I am leaving it in this state so that you can see what kind of code is possible in Smalltalk/V. The code may be more like that of traditional imperative languages, with long procedures (methods), many loops and local variables, but it works. I emphasize that you cannot convert to a Smalltalk/V style of coding at once. Neither do you have to nor actually can you. Only later do you see how to create those two line methods that seem so small but do so much. Be sure to compare this program with the differential equations solver in this same chapter. There you will find a proper code written in true Smalltalk/V spirit.

4.10 HOW CLASS P3 WORKS

Smalltalk/V automatically sorts class methods by name, as they are listed here. However, the first executed method is always **open** or **openOn:**, and all others branch from them. You should always start reading a class from the **open** or **openOn:** method, taking into account what global class variables are declared. In this case, instance class variables are:

- **data,** declared as Polygon in method **initializeData,**
- **lPane,** the ListPane for **data,**
- **originalData,** the GraphPane for graph and the corresponding straight line approximation,
- **reducedData,** the GraphPane for residuals,
- **a** and **b,** the computed straight line coefficients,
- **x** and **y,** auxiliary arrays which hold the *x* and *y* coordinates of **data.**

Just as in any lengthy program, the choice of data structures is somewhat arbitrary. The base structure here is **data,** which must be of type Polygon since that is what a ListPane requires in this case. The **x** and **y** arrays are merely a shorthand. It can be argued that only those two arrays are needed, while the interface to the ListPane could have been implemented as a series of **printString** messages. Both solutions are quite valid, though.

It is common Smalltalk/V practice to declare pane names (**lPane, originalData, reducedData**) as global for the whole class while the window (**TopPane**) variable is local to the **open** method. Therefore, all methods can address panes directly, which significantly eases program development.

The ListPane methods are practically the same as for class **P.** The major developments are new methods for the GraphPanes. The 'name' methods **initOrigi-**

nalGraph: and **initReducedGraph:** are new. They share coefficients **a** and **b** and arrays **x** and **y.** To plot a data graph you need to draw visible points instead of connecting them with straight lines. Therefore, we now draw small ellipses in a loop:

```
"Draw points as small circles."
1 to: n do: [ :i |
    pen place: ((x at: i) @ (y at: i)) truncated.
    pen ellipse: 2 aspect: 1 . ].
```

The straight line is first calculated in a straightforward manner and is then drawn in the upper GraphPane, **originalData.**

The code in **initReducedGraph:** is simpler and mimics the code in **initOriginalGraph:.** Array **r** is computed first, and only then are the scaling constants **c1, c2, c3, c4** found.

4.11 EXTENSIONS

Like all Smalltalk/V programs, extensions and improvements are easy to spot. The **pointsMenu** can be significantly enhanced. You could place new options there for changing x and y values separately. The usefulness of this application strongly depends on the availability of either a separately available floating-point kit or a numerical co-processor. If you have either, you could apply logarithms, exponential functions, and others to make more sense of the experimental data.

Technically, additional transformations could be implemented in two ways. In the first, you would extend the existing **pointsMenu** method with new submenus such as **changeX** and **changeY,** from which the user would select separate functions. The other way would be to incorporate fixed menus in the shape of two additional ListPanes. This would demand interventions in the **openOn:** menu. One pane could be for operations on the x-coordinates, the other for the y-coordinates: selecting one of those items would automatically transform **data.**

4.12 BUSINESS GRAPHICS — HISTOGRAMS AND PIES

One way of increasing the visual appeal of graphical output is shading. Let us see how to shade rectangles, as the simplest figures that Smalltalk/V offers.

Basically, there are just two kinds of shading: using lines and using points. Both are useful and come as a standard part of any interactive graphics editor. They are particularly useful for business graphics.

The simplest shading is achieved by drawing a series of equidistant parallel horizontal or vertical lines. Should the distance between them be less than or equal to the physical dimension of a screen point, the shading turns into filling.

Shading could be described in the following general fashion:

General shading algorithm

(i) Calculate the increment, i.e. the position of a new line.
(ii) Repeat the following procedure, starting with one rectangle side and finishing with the opposite side:

(a) Draw a shading element
(b) Calculate a new increment, and then
(c) Calculate the new position of the shading element.

The shading element in this algorithm can be either a straight line (horizontal, vertical, angled) or a point. Class **PR** can give examples of all these shadings, as can be seen in Fig. 4.6.

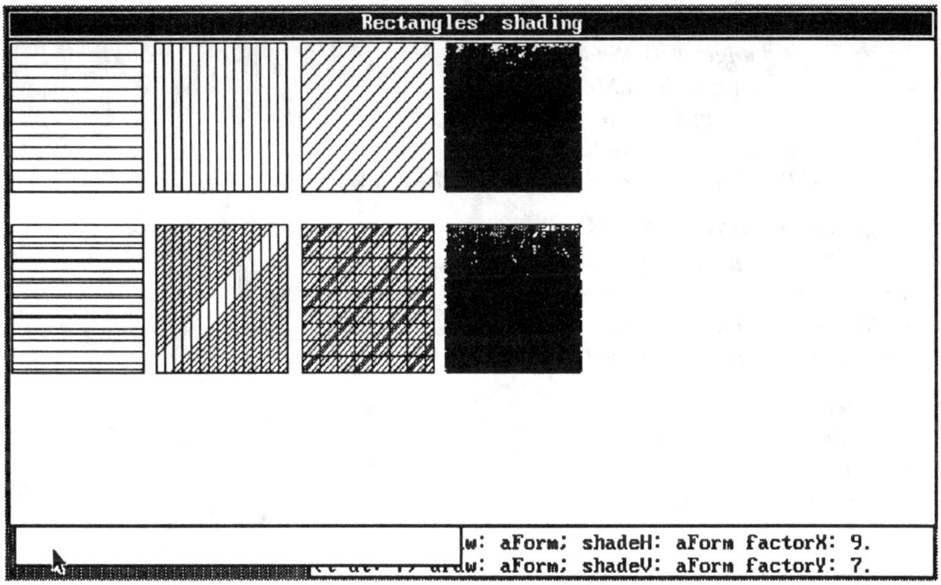

Fig. 4.6 — Shaded rectangles.

```
Object subclass: #PR
    instanceVariableNames:
        'sPane t'
    classVariableNames: ''
    poolDictionaries: ''

initializeRectangles
t := Array new: 8.
t at: 1 put: (0   @ 0 extent: 90 @ 90).
t at: 2 put: (99  @ 0 extent: 90 @ 90).
t at: 3 put: (199 @ 0 extent: 90 @ 90).
t at: 4 put: (299 @ 0 extent: 90 @ 90).
t at: 5 put: (0   @ 110 extent: 90 @ 90).
t at: 6 put: (99  @ 110 extent: 90 @ 90).
t at: 7 put: (199 @ 110 extent: 90 @ 90).
t at: 8 put: (299 @ 110 extent: 90 @ 90).
```

```
 ^t!
openOn: aRectangle
   | aTopPane |
        aTopPane := TopPane new
        label: 'Rectangles'' shading'.
      self initializeRectangles.
      aTopPane addSubpane:
      (sPane := GraphPane new
            model: self;
            name: #shadePane:;
            change: #plotShadePane:;
            menu: #shadeMenu;
            framingRatio: (0 @ 0 extent: 1 @ 1 )).
      aTopPane reframe: aRectangle.
      aTopPane dispatcher openWindow scheduleWindow!

plotShadePane: aPoint
      "Plot the data in a XY-coordinate system."
CursorManager execute change.
self shadePane: sPane frame.
CursorManager normal change.!

shadeMenu
      "Select menu operation empty for now."
 ^Menu
      labels: '' withCrs
      lines: Array new
      selectors: #().!
shadePane: aaForm
      | aForm |
      CursorManager execute change.
      aForm := Form new
            width: aaForm width
            height: aaForm height; white.
      (t at: 1) draw: aForm; shadeH: aForm factorX: 12.
      (t at: 2) draw: aForm; shadeV: aForm factorY: 15.
      (t at: 3) draw: aForm; shadeA: aForm factorN: 10.
      (t at: 4) draw: aForm;
                  shadeP: aForm noOfPoints: 10 enlargement: 5.
      (t at: 5) draw: aForm; shadeH: aForm factorX: 12.
      (t at: 5) draw: aForm; shadeH: aForm factorX: 8.
      (t at: 6) draw: aForm; shadeV: aForm factorY: 15.
      (t at: 6) draw: aForm; shadeV: aForm factorY: 5.
      (t at: 6) draw: aForm; shadeA: aForm factorN: 20.
      (t at: 7) draw: aForm; shadeA: aForm factorN: 10.
      (t at: 7) draw: aForm; shadeH: aForm factorX: 9.
      (t at: 7) draw: aForm; shadeV: aForm factorY: 7.
      (t at: 7) draw: aForm; shadeA: aForm factorN: 22.
```

```
        (t at: 8) draw: aForm;
                shadeP: aForm noOfPoints: 5 enlargement: 2.
        (t at: 8) draw: aForm; shadeH: aForm factorX: 19.
        (t at: 8) draw: aForm; shadeV: aForm factorY: 12.
        (t at: 8) draw: aForm; shadeA: aForm factorN: 32.
aForm displayAt: sPane frame origin.
CursorManager normal change.
 ^aForm!
```

4.13 COMMENTS ON CLASS PR

There are just two global instance variables, **sPane** and **t,** the former acting as a single GraphPane for the window, the latter being an array of Rectangles that are to be shaded. Method **initializeRectangles** does just what you think it might do. The first four Rectangles will be shaded with only one type of shading, and thus illustrate the four basic shading types. Other usual methods are barely represented, some action being found only in the **shadePane:** method. It just shows the basic formats of shading messages. Four messages **shadeH:factorX:, shadeV:factorY:, shadeA:factorN:** and **shade:noOfPoints:enlargement:** implement vertical, horizontal, angled shading, and shading by random points, respectively. The **draw:** takes a Rectangle as a receiver, and draws it on an argument of type **Form.** Since these five messages have Rectangles as receivers, we had to add them directly to class **Rectangle.** Here they are:

```
"Rectangles" draw: aForm
            'APS — Draw a border around the self,
            using aForm as a Form.''
      | i aPoint aPen |
      aPen := Pen new: aForm.
      aPen
            place: (aPoint := self origin);
            goto: (i := self right) @ self top;
            goto: i @ (i := self bottom);
            goto: aPoint x @ i;
            goto: aPoint!

"Rectangles" shadeA: aForm factorN: n
      "APS — Shade the rectangle vertically."
      | x1 x2 y1 y2 incrementX incrementY pen |
   pen := Pen new: aForm. pen black.
   x1 := (self origin) x. y1 := (self origin) y.
   x2 := (self corner) x. y2 := (self corner) y.
   incrementX := ((x2−x1) abs) // n.
   incrementY := ((y2−y1) abs) // n.
   1 to: n do: – :i
            pen down.
            pen place: ((x1+(i*incrementX)) @ y1).
            pen goto: (x1 @ (y1+(i*incrementY))).].
```

```
1 to: n do: [ :i |
            pen down.
            pen place: ((x2-(i*incrementX)) @ y2).
            pen goto: (x2 @ (y2-(i*incrementY))).].!

"Rectangles" shadeH: aForm factorX: fx
    "APS — Shade the rectangle horizontally."
    | x1 x2 y1 y2 currentY incrementY pen |
  pen := Pen new: aForm. pen black.
  x1 := (self origin) x. y1 := (self origin) y.
  x2 := (self corner) x. y2 := (self corner) y.
  incrementY := ((y2-y1) abs) // fx.
  currentY := y1+incrementY.
  [currentY < y2 and: [ incrementY > 0]]
        whileTrue: [
                    pen down.
                    pen place: (x1 @ currentY).
                    pen goto: (x2 @ currentY).
                    pen down.
                    currentY := currentY+incrementY.].!
"Rectangles" shadeP: aForm noOfPoints: number enlargement: blowUp
    "APS — Shade the rectangle using random points."
    | x1 x2 y1 y2 randomX randomY incrementY pen no rb ro rm |
  pen := Pen new: aForm. pen black.
  x1 := (self origin) x. y1 := (self origin) y.
  x2 := (self corner) x. y2 := (self corner) y.
  incrementY := 1.
  randomY := y1+incrementY.
  no := number. rb := 1409.
  ro := 15537. rm := 32749.
  [ randomY < y2 ] whileTrue: [
            1 to: no do: [ :i |
                ro := rb * ro-((rb * ro / rm) truncated * rm).
                randomX := x1+((ro * (x2-x1) abs) quo: rm).
                pen down; place: (randomX @ randomY);
                        ellipse: 2 aspect: 1].
            randomY := randomY+incrementY.
            no := no+blowUp.]!
"   1409 * 15537-((1409 * 15537 / 32749) truncated * 32749)
    15301 * 90 quo: 32749 42
"

"Rectangles" shadeV: aForm factorY: fy
    "APS — Shade the rectangle vertically."
    | x1 x2 y1 y2 currentX incrementX pen |
  pen := Pen new: aForm. pen black.
  x1 := (self origin) x. y1 := (self origin) y.
  x2 := (self corner) x. y2 := (self corner) y.
```

```
incrementX := ((x2-x1) abs) // fy.
currentX := x1+incrementX.
[currentX < x2 and: [ incrementX > 0]]
        whileTrue: [pendown.
                pen place: (currentX @ y1).
                pen goto: (currentX @ y2).
                pen down.
                currentX := currentX+incrementX.].!
```

4.14 COMMENTS ON SHADING METHODS AND TECHNIQUES

draw: is practically identical to the original **drawBox** method in class **PointDispatcher,** except that parameter **aForm** has been added. Note how functionality helped create concise yet understandable program text. The simplest of the other four methods is **shadeH:factorX:**—it goes from the top of the Rectangle downwards, binding vertical sides with parallel horizontal lines. Parameter **fx** determines how many horizontal slices are drawn.

shadeV:factorY: and **shadeA:factorN:** are variations of the same technique as in **shadeH:factorX:,** but shading by points differs. **shadeP:noOfPoints:enlargement:** is similar to **shadeH,** except that we now draw a series of randomly positioned points instead of a continuous horizontal line. Instead of a full line we draw only a **number** of points, increasing it after every line with **blowUp. shadeP** contains a random number generator. Here it is, distilled from the rest:

```
rb := 1409. ro := 15537. rm := 32749.
ro := rb * ro-((rb * ro / rm) truncated * rm).
(ro * (x2-x1) abs) quo: rm
```

We shall devote more space to random numbers in Chapter 5, but here it suffices to note that this is Lehmer's congruential random number generator (contained in the second line above), that it yields the "next" random number between 0 and **rm,** and that the third line digests it further into the Rectangle width. The values of **rb, ro,** and **rm** are chosen in accord with well-defined rules, the reliability of which guarantees the quality of the random number generator.

If you do not have (or do not want to use) a co-processor, and type **Float** is not available, coding of certain operations becomes trickier than in other languages. But Smalltalk/V compensates in a magnificent way: it is, after all, an interpreter, and you can try out actual examples before executing **save.** The two commented lines after the **shadeP** method are an example of this. There we see that the result of the first line would be 15301, which is correct for a general random number but is still not sufficient for the task in hand. In the second line we further experimented to see what kind of integer division would return a meaningful result. We are leaving this interactive code as testimony to an unusual degree of productivity that programmers can achieve using Smalltalk/V.

It is easy to see how shadings could be used to build any kind of histograms: they are just combinations of shaded Rectangles. However, other types of shading can be extremely complicated, since we might rely on them to show depth and third dimension in the picture. Such shadings are beyond the scope of this book. Also, we have here shaded merely the simplest of all figures — rectangles. There are other far more elaborate algorithms for shadings of arbitrary planar polygons — again beyond the scope of this book.

4.15 STATISTICAL HYPOTHESES

The difference between sample and population is the first source of doubt when dealing with statistical inference. It would be nice if we were able to draw conclusions about the population as a whole. We can only presume that future data will be generated under the same circumstances as in the past and that, therefore, it makes sense to study historical data.

In practice, decisions have to be made. Suppose we are testing a new serum: is it really effective? (Statistical conclusions in situations like this can literally make all the difference between life and death.) It is useful to make assumptions about the populations involved. They may or may not be true, and are called *statistical hypotheses*. Usually, they state something about the probability distributions of populations.

There are two types of such hypothesis. One is called *null hypothesis* and usually exists only to be negated somehow. It is denoted H_0. Any other hypothesis is called an alternative *hypothesis* and is denoted H_1. If the task is (and it often is in statistics!) to decide whether a given coin is loaded, the null hypothesis can be that the coin is fair. This translates into $p=0.5$, where p is the probability of 'heads'. Examples of alternative hypotheses would be $p=0.9$, $p>0.5$ and so on — there is an infinite number of alternative hypotheses.

We always adopt one hypothesis as being true, then somehow gather data and compare them against it. In case of significant differences the hypothesis is rejected. The testing procedure itself is called *the test of hypothesis*, or *test of significance*, or *rule of decision*.

There are two types of error that one can make. We can reject a hypothesis when it should have been accepted, and, conversely, we can accept the hypothesis when it should have been rejected. Both cases are errors, and to distinguish between them we call the former a *Type I error*, and the latter a *Type II error*. Both should be minimized but this is usually not possible. Several rules of decision can exist but with various degrees of risks of errors.

The maximum probability with which we are prepared to risk a Type I error is called the *level of significance* of the test. Probabilities of 0.05 and 0.01 are customary. Their meaning is this: there are about 5 (or 1, respectively) cases in 100 repeated tests of significance in which we would reject the hypothesis when it should have been accepted.

We can graphically depict the level of significance as a shaded area between some probability curve and the x axis. There is a large number of probability curves that can be tested against, the normal being the most popular. For example, in the chi-square test we use the chi-square distribution function.

4.16 THE CHI-SQUARE TEST

This test tries to resolve whether there are some significant differences between population and sample values. Such tests are called the *goodness of fit* tests.

The chi-square test is very ambitious and (occasionally) useful. Data are the only means for relaxing uncertainty. The question is how to extrapolate them. It would be excellent if we could ascertain that the data belong to some probability distribution that we know all about. This would be the *theoretical distribution*. The knowledge of the properties of theoretical distribution entitles us to think that the same phenomenon will take place in the same way some time in future.

The test consists of computing the values as if it were a real distribution and then comparing them with the measured data. The technique of comparison is another metric — the sum of the squares of differences between the data and the theoretical values. More precisely, this is the statistics to compute:

$$\chi^2 = \frac{(X_1 - E_1)^2}{E_1} + \frac{(X_2 - E_2)^2}{E_2} + \ldots + \frac{(X_n - E_n)^2}{E_n} \tag{4.7}$$

where the values of X are the measured data and E are the expected (computed) data. For example, suppose that a die is tossed 120 times. Let us test the hypothesis that the die is fair, with a significance level of 0.05. The measured data — frequencies of each of six possible outcomes — are:

face	1	2	3	4	5	6
data	25	17	15	23	24	16
theoretical	20	20	20	20	20	20

The above general formula in the case of the binomial distribution is:

$$\chi^2 = \frac{(X_1 - np_1)^2}{np_1} + \frac{(X_2 - np_2)^2}{np_2} + \ldots + \frac{(X_n - np_n)^2}{np_n} \tag{4.8}$$

or, for values in the table:

$$\begin{aligned}\chi^2 &= \frac{(25\text{–}20)^2}{20} + \frac{(17\text{–}20)^2}{20} + \frac{(15\text{–}20)^2}{20} + \\ &\quad + \frac{(23\text{–}20)^2}{20} + \frac{(24\text{–}20)^2}{20} + \frac{(16\text{–}20)^2}{20} \\ &= 5.00\end{aligned}$$

Here is the Smalltalk/V code for this calculation:

```
"Array" chiSquare: expectedData
        "APS"
        | chiSquare x e |
chiSquare := 0.
1 to: self size do: [ :i |
```

```
        x := self at: i.
        e := expectedData at: i.
        chiSquare := chiSquare +
                ((x−e) * (x−e) / e).
        ].
    ^ chiSquare
```

For example:

```
    #(25 17 15 23 24 16) chiSquare: #(20 20 20 20 20 20 ) 5
```

The value of χ^2 is zero if observed and expected frequencies agree exactly, and is positive otherwise. As with any difference, the greater the value of this sum, the greater the discrepancy between the data and the theoretical values.

As far as a die is concerned, there are only six possibilities. There may be only a finite number of summands. However, the usefulness of the chi-square test stems from a theorem stating that for an infinite number of addends the distribution of the above sum is a well-known theoretical distribution, called the chi-square distribution, after which the test itself was named. From that specific distribution we can compute levels of significance. Actually, a whole table of such numbers exists but in practical applications only two are important, i.e. levels of 0.05 and 0.01. There are some additional rules because the chi-square distribution depends not only on its argument but also on k, called the *degrees of freedom*. It is computed as

$$\nu = k - 1 - m \tag{4.10}$$

where k is the number of classes (possible outcomes) and m is the number of parameters that must be determined while computing theoretical values. For a random distribution, no parameters were needed so there $m=0$. For a Poisson distribution, we need one parameter (arithmetic mean), and for a normal distribution we need two parameters (arithmetic mean and standard deviation).

The values of k act as indices into arrays of levels of significance. For 0.01 and 0.05 the values are:

ν	*0.1*	*0.05*
1	*0.002*	*0.0039*
2	*0.201*	*0.103*
3	*0.115*	*0.352*
4	*0.297*	*0.711*
5	*0.554*	*1.15*
6	*0.872*	*1.64*
7	*1.24*	*2.17*
8	*1.65*	*2.73*
9	*2.09*	*3.33*
10	*2.56*	*3.94*
11	*3.05*	*4.57*
12	*3.57*	*5.23*
13	*4.11*	*5.89*
14	*4.66*	*6.57*
15	*5.23*	*7.26*

16	5.81	7.96
17	6.41	8.67
18	7.01	9.39
19	7.63	10.1
20	8.26	10.9
21	8.90	11.6
22	9.54	12.3
23	10.2	13.1
24	10.9	13.8
25	11.5	14.6
26	12.2	15.4
27	12.9	16.2
28	13.6	16.9
29	14.3	17.7
30	15.0	18.5
40	22.2	26.5
50	29.7	34.8
60	37.5	43.2
70	45.4	51.7
80	53.5	60.4
90	61.8	69.1
100	70.1	77.9

The chi-square table is precise for the first 30 degrees of freedom. (For ν>30 it is usually replaced by the ubiquitous normal distribution.) Here is one possible Smalltalk/V implementation:

```
"numberOfClasses" chiSquareSignificance: level
        "APS ChiSquare"
        | data lev |
lev := level.
level=5 ifTrue: [ lev := 2 ]
                ifFalse:[ lev := 1 ].
data := #(
 1 0.002  0.0039  2 0.201  0.103  3  0.115  0.352
 4 0.297  0.711   5 0.554  1.15   6  0.872  1.64
 7 1.24   2.17    8 1.65   2.73   9  2.09   3.33
10 2.56   3.94   11 3.05   4.57  12  3.57   5.23
13 4.11   5.89   14 4.66   6.57  15  5.23   7.26
16 5.81   7.96   17 6.41   8.67  18  7.01   9.39
19 7.63  10.1    20 8.26  10.9   21  8.90  11.6
22 9.54  12.3    23 10.2  13.1   24 10.9   13.8
25 11.5  14.6    26 12.2  15.4   27 12.9   16.2
28 13.6  16.9    29 14.3  17.7   30 15.0   18.5).
1 to: data size do: [ :i |
        (data at: i)=self
                ifTrue: [  ^(data at: (i+lev))].
        ].
```

```
^nil
```

We can test it thus:

5 chiSquareSignificance: 5 1.15

The number of classes, *k*, is the number of natural groups the original data can be split into. The data are then transformed into frequencies per class. The frequencies are taken as the original data, *E*, in the chi-square calculation.

How many classes are needed? This depends on the situation; when casting a die, there are exactly six possible outcomes, hence, exactly six classes. In the case of an array of numbers, the number of classes is not uniquely defined, but there are guidelines. The number of classes is taken to depend on sample size, according to the following table:

N	*k*
40–60	*6–8*
60–100	*7–10*
100–200	*9–12*
200–500	*12–17*
500>	*21*

This is strictly an empirical recommendation. A further complication is that the number of frequencies may be smaller than five in some classes. They should then be included in other classes. Finally, the test as a whole makes no sense for less than 25 items of data.

The following code computes *k*:

```
"Integer" chiSquareClassesNumber "APS"
(self between: 1    and: 39)     ifTrue: [ ^5].
(self between: 40   and: 59)     ifTrue: [ ^8].
(self between: 60   and: 99)     ifTrue: [ ^10].
(self between: 100  and: 200)    ifTrue: [ ^12].
(self between: 200  and: 500)    ifTrue: [ ^17].
(self between: 500  and: 1000)   ifTrue: [ ^29].
(self between: 1000 and: 5000)   ifTrue: [ ^40].
(self between: 5000 and: 10000)  ifTrue: [ ^60].
(self > 10000)                   ifTrue: [ ^80].
66 chiSquareClassesNumber  10
```

Here is a complete program for the chi-square test. The input consists of a data array with an empirical distribution. From them we make the frequencies as follows:

```
"Array" chiSquareFrequency "APS"
        | ind noOfClasses min max step freq result base s |
min := self min.
max := self max.
noOfClasses := self size chiSquareClassesNumber.
step := (max−min) abs // noOfClasses.
base := min−(step / 2) truncated+1.
```

```
freq := Array new: (noOfClasses+1).
freq zero.
1 to: self size do: [ :j |
        s := self at: j.
        ind := 1+((s−base) abs // (step+1)).
        freq at: ind put: ((freq at: ind)+1)
        ].
result := Array new: noOfClasses.
1 to: noOfClasses do: [ :i | result at: i put: (freq at: i)].
result at: noOfClasses put:
        (freq at: noOfClasses)+
        (freq at: (noOfClasses+1)).
^result
```

This 197 array is the test example:

```
#( 290 238 259 219 246 251 292 254 242 205 280 260 230 210 174 270 258
227 258 250 234 392 231 300 219 227 292 230 238 312 150 240 272 258
310 252 210 262 270 235 250 199 226 238 226 278 234 300 259 215 280
234 252 208 242 334 290 260 300 251 234 272 234 246 272 207 270 230
278 231 200 240 126 210 222 232 260 250 200 310 220 259 256 192 241
340 194 244 259 210 276 190 250 206 242 302 212 270 252 216 250 292
226 234 144 206 254 214 241 246 286 262 215 230 270 242 250 266 216
252 240 262 240 250 262 207 278 238 231 218 226 272 222 190 250 232
242 290 260 302 250 220 206 300 219 292 227 227 210 294 292 231 259
190 280 226 252 250 272 228 273 270 252 245 302 269 219 230 243 300
243 300 234 256 278 240 375 285 216 270 266 264 204 242 230 215 326
236 210 215 300 230 297 288 259 200 270) chiSquareFrequency.
#(1 2 1 16 42 57 40 20 13 3 0 2)
```

The last row contains the resulting array of frequencies.

All that remains to do now is to write the main program for the chi-square test. The following code is executed from the **Transcript Window,** with the above array copied after the := sign in the second row:

```
| rawData freq theoretical chiSquare level |
rawData := "copy the above array here"
freq := rawData chiSquareFrequency.
theoretical := Array new: freq size.
" Uniform distribution"
1 to: freq size do: [ :i |
        theoretical at: i put: (1 / freq sum) ].
chiSquare := freq chiSquare: theoretical.
level := (rawData size chiSquareClassesNumber) significance: 5.
chiSquare < level
false
```

The result, **false,** means that the hypothesis — that the sample was taken from a population with a uniform distribution — is false. Other hypotheses could be tried out.

You have to change the way the **theoretical** array is computed and instead of **(1/freq sum)** for a uniform distribution, something else could be tried. One line might not be enough, though, because for a normal distribution, for example, you would have to find the mean and standard deviation first, and then use them to find values of a new **theoretical** array.

4.17 NUMERICAL SOLUTION OF DIFFERENTIAL EQUATIONS

Differential equations are one of the main areas of numerical mathematics. So few differential equations can be solved analytically that numerical methods are generally used, and — thanks to computers — can be performed up to the required degree of accuracy. The classical initial-value problem is to find a function $y(x)$ which satisfies the first-order differential equation $y'=f(x)$, and takes an initial value $y(x_0)=y_0$. There are many methods for solving this problem:

— the method of isoclines,
— Euler's method
— various polynomial approximations,
— Taylor's series,
— Runge–Kutta methods,
— predictor–corrector methods,
— Milne's method,
— Adams' method, and others.

The final outcome of any of these methods should be either a function in a closed form or a table of numbers that — within given precision — represents discrete values of the solution. Therefore, all numerical methods consist of a series of computations according to a given approximation, starting from one or more initial values and progressing along the solution curve to the end of some interval.

The methods mentioned differ in the choice of approximation. For example, Euler's method computes a discrete set of y_k values using the difference equation:

$$y_{k+1}=y_k+hf(x_k, y_k), \quad \text{where } h=x_{k+1}-x_k. \tag{4.11}$$

This is derived from the very definition of the derivative on the left-hand side of the equation. Although too slow for everyday numerical work, this method provides proof that the solution exists under some very reasonable hypotheses on $f(x,y)$.

Taylor's series is very popular. The idea is to use $p(x+h)$ instead of $y(x+h)$, where $p(x+h)$ is the Taylor polynomial for argument x. After this, the higher derivatives needed for a full Taylor series are computed from the given differential equation. The need to compute higher derivatives is a potential source of error in this method. In most cases, finding those derivatives is burdensome or error-prone.

4.18 THE RUNGE–KUTTA METHOD FOR ORDINARY DIFFERENTIAL EQUATIONS

A better idea is to use something similar to Taylor's expansion but without higher derivatives. This is the idea behind the Runge–Kutta method. Extra values of function $f(x,y)$ are used instead of these derivatives, in a way that essentially duplicates the accuracy of the Taylor polynomial. There are several such formulae, the most popular of which is this set:

$$\begin{aligned} k_1 &= hf(x,y) \\ k_2 &= hf(x + 1/2\ h,\ y + 1/2\ k_1) \\ k_3 &= hf(x + 1/2\ h,\ y + 1/2\ k_2) \\ k_4 &= hf(x + 1/2\ h,\ y + k_3) \\ y(x+h) &\sim y(x) + (1/6)\ (k_1 + 2k_2 + 2k_3 + k_4)\ . \end{aligned} \tag{4.12}$$

It can be proved that Runge–Kutta methods are convergent and that the truncation error depends upon the fifth derivative of $y(x)$. As an example, let us apply the Runge–Kutta method to the following equation:

$$y' = f(x,y) = xy^{1/3},\ y(1) = 1. \tag{4.13}$$

Since $x_0=1$, we can take step h=0.1. (Its value is arbitrary and reflects how much of the computer's resources we need or have to devote to solving one particular differential equation.) With these two data we enter equations for the above four coefficients, producing the following Smalltalk/V code in the process:

```
        | k1 k2 k3 k4 h x y y1 |
x := 1.0. y := 1. h := 0.1.
k1 := h * (x function: y). "'Float' function: y"          "0.1"
k2 := h * ((x+(0.5 * h)) function: (y+(0.5 * k1)) ).    "1.0672162e-1"
k3 := h * ((x+(0.5 * h)) function: (y+(0.5 * k2)) ).    "1.0683536e-1"
k4 := h * ((x+h) function: (y+k3)).                       "1.1378553e-1"
y1 := y+((1/6) * (k1+(2 * k2)+(2 * k3)+k4)).             "1.1068166"
```

The intermediate values are shown on the right, as comments. This code requires the existence of a method called **function:** in class **Float.** Here it is:

```
"Float" function: y
        "APS"
  ^self * (y raisedTo: (1/3))
```

All this is easy, and the complete coding appears to be the same as in any other traditional language. No object-oriented features of Smalltalk/V have been used. So it seems there are not many advantages in using Smalltalk/V for the Runge–Kutta method or for performing the chi-square test on a group of data, for that matter. Such remarks lead into deeper waters. You do not have to use the object-oriented features of a language if you do not want to. You can just as happily use Smalltalk/V merely as a powerful interactive calculator. But object-oriented program development is essentially a bottom-up approach, and the surest way to see what should go into a new class is by playing with the subject interactively. All that we do can sooner or later be expressed as a class. To illustrate, let us make a new class, **DiffEqSolver,** for solving differential equations. We can use the Runge–Kutta method, since we already know how to program it.

In this particular example, we have four intermediate constants (**k1, k2, k3, k4**), three input parameters (**h, x, y**) and the result after each step (**y1**). The class output should at least be an Array of calculated numbers. Other kinds of output could be a window to represent the solution(s) graphically, or a data file on disk to facilitate exchange with other programs.

Let us add **DiffEqSolver** as a subclass of **Object,** choosing type **subclass.** We can immediately include all those names as its instance variables. Later we shall probably discover the need for additional instance variables, but these are a good start. Those additional instance variables are **function, start, end,** and **solution. start** and **end** are edges of the interval over which the equation is solved. Variable **solution** is an Array of function values that numerically represent the solution. Finally, **function** enables us to specify the equation itself as an input datum.

Here is the complete code for class **DiffEqSolver:**

```
Object subclass: #DiffEqSolver
   instanceVariableNames:
      'k1 k2 k3 k4 x y y1 h function start end solution '
   classVariableNames: ''
   poolDictionaries: ''

DiffEqSolver class methods

new
 ^super new!

DiffEqSolver methods

end: aValue
end := aValue asFloat!

function: aBlock
function := aBlock!

h: aValue "set step"
h := aValue asFloat!

solveEquation
      | dim j |
dim := (start — end) abs // h .
j := 1.
solution := Array new: dim.
start to: end by: h do: [ :i |
    self x: i;
          valuePerStepWithBlockFunction;
          y: y1.
    solution at: j put: y.
    j := j+1.
    ].
^solution!
```

```
start: aValue
start := aValue asFloat!

valuePerStep
k1 := h * (x function: y).
k2 := h * ((x+(0.5 * h)) function: (y+(0.5 * k1)) ).
k3 := h * ((x+(0.5 * h)) function: (y+(0.5 * k2)) ).
k4 := h * ((x+h) function: (y+k3)).
y1 := y+((1/6) * (k1+(2 * k2)+(2 * k3)+k4)).!

valuePerStepWithBlockFunction
k1 := h * (function value: x value: y).
k2 := h * (function value: (x+(0.5 * h)) value: (y+(0.5 * k1)) ).
k3 := h * (function value: (x+(0.5 * h)) value: (y+(0.5 * k2)) ).
k4 := h * (function value: (x+h) value: (y+k3)).
y1 := y+((1/6) * (k1+(2 * k2)+(2 * k3)+k4)).!
x: aValue "APS"
x := aValue asFloat!

y1: aValue
y1 := aValue!

y: aValue
y := aValue asFloat!
```

We solve an equation by executing the following code from the **Transcript Window:**

```
        | aaa | "Main program for DiffEqSolver"
aaa := DiffEqSolver new.
aaa function: [ :x :y | x function: y ];
        x: 1;
        y: 1.0;
        h: 0.1;
        start: 1.0;
        end: 2.0.
aaa solveEquation.
```

Simple, isn't it?

4.19 INSIDE CLASS DiffEqSolver

There is just one class method, **new,** which is quite standard. For each variable there is a "set" method, i.e. a method for setting the variable value. Most of these methods are two-liners, such as **end:, h:** and others. Since the numerical solution of differential equations must be done with real numbers, we need to ensure that all relevant input parameters become Floats, by sending a message **asFloat.** The method **solveEquation** solves the differential equation by computing function values according to the Runge–Kutta rules. The main work is done in method **valuePerStepWith-**

BlockFunction. We shall explain its long and unusual name shortly. The solution array contains the computed points and that is what this class returns as its result.

There are two equivalent methods called **valuePerStep** and **valuePerStepWithBlockFunction.** The former is merely how we computed the values of **k1, k2, k3** and **k4** interactively, from the **Transcript Window.** It is a perfect solution in the sense that it works and that is quite easy to write. Its drawback is that it uses a method **function:** from class **Float.** This means that we cannot change the equation we want to solve from outside of the Smalltalk/V environment. This doesn't matter provided that the programmer is the end-user of his own programs, on the same copy of the Smalltalk/V system. But suppose you were making a commercial program for an unknown end-user. Clearly, the user would have to be able to specify new differential equations without meddling with the program itself. Otherwise, the package would be abandoned. Blocks are the way to let the user specify new functions from the outside of the computing class, **DiffEqSolver** in this particular case.

The method **valuePerStepWithBlockFunction** is similar except that it uses a block that has previously been poked into a variable **function.** A block can have zero, one or two parameters. These three kinds of block are activated by messages **value, value:**, and **value:value:**. The arguments of the latter two messages pass on to the block and become its own arguments. In this example, the block is:

[*:x :y / x function: y*]

which again executes the message **function:** from **Float.**

How do we specify a new differential equation? It would be enough to send another message **function:** to an instance of class **DiffEqSolver** (for example, variable **aaa**), changing the block at the same time. The block could look like any of these:

[*:a :b / a function: b*]
[*:x :y / x anyOtherMethod: y*]
[*:a :y / a * y*]

or whatever. The first block acts in the same way as the above, only the internal block variables having other names. The second line illustrates that some other message could be used instead of **function:** from **Float** (lest you are confused into thinking that the coincidence of names has some real effect). The third line would solve this equation:

$$y' = xy \; . \tag{4.14}$$

By the way, the solution of the example, as calculated in class **DiffEqSolver**, is:

(1.1068166 1.2278795 1.3641359 1.5165644 1.6861705 1.8739817 2.0810445 2.3084209 2.5571862 2.8284268)

4.20 DIFFERENTIAL EQUATIONS OF SECOND ORDER

Inheritance makes it dead easy to write further code for the numerical solution of differential equations of the second order. The code will be in descendant class **DiffEqSolver2,** in order to inherit everything from **DiffEqSolver.** The numerical method of solution will also be of a Runge–Kutta type. It is quite easy to show that a second-order differential equation may be replaced by a system of two first-order equations. Let the second-order equation be $y''=f(x,y,y')$. A simple substitution $p=y'$ leads to a system $y'=p$, $p'=f(x,y,y')$. Therefore, any second-order equation may be treated as a pair of two first-order differential equations, meaning that the Runge–Kutta method can be used. Let the equations be

$$y'=f_1(x,y,p), \quad p'=f(x,y,p) \tag{4.15}$$

with initial conditions

$$y(x_0)=y_0, \quad p(x_0)=p_0 \,.$$

The most general formulae are:

$$\begin{aligned}
k_1 &= hf_1(x_n, y_n, p_n) \\
l_1 &= hf_2(x_n, y_n, p_n) \\
k_2 &= hf_1(x_n+0.5h,\ y_n+0.5k_1,\ p_n+0.5l_1) \\
l_2 &= hf_2(x_n+0.5h,\ y_n+0.5k_1,\ p_n+0.5l_1) \\
k_3 &= hf_1(x+0.5h,\ y_n+0.5k,\ p_n+0.5l_2) \\
l_3 &= hf_2(x_n+0.5h,\ y_n+0.5k_2,\ p_n+l_2) \\
k_4 &= hf_1(x_n+h,\ y_n+k_3,\ p_n+l_3) \\
l_4 &= hf_2(x_n+h,\ y_n+k_3,\ p_n+l_3) \\
y_{n+1} &= y_n + 1/6\ (k_1+2k_2+2k_3+k_4) \\
p_{n+1} &= p_n + 1/6\ (l_1+2l_2+2l_3+l_4) \,.
\end{aligned} \tag{4.17}$$

As an example, let us compute the solution of van der Pol's equation:

$$y'' - 0.1(1-y_2)y' + y = 0 \,.$$

The equivalent system of first-order equations is:

$$\begin{aligned}
y' &= p \\
p' &= -y + 0.1(1-y_2)y' + y \,.
\end{aligned} \tag{4.19}$$

According to formula (4.17), the first coefficents are

$$\begin{aligned}
k &= hp_n \\
l_1 &= h(-y_n + 0.1(1-y_n \cdot y_n)\ p_n^2)
\end{aligned}$$

and so on. These are the formulae that we have to capture in class **DiffEqSolver2.** Here it is:

```
DiffEqSolver subclass: #DiffEqSolver2
    instanceVariableNames:
        'p p1 '
    classVariableNames:
        'Solution '
    poolDictionaries: '' !
```

```
!DiffEqSolver2 class methods !
getSolution
        "Answer the value of Solution."
 ^Solution!

new
 ^super new! !

!DiffEqSolver2 methods !

p1: aValue
                "Set the value of p1."
        p1 := aValue asFloat!

p: aValue
                "Set the value of p."
        p := aValue asFloat!

solveEquation
        | dim j |
dim := 3 * ((start — end) abs quo: h)+3.
j := 1.
solution := Array new: dim.
start to: end by: h do: [ :i |
        self x: i;
                valuePerStepWithBlockFunction;
                p: p1;
                y: y1.
        solution at: j put: i.
        j := j+1.
        solution at: j put: y1.
        j := j+1.
        solution at: j put: p1.
        j := j+1.
        ].
Solution := solution.
 ^solution!

valuePerStepWithBlockFunction
        "Definition for system of two differential
        equations of first order — or a system of
        second order"
        | l1 l2 l3 l4
k1 := h * p.
l1 := h * (function value: y value: p).
k2 := h * (p+(0.5 * l1)).
l2 := h * (function value: (y+(0.5 * k1))
                        value: (p+(0.5 * l1)) ).
k3 := h * (p+(0.5 * l2)).
```

```
l3 := h * (function value: (y+(0.5 * k2))
                    value: (p+(0.5 * l2)) ).
k4 := h * (p+l3).
l4 := h * (function value: (y+k3)
                    value: (p+l3)).
y1 := y+((1/6) * (k1+(2 * k2)+(2 * k3)+k4)).
p1 := p+((1/6) * (l1+(2 * l2)+(2 * l3)+l4)).

"Transcript cr; show: 'y1=', y1 printString;
            show: ' p1=', p1 printString."! !
```

There are two additional instance variables, **p** and **p1.** They are analogous to **y** and **y1** from **DiffEqSolver** — the final and intermediate values of the Runge–Kutta algorithm. The main computing method, **solveEquation,** is practically the same as before, except for variables **p** and **p1,** and except for a new array, **solution.** This is a normal array but we impose further structure upon it. It is divided into 3-tuples. The first element is for argument i, the second is for the value of **y1** and the third is for **p1.** The complete solution of the numerical process is contained in just one variable, **solution.** We reach its value in two ways: as a result of the method itself (the value that follows the caret) and, indirectly, through class variable **Solution.** This is a typical usage of class variables. It serves as an outlet of some instance variable but must be assigned its value within instance methods and not within class methods. On the other hand, there must also be a class method such as **getSolution,** so that outside classes and methods can reach the value of **Solution** and **solution.**

The main computational change is in the **valuePerStepWithBlockFunction** method. It directly corresponds to equations (4.17). Note that the computing rule is still in block **function.** It will be very important in our next class, **DrawCurveWindow.**

4.21 VISUAL RELATIONSHIP WITH DIFFERENTIAL EQUATIONS — CLASS DrawCurveWindow

So far, so good. We have code to solve practically any type of ordinary differential equation, of any order. This is as far as other languages would let you go. But in Smalltalk/V it is so easy to add windows and draw curves. Class **DrawCurveWindow** solves the problem of the human interface and is a rather complete editor for **DiffEqSolver2** class. The 'editor' in this context means that the user can control and interactively change all input parameters: the function itself, the interval over which the curve is drawn, the step, and so on. And since the curve will be drawn in a separate window, Smalltalk/V itself automatically adds actions such as window movement, delete, change, and the like. The following code expects one variable from the **DiffEqSolver2** class — **solution.** That is why **solution** must have an artificial, internal organization, with three elements instead of two.

The code seems a bit long but was very straightforward to write. The only significant and new bit of information is in method **evaluate:**, which enables the user to dynamically change the input equation itself.

Object subclass: #DrawCurveWindow

```
    instanceVariableNames:
        'explicitPane condX condY condP h start end label functionBlock
            stringForBlock pen stretch xMin xMax
yMin yMax n aRect c1 c2 c3 c4 x y z x1 y1 points '
    classVariableNames: ''
    poolDictionaries: ''

!DrawCurveWindow class methods !

!DrawCurveWindow methods!
auxArrays
n := points size // 3-1.
x := Array new: n.
y := Array new: n.
z := Array new: n.
1 to: n do: [ :i |
        x at: i put: (points at: (3 * (i-1)+1)).
        y at: i put: (points at: (3 * (i-1)+2)).
        z at: i put: (points at: (3 * (i-1)+3)).
        ].
"x := y. y := z. " "Place to change at will."!
boundaryP
condP := Prompter
        prompt: 'Boundary value for derivative ?'
        defaultExpression: (condP printString).!

boundaryX
condX := Prompter
        prompt: 'Boundary value for argument x ?'
        defaultExpression: (condX printString).!

boundaryY
condY := Prompter
        prompt: 'Boundary value for function Y?'
        defaultExpression: (condY printString).!

calc: aaRect
CursorManager execute change.
aRect := Form new
            width: explicitPane frame width
            height: explicitPane frame height;
            white.
aRect displayAt: explicitPane frame origin.
pen := Pen new: aRect. pen black; down.
self initStretch; "shrink the curve a bit"
        computeAndDraw.
aRect displayAt: explicitPane frame origin.
self labelDrawing.
```

```
CursorManager normal change.
 ^aRect!

computeAndDraw
self solveEquation;
         auxArrays;
         setConstants;
         scaleArrays;
         drawCurve;
         drawVerticalAxis;
         drawHorizontalAxis.!

drawCurve
1 to: (x1 size-1) do: - :i /
      pen drawFrom: ((x1 at: i) @ (y1 at: i)) truncated
                to: ((x1 at: (i+1)) @ (y1 at: (i+1))) truncated.].!
drawHorizontalAxis
      / y /
y := c4-(c2 * (0-yMin)).
pen
   defaultNib: 2;
   drawFrom: ( 0 @ y ) truncated
          to: ( c3-1 @ y ) truncated;
   defaultNib: 1.!

drawIt
self calc: explicitPane frame.!

drawVerticalAxis
pen
   defaultNib: 2;
   drawFrom: ( (c1 * (0-xMin)) @ 0) truncated
          to: ( (c1 * (0-xMin)) @ (c4-1)) truncated;
   defaultNib: 1.!
end
end:= Prompter
      prompt: 'Right interval edge ?'
      defaultExpression: (end printString).!

evaluate: string
functionBlock := Compiler
            evaluate: string trimBlanks
            in: nil class
            to: nil
            notifying: Transcript
            ifFail: [ ^false].!

initCondP
condP := 0.0.!
```

```
initCondX
condX := 0.0.!

initCondY
condY := 1.0.!

initEnd
end := 18.8.!

initEquation
self initFunctionBlock;
        initCondX;
        initCondY;
        initCondP;
        initH;
        initStart;
        initEnd.!

initFunctionBlock
self initFunctionBlock:
    '[ :y :p | y negated+(0.1 * (1-(y * y)) * p) ]'.!

initFunctionBlock: string
stringForBlock := string.!
self evaluate: string.!
initH
h := 0.2.!

initLabel
label := 'Solutions for DiffEqSolver2'.!

initStart
start := 7.0 negated.!

initStretch
stretch := 1.04!

labelDrawing
        | rec x |
rec := explicitPane frame.
yMax truncated printString displayAt:
        rec center x @ (rec top+4).
yMin truncated printString displayAt:
        rec center x @ (rec bottom — SysFont height).
xMin truncated printString displayAt:
        (rec left+4) @ (rec center y).
xMax truncated printString displayAt:
        (rec right — (SysFont width * 2)) (rec center y).!

menu
^Menu
```

```
        labels: 'Draw it\New equation\Boundary X\Boundary Y\Boundary P\Step-
\Start\End' withCrs
        lines: Array new
        selectors: #(drawIt newEquation boundaryX boundaryY boundaryP step
start end)!

newEquation
        | prompt |
prompt := Prompter
        prompt: 'New equation ?'
        default: stringForBlock.
prompt size = 0
        ifFalse: [
                self initFunctionBlock: prompt.
        ].!
openOn: aRectangle
    | aTopPane |
    self initLabel;
                initEquation.
    aTopPane := TopPane new
                        label: label.
    aTopPane addSubpane:
    (explicitPane := GraphPane new
                    model: self;
                    name: #calc:;
                    change: #calc:;
                    menu: #menu;
                    framingRatio: (0 @ 0 extent: 1 @ 1) ).
        aTopPane reframe: aRectangle.
        aTopPane dispatcher openWindow scheduleWindow!

scaleArrays
x1 := Array new: x size.
y1 := Array new: x size.
1 to: x1 size do: [ :i |
        x1 at: i
                put: (c1 * ( (x at: i)-xMin ) ).
        y1 at: i
                put: (c4-(c2 * ( (y at: i)-yMin) ) ). ].!

setConstants
xMax := x max * stretch. xMin := x min * stretch.
yMax := y max * stretch. yMin := y min * stretch.
c3 := (aRect width).
c1 := ( c3 / (xMax-xMin) ).
c4 := (aRect height).
c2 := ( c4 / (yMax-yMin) ).!
```

```
solveEquation
DiffEqSolver2 new
        function: functionBlock;
        x: condX;
        y: condY;
        p: condP; "new"
        h: h;
        start: start;
        end: end;
        solveEquation.
points := DiffEqSolver2 getSolution.!

start
start := Prompter
        prompt: 'Left interval edge ?'
        defaultExpression: (start printString).!

step
h := Prompter
        prompt: 'Step ?'
        defaultExpression: (h printString).!

stretch: aValue
stretch := aValue!
```

4.22 COMMENTS ON CLASS DrawCurveWindow

This class was actually composed by rewriting class **P3.** Most of the variables are explained there. These two classes are a good example of how a piece of software can do the same thing but thoroughly differ within its inner self. The code in **DrawCurveWindow** is written as it should be in a modular language: lots of small subroutines instead of one big one, as was the case in **initOriginalGraph:** of **P3.** And this leads to a fine distinction in regard to inheritance. What most programmers do all day long is **manual inheritance,** i.e. they take a part of the working code and manually transfer from the old part of the program to the new one. There they change it, but all connection between program parts is lost. More often than not, it remains only in the programmer's head — usually for a quite short period of time! And changes in one part of the program are no longer reflected in the whole . . . more effort is required of the programmer. Everybody senses that something is profoundly wrong but the solution is usually found only by using better tools for manual cut and paste — instead of turning to object-oriented languages!

Class **DrawCurveWindow** is an example. It can be successfully inherited and is particularly written with that purpose in mind. Smalltalk/V will not automatically produce anything for you if you do not want it! For example, there is a method **initLabel,** to set up a window name. Since it is a separate method, any descendant of

DrawCurveWindow can merely supply its own method **initLabel** and thus rename the window. Such a convenience did not exist at all in **P3.**

Several other methods are products of the same approach and all begin with 'init': **initCondP, initH,** and so on. The main initializing method, **initEquation,** calls them all to initialize instance variables **condP, h,** etc. There are also methods for interactive redefinition of all such variables: **boundaryP, boundaryX,** etc. These use **Prompter** windows to receive new parameter values from the user. Since those variables are numbers and Prompters always expect strings, the **printString** message is used. As usual, the method **menu** binds all those interactive methods into standard user interface. Let us look at the option **Draw it.** After you select it, the method **drawIt** is executed. This is curious, because **drawIt** consists of one further line only:

drawIt
self calc: explicitPane frame.!

It turns out that you can't put a message with one or several arguments into the **selectors:** part of the **labels:line:selectors:** message to **Menu.** Ergo, you must use an intermediate two-line method. This is annoying but is mandatory so you had better get used to it!

By far the most interesting piece of code concerns the ability to interactively change the equation itself. Two facts make this possible:

— code blocks in variables can be excited by **value** messages, and
— you have direct access to the Smalltalk/V compiler itself!

The latter fact is a rarity among programming languages, both in compilers and in interpreters.

There are just two variables for this: **functionBlock** and **stringForBlock.** The corresponding methods are **initFunctionBlock** and **initFunctionBlock:. stringForBlock** contains the string which is an expression block according to which the equation is to be computed. A maximum of two input variables is allowed since only **value:** and **value:value:** methods exist. (Of course, you can always use blocks inside blocks.) Since it is unquestionably a string, Prompter can usually offer it to the user, just as if it were any other string or number. As it stands now, the user could change everything — even to the point of deleting block or block variables altogether. After pressing Enter, the user can still select other options from the menu, and only after **Draw it** is selected does the actual drawing start.

The link to the Smalltalk/V internal compiler is in **evaluate:**. This method can be used 'as is' in other situations as well. If it were not available, you would have to make your own parser, which is quite counterproductive — your programming system does it better so why should you bother?

Drawing is dispersed throughout many small methods but remains essentially the same. Method **computeAndDraw** tells the whole story, while **calc**: attaches pens and forms and labels the drawing.

This class is very close to what you could pay hundreds of dollars for in some stand-alone commercial scientific package. You can make several smaller windows and visually compare the effects of changes in input parameters or the equation itself. You can even draw arguments and the equation in one window, or the first derivative against the equation in another window — the place to change those assignments is in **auxArrays,** which unpacks the results of the **DiffEqSolver2** class (Fig. 4.7).

4.23 HEAT TRANSFER — SOLVING A PARTIAL DIFFERENTIAL EQUATION

Differential equations with partial derivatives might easily be the most important practical area of numerical mathematics. The concept of studying change of several variables within the same equation leaves room for limitless applications in all branches of science and engineering. The more variables we include in the equation, the more precise will be our knowledge of the process modelled. However, there is a practical limit to computer resources: each new variable increases computational complexity, sometimes by orders of magnitude. The most important practical case is limited to linear differential equations of second order with two independent variables. Their general form is:

$$Au_{xx} + Bu_{xy} + Cu_{yy} + Du_x + Eu_y + Fu = G \ , \tag{4.20}$$

where A, B, C, D, E, F and G are functions of independent variables x and y. The dependent variable is u, and indices denote partial derivatives, for example,

$$u_{xy} = \frac{\delta^2 u}{\delta x \ \delta y} \ . \tag{4.21}$$

There are three types of equation with partial derivatives, depending on the coefficients:

$$\begin{aligned} &B^2 - 4AC < 0, \text{ elliptic} \\ &B^2 - 4AC = 0, \text{ parabolic and} \\ &B^2 - 4AC > 0, \text{ hyperbolic.} \end{aligned} \tag{4.22}$$

We shall restrict ourselves to the parabolic type. The other two types are similar. A typical parabolic equation is the mixed boundary-value problem for the heat conductivity equation. The problem is to find the function $u(x,y)$ which satisfies the equation

$$u_t = u_{xx} \tag{4.23}$$

where t is time and x is the argument as usual. The initial condition is

$$u(x,0) = f(x) \ (0 < x < s) \tag{4.24}$$

and the boundary conditions are:

$$u(0,t) = \phi(t), \ u(s,t) = \psi(t) \ . \tag{4.25}$$

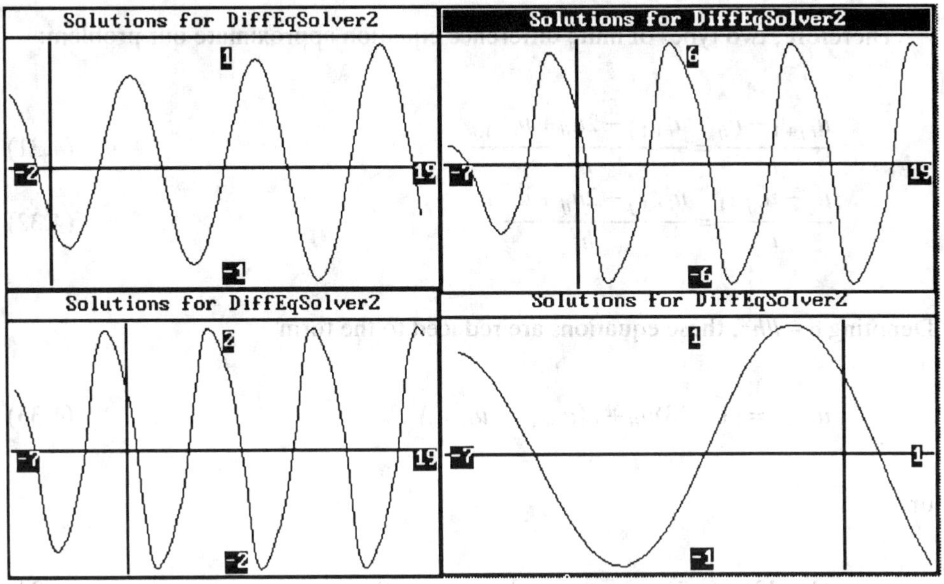

Fig. 4.7 — Experiments with **DrawCurveWindow** windows.

The problem of heat propagation in a uniform bar of length s can be reduced to these equations. Let us solve this equation numerically. Construct in the half-strip $t \geqslant 0$, $0 \leqslant x \leqslant s$, two families of parallel straight lines:

$$x = ih \ (i = 0, 1, 2, \ldots), \ t = jl \ (j = 0, 1, 2, \ldots) . \tag{4.26}$$

The following notation is handy:

$$x = ih, \ t_j = jl, \ u(x_i, t_j) = u_{ij} , \tag{4.27}$$

and we use it to replace derivatives in each interior point (x_i, t_j). First, replace the second derivative:

$$\left(\frac{\delta^2 u}{\delta x^2}\right)_{ij} \sim \frac{u_{i+1,j} - 2u_{ij} + u_{i-1,j}}{h^2} \tag{4.28}$$

then the first ones. There are two possibilities:

$$\left(\frac{\delta u}{\delta t}\right)_{ij} \sim \frac{u_{i,j+1} + u_{ij}}{l} \tag{4.29}$$

$$\left(\frac{\delta u}{\delta t}\right)_{ij} \sim \frac{u_{ij} - u_{i,j-1}}{l} . \tag{4.30}$$

Therefore, two types of finite difference equation approximate our problem:

$$\frac{u_{i,j+1}-u_{ij}}{l}=\frac{u_{i+1,j}-2u_{ij}+u_{i-1,j}}{h^2} \tag{4.31}$$

$$\frac{u_{ij}-u_{i,j-1}}{l}=\frac{u_{i+1,j}-2u_{ij}+u_{i-l,j}}{h^2} . \tag{4.32}$$

Denoting $\delta = l/h^2$, these equations are reduced to the form

$$u_{i,j+1}=(1-2\delta)u_{ij}+\delta(u_{i+1,j}+u_{i-1,j}) , \tag{4.33}$$

or

$$(1+2\delta)u_{ij}-\delta(u_{i+1,j}+u_{i-1,j})-u_{i,j-1}=0 . \tag{4.34}$$

The number δ usually has to satisfy the following conditions:

(1) the error due to the replacement of a differential equation by a difference equation must have the smallest value, and
(2) the difference equation must be stable.

The former equation will be stable if $0<\delta\leq 1/2$, while the latter equation will be stable for any value of δ. The most convenient form is for $\delta = 1/2$:

$$u_{i,j+1}=\frac{u_{i-1,j}+u_{i+1,j}}{2} . \tag{4.35}$$

The solution is once again packaged as a class; this time it is called **ParabolicEquation.** Here it is:

```
Object subclass: #ParabolicEquation
  instanceVariableNames:
    'stepsOnX stepsOnT sigma initialCondition
    leftBoundaryCondition rightBoundaryCondition
    stripWidth h l timeRange u '
  classVariableNames: ''
  poolDictionaries: ''

ParabolicEquation class methods

new
 ^super new!
```

ParabolicEquation methods

```
computeL
l := h * h * sigma!

defineSolutionMatrix
stepsOnX := (stripWidth / h) rounded.
stepsOnT := (timeRange / l) rounded.
u := EnhancedMatrix
        new: (0 @ stepsOnX)
        with: (0 @ stepsOnT).!

fillInLeftBoundary
0 to: stepsOnT do: [ :j |
    u at: 0 at: j put:
        (leftBoundaryCondition value: (j * l)).
    ].!

fillInRightBoundary
0 to: stepsOnT do: [ :j |
    u at: stepsOnX at: j put:
        (rightBoundaryCondition value: (j * l)).
    ].!

fillInZeroethLayer
0 to: stepsOnX do: [ :i |
    u at: i at: 0 put:
        (initialCondition value: (i * h)).
    ].!

fillLayer: j "j is layer"
    | a b |
1 to: (stepsOnX-1) do: [ :i |
  a := u at: (i+1) at: (j-1).
  b := u at: (i-1) at: (j-1).
  u at: i at: j put: ((a+b) / 2).
  ].!

h: aValue
        "Set the value of h."
    h := aValue asFloat!

initialCondition: aValue
        "Set the value of initialCondition."
    initialCondition := aValue!
l: aValue
        "Set the value of l."
    l := aValue!

leftBoundaryCondition: aValue
        "Set the value of leftBoundaryCondition."
```

```
        leftBoundaryCondition := aValue!

rightBoundaryCondition: aValue
                "Set the value of rightBoundaryCondition."
        rightBoundaryCondition := aValue!

show
u show.!

sigma: aValue
                "Set the value of sigma."
        sigma := aValue asFloat!

solveEquation
self defineSolutionMatrix;
            fillInLeftBoundary;
            fillInRightBoundary;
            fillInZeroethLayer.
1 to: (stepsOnT+1) do: [ :j |
        self fillLayer: j.
        ].
 ^u!

stripWidth: aValue
                "Set the value of stripWidth."
        stripWidth := aValue asFloat!

timeRange: aValue
                "Set the value of timeRange."
        timeRange := aValue asFloat!
```

and here is the code with which we shall use it from the **Transcript** window:

```
        | aaa u | "Testing for parabolic equation"
aaa := ParabolicEquation new.
aaa initialCondition: [ :x | (Float pi * x) sin ];
        leftBoundaryCondition: [ :x | 0 ];
        rightBoundaryCondition: [ :x | 0 ];
        stripWidth: 1.0;
        sigma: 0.5;
        h: 0.1;
        computeL;
        timeRange: 0.025;
        solveEquation;
        show.
```

Example. Approximate the solution of the equation

$$u_t = u_{xx} \tag{4.36}$$

satisfying the following conditions:

$$u(x,0) = \sin \pi x \qquad (0 \leqslant x \leqslant 0.5) \tag{4.37}$$
$$u(0,t) = u(1,t) = 0 \qquad (0 \leqslant t \leqslant 0.025)\ . \tag{4.38}$$

Choose the spacing $h=0.1$ for the argument x. Since $\delta=1/2$, we get $l=0.005$. Then enter the initial and boundary values to form a table. The following table is the required solution. More precisely, we give here only the left half of the table since the initial condition is symmetric anyway on [0,1]:

0	*3.0901699e-1*	*2.2867586e-1*	*4.3496733e-1*	*5.9868117e-1*	*7.0379192e-1*
0	*2.9389263e-1*	*5.5901699e-1*	*7.6942088e-1*	*0.9045085*	*9.5105652e-1*
0	*0.2795085*	*5.3165676e-1*	*7.3176275e-1*	*0.8602387*	*0.9045085*
0	*2.6582838e-1*	*5.0563562e-1*	*6.9594773e-1*	*8.1813562e-1*	*0.8602387*
0	*2.5281781e-1*	*4.8088805e-1*	*6.6188562e-1*	*7.7809321e-1*	*8.1813562e-1*
0	*2.4044403e-1*	*4.5735172e-1*	*6.2949063e-1*	*7.4001062e-1*	*7.7809321e-1*

Class **ParabolicEquation** centres around the method **solveEquation.** It first sets up the necessary preconditions — boundary and initial conditions. Method **fillIn-ZeroethLayer** is for the initial condition and methods **fillInLeftBoundary** and **fillInRightBoundary** set up the left and the right boundary conditions. Then method **fillLayer:** computes the interior points, taking its values from the previous row and working downwards.

4.24 PARAMETRIZED MATRICES — CLASS EnhancedMatrix

We see another new type, **EnhancedMatrix,** in class **ParabolicEquation.** It is a subclass of **Matrix** and is its generalization at the same time. **EnhancedMatrix** takes two points as input parameters and generates a matrix with variable lower and upper bounds. For example, a declaration such as:

```
      | aaa |
aaa := EnhancedMatrix new: (5 negated @ 7) with: (0 @ 6)
```

would in Pascal be written like this:

```
bbb=ARRAY [0..6];
aaa=ARRAY [-5..7] OF bbb.
```

We need this enhancement for solving a parabolic equation because of the boundary and initial conditions. It is very easy to inherit almost everything from class **Matrix.** The only new idea is in method **loc:with:**, where a new, two-dimensional address function is given. The following code could be used to get the feel of this type:

```
| aaa | "Testing for the EnhancedMatrix"
aaa := EnhancedMatrix new: (2 negated @ 6) with: (2 @ 3).
aaa at: 0 at: 3 put: 3.
aaa show
```

Here is the complete code for this class:

```
Matrix variableSubclass: #EnhancedMatrix
  instanceVariableNames:
    'x1 x2 y1 y2 '
  classVariableNames: ''
  poolDictionaries:
    'CharacterConstants '

EnhancedMatrix class methods

new: range1 with: range2
    | answer |
answer := super new: (range1 y-range1 x+1)
                with: (range2 y-range2 x+1).
answer x1: range1 x. answer x2: range2 x.
answer y1: range1 y. answer y2: range2 y.
 ^answer!

EnhancedMatrix methods

at: i at: j
      "Access matrix element in (i,j)."
      | value |
value := self loc: i with: j.
 ^(self at: value)!

at: i at: j put: k "Assignment for matrices."
      | value |

value := self loc: i with: j.
self at: value put: k.
 ^self!

columns
 ^(y2-x2+1)!

loc: i with: j
      " Locate the (i,j) matrix element in Matrix."
" ^((i-x1) * (y2-x2+1)+(j-x2)+1)"
 ^((j-x2) * (y1-x1+1)+(i-x2)+1)!
rows
 ^(y1-x1+1)
show
      "Print matrix row by row."
x2 to: y2 do: [ :j |
      x1 to: y1 do: [ :i |
            Transcript show: (self at: i at: j)
                  printString , ' '.
            ].
      Transcript show: Lf printString.
      ].!
```

```
x1
  ^x1!

x1: x
x1 := x!

x2
  ^x2!

x2: x
x2 := x!

y1
  ^y1!

y1: x
y1 := x!

y2
  ^y2!

y2: x
y2 := x
```

4.25 COMMENTS ON CLASS EnhancedMatrix

Class **EnhancedMatrix** has four instance variables: **x1** and **y1** are the range for the first matrix index while **x2** and **y2** are the range for the second index. The only class method is **new:with:**. It reserves as much space as is needed and uses variable **super** to inherit from **Matrix**. Essentially the only new idea is in **loc:with:**. Actually, there are two methods in it, but the first is commented out. They correspond to two possible schemes: the enhanced matrix can be laid out column-wise or row-wise in the Array that reserves in memory. The second, active formula denotes row-wise memory management. The **show** method had to be patched, too.

It might be said that class **EnhancedMatrix** gives you the full power of Pascal as far as matrices are concerned.

4.26 CLASSES OR METHODS?

The manual gives an example of a class called **MonitoredArray,** which enhances **Array** to compute the arithmetic mean whenever the **at:** message is executed. Following this idea, we could have made a special class to house all descriptive statistics. The solution in the text consists of methods dispersed in various classes. This is as good a way to use an object-oriented language as any. However, its main benefits — inheritance and polymorphism — exist only if proper class organization is present. Such examples are **DiffEqSolver** and **ParabolicEquation.** The choice is yours, though.

PROBLEMS

4.1 What are errors of rounding-off and truncation? What are stable numerical processes? Can a larger number of significant digits increase the stability of a numerical process?

4.2 Solve the following equation:

$$\begin{aligned} 1x+1/2y+1/3z+1/4t&=1\\ 1/2x+1/3y+1/4z+1/5t&=0\\ 1/3x+1/4y+1/5z+1/6t&=0\\ 1/4x+1/5y+1/6z+1/7t&=0 \end{aligned}$$

4.3 Find the dominant eigenvalues of the matrices:

$$\text{(a)}\quad \begin{bmatrix} 1 & 2 & 3 & 4 \\ 12 & 12 & 3 & 5 \\ 3 & 5 & 8 & 9 \end{bmatrix} \qquad \text{(b)}\quad \begin{bmatrix} 0.5000 & 0.7071 & 0.5000 \\ 0.7071 & 0.0000 & -0.7071 \\ 0.5000 & -0.7071 & 0.5000 \end{bmatrix}$$

Experiment with different matrix exponents in method **highestEigenValue** of class **SquareMatrix.**

4.4 Rewrite the method **highestEigenValue** in class **SquareMatrix** so that only a minimal number of matrix multiplications is executed. The process should be stopped when two consecutive eigenvalues are practically the same. Would you prefer writing a method called **highestEigenValue: epsilon** ?

4.5 Invent at least two good reasons why speed is better than precision?

4.6 Why can't we put method **mean** into class **IndexedCollection**? What method is lacking?

4.7 Write a method **'Integer' sqrt** that will compute the square root of an integer as a fraction.

4.8 Enhance class **P3** with more operations on data. Insert another ListPane to expose the effect of transformation on data.

4.9 Use blocks to pass a function for data transformation directly to the class **P3** instead of changing it directly in method **initializeData.**

4.10 As it stands, method **initOriginalGraph: aaRect** is unusually long. Rewrite it as a series of several short messages. Do the same for **initReducedGraph: aRect.** How many similar methods can you use that way?

4.11 Create a new class called **RegressionEquation** and then do the previous exercise sending messages to it. Are there any advantages in writing programs through many 'small' classes?

4.12 Create a new class called **ExperimentalPoints** to capture the behaviour of experimental data. Rewrite class **P3** using it instead of writing messages directly to **data.** Would that make adding another such entity to represent transformed data much easier?

4.13 Draw a histogram using shaded areas. The data are:

1 3 5 9 11 14 19 16 13 10 8 7 4 31

4.14 Make a class **ChiSquare** and use it to perform goodness-of-fit tests. Enhance it so that the user can specify theoretical distribution as an input block.

4.15 Enhance class **ChiSquare** to have values of the chi-square distribution other than 0.01 and 0.05.

4.16 Can theoretical values for a chi-square test be input as a block that consists of a constant array? Must such block have two input parameters?

4.17 Use shaded histograms to graphically represent empirical and theoretical frequencies for the chi-square test.

4.18 Write a class called **Euler,** as a subclass of **DiffEqSolver,** to solve an ordinary differential equation using Euler formulae. How many methods can you inherit from **DiffEqSolver** and what methods exactly need to be changed? Can the main program remain practically the same (besides the obvious change of **aaa:=DiffEqSolver new.** into **aaa:=Euler new.**?

4.19 Find out what other numerical methods for solving ordinary differential equations look like and implement them also as subclasses of **DiffEqSolver.**

4.20 Change **DiffEqSolver** to be an abstract class and delegate actual routine **valuePerStepWithBlockFunction** to its subclasses. Create new class **Runge-Kutta** as one of its subclasses, together with **Euler, Adams, PredictorCorrector, Taylor** and others.

4.21 Use class **DrawCurveWindow** to draw solutions of the following second-order equations:

$$(1-x2)y''-xy'+25y=0, \quad y(0)=0, \quad y'(0)=5$$
$$(1-x2)y''-xy'+16y=0, \quad y(0)=1, \quad y'(0)=0.$$

4.22 Compute $y(0.25)$, $y(0.50)$ and $y(1)$, given

$$(1-x2)y''-2xy'+5y=0, \quad y(0)=0.375, \quad y'(0)=12$$
$$(1-x2)y''-2xy'+6y=0, \quad y(0)=-0.5, \quad y'(0)=8.$$

4.23 Is it possible to have blocks with three arguments? Does a message like **value:value:value:** exist? Can you write it?

4.24 Rewrite **DrawCurveWindow** to work with classes from Problem 4.20.

4.25 Is **DrawCurveWindow** general enough to serve as a postprocessor for all curves one might want to draw? Finish it.

4.26 Class **ParabolicEquation** implements approximation by equation (4.33). Rewrite it so that equation (4.34) and its consequences are used.

4.27 Find out about other methods for the numerical solution of the parabolic equation and implement them as subclasses of **ParabolicEquation.** Represent their solutions graphically, as a special window for solving parabolic equations.

4.28 Solve the parabolic equation

$$u_t = u_{xx} + F(x,t)$$

instead of (4.23), with the same initial and boundary conditions.

4.29 Try out column-wise memory management for class **EnhancedArray.** What would be the difference inside it? Would there be any difference outside of it? Would you say that information hiding is one of the best features of Smalltalk?

4.30 Other languages also have multi-indexed arrays. Write a class that will have matrices with three and four indices. Could a Point3D be used by analogy with class **EnhancedMatrix** and its input parameters as a way of passing index ranges? What solution would you adopt for matrices with four indices? With seven? What would be the best place in the Smalltalk/V hierarchy to put this new class into?

4.31 Why are complete classes better than methods scattered around within the Smalltalk/V image?

5

Smalltalk/V for discrete simulations

Exposure to SIMULA helped Alan Kay to distil the essence of object-oriented programming. Object-oriented languages have remained closely linked to computer simulation ever since.

SIMULA appeared in 1967. GPSS, a language for General Purpose Systems Simulation, already existed in 1961. It was popular but limited in scope and approach. For example, arithmetic operations were quite difficult to write in it. Therefore, the main consideration while designing SIMULA was to gain simulation capabilities without wasting the desirable qualities of a general-purpose programming language. SIMULA was conceived as an ALGOL 60 with simulation extensions. It featured data hiding, virtual routines, polymorphism, coroutines, garbage collection. Coroutines were not directly related to object-orientation but virtual routines preceded the notion of inheritance.

5.1 DEFINITION OF SIMULATION

There are several definitions of simulation. It is undeniably a technique for conducting experiments on system models. Indeed, one school of thought has it that computer simulation is the art of making and playing with computer models. Virtually every program would then be a simulation of something, even if only of mental processes. But that is rather an exaggeration. We therefore adopt the following definition:

Simulation is an experiment with an abstract model of a system. In computer simulation, a model is a computer program in which all processes last for a certain time.

The word simulation, in its broadest sense, also means the following set of activities:

— measuring the data on a real system,
— experimenting on a real system,
— formulating a theory,
— creation of model(s),
— coding a computer program,
— planning experiment(s) on the computer,
— verifying the results obtained,

— analysing, interpreting and, eventually,
— using the simulation output.

5.2 SYSTEMS

A system consists of a set of parts organized functionally to form a connected whole. Every system has these properties:

— **entity**, an object of interest in the system,
— **attribute**, a property of an entity,
— **activity**, any process that causes a change in the system, and
— **event**, the start or completion of an activity; alternatively, event is the occurrence of a change.

We measure the frequency of system attributes, activities and events, and thus gather system statistics in an organized manner.

A subsystem is a component of the total system that is either a part of the whole or an independent system itself. A subsystem can further consist of its own subsystems, *ad infinitum*. From the other side, a supersystem is a system that contains subsystem(s). It is important to isolate subsystems that are easier to study or whose analytical solutions we already know. For instance, a dockyard. It has many components: wharves, cranes, transport, ships, cargoes, passengers. Every dockyard part is, essentially, a subsystem. A ship consists of decks, cabins, boats, each of which can be further studied as a system. Looking at it in a reverse direction, a dockyard is a subsystem of a complete harbour.

The historical link between simulation and object-oriented languages is clear in terminology. For example, systems are classes; subsystems inherit properties of systems, etc.

5.3 MODELS

A model of a system is any representation of the system. Usually, there are two natural requirements:

— a model should enable the system behaviour to be predicted, and
— it must be easier to deal with than the system itself.

A theory is a general statement of a principle that is extracted from the system and/or the data obtained from observations of the system. Theory aims to explain system behaviour and, eventually, to forecast its future. A model is always both a representation of the system and a representation of the corresponding theory. The theory explains the system, forming a basis for model building at the same time, and links the model to its system. A model has only one function: to check the theory in practice. Each model is a compromise between simplification of the system and the number of features that we intend to study. A model must be easier to handle than the system itself.

According to the nature of the system, two distinct types of variable exist: deterministic and stochastic.

Deterministic variables represent quantities that can be precisely measured or computed. Stochastic variables stand for system quantities that we do not know exactly in advance, but a general notion of their behaviour exists. They capture random features of the system.

While creating a model we must decide whether it will be deterministic or stochastic. Proper diagnosis of a system's nature in this aspect is crucial. Deterministic models usually use calculus and differential equations. Stochastic models use probability, statistics, and random processes. It takes only one stochastic variable to turn a deterministic system into a stochastic one.

There are also continuous and discrete models. States in continuous models change continuously in time, and measurements are not restricted to integers. A rocket in flight continuously changes trajectory in time, so its model must be continuous.

Another very important classification depends on advancing the clock in the model. There are models with continuous and discrete time. Models with discrete time further divide into:

- — models of critical events, in which movements of the model clock depend on the events in the model, and
- — models of constant time periods, in which the model clock always advances in regular increments, regardless of whether events happen or not.

The constant time periods approach is useful when there is a high probability of a critical event taking place in every moment. A top-level design for this could look be:

SIMULATION DESIGN 1

S = 0 (*start-up state*)
REPEAT (**V** *times*)
    S = ***S*** + 1 (*system clock is advanced*)
    IF there are events scheduled for this moment
        THEN perform all of them
            and schedule the following events
UNTIL ***S*** = ***V***

This is a sure but slow way. The IF statement is performed even if nothing should happen. The whole process can be much speeded up if the system clock is advanced immediately to the time to which the next event is scheduled. The above algorithm then changes to:

SIMULATION DESIGN 2

S = 0 (*start-up state*)
WHILE ***S*** < ***V*** *do*
    S = ***S*** + *ADVANCE* (*system clock is advanced*)
    PERFORM all events scheduled for this moment
        and schedule the following events
END WHILE

This is the preferred solution if execution speed is important.

A discrete model matches two conditions:

— there are (large) blocks of time in which system states do not change, and
— all units that move through the system are integer.

Various traffic situations are naturally discrete. The same holds for queueing systems. Very many models reduce to that simulation type. The supermarket is a classic example of a queueing system.

A discrete system jumps from one state to another. Such a system consists of a series of states, together with actions that lead from one state to another.

The selection of model types depends on the investigator's personality, knowledge, scientific background, available time, hardware, etc. Continuous systems have dominated ever since the introduction of calculus in the seventeenth century. Statistics and discrete mathematical structures have become fashionable more recently.

5.4 SOLVING THE MODEL

Having built a model, the next task is to extract as much information as possible about the system. Model solution can be analytical or numerical.

A model is analytical if it describes the system through a set of mathematical formulae or relations. Finite formulae are easy to compute by hand and are also trivial in programming terms. Formulae introduce a touch of elegance and power. The problem is (we are sure) under control: prediction reduces to finite computations, and these are always possible. Model input automatically trims down to various controlled combinations of variables and parameters that take part in the formulae.

Modelling implies a certain degree of idealization, regardless of the type of model. Mathematical models carry such abstraction to extremes, so models of this type can be unrealistic. There is an obvious risk that the model does not reflect important parts of the system, which are left out as 'difficult to compute'. Analytical solutions can be very complex and sometimes the model itself introduces a formula that is not directly computable. What if a nonlinear partial differential equation models the system? Most of these equations have purely numerical solutions, which brings the error of the mathematical method into the whole procedure.

We can simulate literally everything. However, mixed models yield the best effects. One part is analytical, while the main part of the system is (usually) stochastic. Calculation within simulation often brings the reward of optimal execution times.

Analytical solutions are rare. Making them is tantamount to inventing new mathematical theories' and most investigators are not able to do this. The results are usually needed immediately, which leaves no time for deep excursions. The usual solutions are 'cheap-and-cheerful' numerical computations. Such are almost impossible to do by hand, so this is where computers come into play. The invention of computers played a decisive role in the acceptance of simulation as a reliable scientific method.

In spite of possible difficulties, closed formulae are always welcome in a mathematical model. Analytical solutions describe the system qualitatively and offer generality. Such generality is strictly in the region of well-defined input assumptions, though. On the contrary, a numerical solution returns only a partial behaviour of the system. We could get a complete chart of system behaviour only after all of the system input is exhausted. This is often impossible in practice, and we can be too easily fooled by incomplete input data that we ourselves created.

5.5 MODEL VERIFICATION AND VALIDATION

Two crucial tests remain after deciding on theory and model type — verification and validation. Verification is proof that the model conforms to the theory. In other words, we check whether the theory is properly translated into the model. Validation is checking that the model acts in the same way as to the system.

Verification is really an iterative process. Thus we make different versions of a computer program to dispose of program errors. The problem of model verification is otherwise known as the problem of program correctness. This is a truly difficult problem. Except for the most trivial programs, we are unable to ensure that the program will work correctly. This is as true for deterministic programs as for programs in which random variables appear. There have been many attempts to solve the problem of program correctness, and so far all of them have failed.

Verification is the problem of the computer programmer. The analyst is more concerned with validation. That phase comes only after a model has been built, so the analyst bears a double burden: if the model does not imitate the system in a satisfactory way, the mistakes can be either in the realization of the model (i.e. program bug), or in the theory that underlies the model. The process of validation is much easier if the designer of the model and the analyst are the same person. This is why almost all analysts learn programming languages and become programmers!

5.6 REQUIREMENTS FOR DISCRETE SYSTEMS SIMULATIONS LANGUAGES

General-purpose languages such as BASIC, FORTRAN, COBOL, PL/1, FORTH, Pascal, C, and others are not particulary well suited for simulations of any kind. There are specialized problem-oriented languages to fill the gap. The model and the program are one and the same in those languages; the verification and validation phase merge into one whole. The program is the model.

A specialized discrete simulation language must take care of:

Time: Delays, passing of the simulated time, change of the simulation clock.

Events: Only significant events should change model state. If many events should happen at the same time, a strategy of priorities must be available.

Random number generator: Must be fast and random.

Management of important statistics: Done automatically, by the language itself. A support for standard statistical printout.

Control of simulation states: Easy access to all internal and external components of the model.

General requirements: Program readability, initialization, debugging facilities, modularity of instructions and model structure, error checking, etc.

A state of a discrete system is a set of system variables, which changes on the occurrence of some event. The event may influence all system variables or just some of them. There can be more than one discrete event in the transition from state to state; such events are simultaneous (parallel) events.

Some popular discrete systems simulations languages are: GPSS, SIMSCRIPT II, SIMULA 67, GASP IV. Any object-oriented language ought to be easily enhanced to a full discrete systems simulation language.

5.7 RANDOM NUMBERS

Computers are deterministic. That is not always what we want. Some degree of randomness must exist in areas of heuristic programming, numerical analysis, cryptography, computer security, decision making, games, education. Random numbers are the easiest way to annihilate the deterministic nature of computers.

Practical use of random numbers imposes two requirements: speed and versatility. Larger simulations use dozens of thousands of random numbers so their generation must be easy on system resources. It suffices to learn how to generate a uniform distribution of random numbers. This is the basis for all other distributions.

There are three methods of generating a series of random numbers that are uniformly distributed over the interval [0,1]:

— Generators of random numbers,
— Tables of random digits, and
— Pseudo-random numbers.

Strictly speaking, random numbers exist only as realizations of stochastic processes. Physical random number generators need no extra memory. Degeneration is, by definition, impossible. The range of numbers is, essentially, unlimited. However, random numbers are really random. They cannot be repeated at will, unless kept in a special file, but then they become tables. The 'quality' of the numbers created is difficult to check. Devices that produce random numbers need special maintenance, and their results should be checked now and then by means of special tests. Finally, most random number generators are much slower than electronic computers.

A random number table ideally contains several million digits. Also, its elements should be retrieved quickly. Tables make sense when several megabytes of RAM are available. Smalltalk/V286 can address up to 16 megabytes of extended memory and can easily use tables of up to several million bytes of length. However, tables can degenerate. For example, a truly large table of random digits is almost sure to contain a series of, say, 100 zeros in a row. Such digits are not random. All in all, tables are of limited use in simulation programs.

Pseudo-random numbers are numbers computed by means of a given formula. They can be used instead of real random numbers in solving certain problems but are not really random. Computers themselves are not able to 'pull a number' out of thin air. The output of a pseudo-random number generator is always one and the same for the same input data. The use of pseudo-random numbers for simulations of stochastic systems on a computer is a contradiction in terms. Why are, then, pseudo-random numbers so often used?

The answer is not simple. A simulation model extracts important features out of the real system. It is not obligatory to have a better series of random numbers than the real system requires! In other words, there is no need for the 'best available' random number generator, only for the most appropriate generator considering the system and the problem in hand. The precise meaning of 'random' thus changes from problem to problem. Random numbers are not a goal in themselves, but are a convenient tool for solving certain classes of problems. If real random numbers are hard to use, then why not take a series of numbers that is easy to compute, but still 'look like' real random numbers? Pseudo-random numbers emerge as a workable compromise between the computer environment and the needs of simulation as a general problem-solving method. The idea is thus to induce a series of random numbers that can be applied to solving the concrete problem, and it does not really matter how the series is assembled if it passes certain statistical tests.

There are also definite advantages when using pseudo-random numbers:

Flexibility. For a new stochastic process, only input data are changed, and not the random number generator itself. Once the generator is certified, it can be used with different input data producing independent random numbers.

Ease of computing. A small number of program statements is sufficient to compute a new pseudo-random number, without additional memory requirements.

No wonder pseudo-random numbers are always used in computer simulations.

From the implementation point of view, the random number generator should be fast in execution, economical in terms of computer memory, easy to use within a program, and reproducible. This last property is vital during program debugging.

Almost all practical algorithms for generating sequences of pseudo-random numbers are given by the following recursive formula:

$$r_{i+1} = f_i(r\ ), \text{ where } i = 0,1,\ldots,n\ . \tag{5.1}$$

The initial number r_0 is called the 'seed' and has to be defined in advance. One efficient function is

$$r_{i+1} = \text{mod}_i(br + c,\ m),\ i = 0,1,2,\ldots,n\ . \tag{5.2}$$

This is Lehmer's linear congruential method. Here is an example:

Let $r_0 = 9$, $b = 4$, $m = 8$, $c = 2$. The sequence is then:

$$\begin{aligned} r_0 &= 9 \\ r_1 &= \text{mod}(4 \times 9 + 3,\ 8) = 7 \\ r_2 &= \text{mod}(4 \times 7 + 3,\ 8) = 7 \\ r_3 &= r_4 = 7 = \ldots\ . \end{aligned}$$

This selection of input parameters has degenerated almost immediately.

The constant c is sometimes left out: $c = 0$. The residual function becomes simpler:

$$r_{i+1} = \text{mod}_i(br,m),\ i = 0,1,2,\ldots,n\ , \tag{5.3}$$

and is known as Lehmer's multiplication generator. Although it yields only integers, we can always divide r_{i+1} by m, the result becoming a realization of the uniform random variable R on interval $[0,1]$.

One of the most frequent errors is to underestimate the length of run needed to obtain meaningful results. Usually a run of 5–6000 is regarded as 'long'. Unfortunately, the following error estimate holds:

$$\text{error} = \sqrt{(D/N)}$$

where D is some constant and N is the run length. It is clear that in order to decrease the error by a factor of 10 (in other words, to obtain another significant digit in the result), an increase in N by a factor of 100 would be necessary. If, say, a length of 5000 gives an accuracy of 0.01, then a length of a formidable 500 000 is needed in order to improve the accuracy up to only 0.001! Nevertheless, there are shortcuts in any particular situation. Different values of D often considerably increase accuracy, decreasing the effort needed to achieve the final result.

And there is another problem. Consider taking cards out of a deck of 52 playing cards. In the beginning, any card is probable, but when 51 cards have been drawn the remaining card is uniquely determined. The case with random generators is similar: the numbers drawn in the second half of the period become less independent with each new generation. This is why in real life, simulation generators with only a half of the whole period should be used.

5.8 IMPLEMENTING RANDOM NUMBERS

There are several ways of incorporating random number generators into Smalltalk/V programs. We have already seen one of them, in method **shadeP:noOfPoints:enlargement:** of class **Rectangles**. We added that method while shading polygons in class **PR**. There we had lines

```
rb := 1409.
ro := 15537.
rm := 32749.
...
ro := rb * ro − ((rb * ro / rm) truncated * rm).
```

that implement equation (5.3). The input data, 1409, 15537, 32749, yield a quality Lehmer's generator. These numbers are optional — we could have taken others, equally good for the purpose.

We should turn this into a proper class, say **RandomNumber**. As usual, a special window will show the effects of the new class. We shall inherit **DrawCurveWindow** and thus cheaply get a slot to test **RandomNumber**. Here is the code for class **TestRandom**:

```
DrawCurveWindow subclass: #TestRandom
  instanceVariableNames:
    'randomNumber '
  classVariableNames: ''
  poolDictionaries: ''
!TestRandom class methods ! !
!TestRandom methods !
auxArrays
```

```
n := 55.
x := Array new: n.
y := Array new: n.
1 to: n do: [ :i |
    x at: i put: randomNumber next.
    y at: i put: randomNumber next.
    ].!
initLabel
label := 'Testing class RandomNumber'.
randomNumber := RandomNumber new.
randomNumber lowerBound: 1;
                upperBound: 100;
                initialize.!
labelDrawing
    "Inheritance blocking."!
menu
 ^Menu
    labels: 'Draw it\New seed' withCrs
    lines: Array new
    selectors: #(drawIt newSeed)!
newSeed
 ^randomNumber newSeed: (
    Prompter
      prompt: 'New seed?'
      defaultExpression:
        (randomNumber seed printString)
    )!
solveEquation
    "Inheritance blocking."!
```

5.9 COMMENTS ON CLASS TestRandom

TestRandom inherits **DrawCurveWindow** adding only one new instance variable, **randomNumber**. It is initialized in an unlikely place, in method **initLabel**. This choice is due to inheritance. We try to inherit everything with as little change as possible. The opening method, **openOn:**, can be inherited automatically if only method **initLabel** were different. In class **DrawCurveWindow** it returns one label but in **TestRandom** it should return another. Therefore, we must write a new **initLabel** method. It is the only method executed from **openOn:**, so it can contain other initializations as well. Instance variable **randomNumber** learns its type here. There is no real need to add a separate method for initialization. Two other methods, **labelDrawing** and **solveEquation**, exist only to block corresponding methods in the ancestor class. The method **auxArrays** is actually changed to receive instances of class **RandomNumber**. Finally, method menu is new and uses **newSeed** to set a new seed value.

This class is an excellent example of inheritance techniques: blocking, rewriting or complete changing. **newSeed** is the only additional method — others are just revisions of the existing code. **DrawCurveWindow** consists of 188 lines against only 36 in **TestRandom**.

Fig. 5.1 contains four different windows with 50 random points. Each window has

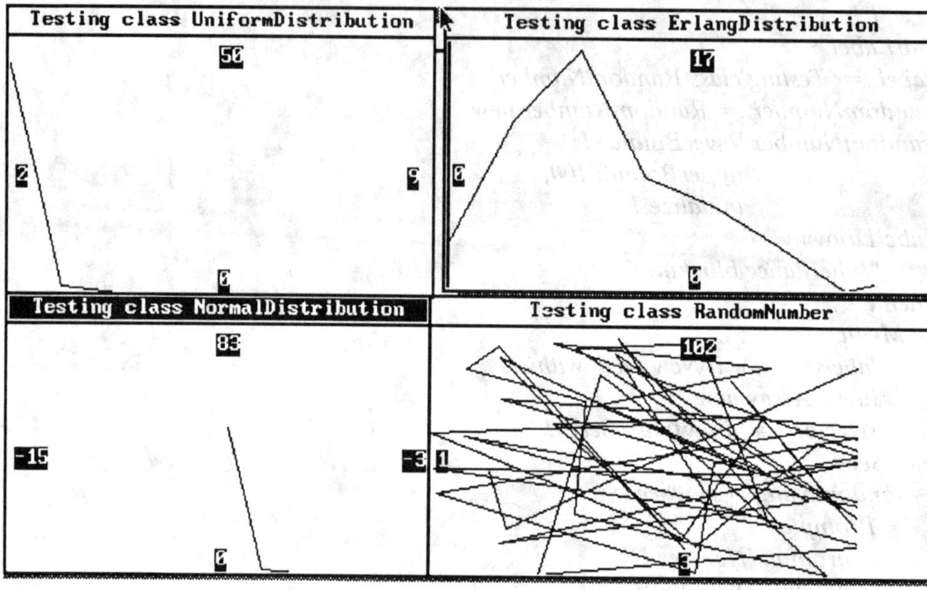

Fig. 5.1 — Different sets of random points.

its own seed. A left click of the mouse in the pane and menu option **Draw it** are equivalent. First calculate random points and then draw them from scratch. Here it is:

```
Integer subclass: #RandomNumber
  instanceVariableNames:
  'ro rb rm lowerBound upperBound range'
  classVariableNames: ''
  poolDictionaries: ''
!RandomNumber class methods !
!RandomNumber methods
initialize
  | u l r|
self initRb; initRm; initRo.
u := upperBound. l := lowerBound.
r := u - l.
range := (upperBound - lowerBound) abs.!
initRb
rb := 1409.!
```

```
initRm
rm := 32749.!
initRo
ro := 15537.!
lowerBound: aValue
lowerBound := aValue!
newSeed: aValue
ro := aValue!
next
ro := rb * ro - ((rb * ro / rm) truncated * rm).
^ro // range + lowerBound!
seed
^ro!
upperBound: aValue
upperBound := aValue!
```

5.10 COMMENTS ON CLASS RandomNumber

The central method in **RandomNumber** is **next**. It returns the 'next' pseudo-random number in the series. Its first line is formula (5.3) rewritten with instance variables **ro, rb, rm**. Methods **initRb, initRm, initRo** set their values separately. Method **newSeed:** can assign a value to **ro** from the outside of the **RandomNumber** itself. **newSeed** of class **TestRandom** uses it to change the random number series.

Random numbers must conform to the nature of the objects they represent. For instance, the random number usually stands for the arrival of a customer. In all practical applications, the customers come every several seconds and the generated numbers must be in that domain. Variables **lowerBound, upperBound** and **range** stretch **ro** to the value of **range** (see second line in **next**).

Let us use random numbers to generate different distributions. The main technique is the inverse distribution method.

5.11 THE INVERSE DISTRIBUTION METHOD

A random variable is defined through its probability density function $f(x)$, which expresses the probability that random variable X takes a value of x. The cumulative function $F(x)$ is defined as:

$$F(x) = \int_{-\infty}^{x} f(t)\,dt = P(X \leqslant x)$$

which in case of a discrete density function becomes

$$F(x) = \sum_{x_i < x} f(x_i),\ i = 1,\ldots,n.$$

The inverse distribution method consists of selecting a random number r (uniformly distributed over interval [0,1]), setting $F(x) = r$, then solving that equation for x. Symbolically, the solution is written as:

$$x^{-1} = F(r). \tag{5.4}$$

A value on the vertical axis is chosen first, after which the corresponding abscissa is computed.

The success of this method strongly depends on the nature of function F, i.e. how easy it is to solve equation (5.4). For all common distributions, the solution can be found using short and efficacious algorithms.

5.12 NORMAL DISTRIBUTION

This is the most important continuous distribution. Whenever a random variable X may be expressed as a sum of a large number of independently acting random variables, the probability function of X is approximately normal. Such is the case, for example, when X represents fluctuations of the voltage developed across a resistor by thermal agitation.

The probability function of a normal variable N(a,b) takes any of the values from the interval ($-\infty$, $+\infty$) according to the following expression:

$$f(x) = \frac{1}{b\sqrt{(2\pi)}} \exp\left(\frac{(x-a)^2}{2b^2}\right) \tag{5.5}$$

$$\mu = a^2, \sigma^2 = b^2 .$$

This function is represented in Fig. 5.2.

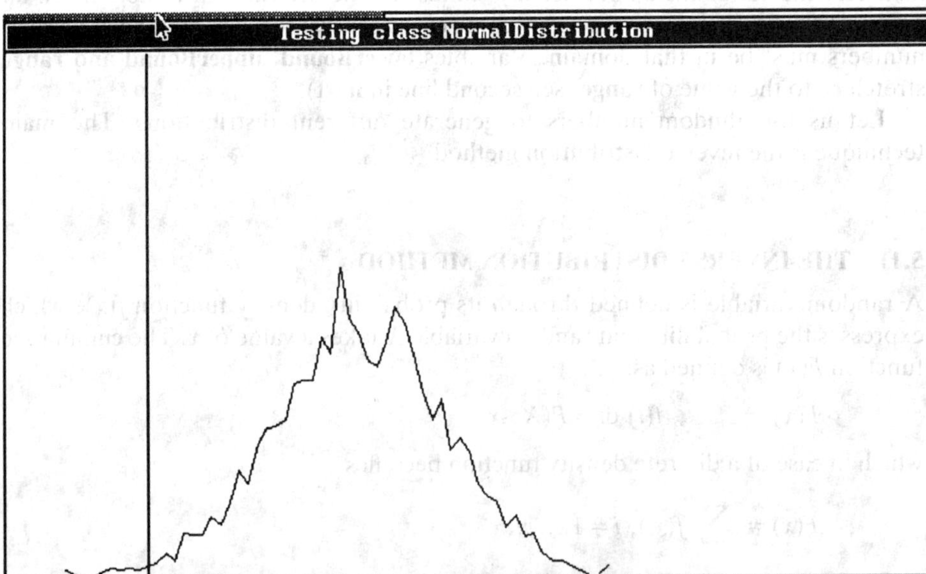

Fig. 5.2 — Normal distribution sampled from class **NormalDistribution**.

The arithmetic mean μ and standard deviation σ^2 completely determine the normal distribution. One particular, but very useful, case is the standardized normal distribution with $\mu = 0, \sigma^2 = 1$. The symbol for this function is N(0,1), and its density function is:

$$f(x) = \frac{1}{\sqrt{(2\pi)}} \exp^2(-x/2) \ . \tag{5.6}$$

There are many algorithms for the computerized generation of normal random variates. The central limit theorem is the most popular. It states that the probability distribution of the sum of n independently and identically distributed random variables R_i with mean μ_i and σ_i, where $i = 1,2,...,n$, approaches the normal distribution with mean $\sum_1^n \mu_i$ and variance $\sum_1^n \sigma_i$, asymptotically as n becomes large.

Variables R_i can be standardized random variables, as in equation (5.5). Thus the sum of R_i has a mean of $n/2$ and a variance of $n/12$ as n becomes large. Quite a good approximation is achieved when n is as small as 12.

The statistic Z defined as

$$Z = \frac{\sum_{i=1}^{n} (R_i - n/2)}{\sqrt{(n/12)}}$$

has an N(0,1) distribution for large n. For $n = 12$ we see that

$$Z = \sum_{i=1}^{12} R_i - 6$$

also has an N(0,1) distribution. A variate z, derived from N(0,1), is calculated as

$$z = \sum_{i=1}^{12} r_i - 6. \tag{5.7}$$

It is easy to show that a variate from an N(μ,σ^2) distribution is computed according to the formula

$$x = \mu + \sigma z \tag{5.8}$$

where z derives from equation (5.1). For these formulae we create a new class, **NormalDistribution**. The line with "***" in method **next** implements the above formula. Here is the code:

```
Integer subclass: #NormalDistribution
  instanceVariableNames:
    'randomNumber arithmeticMean standardDeviation '
  classVariableNames: ''
  poolDictionaries: ''
!NormalDistribution class methods !
```

```
!NormalDistribution methods !
arithmeticMean: aValue
arithmeticMean := aValue
initialize
randomNumber := RandomNumber new.
"Special setting to neutralize code
  in RandomNumber's next method'. "
randomNumber lowerBound: 0;
                    upperBound: 1;
                    initialize.!
next
    | sl |
sl := 0.
1 to: 12 do: [ :i | sl := sl + randomNumber next. ].
 ^standardDeviation * (sl - 6) + arithmeticMean " ***"!
standardDeviation: aValue
standardDeviation := aValue!
```

Class **TestNormal** produces Fig. 5.2. The code is quite short because everything is inherited from **TestRandom** and **DrawCurveWindow**. Note that we use one of the previous methods from **Array, chiSquareFrequency**. We wrote this for the chi-square test.

Method **initStretch** is interesting. It overrides **initStretch** from **DrawCurveWindow**, two classes above. Method **initStretch** was written with only one purpose in mind: to be overriden by a descendant method!

```
TestRandom subclass: #TestNormal
  instanceVariableNames: ''
  classVariableNames: ''
  poolDictionaries: ''
!TestNormal class methods !
TestNormal methods
auxArrays
    | z |
n := 8000.
z := Array new: n.
1 to: n do: [ :i | z at: i put: randomNumber next.].
y := z chiSquareFrequency.
x := Array new: y size.
1 to: y size do: [ :i | x at: i put: (i - 10).].!
initLabel
label := 'Testing class NormalDistribution'.
randomNumber := NormalDistribution new.
randomNumber arithmeticMean: 100;
                    standardDeviation: 1;
                    initialize.!
initStretch
```

stretch : = *1.7!*

Writing new generators and testing them becomes child's play. So let's play!

5.13 UNIFORM DISTRIBUTION ON THE INTERVAL *[a,b]*

The uniform distribution is the simplest continuous distribution for a random variable X defined over $[a,b]$. Its functions are:

$$f(x) = \frac{1}{b-a},\ a \leqslant x \leqslant b$$
$$0,\ x<a \text{ and } x>b$$
$$0,\ x<a$$

$$F(x) = \frac{x-a}{b-a},\ a \leqslant x < b$$
$$1,\ x \geqslant b$$

$$\mu = \frac{a+b}{2},\ \sigma^2 = \frac{(b-a)^2}{12}\ .$$

They are represented in Fig. 5.3. To generate a variate we use the following relation:

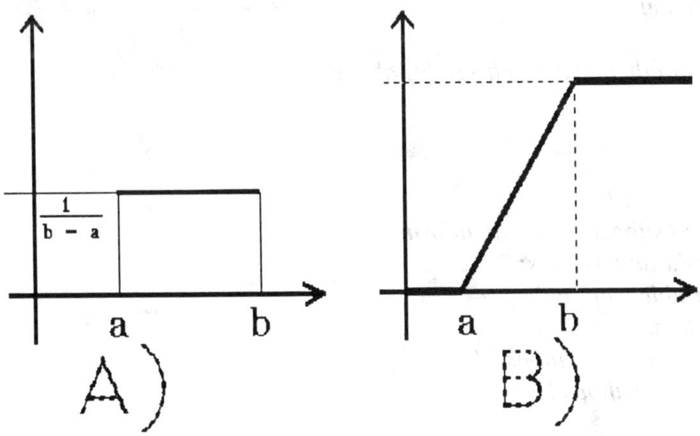

Fig. 5.3 — (a) $f(x)$ (b) $F(x)$ for a uniform distribution over $[a,b]$.

$$F(x) = r = \frac{x-a}{b-a}\ .$$

Its inverse function is

$$x = F(r)^{-1} = a + (b-a)r\ . \tag{5.9}$$

The plan for computation is very simple: define interval edges *a* and *b* and use formula (5.9). Once again, we have two classes, **UniformDistribution** to compute, and **TestUniform** to draw in a window. Here they are:

```
Integer subclass: #UniformDistribution
  instanceVariableNames:
    'randomNumber left right '
  classVariableNames: ''
  poolDictionaries: ''
!UniformDistribution class methods ! !
!UniformDistribution methods !
initialize
randomNumber := RandomNumber new.
"Special setting to neutralize
    code in RandomNumber's
    next method'. "
randomNumber lowerBound: 0;
             upperBound: 1;
             initialize.!
left
 ^left!
left: aValue
left := aValue!
next
 ^randomNumber next * (left - right) abs + left!
right
 ^right!
right: aValue
right := aValue! !
TestRandom subclass: #TestUniform
  instanceVariableNames: ''
  classVariableNames: ''
  poolDictionaries: ''
!TestUniform class methods ! !
!TestUniform methods !
auxArrays
    | z w |
n := 800.
z := Array new: n.
1 to: n do: [ :i |
    z at: i put: randomNumber next.].
y := z chiSquareFrequency.
x := Array new: y size.
start := randomNumber left.
end := randomNumber right.
w := (start - end) abs / x size.
1 to: x size do: [ :i |
```

```
    x at: i put: (i - 1) * w + start].!
initLabel
label := 'Testing class UniformDistribution'.
randomNumber := UniformDistribution new.
randomNumber left: 2;
             right: 10;
             initialize.!
```

UniformDistribution again has three instance variables, but the names are changed. **left** and **right** contain the left and right domain edge. Method **next** is very simple and directly corresponds to formula (5.9). There is a slight change in **auxArrays** of **TestUniform:** array x actually contains arguments of function $F(x)$.

5.14 EXPONENTIAL DISTRIBUTION

One particularly frequent event in discrete simulations is the arrival of a transaction. For instance, a customer arrives at the theatre booth, or cars arrive to form a queue at the traffic light. The time interval between two consecutive arrivals is exponentially distributed:

$$f(x) = \lambda \exp(-\lambda)$$
$$f = \frac{1}{\lambda},\ e^2 = \frac{1}{\lambda^2}\ .$$

The distribution function is

$$F(x) = 1 - \exp(\lambda - x)\ .$$

Let us use the inverse distribution method. First put:

$$r = F(x) = 1 - \exp(\lambda - x)$$

then solve it for x:

$$x = -\frac{1}{\lambda}\ \ln(1 - r)\ .$$

Since random variable $(1 - r)$ has the same uniform distribution over the interval $[0,1]$ as r itself, the expression is simplified to:

$$x = -\frac{\ln(r)}{\lambda}\ . \tag{5.10}$$

5.15 ERLANG DISTRIBUTION

The Erlang distribution has the following density function:

$$f(x) = \frac{1}{(k-1)!}\ \lambda^k\ x^{(k-1)}\ \exp(-\lambda x)\ .$$

This is really a family of distributions; to each k there corresponds one particular density distribution. The most important case is $k = 1$, when the Erlang distribution reduces to the exponential distribution (see above). For $k>30$, the Erlang distribution is best replaced by the normal distribution. In Fig. 5.4, we see a curve for $k = 20$.

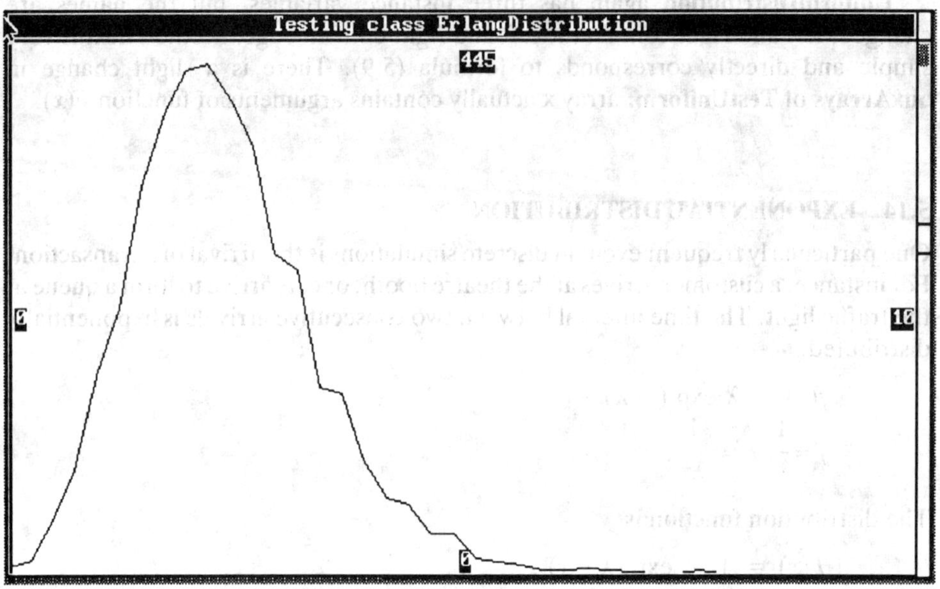

Fig. 5.4 — Erlang distribution for various values of k.

The Erlang distribution describes random arrivals. If λ is the average number of arrivals in a time unit, then $1/\lambda$ is the average time between two consecutive arrivals. Lower values of k (say, $k = 2$) mean that the process is governed by strong influences of manual labour. On the contrary, larger values of k (say, $k = 30$) reflect the influence of automatic devices (cranes, for example).

The Erlang distribution $E(k,\lambda)$ is the sum of k exponential distributions. The Erlang variate $E(x)$ can, therefore, be generated by a very simple formula:

$$E(x) = \sum_{1}^{k} -\ln(r_i)/\lambda$$

which is further rewritten as:

$$E(x) = -\frac{1}{k\lambda} \ln \sum_{i=1}^{k} r_i \qquad (5.11)$$

The corresponding classes are **ErlangDistribution** and **TestErlang**:

```
TestRandom subclass: #TestErlang
  instanceVariableNames: ''
  classVariableNames: ''
  poolDictionaries: ''
!TestErlang class methods !
!TestErlang methods
auxArrays
     | z w |
n := 4000.
z := Array new: n.
1 to: n do: [ :i |
     z at: i put: randomNumber next.].
y := z chiSquareFrequency.
x := Array new: y size.
start := 0.
end := 10.
w := (start - end) abs / x size.
1 to: x size do: [ :i |
     x at: i put: (i - 1) * w + start]..!
initLabel
label := 'Testing class ErlangDistribution'.
randomNumber := ErlangDistribution new.
randomNumber lambda: 20;
                k: 20;
                initialize.! !
Integer subclass: #ErlangDistribution
  instanceVariableNames:
     'randomNumber lambda k '
  classVariableNames: ''
  poolDictionaries: ''
!ErlangDistribution class methods !
!ErlangDistribution methods
initialize
randomNumber := RandomNumber new.
"Special setting to neutralize
     code in RandomNumber's
     next method'. "
randomNumber lowerBound: 0;
                upperBound: 1;
                initialize.!
k: aValue
k := aValue!
lambda: aValue
lambda := aValue!
next
     | sl |
sl := 1.
```

```
1 to: k do: [ :i /
     sl := sl * randomNumber next.].
 ^(1 / (lambda negated / k)) * (sl ln)!
```

Method **next** is a direct transcription of formula (5.11). The rest of the code is self-evident.

This is a technical summary of the statistics and Smalltalk/V classes that will be used in the forthcoming programs. With this background, we are ready to start studying the simulation of technical systems.

5.16 DATA STRUCTURES, CLASSES Stack AND Queue

Several data structures appear in almost any application. Linear arrays, matrices and strings are ubiquitous. All general-purpose languages support them. However, they are just the beginning. Thick books have been written on data structures and algorithms to access, change or edit data in them. It would be very difficult to differentiate between programming languages if all they offered were integers and reals. Programming languages actually differ according to the structures they support best. A tendency towards certain structures, and the absence of others is what makes languages dissimilar. For example, the main data structure in FORTH is stack. FORTRAN is all arrays and matrices. PROLOG is about trees and so on. Object-oriented languages put things into perspective because all data structures are of equal significance. That is not to say that any particular language implementation will come with all the existing data structures. No. But we can add them when the need arises and in a well-organized manner.

Let us now add two classical data structures, **Stack** and **Queue**. **Stack** is used inside literally all language processors, only its workings (except in FORTH) are well concealed. **Stack** is also useful in simulations. On the other hand, **Queue** is almost always used in simulations of discrete systems. Both **Stack** and **Queue** are very easy to implement in Smalltalk/V, because both will inherit from **OrderedCollection**. Both classes will be totally generic, meaning that mixed types of objects can be stored in a single instance of either. This feature is unique to Smalltalk.
Here is class **Stack**:

```
OrderedCollection variableSubclass: #Stack
  instanceVariableNames: ''
  classVariableNames: ''
  poolDictionaries: ''
!Stack class methods !
!Stack methods
clear
1 to: self size do: [ :i /
     self pop ].
 ^self!
cr
Transcript cr.!
example
```

```
" | stack |
stack := Stack new.
1 to: 6 do: [ :i |
      stack push: i * i. ].
stack cr; print;
        reverse; cr; print.
1 4 9 16 25 36
36 25 16 9 4 1
"
isEmpty
 ^self size = 0!
pop
 ^self removeLast!
print
self do: [ :stackElement |
      Transcript show:
      (stackElement printString , ' ').].!
push: aValue
self add: aValue!
reverse
      | r |
r := Stack new.
self size to: 1 by: 1 negated do: [ :i |
      r add: (self at: i). ].
1 to: self size do: [ :i |
      self at: i put: (r at: i).].
 ^self!
stackTop
self last!
```

5.17 COMMENTS ON CLASS Stack

Stack contains classic stack operations: **clear** (make a fresh Stack), **isEmpty** (check to see if it contains any elements at all), **pop** (remove the top of the Stack; return its value), **push** (put something on the Stack) and **reverse** (reverse stack). A couple of methods serve only for testing. These are **cr** (new line on **Transcript** window), **example** (the main program for testing), and **print** (print Stack contents on the **Transcript** window).

Coding class **Stack** is very easy. **OrderedCollection** can do much more than **Stack**. Actually, all these classical stack operations already exist in **Collection**. The main improvement and the reason to have **Stack** as a separate class is convenience. With **Stack** existing, you can express yourself directly in stack terms. This allows you to think at a higher level than before. And this is the main advantage of object-oriented languages: they let you think one, two or several levels higher, closer to reality, further away from the hardware.

Class **Queue** is even smaller:

```
OrderedCollection variableSubclass: #Queue
  instanceVariableNames: ''
  classVariableNames: ''
  poolDictionaries: ''
!Queue class methods !
!Queue methods
clear
1 to: self size do: [ :i |
     self removeLast ].
 ^self!
cr
Transcript cr.!
example
"| queue |
queue := Queue new.
1 to: 6 do: [ :i |
     queue add: i * i. ].
queue cr; print;
        remove; cr; print;
        add: '4567'; cr; print.
queue last.
1 4 9 16 25 36
1 4 9 16 25
1 4 9 16 25 '4567' "!
isEmpty
 ^self size = 0!
print
self do: [ :queueElement |
     Transcript show:
     (queueElement printString , ' ').].!
remove
self removeLast!
```

5.18 COMMENTS ON CLASS Queue

Class **Queue** is extremely simple. **OrderedCollection** contains almost everything a proper Queue should have, except printing messages. The only message specific for Queues is **remove (add** already exists in **OrderedCollection**).

There is a difference in the implementations of **Stack** and **Queue**. The top of **Stack** is the element with the highest ordinal number, while the top of **Queue** is element 1. But that does not really matter. Both classes function correctly as they are.

Class **Queue** is very general. It needs to know more about simulations to be useful in discrete simulations programs. Let us create a descendant class **SimulationQueue**.

5.19 QUEUEING SYSTEMS AND CLASS SimulationQueue

There are many systems in which entities 'move' to and from various parts of the system. For example, all traffic systems, all systems that pass messages (PTT), computers, banking transactions, and so on. They are very common and are frequently simulated. The moving entity is called a 'transaction', which is a term borrowed from the world of finance. Anything in the system that changes states, anything that forces actions, events about to happen, can be regarded as a transaction.

To every transaction we attach a series of parameters. A parameter is usually either an attribute or a statistic. There is no limit to the number of parameters; it only depends on what system performances we want to observe. Attributes keep track of where in the system the transaction is, but usually the aim of a simulation is to find out how many time units a transaction has spent in certain states. Therefore, transaction statistics are updated whenever a transaction passes from one state to another.

Since transactions are practically identical to events, it is also customary to talk of 'critical events' instead of 'transactions with defined execution times'.

The essence of every queueing system is a server which is too busy to accommodate everybody and everything at once. Therefore, some waiting occurs in front of the server—a queue forms. The nature of server and transactions (entities waiting to be served) varies wildly: a ticket booth and people eager to see a new film or show; a aircraft and its passengers; an airport runway and planes waiting to land or take off; a time-sharing computer and terminals; CPU and multitasking programs.... Examples abound. Whenever you wait, you are a part of a 'queueing system'.

Once in a queue, a transaction is waiting to reach the desired server facility (repair, reserves, ticket booth, etc.). Waiting implies two questions: (1) Which particular transaction is drawn out of the queue? and (2) How the timings of critical events are generated? We devote class **SimulationQueue** to these issues. It defines operations on queues, i.e. how a selected unit transits from the queue to the server, the timing of a next critical event, and other similar events.

Critical events are taken care of by any of the two top-level designs that we have already considered.

A queue discipline is a criterion by which a waiting transaction proceeds to the service. The following disciplines are common:

LIFO, Last In, First Out (trays in a cafeteria),
FIFO, First In, First Out (a customer at the supermarket checkout counter),
Random discipline, the 'next' transaction is picked up in a random manner. The probability is equal for all transactions, as for example the drawing of a ticket at a raffle,
Priority discipline, any transaction attribute can be a basis for priority: the shortest or the longest waiting time, transaction type, the easiest letter to answer, or anything else, such as the shortest or the fastest road between two cities in a network.

Fig. 5.5 shows several queue disciplines.
Class **SimulationQueue** implements them:

Queue variableSubclass: #SimulationQueue
instanceVariableNames:

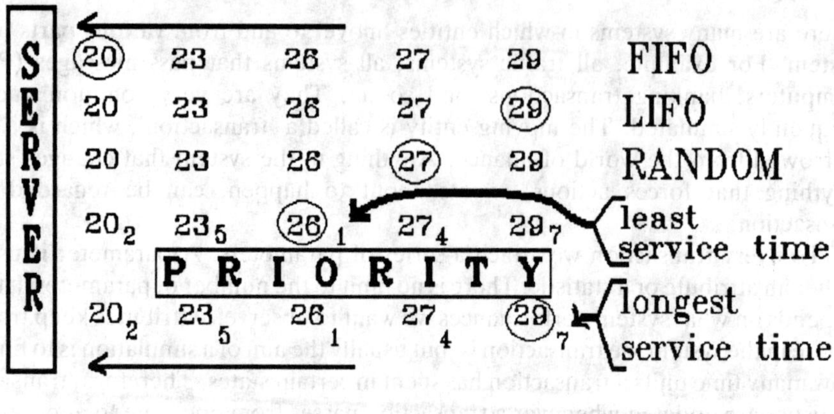

Fig. 5.5 — Queueing disciplines.

```
    'sd randomNumber disciplineName selectedDiscipline tagged '
  classVariableNames: ''
  poolDictionaries: '' !
!SimulationQueue class methods ! !
!SimulationQueue methods !
disciplineName
 ^disciplineName!
disciplineName: aValue
 ^disciplineName at: aValue!
fifo
 ^tagged := (self at: self size) "Answer the very last"!
initialize: aPoint
randomNumber := RandomNumber new.
randomNumber lowerBound: aPoint x;
                upperBound: aPoint y;
                initialize.
disciplineName := OrderedCollection new.
disciplineName add: 'FIFO'.
disciplineName add: 'LIFO'.
disciplineName add: 'Random'.
disciplineName add: 'Priority, shortest service time'.
disciplineName add: 'Priority, longest service time'.!
lifo "Stack discipline"
 ^tagged := (self at: 1) "Answer the very first."!
longestServiceTime
 ^tagged := self max!
random "Take transaction at will."
    | md |
md := randomNumber next truncated.
[(md between: 1 and: self size)]
```

```
        whileFalse: [
            md := randomNumber next truncated. ].
tagged := (self at: md).
 ^tagged!
remove
self remove: tagged ifAbsent: [ ^nil ].!
sd: aValue
sd := aValue!
selectDiscipline
selectedDiscipline := disciplineName at: sd.
sd = 1 ifTrue: [ self fifo ].
sd = 2 ifTrue: [ self lifo ].
sd = 3 ifTrue: [ self random ].
sd = 4 ifTrue: [ self shortestServiceTime ].
sd = 5 ifTrue: [ self longestServiceTime ].!
selectedDiscipline
 ^selectedDiscipline!
selectedDiscipline: aValue
selectedDiscipline:= aValue!
shortestServiceTime
 ^tagged := self min! !
```

5.20 COMMENTS ON CLASS SimulationQueue

The central methods are **fifo, lifo, random, longestServiceTime** and **shortestServiceTime**. Each is a specific way of deleting an element from the queue. All of them keep the index of the requested element in variable **tagged**. Only the method **remove** uses **tagged** to actually remove anything.

Method random loops over a series of random numbers in order to ensure that the generated number is in the current queue range.

These three methods locate an element according to its position in the queue. The remaining two methods actually look into the element value. It can mean anything, but in a queueing system it is convenient that the element is duration of service time. In other words, the numbers in queue tell how long the server will be occupied. Minimal or maximal strategies are usual; therefore methods **shortestServiceTime** and **longestServiceTime** just take the minimal or maximal element of the queue. Note the remarkable conciseness of the code of these two methods.

Important class instance variables are **randomNumber** and **disciplineName. randomNumber** serves only in method **random**, to select a random queue element, while **disciplineName** is an array of the distributions names. Method **selectDiscipline:** selects the criterion and calls the appropriate method (**fifo, lifo, random, shortestServiceTime, longestServiceTime**).

5.21 ANIMATED QUEUEING SYSTEM

This will be the simplest possible queueing system. There are no transactions here. The system has two parts: a queue and a server. They are represented in Fig. 5.6 as a

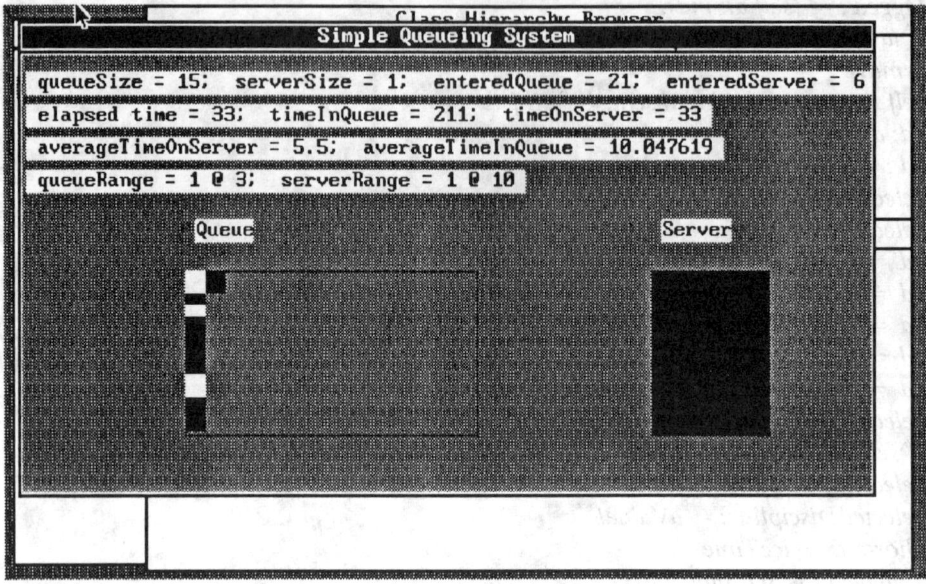

Fig. 5.6 — An output from the **AnimatedQueueingSystem**.

pair of boxes. To both, something comes and from both, something goes away. Queue elements (customers) come in random time intervals, join the queue and remain there as long as they are not withdrawn from it. Queue output is server input. There are many ways of selecting the queue element that will continue to the server, but in this model it boils down to a pure random distribution.

The aim of this simulation is to gather system statistics — how many customers entered the queue, were served by server, how much time was spent there, average time waiting in the queue, how long was the overall waiting, and the like.

There are two simulation designs, one that checks events in every clock movement and the other with future-event chains. The former is easier to implement, so let us decide to use that. We already know that there will be one main loop with IF statements dispersed within. Here is the algorithm:

Algorithm: Single-queue, single-server system

(1) Initialize variables to hold statistics; initialize random number generators for queue input and server-starting service times.

Start a loop:

(2) Create new customer.

(3) Schedule for new arrival, for some later time.

(4) If the server is free and there is someone in the queue, remove a customer from the queue and let it go to the server. Update server statistics.

(5) Update timing statistics.
End loop.
(6) Print the statistics.

The algorithm remains the same regardless of the language and programming environment. But Smalltalk/V windows and graphics facilities suggest creating a graphics window and some kind of animation. A GraphPane window is the expected choice. The class name is long but appropriate: **AnimatedQueueingSystem**. Here it is:

```
Object subclass: #AnimatedQueueingSystem
  instanceVariableNames:
    'elSize elNum elForm elPos scanner queuePane aRect
    pen queueRectangle serverRectangle '
  classVariableNames: ''
  poolDictionaries: '' !
!AnimatedQueueingSystem class methods ! !
!AnimatedQueueingSystem methods !
activate: aPoint
        |simulationEnd
        rnEnter tsEnter
        serverSize queueSize
        enteredServer enteredQueue
        timeInQueue timeOnServer
        averageTimeOnServer averageTimeInQueue
        s sLen ts tn upperLeft queueRange serverRange |
CursorManager execute change.
simulationEnd := 33. "Duration"
queueRange := 1 @ 3.
serverRange := 1 @ 10.
rnEnter := RandomNumber new.
rnEnter lowerBound: queueRange x; "Queue range"
         upperBound: queueRange y;
         initialize.
tsEnter := RandomNumber new.
tsEnter lowerBound: serverRange x; "Server range"
        upperBound: serverRange y;
        initialize.
queueSize := 0.
serverSize := 0.
enteredServer := 0.
enteredQueue := 0.
timeInQueue := 0.
timeOnServer := 0.
"Main program loop."
tn := rnEnter next truncated. "First arrival."
ts := tsEnter next truncated. "First service."
1 to: simulationEnd do: [ :time |
```

```
    tn = time
      ifTrue: [ "Join the queue."
                self toQueue.
                queueSize := queueSize + 1.
                enteredQueue := enteredQueue + 1.
      ].
    tn := time + (rnEnter next truncated). "Next arrival."
    ts = time "Server time."
      ifTrue: [ serverSize := 0. self fromServer. ].
    serverSize = 0
      ifTrue: [
        queueSize > 0
          ifTrue: [
            self fromQueue.
            self toServer.
            queueSize := queueSize - 1.
            serverSize := 1.
            ts := time + (tsEnter next truncated).
            enteredServer := enteredServer + 1.
            ].
      ].
    "Calculate statistics."
    timeInQueue := timeInQueue + queueSize.
    timeOnServer := timeOnServer + serverSize.
    ].
  averageTimeOnServer := timeOnServer / enteredServer.
  averageTimeInQueue := timeInQueue / enteredQueue.
  upperLeft := queuePane frame origin.
  s := (' queueSize = ', queueSize printString), '; ',
       (' serverSize = ', serverSize printString), '; ',
       (' enteredQueue = ', enteredQueue printString), '; ',
       (' enteredServer = ', enteredServer printString), ' '.
  self printString: s
      at: ( upperLeft + (3 @ 10)).
  s := (' elapsed time = ', simulationEnd printString), '; ',
       (' timeInQueue = ', timeInQueue printString), '; ',
       (' timeOnServer = ', timeOnServer printString), ' '.
  self printString: s
      at: ( upperLeft + (3 @ 30)).
  s := (' averageTimeOnServer = ',
           (1.0 * averageTimeOnServer) printString), '; ',
       (' averageTimeInQueue = ',
           (1.0 * averageTimeInQueue) printString), ' '.
  self printString: s
      at: ( upperLeft + (3 @ 50)).
  s := (' queueRange = ', queueRange printString), '; ',
       (' serverRange = ', serverRange printString), ' '.
```

```
self printString: s
    at: ( upperLeft + (3 @ 70)).
CursorManager normal change.!
drawQueue
    "Draw a rectangle that is a queue
    and stick it to the queuePane."
queueRectangle := (100 @ 100) + queuePane frame origin
        corner: ((300 @ 200) + queuePane frame origin).
self drawRectangle: queueRectangle.!
drawRectangle: r
pen place: r origin;
    goto: r corner x @ r origin y;
    goto: r corner x @ r corner y;
    goto: r origin x @ r corner y;
    goto: r origin.!
drawServer
    "Draw a rectangle that is a queue
    and stick it to the queuePane."
serverRectangle :=
      (420 @ 100) + queuePane frame origin
        corner: ((500 @ 200) + queuePane frame origin).
self drawRectangle: serverRectangle.!
fromQueue
    "Erase a queue element graphically."
    | temp5 temp6 |
elNum := elNum - 1.
temp5 := elNum - elSize.
temp6 := elNum quo: elSize.
elForm white displayAt: (elPos at: temp5 at: temp6).!
fromServer
    "Erase server graphically."
    | temp5 |
temp5 := Form width: serverRectangle width
                height: serverRectangle height.
temp5 copy: (serverRectangle origin
temp5 white displayAt: serverRectangle origin +
              (queuePane frame origin).!
initialize: aaRect
    | temp1 temp2 temp3 temp4 |
CursorManager execute change.
elSize := 14.
aRect := Form new
            width: queuePane frame width
            height: queuePane frame height;
            white.
aRect gray.
scanner := CharacterScanner new
```

```
        initialize: aaRect
        font: SysFont.
pen := Pen new: aRect.
pen black; down.
self drawQueue; drawServer.
aRect displayAt: queuePane frame origin.
self labelQueue; labelServer.
elNum := 0.
temp1 := (queueRectangle width) // elSize.
temp2 := (queueRectangle height) // elSize.
elForm := Form width: temp1 height: temp2.
elForm black.
temp3 := (queueRectangle origin x) + (queuePane frame origin x).
temp4 := (queueRectangle origin y) + (queuePane frame origin y).
elPos := EnhancedMatrix new: (0 @ elSize) with: (0 @ elSize).
0 to: elSize do: [ :i |
  0 to: elSize do: [ :j |
    elPos at: i at: j
      put: (
        (temp3 + (j * temp1))
        @
        (temp4 + (i * temp2))
        )
      ].
    ].
CursorManager normal change.
 ^aRect!
labelQueue
self labelQueue: 'Queue'.!
labelQueue: aString
self printString: aString
    at: queueRectangle origin + (20 @ 0)!
labelServer
self labelServer: 'Server'.!
labelServer: aString
self printString: aString
    at: serverRectangle origin + (20 @ 0)..!
menu
 ^Menu
    labels: 'Nothing' withCrs
    lines: Array new
    selectors: #(noOp)!
noOp
    "No operation."! |
open
self openOn: ( 10 @ 10 corner: 600 @ 300)!
openOn: aRectangle
```

```
    | aTopPane |
    aTopPane := TopPane new
                label: 'Simple Queueing System'.
    aTopPane addSubpane:
    (queuePane := GraphPane new
            model: self;
            name: #initialize:;

            change: #activate:;
            menu: menu;
            framingRatio: (0 @ 0 extent: 1 @ 1) ).
    aTopPane reframe: aRectangle.
    aTopPane dispatcher openWindow scheduleWindow!
printString: aString at: cursorOffset
scanner
  display: aString
  from: 1
  to: aString size
  at: cursorOffset - scanner frame origin!
toQueue
    "Show a new queue element graphically."
temp5 temp6
elNum := elNum + 1.
temp5 := elNum \\ elSize.
temp6 := elNum quo: elSize.
elForm black displayAt: (elPos at: temp5 at: temp6).!
toServer
    "Erase server graphically."
    | temp5 |
temp5 := Form width: serverRectangle width
                height: serverRectangle height.
temp5 displayAt: serverRectangle origin +
                    (queuePane frame origin).! !
```

5.22 COMMENTS ON CLASS AnimatedQueueingSystem

The main procedure is in method **activate**:. It implements both the above algorithm and its graphical presentation. The graphics are nothing fancy: two Rectangles representing the queue and the server. The queue rectangle fills with small Forms, thus visually depicting the customers. Black indicates the presence of a customer in a particular position within the queue; white is a queue vacancy.

The box on the right is the server. Its colours alternate black and white to show whether it is busy or not.

When the simulation time has expired, the results are written onto the same GraphPane and remain in view if the window is resized or moved to another position on the sceen.

Variables **rnEnter** and **tsEnter** are random number generators. They generate random numbers in ranges that are kept in variables **queueRange** and **serverRange**. These are actually Points, but only because it is the most concise syntax for a pair of numbers. The ranges are the main means of playing with the model. In this particular case, customers arrive every one, two or three time units while the server takes much longer (up to ten time units) to do whatever it is that it does in this model. Without Smalltalk/V and even without a computer we can expect rather a crowd here!

Variables **queueRectangle** and **serverRectangle** are Rectangles. To draw a Rectangle, obviously, we have to place it upon a surface, or, in Smalltalk/V terms, upon a Form. There is just one subpane in the **AnimatedQueueingSystem** window. Since it is of type **TopPane**, we cannot access it directly as a Form. Instead, we create a Form which is exactly of the same dimensions as the GraphPane.

Method **initialize:** contains that code. Its input is a Rectangle called **aaRect**. We create a Form called **aRect** on which we shall consequently draw everything. Variable **pen** is a Pen. It is defined in **initialize:** but is actually used later, in method **drawRectangle:**. Therefore, it has to be an instance variable, global for the whole class.

Methods **drawQueue** and **drawServer** draw the Rectangles that represent the queue and the server. Both call upon **drawRectangle:** for actual drawing. Normally, one would expect a method that draws a **Rectangle** to be a message defined in class **Rectangle**. If this were a real program, that would be the way to go. The advantage would be that all other classes could use it freely. But, there are two counter arguments. First, for the purposes of this book, it is better that all the code is in one class (it is easier for me to explain things that way). Second, the amount of coding is about the same. There are actually two parameters: the Rectangle to draw and the Form on which to draw. Even if **drawRectangle:** were part of another class, it would still need to spell out the second argument, the Form **aRect** which the class **AnimatedQueueingSystem** already knows about. All in all, these are two equal choices in coding style.

Definitions of the **serverRectangle** and **queueRectangle** are interesting. Both contain a phrase **queuePane frame origin** to offset them into the pane. Were that missing, the Rectangles would not transfer properly when resizing and moving the complete **AnimatedQueueingSystem window**.

The drawings are thus a consistent part of the window. So should be the labels and results — more precisely, the text that spells them out. We had textual labels before (ranges in class **DrawCurveWindow**) but they were put on the screen in a rather crude way, through a **displayAt:** message. This writes directly to **Display**, that is, directly to the screen, erasing its contents. Such strings appear as white letters on black. They are not part of the Form of the **AnimatedQueueingSystem** window but are a part of another Form, the **Display**. In this class, we write directly to the window's Form.

So what? The only visible difference is that the letters will be black on white (or whatever the colour of the queuePane's Form is). This looks better but only marginally. The main advantage of this new technique is that we can specify a quite different font for our window. Moreover, every window can have its own font, quite independently. If you think of writing an application that has to use different fonts, then Smalltalk/V is the best choice. Later in this book I'll give you a class for editing fonts, so you can easily put this advantage to work for you.

Technically, all fonts are based on two arrays. One is the array of ASCII codes, saying for example that number 65 corresponds to letter A. The other array is an array of pictures representing the letter. Smalltalk/V Forms are a convenient way of playing the role of such pictures. Class Font contains just such Forms, together with some additional information about them. But the actual connection between the number of a letter and its visual representation is in another class, **CharacterScanner**. You must have an instance of that class if you want to write normally on a GraphPane (or on any Pane, for that matter). In this class, such a variable is called **scanner**.

scanner has two input parameters: a Rectangle to which the output will be bound and a font according to which the letters will be shaped. There are four system fonts in Smalltalk/V but the most profound is **SysFont**, so that is what we use. There is only one method in **AnimatedQueueingSystem** devoted to the scanner, called **printString:at:**. It displays a string at the given position. Note the phrase **scanner frame origin**, which again offsets from the current **queuePane** screen position. Several other methods build upon the **printString:at:** method directly (**labelServer:**, **labelQueue:**, **activate:**) or indirectly (**labelServer**, **labelQueue**).

Provided you have already prepared some new font for use, you need only declare **scanner** with that font instead of **SysFont**. Everything else is the same. Using existing fonts is so easy in Smalltalk/V.

I'll admit that animation in this class is not all that it could be. However, class **Animation** is very well explained in the manual and there is the demo option in the main system menu, so there is not much point in repeating it all here. The graphics in this program just emphasize the events in the queue. The queue itself is represented as a Rectangle, so smaller Rectangles fit in nicely. That is why customers are represented through an instance variable **elForm**. Internally, the **queueRectangle** is divided into an EnhancedMatrix (we need these zero matrix elements for rectangle boundaries) of rectangle coordinates. Methods **toQueue** and **fromQueue** put **elForm** into **queueRectangle**. The only difference is in colour: **toQueue** draws a 'customer' (**elForm** in black), while **fromQueue** puts a white **elForm** somewhere into the queue to show the vacancy.

Variable **elNum** is the 'next' absolute position that should be occupied by the incoming customer. It corresponds to the usual notion of a queue as that of a waiting line. But the queue in this case is a Rectangle, so the 'line' has to be broken into bins whose origins correspond to elements of enhanced matrix **elPos**. Black and white instances of **elForm** fill the bins. The actual drawing is due to the **displayAt:** message at the end of **toQueue**, **fromQueue**, **toServer**, and **fromServer**. Temporary variables act as indices into **elPos**.

5.23 CONCLUSION

This chapter is no more than an introduction to writing discrete simulations in Smalltalk/V. It gives the tools to do the job but does not elaborate on the simulation techniques themselves. That would fill another book. If all you want is to write simulations, then Smalltalk/V will fill the bill magnificently.

PROBLEMS

5.1 Consider your favourite computer game and try to figure out how many random processes are built into it?

5.2 Can you treat a full page of text as a table of random letters? Can a page of text be a uniform generator? Do all letters occur with the same frequency in text?

5.3 Make an array of 10–20 strings with descriptions of the various organs of an extraterrestrial being. Use random numbers to generate several descriptions of aliens, and see which of them is the most horrible.

5.4 Many other random generators are possible. The linear congruential method can be replaced by a quadratic congruential method:

$$r_{i+1} = \text{mod}(ar_i^2 + br_i + c, m) .$$

It has been proved that this method can produce proper random numbers.

5.5 Introduce alternating finite and infinite queues in front of the queue of the **AnimatedQueueingSystem** class.

5.6 Give several examples of real systems to which the class **AnimatedQueueing-System** can be applied.

5.7 Devise a series of random numbers that are exponentially distributed and draw the corresponding histogram.

5.8 Both exponential and Erlang distributions belong to the family of Gamma distributions. Make a new class for Gamma distributions. Where should it be in the class hierarchy?

5.9 Demonstrate that the normal distribution is really a good approximation of most other distributions when the population size exceeds 30.

5.10 Is it always possible to apply inverse distribution methods? What about the numerical solution of the equation that arises in the inverse distribution methods. Is is practical?

5.11 What is the connection between the chi-square test and the normal distribu-tion?

5.12 Use **Stack** to add numbers in Reverse Polish Notation.

5.13 Use **Stack** to implement recursive computations.

5.14 Make a graphical representation of one real CPU (8088, Z80, 8088) and its stacks.

5.15 Simulate a time-sharing computer system. It usually consists of a CPU, main memory, selector channels that lead to auxiliary storage and control units, and multiplexors for terminals. The auxiliary storage and terminals compete for CPU attention. If the CPU is busy doing something else, a queue forms. There can be several such queues at any time. The goal of the simulation project is to see how many terminals the system can carry, or 'conversely' — the quantity of the storage that the system must have in order to satisfy all the attached terminals.

5.16 Simulate a light-controlled traffic intersection. The goal of the simulation would be to see the length of time the motorists spend waiting at the intersection. The performance of the intersection would be measured by the average and maximum waiting times experienced by the motorists.

5.17 Create special windows for the two previous simulations. Use class **Animation** to enhance visual impact.

6

Elements of a building schedule program

6.1 LANGUAGES AND APPLICATIONS PROGRAMMING

How do we choose a programming language to write a specific type of program? Many factors influence that decision. Considering language factors only, you can select from:

— languages to which you have access,
— languages that you already know,
— languages that you might find most suitable for the job.

The choice of languages on personal computers is overwhelming. Practically all languages of any importance are available. The real choice is between the languages that you know and the languages that you only know to be suitable for the purpose. This can be tantalizing, but the reward for writing the program in it may be so great that you decide to learn a new language.

Is Smalltalk/V good enough for writing a commercial program? Are there programs that cannot be written with Smalltalk/V? What will the finished program look like? Will the speed be adequate? Will the program be transportable across operating systems and machines? If I take the plunge into Smalltalk/V, what do I gain?

These are the questions that any serious programmer ought to ask, though I admit that I did not pose them to myself in the beginning. I was simply seduced by Smalltalk/V graphics, menu and mouse control, windows, and carefree memory allocation. I reckoned that whatever program I write it will be, somehow, *automatically beautiful*, without any effort on my part. Little did I care what I was throwing myself into. After long hours, days, weeks, months (and years!) I now know how to write a meaningful Smalltalk/V program. In this chapter I want to share that knowledge with you.

At times I was desperate. At times I was ecstatic. Most of the time I was extremely productive. The Billings Schedule (BS) program was written within six months. It took several thousand lines to demonstrate its capabilities. The main program interface was changed no fewer than four times! And, typically, there were false leads like the following one. One potential user suggested that BS should have a means of direct calculation of numbers. The clerks that routinely create billings schedules without the computer calculate all day long with hand-held calculators, and write down the result on paper for further calculation. So our potential customer casually mentioned the word 'calculator'. I took it as a serious end-user request and spent three weeks conceiving, writing, debugging and testing a window which emulates a pocket calculator. That window remained as one of the BS's 'fortes' until several months later when another potential end-user said something like: 'OK, it can calculate and I do want that, but only in such a way that all the input values can be checked'. And that was, in all probability, the true intention of the first suggestion. Unfortunately, the wrong word was mentioned . . . so I simply erased a month of my life.

The calculator was left out of the program, but nevertheless it turns up later in this chapter, quite intact!. And the beauty of Smalltalk/V is that you can key it in, and use it without any change in any of your other projects. All your programs from now on can have a simulation of an RPN hand-held calculator, with even more programming power than in the original! Not to mention that all your programs can use the already delivered windows for freehand drawing and file/directory browsing!

A Smalltalk/V application is best organized as a series of autonomous windows. Windows are separate objects and that is the secret of reusability. One class is allocated to every window. Of course, every class will depend on many other classes, but, conceptually, it is just the 'one window, one object, one class' approach. This concept has a tremendous practical influence on how you write Smalltalk/V programs. The end-user design should consist of as many windows as you need. When you write all those windows, the application is finished. And how do you create a window? You simply

(1) write the code to create a window,
(2) create its subpanes (if more than one),
(3) assign a method attached to the left mouse button,
(4) assign menus to all subpanes,
(5) write one method per option from those menus,
(6) create internal data structures to augment those methods, and
(7) write private methods to manipulate the internal data structures.

This is a fixed methodology for writing a window. And just because it is fixed, programming in Smalltalk/V is an easy, routine activity.

You'll frequently hear a phrase 'prototype programming' in connection with Smalltalk/V. It is a direct consequence of the fact that steps (1)–(4) are taken so easily that you almost immediately come up with the finished application, with one difference: the code for options is not yet written. And that is exactly what a prototype is — a program in which only the user interface is programmed, without any real code behind it. Old hands might like to compare this programming methodology with the 'stubs' method for program testing and debugging. The empty 'options' methods act as stubs.

The benefits of this approach are immense. For example, you can show the program to your end-user and receive swift feedback. Once your end-user approves the design, you can go on coding and the program should be finished in no time at all.

Technically, steps (1)–(4) are all placed in one method. By convention, it is called

openOn: — we've already seen many such methods in this book. Internal data structures are instance variables (globals for a class) while windows share data through class or global Smalltalk/V variables. Alternatively, the data can be shared through disk files. Finally, an application is a series of windows. This poses a natural question:

(1) should you design a window and immediately write its internal code, then design another window and write its internal code and so on, or
(2) should you design all the windows first and only then write the corresponding code, in classes?

You'll soon discover that your productivity will be even greater if you adopt the second approach, that is, 'design all, code all'.

6.2 Smalltalk/V AND SOFTWARE CATEGORIES

The most important software categories are:

— operating systems,
— word processors,
— utilities,
— databases,
— spreadsheets,
— communications,
— integrated programs,
— CAD,
— games and others.

How does Smalltalk/V rate in these categories? In other words, what would be better and more easily written in Smalltalk/V than in other languages? Let us analyse how software categories relate to Smalltalk/V.

Operating systems

From the very beginning, Smalltalk was intended to be not only a language but a complete environment for the end-user. Could you make Smalltalk/V an operating system for PC computers? Actually, you could. It is possible to unload the complete Smalltalk/V (except some 37K) to disk, invoke a new copy of COMMAND.COM and run any program. So far no one appears to have done this seriously. For one thing, there aren't any real advantages although the capacity exists. In one of the additional Goodies packages for Smalltalk/V and in the Smalltalk/V286 right from the start you can find multitasking classes. It would be interesting to see whether a meaningful operating system could be made out of the Smalltalk/V286 version, since it treats extended memory in a linear fashion.

By the way, Digitalk, the maker of all Smalltalk/V versions, has an interesting policy: Smalltalk/V never takes over the host operating system but, instead, uses the hosts's own graphics and windowing facilities. So on Macintosh computers you get Macintosh windows and under Presentation Manager you get PM windows, all from (almost) the same source code.

But many more services are expected from an operating system: computer resources allocation, underlying file system, easy data interchange between applications, and so on. Even if you had all that, it would still take a major commercial backer for this idea, to be accepted by the millions of users and potential users.

One of the options in the main BS menu will be '**goto to DOS**'. This illustrates the techniques of leaving Smalltalk/V in favour of another program.

Word processors

Smalltalk/V would be an ideal language to write any kind of word processor, provided the hardware platform is at least an XT with a clock of 10 MHz or greater. Of course, on AT, 386, 486, 680x0 and other more powerful computers and CPUs, Smalltalk/V makes an even better contender.

You already have most of the text editor code within TextPane windows, not to mention the mouse. To make it a decent editor or word processor, you only need to link the keyboard to editing commands. The link between the screen, the keyboard and the commands that the user wants executed is divided among three different classes. (In the BS program we shall see a complete example. That knowledge was particularly difficult to grasp!)

Apart from this, it would take a lot of code to reach the quality of any commercial word processing tool, not to mention the drivers needed for screen adapters and printers. And yet, it would be easier to complete a word processor from Smalltalk/V as delivered than from scratch using other languages.

Utilities

For DOS users, the class of utility programs actually means levelling out the deficiencies of the DOS itself: denoting multiple files for one operation (copying, deleting, moving), killing directories, listing and printing files, and the like. Smalltalk/V has a special windowing class for browsing files and it can be a part of every application that you write. This is very important, because it enables you to do DOS chores without ever leaving the application program.

Other than that, a utility could be a program for any technical service that you need: file conversions and comparisons, backups, global replacements and deletions, cryptography, etc. All of this can be written in Smalltalk/V, just as in any other programming language. The only difference is that you would have to initiate the utility from the Smalltalk/V environment itself, rather than directly from DOS.

Such utilities often take the form of TSR programs — memory-resident programs under DOS. I do not know how a TSR program could be produced from Smalltalk/V. If you want to create TSRs under DOS, then look somewhere else. That is not to say that Smalltalk/V won't work with TSRs from other sources. Smalltalk/V under DOS co-exists with different cache emulators and other TSR software written in other languages, but note that TSRs are a peculiarity of DOS. In other operating systems they are replaced by true multitasking utility programs.

Databases

There are at least three different ways of thinking and writing databases in Smalltalk/V terms:

— object-oriented databases,
— using data from the already existing databases (dBASE format, in particular), and
— writing classical databases anew.

Object-oriented databases have two important ingredients: data persistence and inheritance. Data persistence is a logical extension of any object-oriented language. Inheritance would mean that the end-user can inherit data types (records) and the data themselves from the already existing (and probably persistent) data.

Reading and writing data in popular file formats is a practical necessity. Time and other resources permitting, there is no reason why you couldn't write those routines from scratch. But for other languages (Modula-2 and C, most notably) functions or modules to read and write data in dBASE, Lotus 1-2-3 and other formats are offered. In the Goodies 1 package there is a class to connect Smalltalk/V with any BIOS call and DOS service, which means that it is possible to call them from Smalltalk/V itself. Perhaps the best use of Smalltalk/V is to serve as a front-end processor, leaving it to the routines from other languages to do the job in a straightforward manner.

Finally, writing a database anew in Smalltalk/V is, in many aspects, easier than in C or similar languages. Any database program is primarily a data editor. And as in any editor, it must have ways to read and write data to the output medium, to organize data input, search, change, insertion and removal. As stated before, the best strategy in Smalltalk/V is to make a separate window for any such editor. Then, armed with inheritance — you can generate as many different database editors as you like. In practice, this means adding only what is different (names of data records, window labels, etc.).

Incidentally, this would solve one of the worst problems that one may encounter in database programming: rewriting essentially similar programs all over again. Database programmers end up with dozens of algorithmically identical programs except for a few lines here and there. They usually copy large segments of source code (at that moment the database programmer wonders if he should switch to a programming editor, with several windows, separate compilation, etc.) and create different program files, indeed different programs for one and the same main program menu.

Writing databases in Smalltalk/V could be easier than in other languages. Additional Goodies packs contain special classes for creation of screen masks, making it possible to input every record field one per line, just as with other data managers.

The other side of the coin is, of course, the speed of data retrieval. For a start, simple OrderedCollections of records will work as underlying data structures for the database. Whether there should be a need for a change later remains to be judged in each particular case. For example, if you organize a database using 2 megabytes of central memory with Smalltalk/V286 or under PM, you will be able to hold hundreds of kilobytes of data directly in memory. Should that be expected on an AT type of computer (or even on faster ones), in all probability a simple linear search will be quite efficacious.

All in all, simple and complicated databases can be created more easily with

Smalltalk/V than with other languages, not to mention the fact that the system automatically takes care of memory allocation and deallocation. A fairly simple database of text lines lies at the core of BS.

Spreadsheets

The beauty of a spreadsheet program is that the internals of that application closely follow the external visual impact on the user. On screen, it is a matrix (table) of numbers or text. In memory, it is also a matrix, a well-known data structure. This book gives many types of 'ready-to-go' matrices.

While on the subject of user interface, it is worth mentioning that one of the Goodies packages contains a window with cells — an ideal front end for our present purpose. Connect the two and you have a rudimentary spreadsheet!

Communications

This is already available. Digitalk markets a communications program, with separate windows for comms services.

CAD

Designing a CAD program is an entirely different matter. You typically need an internal database of geometric objects and a display file (actually, another database of instructions that the program will interpret and thus draw). The main problems of user interface are already solved for you if you take the already existing **FreeDrawing** class as a starting point and add the graphics commands that you need. It goes without saying that you can create your own windows (as demonstrated in this book) for various graphics displays.

There is a three-dimensional editor in one of the Goodies.

Games

Smalltalk/V is ideal for adventure games. Should you want to write a fantasy game with dwarves, men, trolls, goblins, elves, orcs, and the like, you could create a genealogy class, relating all of them to one archetype. Such a creature could have two legs, two arms, one head, a body, — and that's about all it would need. From there you could inherit, add or block the number of eyes in the head, the character, the weapons, magic capabilities, current position, sense of direction, etc. Another object you would probably need would be a window to display the map, what the character carries with him, the energy score, and the like. Such a window would also handle communication with the user. With the **FreeDrawing** window you could easily draw the scenery, and on faster machines you could use the **Animation** class to show fighting duels . . . .

You would have to consider many other objects, for example, the building in which the action takes place. Nevertheless, Smalltalk/V gives you all you need for writing quality fantasy games. But writing arcade games on slower machines (XT) is not recommended — too much graphics slows everything to the point of impractibility.

Integrated programs
Create all the above windows (one or more per type), make them interchange data if necessary and, voila! — you have an integrated program — with games!!

As a conclusion, the biggest advantage of Smalltalk/V is that it elevates programming from machine level to application level. The Smalltalk/V programmer does not think in terms of bytes, ports, dots, memory addresses, program interrupts, and the like. He or she could and should think in terms of windows, prompters, menus, panes, text editors, lists, figures, ordered collections, matrices, and so on. The Smalltalk/V programmer immediately thinks in the same terms as the end-user.

6.3 THE BILLINGS SCHEDULE SPECIFICATION

Let us see what ideas lie behind an original application in Smalltalk/V. Please note that this is an *attempt* to write a commercial program, that is, a program that tries to guess what the needs of a broad class of users are. It is one thing to write a 'commercial' program in a theoretical sense, and quite another to make it commercially viable. At the time of writing, I was looking for a publisher .... If you see it advertised somewhere, you'll know I made it!

The acid test of a general programming language is its ability to produce a real-life application. The effort of writing a new program is usually undertaken only if the appliation is not satisfed by typical software categories. What application would be suitable? I chose one particularly important but mundane task in all technical projects - a billings schedule. Say, you were a builder starting work on a building: you would know what materials are required for the project and you would have a list of current prices. Since a labour force of tradesmen is required, you also need to know what wages you must pay. The total cost comprises the cost of materials and the cost of labour. Once you fill in all the positions (descriptions in words or pictures, with quantities and prices per unit), you can compute the final sum and see where you stand. Then you can increase or 'mark up' the total to allow room for contingencies and profits. You might want to do that when tendering for a new construction deal, for example. Not all the materials are actually available all the time, so the Billings Schedule program should allow for quick changes in quantities and prices, both for materials and for labour.

The printout should look reasonably impressive and professional. Printing by means of ASCII characters often won't do since in many technical applications (in thermodynamics, for example) many crucial items are coefficients conventionally expressed in Greek. Such a program should be useful to engineers all over the world and not only in English-speaking countries. It would be shortsighted to develop a program that could not be sold only because it could not be printed in French or Russian! There is a definite need for different sets of characters in this program — both on the screen and on the printer. (Epson-compatible printers will do.)

Foreign character sets do not terminate the printing specification. Engineers are used to having those billings schedules printed as neat forms, with headers or footers (or both) on each page, so that the company and the purpose of a billings schedule are clearly defined. After the data are filled in (text, drawings, prices and calculation) it may turn out that the normal portrait mode is not wide enough. It is essential that all the figures (which mean money!) are visible, so printing in a sideways fashion (landscape mode) is not just an idle wish.

Finally, the program should be easy to use — whatever that means. A good way to make such a program is to build uniform rules for conversation with the program. One such rule, notably enforced by Smalltalk itself, is that all commands should be visible in menus. The menus should be easy to invoke, too.

The Billings Schedule program is thus a blend of a drawing program, a spreadsheet, a database, a data entry program, word processing (confined to lines only in input but block oriented in exploitation) and so on. You could do parts of it with existing programs but you can't draw symbols for doors and windows with a word processor and you can hardly add two numbers in a drawing program. In other words, there is a definite need for a separate, new program.

Before anything else, I must emphasize that what follow are only excerpts from the real thing. There is about 140K of source code in the full version of the Billings Schedule and that simply cannot be put into this book — any book. I'll give as much of the code as is meaningful but the accent is on solving technical problems that arise from predefined objects in the Smalltalk/V system, most notably, from windows and panes. Don't worry: once you get the knack of it, Smalltalk/V fulfils its promise — relatively easy writing of beautiful and powerful programs.

Some of this information has really been won the hard way and I am happy I can share it with others — you can *inherit* it from this book, if you'll forgive that object-oriented buzzword! On some occasions I shall reveal how I arrived at the code presented here. By no means did it fall from thin air!

6.4 THE GENERAL APPROACH

Since we are using Smalltalk/V, we should think in terms of objects from the very start. But as everything can be an object, we have to consider other factors. We can start with the user — what he sees, in what ways he controls the system, and so on. Smalltalk/V provides windows as the main means of communicating with the user. Therefore, our first concern is to make a window through which the user can interact with the main program variables. The complete application will then consist of a series of windows that somehow — if at all — interact among themselves. Writing such objects (mini-programs, in fact) is much easier than developing one huge pile of code. BS consists of less than a dozen classes (modules), not all of which have their own windows.

We devote a special window to the input of the Billings Schedule. A separate window for data is an obvious choice. The user spends most of the time in it so we must design it with special care. From that window must also come the numerical results. It was the very first window written for this application.

That said, we still have to decide what the input is going to be like. The real question is what subpanes a window should consist of. There are three main subpane types that come with Smalltalk/V: ListPane, TextPane and DrawPane. We can inherit from them and that should always be the first consideration. We can also make our own pane types.

In BS, the role of text subpanes is limited to data input and the Help window.

TextPanes are excellent for notes, jottings, longer unstructured texts, and the like. In this particular program we do not need florid descriptions of parts and elements, we only want to input text one or more lines long. On the other hand, it is essential that the user can read the help file instead of thumbing through the manual. The help file will be a text window that can be listed but not changed.

A useful drawing class, **FreeDrawing**, is shipped with Smalltalk/V. The user will draw headers and footers with it. The drawing window is a boon to software developers and is one of the strengths of Smalltalk/V.

Saving the best for the last — the ListPanes. In the heart of every program lies a database, i.e. a collection of records. ListPanes represent them on the screen and — without any programming — offer the programmer an excellent data editor. This is why this application will use ListPanes and their enhancements in virtually all data windows.

The prime example of a multitude of ListPanes is class **Pa**. It is a window through which the data come alive, imitating the final printout form. Most companies are interested only in columns for quantity and price of materials so I'll include only four columns per window. It would take much more space to add the actual code for the labour units and price, and would not demonstrate any new principles. Once you understand the columns for materials you will be able to apply the principle to whatever you want.

The **Pa** window (Fig. 6.1) is a general data editor. It is very easy to change its data

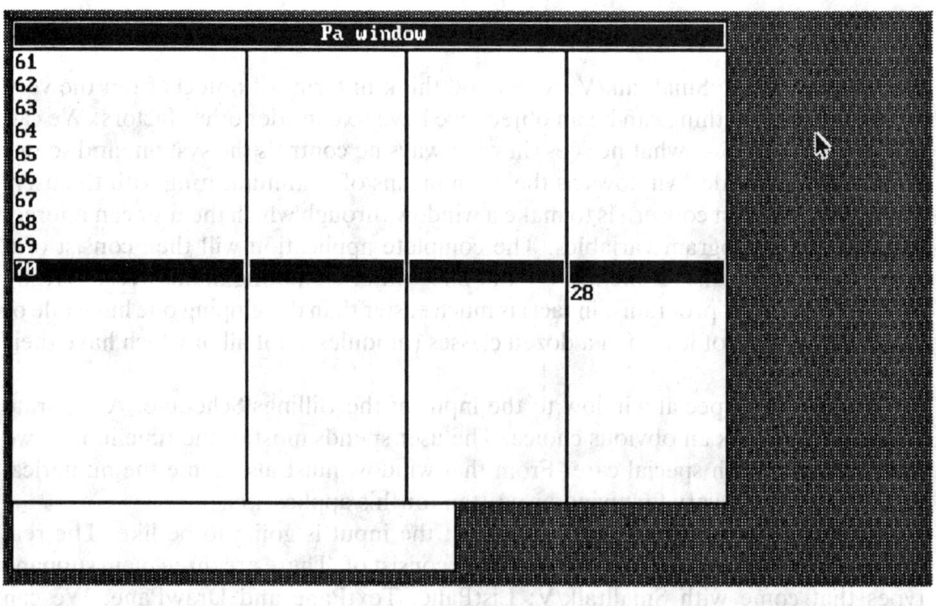

Fig. 6.1 — The **Pa** window.

to any other records, for example, to simulate your personal chequebook. The name, **Pa**, for this class is purely coincidental. I was trying to extend code from some other class in which a ListPane already existed. It just so happened that its class name was **Pa**. This turned out to be an unexpected boon: almost all classes made for this application use **Pa** as prefix. The advantage here is that such classes are brought together in the Class Hierarchy Browser window. Also, most of the classes are inherited from existing base classes of Smalltalk/V itself, so adding **Pa** in front of the name helps to distinguish them from the others.

There are four columns in a **Pa** window. The columns are all instances of a class called **PaListPane** while the horizontal subpanes are of type **PaTextPane**. It is easy to guess that **PaListPane** and **PaTextPane** are subclasses of **ListPane** and **TextPane** classes.

6.5 CLASS PaListPane

The **ListPane** class as delivered with Smalltalk/V is suitable for browsing data, but has no editing capabilities. You cannot change the data the cursor is on. Everything else is there, though: easy scrolling, mouse support, etc. This is a perfect situation for inheritance: PaListPane is a ListPane for sure, but with some practical enhancements.

The **TextPane** class is probably the most common class in Smalltalk/V: we write in it, move and copy the text around, compile from it, and the like. But the subpanes in the Pa windows exist only to show parameter values (block start and end, sums, record line number) so the user should not be able to alter them. We need a TextPane that is actually less than a normal TextPane — class **PaTextPane** is just that. It blocks certain functions of a normal TextPane, but is still is a proper TextPane.

From these two classes we see that inheritance is useful both for enhancements and for reductions of the original class.

Here is **PaListPane**:

```
ListPane subclass: #PaListPane
      instanceVariableNames: ''
      classVariableNames: ''
      poolDictionaries: '' !!

!PaListPane class methods ! !

!PaListPane methods !

curFont
 ^curFont!

curFont: a
curFont := a!

defaultDispatcherClass
      "Answer ListSelector which is the
      default dispatcher of a ListPane."
      ^PaListSelector!
```

```
initializeFont
curFont := FontDes activeFont. ! !
```

This subclass has only a handful of methods. They are mostly concerned with the keyboard and fonts.

Class **PaTextPane** is similarly short:

```
TextPane subclass: #PaTextPane
    instanceVariableNames: ''
    classVariableNames: ''
    poolDictionaries: '' !

!PaTextPane class methods ! !

!PaTextPane methods !

curFont: p
curFont := p!
defaultDispatcherClass
        "Answer PaTextEditor which is the
        default dispatcher of a PaTextPane."
    ^PaTextEditor!
initializeFont
curFont := FontDes activeFont. ! !
```

We installed two new classes only to point to another two new classes, **PaListSelector** and **PaTextEditor**. Both are subclasses of the **Dispatcher** class. **Dispatcher** and its descendants analyse keyboard and mouse events, then react to them. The keys are divided into several categories:

— control keys,
— function keys,
— input keys (meaning all others that are not control and function keys).

The corresponding method names start with 'process' and then describe what they do. Such are the methods **processControlKey:**, **processFunctionKey:** and **processInputKey:.** All of these methods are just one big CASE statement, saying in effect: only one key was depressed; bind exactly one action to that keyboard event. In Smalltalk/V there isn't such a thing as an explicit CASE. This is why these three methods make do with a series of *ifTrue*: questions. (This is not really an omission. CASE statements are usually the main source of problems in programs. One could say that the only idea behind object-oriented methodology of programming is a desire to make CASEs abundant — the classes' internal structure is essentially one huge CASE. However, at this relatively low level of routines, a CASE is a must, one way or the other.)

```
TextEditor subclass: #PaTextEditor
```

```
    instanceVariableNames: ''
    classVariableNames: ''
    poolDictionaries:
        'FunctionKeys CharacterConstants ' !

!PaTextEditor class methods ! !

!PaTextEditor methods !

processFunctionKey: aCharacter
        "Private — Process function keys
        from the keyboard or mouse."
    pane
        displayChanges;
        showSelection.
    SelectFunction == aCharacter
        ifTrue: ≈^self "pane selectAtCursor"].
    SelectToFunction == aCharacter
        ifTrue: [^self "pane selectToShifted"]].
    SetLoc == aCharacter
        ifTrue: [
        Terminal mouseSelectOn
            ifTrue: [^self "pane selectToCursor"]].
        super processFunctionKey: aCharacter! !
```

PaListSelector contains a lot of examples of translating keys into meaningful actions. This class is a mix of three different groups of methods. The first is **processControlKey**. It scans the keyboard and decides what method to invoke next. The methods differ only in the last letter, which corresponds to the key pressed.

The method of distinguishing whether the key was pressed together with the **Control** key is **asControl** from class **Character**:

```
asControl
    (self isUpperCase or: [self isLowerCase])
        ifTrue: [^(asciiInteger bitAnd: 16r1F) asCharacter].
    ^self!
```

Here is the main code:

```
ListSelector subclass: #PaListSelector
    instanceVariableNames:
        'model '
    ClassVariableNames: ''
    poolDictionaries:
        'FunctionKeys CharacterConstants ' !

!PaListSelector class methods ! !

!PaListSelector methods !
```

```
doControlB
self model perform: #blockInsertBefore.!

doControlC
self model perform: #gotoEnd.!

doControlD
self model perform: #blockEndd.!

doControlE
self model perform: #read.!

doControlF
self model perform: #blockRemove.!

doControlG
self model perform: #blockAll.!

doControlH
self model perform: #rowAdd.!

doControlI
self model perform: #insertYesNo.!

doControlJ
self model perform: #gotoLine.!

doControlK
self model perform: #replaceMenu.!

doControlL
self model perform: #dataToDisk.!

doControlM
self model perform: #searchItemPrompt.!

doControlN
self model perform: #dataFromDisk.!

doControlO
self model perform: #searchNextUp.!

doControlP
self model perform: #replaceItemPrompt.!

doControlQ
self model perform: #searchNextDown.!

doControlR
self model perform: #gotoStart.!

doControlS
self model perform: #blockStart.!

doControlT
```

```
self model perform: #rowRemove.!

doControlU
self model perform: #blockBlankOut.!

doControlV
self model perform: #blockInsertAfter.!

doControlW
self model perform: #gotoOneUp.!

doControlX
self model perform: #gotoOneDown.!

model
    | sch |
sch := Scheduler dispatchers at: 1.
 ^(model := sch pane model).!

processControlKey: aCharacter
    aCharacter == $W asControl
        ifTrue: [^self doControlW].
    aCharacter == $R asControl
        ifTrue: [^self doControlR].
    aCharacter == $C asControl
        ifTrue: [^self doControlC].
    aCharacter == $E asControl
        ifTrue: [^self doControlE].
    aCharacter == $Q asControl
        ifTrue: [^self doControlQ].
    aCharacter == $X asControl
        ifTrue: [^self doControlX].
    aCharacter == $G asControl
        ifTrue: [^self doControlG].
    aCharacter == $T asControl
        ifTrue: [^self doControlT].
    aCharacter == $V asControl
        ifTrue: [^self doControlV].
    aCharacter == $S asControl
        ifTrue: [^self doControlS].
    aCharacter == $D asControl
        ifTrue: [^self doControlD].
    aCharacter == $U asControl
        ifTrue: [^self doControlU].
    aCharacter == $F asControl
        ifTrue: [^self doControlF].
    aCharacter == $H asControl
        ifTrue: [^self doControlH].
    aCharacter == $J asControl
```

```
        ifTrue: [^self doControlJ].
    aCharacter == $I asControl
        ifTrue: [^self doControlI].
    aCharacter == $O asControl
        ifTrue: [^self doControlO].
    aCharacter == $P asControl
        ifTrue: [^self doControlP].
    aCharacter == $B asControl
        ifTrue: [^self doControlB].
    aCharacter == $N asControl
        ifTrue: [^self doControlN].
    aCharacter == $M asControl
        ifTrue: [^self doControlM].
    aCharacter == $K asControl
        ifTrue: [^self doControlK].
    aCharacter == $L asControl
        ifTrue: [^self doControlL]. ! !
```

6.6 SCHEDULER AND OTHER MYSTERIES

Decoding of keys looks straightforward enough. A typical action method looks like this:

```
doControlJ
self model perform: #gotoLine.
```

When the user presses Ctrl-J, the method **doControlJ** executes another method, **gotoLine**. Note that you cannot see from this code where **gotoLine** actually is. The message **self model** returns the name of the class that contains the method **gotoLine** and within which it will have the required effect. Also note the **perform:** message. It was extremely difficult to find out how to use it properly. The following method is the key:

```
model
    | sch |
sch := Scheduler dispatchers at: 1.
 ^(model := sch pane model).!
```

Quite a lot of experimenting went into this discovery. First of all, **Scheduler** is a global Smalltalk/V variable. Everybody and everything can access it, query it, change it. Any indiscriminate change of **Scheduler** would literally ruin your work — **Scheduler** is actually the array of all windows that you see on the screen. Perhaps that is why it is scarcely mentioned in the manual. **Scheduler** is the only instance of class **DispatchManager** that should exist in the system. Nothing will prevent you from creating parallel window chains but it is best to play clean.

Knowing that **Scheduler** exists gives you a clue about the control of the complete

Smalltalk/V system. Message **Scheduler dispatchers** returns an array of all windows, more precisely, of all existing dispatchers. Another fact of life is that the active window always gets the very first position in that array. Variable **sch** in the above code is the dispatcher (the class that connects the keyboard and some window on the screen) of the currently active window. And that is just what is needed because **PaListSelector** serves only one purpose: to allow input of characters into the Pa window. In other words, we press the keys to which this class answers while in the data entry window itself, and that is why it is also No. 1 in the **Scheduler**.

Variable **sch** is a dispatcher, message **sch pane** discovers the subpane to which the dispatcher belongs, and then message **model** finds out the name of the class. All of this is a rather involved way of discovering how to address the window that you input your data into.

However, that is not the end of the story. The message **model** cannot find a name if it is not already there. At some point we have to arrange for the name (**#Pa** in this case) to appear in some handy place so that we can retrieve it later. Inspecting the code, we see that class **TopPane** contains instance variable **model** and messages to access its value. Therefore, the name of Pa must be its default value. We shall eventually study the code for the complete class **Pa**, so here we just give the actual code from method **openOn9**:

```
pointWindow := TopPane new.
pointWindow model: self.
```

Variable **pointWindow** is the working part of the window and the second line serves only to put the window name into **TopPane**'s instance variable **model** so that later it can be retrieved in a method such as **model** in a class **PaTextEditor**.

And all this started because **perform:** will not work unless its receiver is a model of a **TopPane** . . .

None of this is too obvious. It illustrates well the pitfalls that a newcomer will face in object-oriented systems: everything depends on everything and it is not easy to think or write in that manner. But a little hacking did it, after all.

6.7 CLASS Pa — DATA INPUT AND MANIPULATION

Here is one possible layout for class **Pa**, the class in which the end-user should spend most of the time. It will have four columns, the leftmost for the data description, the second for the quantity, the third for the price and the fourth for the product of the second and third. In Smalltalk/V jargon, **Pa** has four subpanes of type **PaListPane**. Each will have its own menu. There are many useful operations that one would like to exercise on this data. For this book, I took the middle road. The menus offer a minimal selection of options, the code offers many more operations and there are some that I have simply cut out in order to save space.

Here are the opening lines for **Pa**:

```
Object subclass: #Pa
    instanceVariableNames:
```

```
        'sum insert lowerLine upperLine
        blockLength low subpanes paRecords
        replaceItem windowLabel blockEnd stopInput
        lists pointList pointWindow'
    classVariableNames:
        'SearchItem'
    poolDictionaries:
        'CharacterConstants' !

!Pa class methods !

searchItem
 ^SearchItem! !

!Pa methods !
```

As already pointed out, the main instance variable is **paRecords**, the sole representative of class **PaRecords**.

The first methods to execute are:

```
open
self openOn: ((5 @ 5) corner: (500 & 300))!

openOn: aRectangle
    | s h |
    s := (16).
    h := (1/(s – 1)). "high end"
    low := 1 – h. "low end"
    pointWindow := TopPane new.
    pointWindow label: ' Pa window ';
                model: self.
    self initializeSubpanes.
    subpanes := pointWindow subpanes.
    self initializeAll.
    pointWindow reframe: aRectangle.
    self showAll: 1.
    pointWindow dispatcher openWindow scheduleWindow.!
```

This is a rather different coding style compared to all other **openOn:** methods so far. Instead of adding the subpanes here and now, their addition is left to the **initializeSubpanes** method. Here it is:

```
initializeSubpanes
    | h x |
    h := (1/9). "Base column width."
    x := Array new: 3.
    x at: 1 put: (3 * h).
    x at: 2 put: (5 * h).
    x at: 3 put: (7 * h).
```

```
    pointWindow addSubpane:
    (PaListPane new change: #showAll:;
        menu: #dutiesMenu;
        returnIndex: true;
        model: self;
        name: #initDuties;
        framingRatio: (0 @ 0 corner: ((x at: 1) 1) )).

pointWindow addSubpane:
    (PaListPane new
        change: #showAll:;
        menu: #qtyMenu;
        returnIndex: true;
        model: self;
        name: #initQty;
        framingRatio: ((x at: 1) @ 0 corner: ((x at: 2) @ 1) )).

pointWindow addSubpane:
    (PaListPane new
        change: #showAll:;
        menu: #rateMenu;
        returnIndex: true;
        model: self;
        name: #initRate;
        framingRatio: ((x at: 2) @ 0 corner: ((x at: 3) @ 1) )).

pointWindow addSubpane:
    (PaListPane new
        change: #showAll:;
        returnIndex: true;
        menu: #amountMenu;
        model: self;
        name: #initAmount;
        framingRatio: ((x at: 3) @ 0 corner: (1 @ 1) )).!
```

Another difference is that no special names (ie variables) are allocated to subpanes. Some digging into the window structure reveals that panes are nothing more than a collection of subpanes. You can address, say, the second pane in the order of adding to the TopPane variable (**pointWindow** here), by a simple

```
subpanes := pointWindow subpanes.
subpanes at: 2...
```

This coding is as effective as it is possibly confusing. There is an instance variable called **subpanes** and it is assigned its value in the first of the above two lines. Then throughout the whole class you can use a line like the second to address the PaListPane subpane with methods **qtyMenu** and **initQty**.

Of course, you would first have to add a method like

```
subpanes
 ^subpanes
```

in the **TopPane** class for all this to work.

Let us analyse **Pa** column by column. For reasons of my own, I named those columns *duties*, *qty*, *rate* and *amount*. Therefore, all methods with *duties* in its names should connect with the leftmost column, the one with the description of the part(s) that come in certain quantities (column *qty*), cost so much apiece (*rate*) and with the total *amount* to pay, in the rightmost column.

6.8 CLASS Pa — DUTIES COLUMN

First of all, here are the three proverbial Smalltalk/V branches into initialization code, left and right mouse methods:

```
initDuties
 ^paRecords at: 1!

dutiesMenu
        "Select menu operation."
 ^Menu
    labels: 'print\remove row\add row\change
        \column input\row input
        \to start\to end\to line\
        search\replace down' withCrs
    lines: #(1 3 4 6 9 12)
    selectors: #(print rowRemove rowAdd dutiesChange
        dutiesColumnInput rowsInput
        gotoStart gotoEnd gotoLine
        searchDown replaceDown)!
showAll
self showAll: lists.!

showAll: anInteger
1 to: paRecords columns do: [ :i |
    (subpanes at: i) changed: #initPoints.
    (subpanes at: i) restoreSelected: anInteger.].!
```

From method **initDuties** we see that **paRecords** is an array of four columns. Method **showAll:** selects the current line (the one with the index **anInteger**). All other **change:** methods in **Pa** also point to this method so whichever column you click with the left mouse button on, a black horizontal line is produced. Note that this method is compactly coded thanks to variable **subpanes**.

Method **showAll** is a shorthand. It also produced the cursor line on position that is contained in numeric variable **lists** (the current line in **Pa**).

Finally, the menu for this column is the most extensive of the four. Even so, it should be larger — that is the place to include calls to all block operations that are otherwise linked only through **Ctrl** keyboard combinations (see class **PaListSelector**).

The **print** method is shown with **PaPage**, because that's where it logically belongs. **rowRemove** deletes the current row (the one with the black cursor line on it). Here it is:

```
rowRemove
    | size |
size := self size.
lowerLine := (subpanes at: 2) selection.
upperLine := (subpanes at: 2) selection.
self blockStart;
    blockEndd;
    blockRemove.
lowerLine > 0
    ifTrue: [ self showAll: (lowerLine := lowerLine — 1)].
lowerLine = 0
    ifTrue: [ self showAll: (lowerLine := 1) ].!
```

The logic is simple: there is a fairly extensive set of block operations in **Pa**: among them is block deletion. To form a block, you decide upon the starting and ending block lines first. Methods **blockStart** and **blockEndd** formally make a block, and **blockRemove** removes it physically. Variables **lowerLine** and **upperLine** denote the start and end of a block.

Of course, this could have been written in a much more direct way. Side-effects make this a plausible solution too: marking a line as a block automatically transfers it into W, a global Smalltalk/V variable, which is a buffer for blocks. Since it is global, we can use it to transfer blocks of data both within one **Pa** window and among many simultaneously existing **Pa** windows. This opens the way for the best use of **Pa** windows. The idea is that the description of typical parts is always the same, except for a small amount of numerical data. In one **Pa** window you put the library of schematic descriptions; then you open another **Pa** window to put fresh data into. From the 'library' window you take schematic text denoting it as a block of lines. Move the cursor into the data window and insert the text. You are then ready to find where exactly to put the new data. If you remember, method **read** is specifically formulated for this use. It will both open the text window and place the cursor behind the string that you previously searched for.

Adding a row means adding one row (**addAll**) and then showing it (**showAll**):

```
rowAdd
lists := (subpanes at: 2) selection.
self addAll;
    showAll.!
```

Perhaps the most frequently ocurring message in **Pa** is **selection**. It is actually a message to the related PaListPane and returns the ordinal number of the selected line. Therefore, **lists** contains the current number of the cursor line. Here is **addAll**:

```
addAll
    (lists = paRecords size)
        ifTrue: [ insert := true.].
    (insert)
        ifTrue: [ paRecords addAllAfter: lists. ].
    lists := lists + 1.!
```

Instance variable **insert** enables the automatic insertion of new lines at the end of the file.

Method **dutiesChange** is very simple:

```
dutiesChange
self read: 1.!
```

It opens exactly one cell in the first column and allows the user to edit its contents. This is practically identical to **Ctrl–E**.

The most important task of a column editor is to enable two types of input: pure 'vertical' input in a column and 'horizontal' input of a data record. This is why methods **dutiesColumnInput** and **rowsInput** exist. First the code for 'horizontal' input:

```
rowsInput
lists := (subpanes at: 2) selection.
StopInput := false.
[StopInput == true ]
    whileFalse: [
        self possibleEnd.
        self rowInput.
        (StopInput == true)
            ifTrue: [self showAll.
                ^ (StopInput := false) ] .
        self finishRowInput. ].!
```

Let us first see what the methods in **rowsInput** do. **possibleEnd** just checks for the end of the data:

```
possibleEnd
(lists = paRecords size)
    ifTrue: [ insert := true.].!
```

rowInput reads the first three cells, horizontally. It constantly checks to see whether the input was stopped from the keyboard:

```
rowInput
```

```
self dutiesChange.
StopInput == true
    ifFalse: [ self qtyChange ].
StopInput == true
    ifFalse: [ self rateChange ].!
```

Who and what raises the value of **StopInput**? Way back in class **PaListSelector** we see that shortcut **Ctrl–A** does nothing except put global variable **StopInput** to **true**. It is a rather obscure way of sensing keyboard events but I found nothing better. And it is certainly a couple of parsecs apart from the way you'd do the same thing in BASIC or Pascal. On the other hand, now that you do know how to do it . . . .

The last method is **finishRowInput**. It adds another row so that you have a place to write a new line into, and shows it visually.

```
finishRowInput
self addAll;
    showAll.!
```

The 'vertical' input requires a similar approach. The method is:

```
dutiesColumnInput
self columnInput: 1.!
```

dutiesColumnInput needs the help of another method, **columnInput:**. It is a general routine and serves all four columns:

```
columnInput: column
StopInput := false.
[StopInput == true ]
    whileFalse: [
        lists := (subpanes at: 2) selection.
        self possibleEnd.
        self read: column.
        (StopInput == true)
            ifTrue: [ self show: column.
              ^ (StopInput := false) ] .
        self finishRowInput].!
```

This is very similar to 'horizontal' input, save for the presence of the **read:** instead of **rowInput**.

The next three methods are kinds of GOTO to specific lines. You can jump to the very start and very end of the file and also to any other line that you care to specify. The methods are:

```
gotoEnd
self showAll: paRecords size.!
```

```
gotoLine
    | line |
line := Prompter
    prompt: 'To line ?'
    defaultExpression: (paRecords size // 2) printString.
line == nil ifTrue: [ ^self ].
(line between: 1 and: paRecords size)
    ifFalse: [ ^self].
self showAll: line.!
gotoStart
self showAll: 1.!
```

The following two methods are not invoked from the menu (though you can incorporate them if you want). They are activated with keyboard shortcuts **Ctrl–X** and **Ctrl–W**. See **PaListSelector** above.

```
gotoOneDown
lists := (subpanes at: 2) selection.
lists := lists + 1.
lists > paRecords size
    ifTrue: [ lists := lists - 1 ]
    ifFalse:[ self showAll ].!

gotoOneUp
lists := (subpanes at: 2) selection.
lists := lists - 1.
lists > 1
    ifTrue: [ self showAll ]
    ifFalse:[lists := lists + 1 ].!
```

You can search quite efficiently. The method **searchDown** prompts you for a **SearchItem** and then uses **searchNextDown** to do the job.

```
searchDown
SearchItem := Prompter
    prompt: 'Search for ?'
    default: SearchItem.
self searchNextDown.!
searchNextDown
    | found |
lists := (subpanes at: 2) selection.
lists >= paRecords size ifFalse: [
    found := paRecords
                search: SearchItem
                from: (lists + 1)
```

```
                    to: self size.
    self searchSuccessful: found ].!

searchSuccessful: found
found > 0
    ifTrue: [ self showAll: found;
                    read: 1 ]
    ifFalse:[ paRecords field replyPane dispatcher doControlA.
                    self showAll: (subpanes at: 1) selection.].!
```

The search depends on **searchSuccessful:**. If there was a match, you are right into the text (first column) and can change it immediately. However, if the search was not successful, it is best to remain on the line from which the search began.

The expression

paRecords field replyPane dispatcher doControlA

really took time to discover. Let us analyse it. First **paRecordsfield** yields the **PaField** type, then **PaField replyPane** yields **PaTextPane**, then PaTextPane dispatcher yields **PaFieldEditor**, and finally, the message **PaFieldEditor doControlA** does what I wanted it originally to do — to simulate the effect of pressing **Ctrl–A** from the keyboard, which, incidentally, stops the input.

The very last menu option for the first column is replacement. It handles the user interface (calls **replaceItemPrompt**) and delegates all the work to **PaRecords**.

```
replaceDown
self replaceItemPrompt.
paRecords replace: SearchItem
    from: (lists := (subpanes at: 1) selection)
    to: paRecords size
    with: replaceItem.
self showAll.!

replaceItemPrompt
SearchItem := Prompter
    prompt: 'Change what ?'
    default: SearchItem.
replaceItem := Prompter
    prompt: SearchItem, ' is changed into ?'
    default: replaceItem.!
```

These were the options from the main Pa menu (Fig. 6.2). Let us now look at menus for other subpanes.

6.9 CLASS Pa — THE OTHER THREE COLUMNS

The three basic methods are **showAll:**, **qtyMenu** and **initQty.**:

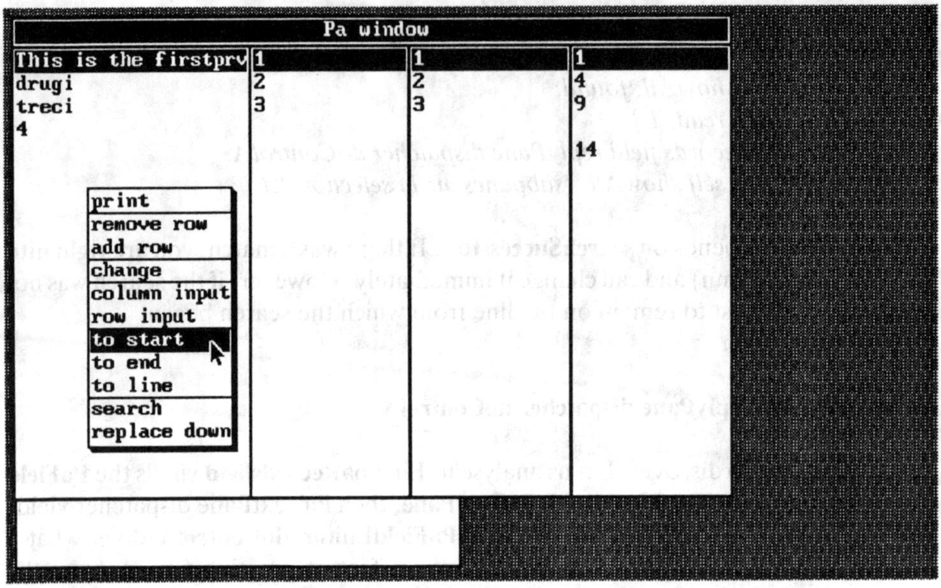

Fig. 6.2 — The main **Pa** menu.

```
initQty
 ^paRecords at: 2!
qtyMenu
 ^Menu
    labels: 'remove row\add row\change\column input\row input' [withCrs
    lines: #(2 3 )
    selectors: #(rowRemove rowAdd qtyChange qtyColumnInput rowsInput)!
```

The first two options and the last are the same as before. The new ones are for the direct change of the cell in this column and for row ('vertical') input.

```
qtyInputColumn
self columnInput: 2.!

qtyChange
self read: 2.
paRecords computeAmount:
    (lists := (subpanes at: 2) selection).!
```

This is conceptually the same as for the duties menu but the new message, **computeAmount:**, is sent to **paRecords**. It updates the state of the fourth column, dependent on the state of the corresponding two horizontal cells.

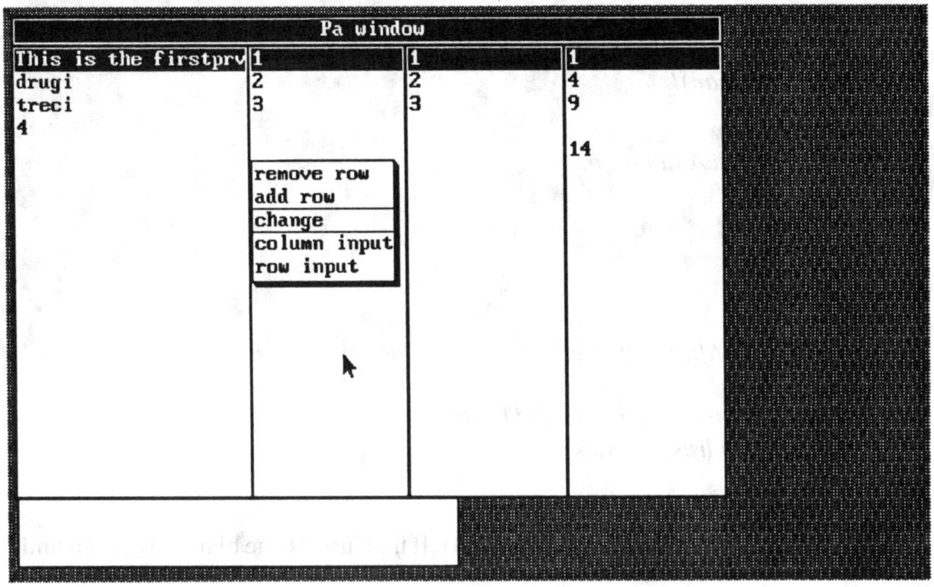

Fig. 6.3 — The second **Pa** menu.

The third column is practically the same:

```
initRate
 ^paRecords at: 3!
rateChange
self read: 3.
paRecords computeAmount:
    (lists := (subpanes at: 3) selection).!
rateInputColumn
self columnInput: 3.!

rateMenu
 ^Menu
    labels: 'remove row\add row\change
        \column input\row input' withCrs
    lines: #(2 3)
    selectors: #(rowRemove rowAdd rateChange
        rateColumnInput rowsInput)!

readRate
self read: 3.!
```

The fourth column is even simpler:

```
amountMenu
 ^Menu
     labels: ' sum ' withCrs
     lines: #()
     selectors: #(sum)!

computeAmount: p
paRecords computeAmount: p.!

initAmount
 ^paRecords at: 4!

sum
     | s |
paRecords addAllAfter: self size.
self showAll: (lists := self size).
s := (paRecords sum: 4) printPaddedTo: 0.
paRecords at: 4 at: lists put: s.
self showAll.! !
```

The only interesting method is **sum** (Fig. 6.4). It first inserts one blank row, then finds

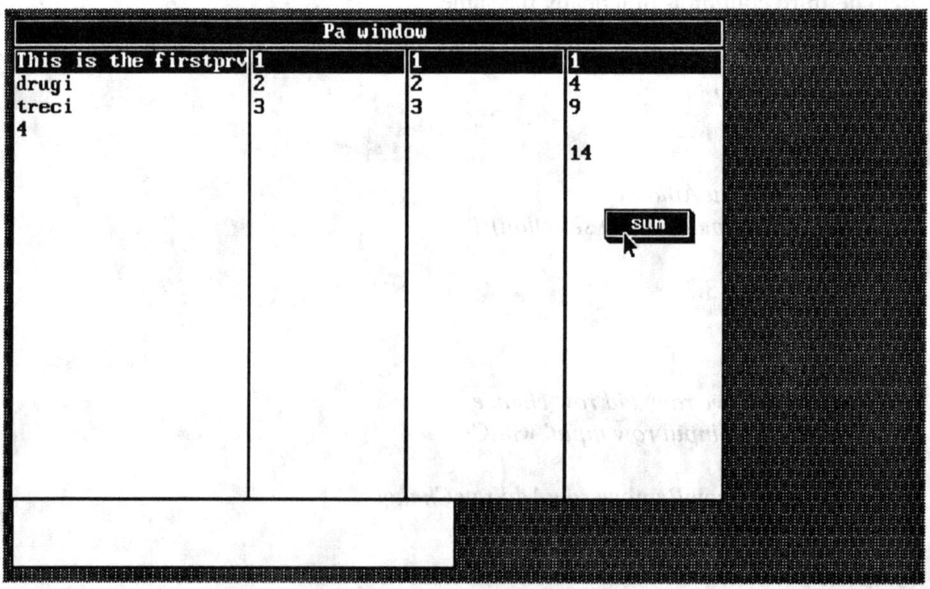

Fig. 6.4 — The fourth **Pa** menu.

the sum (using **paRecords** once again!) and puts it back as the only entry in the last row.

6.10 — CLASS Pa — BLOCK AND AUXILIARY METHODS

Here are the remaining methods for this version of **Pa**. The original had many more, by the way. Most of these methods are about blocks, that is, they prepare **paRecords** for performing low-level operations.

```
at: column
 ^ (subpanes at: column)!

blockAll
self showAll: 1;
     blockStart;
     showAll: paRecords size;
     blockEndd.!

blockBlackOut
lowerLine to: upperLine do: [ :line |
     (subpanes at: 2) boldLine: line.].!

blockBlankOut
CursorManager execute change.
paRecords blockBlankOut.
self showAll: lowerLine.
CursorManager normal change.!

blockEndd
self blockEndd: (subpanes at: 2) selection.!

blockEndd: aValue
blockEnd := aValue.
(lists == nil)
     ifTrue: [^Terminal bell]
     ifFalse: [
          lowerLine := lists min: blockEnd.
          upperLine := lists max: blockEnd.
          paRecords blockStart: lowerLine;
               blockEndd: upperLine.
          self blockBlackOut.
          lists >= blockEnd ifTrue: [
               (subpanes at: 2) boldLine: lowerLine. ]
               ifFalse: [ (subpanes at: 2) boldLine: upperLine. ].
     ].
blockLength := (upperLine — lowerLine) abs.
self blockToBuffer.!

blockFromBuffer
CursorManager execute change.
```

```
paRecords blockFromBuffer:
    (lists := (subpanes at: 1) selection).
self showAll: lists + (W at: 1) size.
CursorManager normal change.!

blockInsertAfter
paRecords addAllAfter:
    (lists := (subpanes at: 1) selection).
self blockFromBuffer;
    showAll: (subpanes at: 1) selection + 1;
    rowRemove.!

blockInsertBefore
paRecords addAllBefore:
    (lists := (subpanes at: 1) selection).
self blockFromBuffer;
    showAll: lists;
    rowRemove.!

blockPosition: line
    | up down |
lists := line.
up := paRecords searchLabelUp: lists.
down := paRecords searchLabelDown: (lists + 1).
down < 0
    ifTrue: [ down := 1 ].
self showAll: up;
    blockStart;
    showAll: down;
    blockEndd.!

blockRemove
CursorManager execute change.
paRecords blockRemove.
self showAll: lowerLine.
CursorManager normal change.!

blockStart
self blockStart:
    (lists := (subpanes at: 2) selection).!

blockStart: aValue
paRecords blockStart: aValue!

blockToBuffer
paRecords blockToBuffer.!

changeFont
    | currentFont |
subpanes collect: [ :subpane |
    subpane initializeFont.].
```

```
currentFont := (subpanes at: 1) curFont.!

initializeAll
self changeFont.
paRecords := PaRecords new.
SearchItem := '$%'.
lists := 1.
insert := true.
paRecords initializeAll.
W := Array new: paRecords columns.
upperLine := 1.
lowerLine := 1.!

insertYesNo     | insert |
insert
    ifTrue: [ insert := false]
    ifFalse:[ insert := true ].!

qtyDelete
    | answer s |
answer := Menu confirm: 'Delete column ?'.
answer
    ifTrue: [
    CursorManager execute change.
    paRecords delete: 2; delete: 4.
    self showAll: lists.
    CursorManager normal change].!

read
self read: 1!

read: column
lists := (subpanes at: 1) selection.
paRecords
    read: column
    atLine: lists
    paListPane: (subpanes at: column)
    searchItem: SearchItem.
self show: column.!

recalc
paRecords foreignColumn: 1.
self showAll; sum.!

rowChange
lists := (subpanes at: 2) selection.
self readDuties;
    readQty;
    readRate.!

searchItemPrompt
```

```
SearchItem := Prompter
    prompt: 'Search for ?'
    default: SearchItem.!

show: i
(subpanes at: i) changed: #initPoints.
(subpanes at: i) restoreSelected: lists.!

size
 ^paRecords size!
```

6.11 CLASS PaRecords

Now we can turn to the internal design of **Pa**, the main data window. It should be an editor for a series of records, where each record has four elements. There are several ways of implementing this. My first attempt was to assign a separate collection to each column. It resulted in slower program writing because I had to look after four different variables, and literally all the methods had to be multiplied by four. Later I thought of other possible data representations: data as an array of records, with four separate variables per record. Both approaches had strong and weak design points so I decided to hide them in a special class, **PaRecords**. Here is how its code starts:

```
Object subclass: #PaRecords
    instanceVariableNames:
        'ext upperLine lowerLine blockLength field
        data columns fileName widths printWindow '
    classVariableNames: ''
    poolDictionaries:
        'CharacterConstants ' !

!PaRecords class methods ! !
```

The rest of the class consists of familiar methods. Smalltalk/V sorts them alphabetically by method name, but that is not the best way to demonstrate what goes on. The most important instance variable is **data**. There are two initialization methods; normally, you would send the message **initializeAll** to a fresh instance of class **PaRecords**. Here is **initializeAll**:

```
initializeAll
ext := 'ext'.
columns := 4.
data := Array new: columns. "the columns themselves"
1 to: columns do: [ :i |
        self initialize: i].!
```

This method calls a private method for initialization, **initialize:**. It is short:

```
initialize: column
```

```
data at: column put: OrderedCollection new.
(data at: column) add: ' '.!
```

Variable **data** is an OrderedCollection of columns, practically an open-ended matrix. Other variables are **columns**, which hold the actual number of columns (here it's four).

Standard "get" and "put" methods are:

```
columns
 ^columns

columns: c
columns := c
```

Variable **widths** holds the widths of each column. There are only three methods directly concerning **widths**:

```
widths
 ^widths!

widthsCompute
     | u m |
1 to: columns do: [ :i |
     u := data at: i.
     m := (u at: 1) size.
     1 to: u size do: [ :j |
          m := m max: (u at: j) size ].
     widths at: i put: m].
1 to: widths size do: [ :i | widths at: i
                              put: ((widths at: i) + 1) ].!
```

There is more on **data**, since it is the main structure in this class. First, there are two standard methods for manipulating an instance variable:

```
data
 ^data

data: h
data := h
```

Then come three essential methods for assessing records in **data**:

```
at: i
 ^data at: i

at: column at: lists put: aValue
(data at: column)
     at: lists
```

```
    put: aValue.

at: i put: d
data at: i put: d
```

The syntax of these methods could be entirely different but it is to the programmer's advantage to use identical names for identical purposes. Therefore, method **at:** returns one of the columns as a **whole**, i.e. an OrderedCollection. Method **at:put:** sets the value of a complete column and method **at:at:put:** puts **aValue** into a specific matrix cell, with coordinates (**column**, **lists**). The name **lists** is from class **Pa** where it is a pointer to the current cursor row. (Since Pa is a data browser window, such a counter there actually 'lists' one specific row, hence the name.)

These three methods enable data hiding. The data will be hidden inside this class if we restrict ourselves to work with data exclusively using those methods. This may or may not be imperative but comes in handy in the long run. Note that the first method would be (inside class **PaRecords**) used like this

```
self at: i
```

There are no advantages in writing **self** instead of **data** except for data hiding. But why not, then, introduce yet another class to hold only **data**? This might be a logical consequence but you must stop somewhere. Smalltalk/V lets you make classes quite easily but that does not mean you should always do so!

Outside the class **PaRecords** these three methods are the only way to reach records. A simplified but typical usage would be this:

```
    | paRecords |
paRecords := PaRecords new.
pRecords initializeAll; at: 1 at: 45 put: 10.
```

and so on.

Similarly, there is a method to delete a complete column:

```
delete: column
1 to: (data at: column) size do: [ :i |
    (data at: column) at: i put: ''.]
```

Method **size** finds out how many records are in the database:

```
size
^(data at: 2) size.
```

This works because all columns are equal in size.

Taking sums across the columns is one of the primary goals of this program. The following method computes it in a standard way:

```
sum: column
    | s d v b |
```

```
s := 0.
1 to: (data at: column) size do: [ :i /
    d := data at: column.
    v := d at: i.
    b := (' ', v) trimBlanks asInteger.
    s := s + b].
^s!
```

Local variable **v** is a cell with coordinates **(column,i)**. All data in columns are strings, even if they represent numbers. ListPanes and their derivatives require all the data to be strings. Immediately before the addition, the string from **(column,i)** is converted into a number, **b**. In the **String** class there is a method **asInteger** which turns strings into integers. A somewhat strange idiom **(' ', v) trimBlanks** prepares the data for **asInteger**. The **trimBlanks** reports an error if there isn't any blank to eliminate, so this code intentionally adds a blank in front of **v** to satisfy **trimBlanks**.

The method **computeAmount:** calculates the product of numbers in the third and fourth rows, i.e. quantity times price. It is called automatically whenever the data in one of those columns are changed. It is also called for the final calculation of the grand total.

```
computeAmount: p
/ q r s g /
(data at: 4) at: p put: ''.
q := (' ', ((data at: 2) at: p)) trimBlanks asInteger.
r := (' ', ((data at: 3) at: p)) trimBlanks asInteger.
(q * r) = 0
    ifTrue: [ (data at: 4) at: p put: '']
    ifFalse:[ (data at: 4) at: p
            put: (( q * r)
               printPaddedTo: 0) ].!
```

The last row is particularly interesting. The ListPane expects its data as strings and we need to convert true integers to strings again. The unlikely answer to that plea is the **printPaddedTo:** method. Its receiver is an integer and its input parameter is the resulting string length. The most economical solution is to put a zero there. Any other number produces that many blanks first and only then the string that is visually identical to the receiver.

6.12 FILE OPERATIONS

There are just two disk-based operations. The method **toDisk:** writes data to disk, using an auxiliary method **toDisk:extension:**. Here they are:

```
toDisk: name
    / ext /
fileName := Prompter
```

```
    prompt: 'Header to disk: file name ?'
    default: name.
self toDisk: fileName extension: ext.
self toDisk: fileName extension: 'bak'.!
toDisk: filename extension: extension
    | dataOut |
fileName := (filename , '.' , extension).
dataOut := File pathName: fileName.
dataOut nextPutAll: (self size printPaddedTo: 10);
        nextPut: Cr.
1 to: self size do: [ :i |
    1 to: columns do: [ :j |
        dataOut nextPutAll: ((data at: j) at: i);
            nextPut: Cr. ].
].
dataOut flush; close.!
```

The main reason for creating this latter method is to write a backup automatically (a file with extension 'bak'). The real output is in **toDisk:extension:**. Note that **fileName** is an instance variable. **dataOut** is a file variable and receives the **data** size first, then the **data** itself, in two loops.

Input must comply with the output structure. First the **fromDisk:** method must read the **data** size and then read its elements, also in two loops:

```
fromDisk: name
    | dataIn dataSize |
fileName := Prompter
    prompt: 'read data, filename?'
    default: name.
dataIn := (File pathName: (fileName , '.' , self class ext)).
dataIn size == 0 ifTrue:
    [ Prompter prompt: 'Doesn't exist!' default: name.
        ^nil ].
dataSize := dataIn nextLine trimBlanks asInteger.
1 to: columns do: [ :i |
    data at: i put: OrderedCollection new. ].
1 to: dataSize do: [ : |
    1 to: columns do: [ :j |
        (data at: j) add: (dataIn nextLine). ].
    ].
lowerLine := 1.
upperLine := dataSize.!
```

Apart from that, this method initializes class variables **LowerLine** and **UpperLine** to embrace all the data so that any further operation would act on the complete file.

6.13 BLOCK OPERATIONS

One of the main advantages of a computer editor is group handling of basic text elements. In this particular editor, a group consists of lines. Therefore, all block operations will act on lines of text. All block routines have names that start with the word 'block'.

The most essential editor operation is insertion of a line. There are two methods for this: one to insert in front of the line with ordinal number **lists**; the other to insert after it:

```
addAllAfter: lists
    | q w |
1 to: columns do: [ :i |
    q := data at: i.
    w := q at: lists.
    q add: '' afterIndex: lists. ].!

addAllBefore: lists
1 to: columns do: [ :i |
    (data at: i) add: '' beforeIndex: lists. ].!
```

All our data are OrderedCollections and we use the methods from that class. For example, it contains methods **afterIndex:** and **beforeIndex:** and I found it easy to use them in methods **addAllBefore:** and **addAllAfter:**. Of course, I could have invented any other method for insertion but given the existence of **afterIndex:** and **beforeIndex:**, the easiest way was to use them. It also shows how the implementation of the chosen language influences practical programming and even design decisions!

Instance variable **columns** is the size of **data.** Variables **lowerLine** and **upperLine** play an important part in most operations. Here is a short description of what the rest of the block methods do:

blockAll, denotes all data as one block,
blockBlankOut, puts blank lines into the block (useful for typing over a couple of lines at once, without disrupting other data),
blockEndd, put the current block end into **upperLine** and computes the block length,
blockRemove, deletes block from **lowerLine** to **upperLine**,
blockStart:, puts the start of the block into **lowerLine**,

Here is the code:

```
blockAll
lowerLine := 1.
upperLine := self size.!

blockBlankOut
lowerLine to: upperLine do: [ :lists |
    1 to: columns do: [ :i |
        (data at: i) at: lists put: '' ]
```

```
    ].!

blockEndd: blockEnd
upperLine := blockEnd.
blockLength := (upperLine − lowerLine) abs.!

blockRemove
(lowerLine = 1 and:
[ (upperLine = self size) ])
    ifTrue: [ self initializeAll.]
    ifFalse:[
        1 to: columns do: [ :i /
            data
                at: i
                put: (self blockRemoveColumn: (data at: i)).
        ].
    ].!

blockRemoveColumn: col
    / n1 n2 /
n1 := col copyFrom: 1 to: (lowerLine − 1).
n2 := col copyFrom: (upperLine + 1) to: col size.
^(n1 , n2).!

blockStart: start
lowerLine := start!
```

There are some interesting coding techniques here. In **blockRemoveColumn:** I used the **copyFrom:to:** method. It appears to be the best choice for fast copying of any kind of collection. In **blockBlankOut** there is this line:

```
(data at: i) at: lists put: ''
```

Earlier in this book, class **Matrix** was invented, with methods such as **at:at:** and **at:at:put:**. The above code is quite similar except **data** is not a **Matrix** but an **OrderedCollection**. Therefore, parentheses apply after the first **at:** message.

There is another global variable, **W**. It is the basis of block interchange between Pa windows. Any block automatically goes to **W** and is ready for insertion at some later moment. Here are the relevant methods **blockFromBuffer:** and **blockToBuffer:**

```
blockFromBuffer: c
1 to: columns do: [ :i /
    1 to: (W at: 1) size do: [ :line /
        (data at: i)
            add: ((W at: i)
            at: line)
                afterIndex: (c + line − 1) ].
    ].!
```

```
blockToBuffer
    | w |
1 to: columns do: [ :i |
    w := OrderedCollection new.
    lowerLine to: upperLine do: [ :line |
        w add: ((data at: i) at: line).].
    W at: i put: w. ].!
```

6.14 LINE INPUT

All editors are keyboard intensive. The user spends most of the time adding, changing or deleting data. Like all others, BS stands or fails by its user interface. Since it is line oriented from the very beginning, the idea is to let the user select the line and edit its contents at will. Whether this is optimal from the end-user standpoint is a matter of contention. Given Smalltalk/V ListPanes and its support for line editing, I chose to enhance a ListPane up to the editor level instead of writing something similar from scratch.

I'll openly admit that it was the easy way out for me, the programmer. And it wasn't a bad choice for the user either, in spite of some things being different. For instance, the line cursor is a black line instead of a white character-sized rectangle. The background in all lines is white, and the characters are black. The line cursor inverts it, so it is a combination of white characters on a black background. Once you press **Ctrl–E** or select any other option to change the contents of a line, you see the usual 'black-on-white' ListPane line. So I faced the dilemma: how to visually denote that the cursor the line is being edited? Of course, the real question was: How to enable the user to change line contents? In true spirit of object-oriented programming, the answer is simple: create a new TextPane window, which will be identical in size with the cursor line on the screen. Let the user do whatever editing operations are possible in a TextPane window even though it is physically just one line. And this was relatively easy to do, especially as among the Goodies packs is a suitable class, **Field**, which I inherited, producing class **PaField.**

It all worked in no time at all (long live inheritance!), with the added advantage that the **PaField** class automatically puts a frame around the PaTextPane. This distinguishes the edited line from others. Undoubtedly, other clues could have been thought of, but this one is good enough.

This is as far as the first version of line input went. Later, I wrote searching routines which influenced the start of line editing. The string that was searched for is kept in an instance variable **searchItem** and was never empty. When you find the string, you actually want to edit it immediately. So editing starts with searching for **searchItem** within the line text. If the search is successful, the editing cursor (an I-shaped beam) is placed right behind the located text. You'd expect it to be placed before, but the **PaTextPane** class handles **Backspace** better than other keys.

Here is the code for all of the above. It is cryptic and the detailed comments follow.

read: column

```
    atLine: lists
    paListPane: dutiesList
    searchItem: searchItem
    | w d k m h a upperLeftCorner |
field := PaField new.
upperLeftCorner := dutiesList frame origin.
a := dutiesList lineToRect: lists.
field offset: a origin + upperLeftCorner.
field width: dutiesList frame width.
field default: ((data at: column) at: lists ).
d := (data at: column) at: lists.
w := d indexOfCollection: searchItem.
w > 0
    ifTrue: [
        k := dutiesList frame left.
        m := FontDes currentFont width * (w + Pa searchItem size).
        h := (k + m) @ ((a origin + upperLeftCorner) y + 5).
        Cursor offset: h.
    ].
field edit.
(data at: column)
    at: lists
    put: field default.!
```

These are the input parameters:

column — which of four columns should the data be read in?
lists — in which row?
dutiesList — actual PaListPane for the column,
searchItem — the string to search for within the cursor line.

Variable **field** is an instance of **PaField**. It will recreate a TextPane for the user, but one down-to-earth question is where to put it on the screen? Not only will **field** be the size of a current PaListPane line, but it must also match it visually. The first step is to find out the upper left corner of the **dutiesList** subpane. That is what the line

upperLeftCorner := dutiesList frame origin.

does. The next line uses method **lineToRect:** from **PaListPane** to find out the true screen coordinates of the line that corresponds to the given row number, **lists**. Variable **a** is the rectangle that surrounds the cursor line. Then three messages to **field** place it on the screen (**offset:**), define **field** width (**width:**) and fill in the line text (**default:**). This completes the setup, and normally the line

field edit.

would follow immediately. It actually opens the mini-window, lets the user interact with the line contents, and puts the amended text back into the corresponding (**column**, **lists**) cell in the **data** OrderedCollection. However, lines

```
d := (data at: column) at: lists.
w := d indexOfCollection: searchItem.
w > 0
    ifTrue: [
        k := dutiesList frame left.
        m := FontDes currentFont width * (w + Pa searchItem size).
        h := (k + m) @ ((a origin + upperLeftCorner) y + 5).
        Cursor offset: h.
    ].
```

were inserted later, in order to place the text cursor right on the required text. The line text is in variable **d**. Method **indexOfCollection:** is a standard way of searching within a string. **w** contains the start of the located string and we have to translate that into screen pixels because the only way to move the text cursor around is message

Cursor offset: h

Computing **h** is easy: first find the left side of the PaTextWindow and keep it in **k**, then multiply **w**, the number of characters to skip, by the width of those characters. This presupposes that the current font in Pa is non-proportional. Variable **m** contains a horizontal cursor offset from **k**, but message **offset:** to **Cursor** requires a Point. Variable **h** is that point.

Message **Pa searchItem** yields the symbol that is to be skipped. This is another degree of freedom for the user, which can insert into the text the symbol that is defined in **Pa** and automatically search for it. The easiest way to start that automatic search is **Ctrl-Q**.

6.15 SEARCH AND REPLACE OPERATIONS

Search and replace operations are straightforward. They all act upon the selected block. Most of the code exists only to ensure that input data will be interpreted correctly. Method **within:replace:with:startingAt:** actually changes the text.

```
replace: str from: from to: to with: replaceItem
    | w d byIncrement |
((str = nil) or: [ str = '' ]) ifTrue: [ ^ 0 ].
((replaceItem = nil)
    or: [ replaceItem = '' ]) ifTrue: [ ^ 0 ].
CursorManager execute change.
from = to ifTrue: [ ^ self ].
from > to ifTrue: [ byIncrement := 1 negated ].
from < to ifTrue: [ byIncrement := 1 ].
from to: to by: byIncrement do: [ :i |
```

```
        d := (data at: 1) at: i.
        w := d indexOfCollection: str.
        w > 0
            ifTrue: [
                (data at: 1) at: i put:
                    (self within: d
                        replace: str
                        with: replaceItem
                        startingAt: w).].
                ].
CursorManager normal change.!

search: str from: from to: to
    | w d increment |
((str = nil) or: [ str = '' ]) ifTrue: [ ^ 0 ].
from = to ifTrue: [ ^ 0 ].
from > to ifTrue: [ increment := 1 negated ].
from < to ifTrue: [ increment := 1 ].
from to: to by: increment do: [ :i |
        d := (data at: 1) at: i.
        w := d indexOfCollection: str.
        w > 0 ifTrue: [ ^ i ].
    ].
 ^0!

within: col
    replace: str
    with: replaceItem
    startingAt: w
| n1 n2 |
n1 := col copyFrom: 1 to: (w - 1).
n2 := col copyFrom: (w + str size) to: col size.
 ^(n1 , replaceItem , n2).! !
```

6.16 CLASS PaField

Here is the code for **PaField** and related classes:

```
Field subclass: #PaField
    instanceVariableNames:
        'replyPane'
    classVariableNames: ''
    poolDictionaries: '' !

!PaField class methods ! !

!PaField methods !

boundingBox
```

```
        "Answer the frame that contains
        the field and its contents."
    ^offset extent: (width @ (font height + 3))!

edit
    | topPane aString |
    topPane := TopPane new.
    topPane model: self.
    topPane addSubpane:
        (replyPane := PaTextPane new
            model: self;
            name: #default;
            dispatcher:
                PaFieldEditor new;
            font: font).
    replyPane
        reframe: (self boundingBox);
        open;
        showWindow;
        selectAtCursor.
    replyPane dispatcher processInput.
    default := replyPane contents trimBlanks.
    replyPane
        refreshAll;
        selectAfter: 0@1;
        forceSelectionOntoDisplay;
        hideSelection;
        close.
    Dependants removeKey: self ifAbsent: [].
    self update.
    ^default!

replyPane
        "Answer the value of replyPane."
    ^replyPane! !

FieldEditor subclass: #PaFieldEditor
    instanceVariableNames:
        'model'
    classVariableNames: ''
    poolDictionaries:
        'FunctionKeys CharacterConstants' !

!PaFieldEditor class methods ! !

!PaFieldEditor methods !

doControlA
StopInput := true.
self accept.
```

```
"self model perform: #showAll."

model
    | sch |
sch := Scheduler dispatchers at: 1.
 ^(model := sch pane model).!

processControlKey: aCharacter
    aCharacter == $A asControl
        ifTrue: [^self doControlA].
    super processControlKey: aCharacter.! !
```

6.17 — FONT DESIGNER — CLASS FontDes

One of the reasons for this program is that the usual text processing tools do not support characters defined in software. I believe that any word processing program must have its own font editor. Suppose you wanted to sell your program in another, non-English-speaking country. You stand a greater chance of succeeding if the natives can use their own alphabet. Technical, chemical, mathematical and engineering texts require several different fonts anyway, regardless of the base language.

We need a special window with which to design fonts. The class behind it is **FontDes** (Fig. 6.5). Here is the beginning of it:

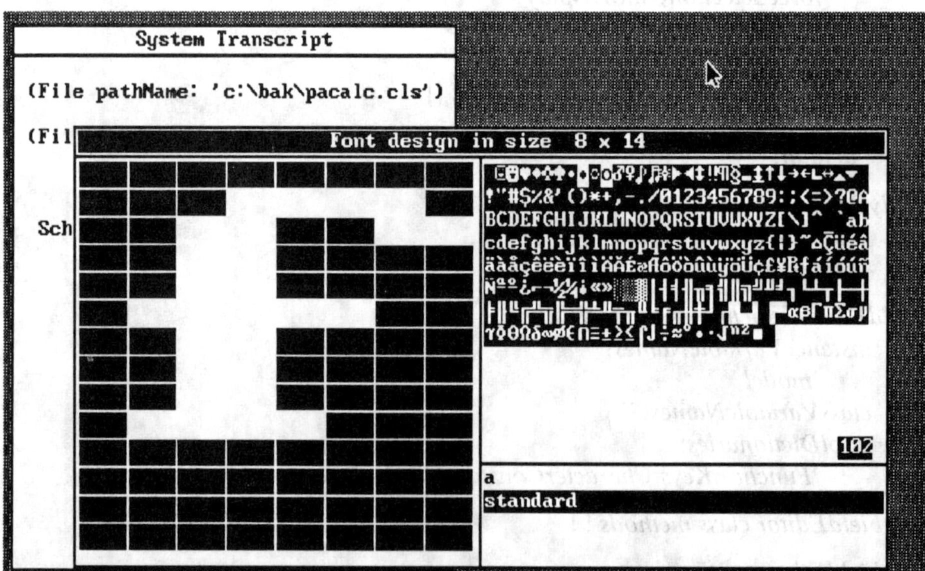

Fig. 6.5 — The **FontDes** window.

```
Object subclass: #FontDes
    instanceVariableNames:
        'ext bakExt maxNoOfChars chars rows
        pane2 form2 pane3 mat matCharNum label
        choiceOfFont blankGlyphs reverseTrue
        charForm char font oldChar pane charWidth
        charHeight pen form asciiCode xRect yRect
        point matrix oldGlyphs newGlyphs'
    classVariableNames:
        'CurrentFont'
    poolDictionaries:
        'CharacterConstants' !

!FontDes class methods !
activeFont
 ^CurrentFont!

currentFont
 ^CurrentFont! !!

!FontDes methods !
```

Let us see how the FontDes window is called into existence. By convention, we use two methods, **open** and **openOn:**. The former usually builds the window by calling the latter, supplying it with screen coordinates. In this case, these two methods are called **open3** and **openOn3:**. Here they are:

```
open3
self openOn3: (50 @ 70 corner:
    ((610 @ (Display boundingBox corner y - 10))))!
openOn3: aRectangle
        "Open a font designer window."
    | topPane hh |
    hh := 3/4.
    self initializeConstants.
    topPane := TopPane new
        model: self;
        minimumSize: 560 @ 270;
        label: label
        yourself.
    topPane addSubpane:
        (pane :=
        GraphPane new
            model: self;
            name: #initialize:;
            menu: #menu;
            framingRatio: (0 @ 0 corner: (1/2) @ 1 );
            change: #change:).
```

```
topPane addSubpane:
    (pane2 :=
    GraphPane new
        model: self;
        name: #initialize2:;
        menu: #menu;
        framingRatio: ((1/2) @ 0 corner: 1 @ hh );
        change: #change2:).
topPane addSubpane:
    (pane3 :=
    PaListPane new
        change: #change3:;
        model: self;
        name: #initialize3;
        menu: #menu3;
        returnIndex: true;
        framingRatio: ((1/2) @ hh corner: 1 @ 1 )).
topPane reframe: aRectangle.
topPane dispatcher openWindow; scheduleWindow!
```

This window has three subpanes. In pane **pane** we draw the character dot by dot. It takes the left vertical half of the FontDes window. The other two panes, **pane2** and **pane3**, contain characters and the corresponding font. The right vertical half is divided between them. The user must visit all three subpanes in order to edit existing or add new characters and fonts.

6.18 FontDes COMMANDS — END-USER INTERFACE

The first pane to visit is the lower right pane, represented by variable **pane3**. It is a PaListPane and contains font names. Pressing the left mouse button selects a font name and makes that font active. The active font is of overall significance, both in **FontDes** and in the complete BS application. Within **FontDes** itself, the selection of font in the lower right subpane automatically shows the complete font, all 255 characters, in the upper right subpane (**pane2**). In BS, the font that is selected in **pane3** becomes the base font for all new TextPanes. If you select Russian and then open the Pa window in order to create a completely new billings schedule, the characters will form the Russian alphabet. Selection of a font from the **FontDes** (Fig. 6.6) window is always the first step in installing BS. Most users do not need specific alphabets as such, but are interested in combinations, for instance, standard IBM character set with all the Greek letters. That is exactly what the menu in **pane3** enables. There are only three operations in it, as can be seen from the following method:

```
menu3
 ^ Menu
    labels: 'add blank font\delete font\copy font'
```

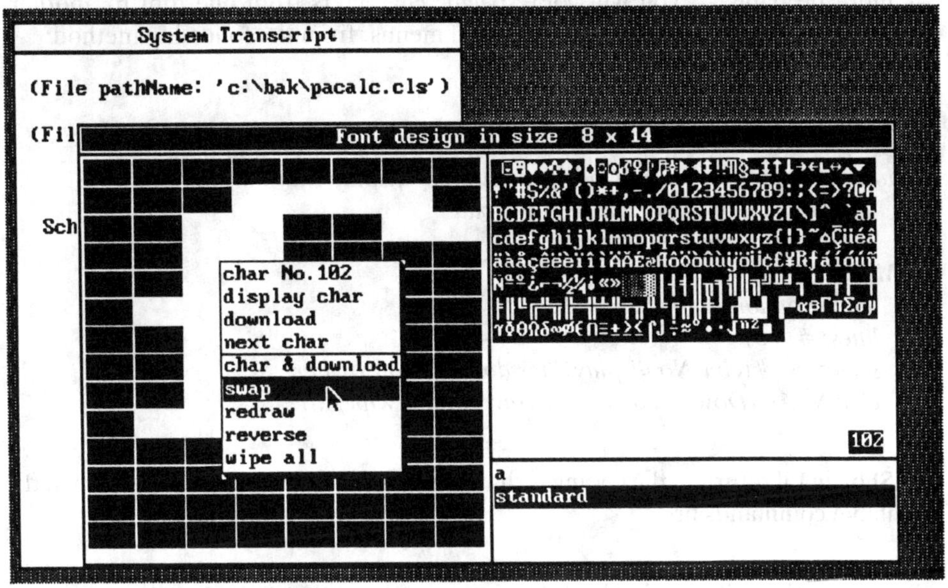

Fig. 6.6 — The main **FontDes** window.

withCrs
lines: #()
selectors: #(fontBlankAdd fontDelete fontCopy).!

You can add a new font, delete one of the existing fonts or copy the existing font into a new font. Adding a new font is actually blanking all the characters out. Then you can use the **pane** subpane to create all characters from scratch. This is not altogether meaningless. For example, the Greek font was created in that way because it contains only Greek letters, and there are not too many of them. The idea is to have one set of characters and to be able to blend them into another character set.

Deleting a font is a radical measure. **FontDes** won't allow you to delete some fonts, otherwise you would risk deleting all the fonts! This prohibitive measure had to be taken, as this version of FontDes does not support storing and reading fonts to and from disk. Those routines are not particularly difficult to write and you have all the tools in **FontDes** code. In other languages, dealing with fonts would be impossible without explicit disk routines, but Smalltalk/V swaps memory contents automatically anyway and I found no reason to try duplicating its effort. Of course, were this a program for true word processing, printer support or character design, those routines would have to exist.

Copying a font is by far the most practical font operation. It creates a whole new font (you supply only its name through a Prompter) and copies all characters from the selected font. Then you can select a character from the new font and redesign it or — more probably — you will copy specific characters from one font to another. Subpanes **pane** and **pane2** contain identical menus, from the following method:

```
menu
    | options |
options := 'char No.' , asciiCode printString, '\display char
    \download\next char\char & download
    \swap\redraw\reverse\wipe all'.
 ^ Menu
    labels: options withCrs
    lines: #(4 5)
    selectors: #(charNo displayChar download nextChar
    charNoAndDownload swap redraw reverse wipeAll).!
```

Shortly I'll return to the coding techniques in this method. Let us run through the available commands first:

char No. — the ASCII ordinal number of the character that we want to 'magnify' and edit in the **pane** subpane;
display char — display the character with the current ASCII number defined in the previous option;
download — you decide that the character design is finished and want to put it back into the font;
next char — make next ordinal ASCII number current — used for designing a series of characters;
char No & download — request the ASCII code to which the design from **pane** should be downloaded into the current font;
swap — swap two characters — you submit their ASCII numbers through two consecutive Prompters;
redraw — if the screen gets too cluttered you can use this command to recreate the character design in **pane**;
reverse — does to the design exactly what it says — every black pixel becomes white and vice versa;
wipe all — wipes the complete character design, allowing you to start the design anew.

The last three commands act only upon **pane**.

These operations are very flexible because the design in **pane** does not depend on the current font. So you can select one font, select one character within it, change font — eventually alter the character — and download it to the changed font. In practice, all this happens faster than can be described, especially with mouse.

The menus correspond to the right mouse button. Panes **pane** and **pane2** have identical menus (see method **openOn3:** above). However, they react differently when the left mouse button is pressed. In **pane**, which contains magnified pixels of a character, the left button just inverts the pixel. Change a pixel at a time and you change the overall character. Once again, this is much faster with the mouse.

In **pane2**, the left mouse button both selects the character and magnifies it in the left vertical subpane, **pane**. You just position the arrow cursor over a character that you want to edit and press the left button. It's the old 'point-and-shoot' idea in action. Whatever the method of character selection, its ASCII number shows in the lower right corner of the **pane2** subpane.

Unfortunately, all this is not enough to solve all the problems that might confront the end-user. The **FontDes** window links characters with the ASCII table, but has no influence over the way the keyboard is mapped into ASCII. The DOS system program KEYB.COM (with its many local variations) usually takes care of that translation. You'll have to dig into it in order to make life easier for your end-user.

And that is all the end-user can see — not much really — and this illustrates how writing a user manual could be much simpler for Smalltalk/V programs than for other languages. The documentation just describes the effects of mouse buttons, eventual menu options and — that's it!

Of course, how it achieves what it does is quite another story. Let us now look at the code.

6.19 MENUS

We have already seen the only two menu methods. The first, **menu3**, is quite straightforward. The second, **menu**, is not. There is one shortcoming and one example of finesse in it. The finesse is that all messages to **Menu** usually have the array of options text integrated within the message itself. In **menu**, I introduced a new local variable, called **options**. It contains the options text but also includes a changeable ASCII code. In this menu, you not only see invariable options, but you also see the ASCII number of the current character in **pane**. That number is in variable **asciiCode**, which has to be converted to a string to become a part of the first option's text. Therefore, the first line contains text

'char No.' , asciiCode printString,

The shortcoming mentioned is in the way the text of the **menu** method is hyphenated to fit into the book. Normally, all those four lines defining **options** would have to be just one line in Smalltalk/V TextPane.

Let us see how all these commands are implemented in **FontDes**.

6.20 CHARACTER COMMANDS

These are the commands from the **pane** and **pane2** pane menus. Some of the supporting methods are very easy to understand. They either use Prompters to ask for new data or call other methods in simple sequences. Their names closely correspond to options themselves. For example, method option **char No.** calls method **charNo**, and so on.

The following code won't work until you add method **glyphs:** to Font:

```
"Font" glyphs: aValue
glyphs := aValue
```

Here are further **FontDes** methods:

```
charNo
    | prompt |
    "Ordinal number of input character."
prompt := Prompter prompt: 'ASCII code?'
          defaultExpression: ''.
(prompt = nil)
    ifTrue: [ ^ self ].
asciiCode := prompt.!

charNoAndDownload
self charNo; download.!

charNoAndUpload
self charNo; displayChar.!

nextChar
asciiCode < 255
    ifTrue: [
        asciiCode := asciiCode + 1.
        self displayChar.
        ].!

swap
    " Swap two characters."
    | first second immediate |
first := Prompter
    prompt: 'Swap: ASCII No. of the first character ?'
    defaultExpression: ''.
(first = nil) ifTrue: [ ^ nil ].
(first between: 0 and: maxNoOfChars) ifFalse: [ ^nil ].
second := Prompter
    prompt: 'Swap: ASCII No. of the second character ?'
    defaultExpression: ''.
(second = nil) ifTrue: [ ^ nil ].
(second between: 0 and: maxNoOfChars) ifFalse: [ ^nil ].
CursorManager execute change.
asciiCode := first.
self displayChar.
asciiCode := 2.
self download.
asciiCode := second.
self displayChar.
```

```
asciiCode := first.
self download.
asciiCode := 2.
self displayChar.
asciiCode := second.
self download.
CursorManager normal change.!
```

swap is longer but its concept is simple. It uses the second character in the IBM ASCII table as an intermediate value. It is quite unlikely that this will cause some side-effect, as ASCII characters with ordinal numbers less than 32 are considered unprintable and are very rarely used.

The above methods rely mostly on two other methods, **download** and **displayChar.** Here is **displayChar:**

```
displayChar
    "Show asciiCode in Font Designer window."
    | aBit |
1 to: charWidth do: [ :i |
    1 to: charHeight do: [ :j |
        aBit := self
            valueAt: (asciiCode * charWidth + i - 1 @ (j - 1))
            form: font glyphs.
        (aBit = 0) ifTrue: [ matrix at: i at: j put: false ].
        (aBit = 1) ifTrue: [ matrix at: i at: j put: true ].
        ].
    ].
self displayOrdNum; redraw.!
```

For the first time we meet the underlying structure of **pane**. Variable **font** contains the current font and message **font glyphs** isolates the Form that contains the characters — the picture of all letters. Instance variable **glyphs** in class **Font** is a Form with all the characters already drawn in. A Form is just a matrix of pixels, and by copying those pixels to the screen, the letters are formed. We can think of the glyphs Form as of a very wide display made up of a series of character images. This imposes a logical structure to the otherwise continuous series of dots. The height of the glyphs Form is equal to the total height of each letter, and the width is computed as the product of the number of letters in the alphabet and the width of each letter. Character widths are normally constant but it is quite possible to create proportional letters. This would complicate horizontal measurements in TextPane windows and editors but is otherwise quite feasible in Smalltalk/V.

Each letter image occupies a certain Rectangle within the glyphs Form in the particular font. Since widths are constant, it suffices to perform the following calculation for horizontal offset:

```
asciiCode * charWidth - 1
```

where **asciiCode** is the ordinal number of the letter in the font and **charWidth** is actual character width. The *displayChar* method has to peek the character image one pixel at a time and transfer it visually into **pane**. So, the big question is: How does one peek a bit from a Form? Scanning the manual and delivered Font and Form classes yields no such method. However, by careful reading of the existing code it is possible to come up with a special method for that — the **valueAt:form:** method from class **FontDes** itself.

The manual does not explicitly state anything about the internal structure of Form representations and I wrote this method imitating the existing code for something else. However, it works. This was the most difficult part while writing **FontDes**.

```
valueAt: aPoint form: aForm
    | byteLoc aByte val |
        "Answer the bit at aPoint in the image (original) form."
    byteLoc := aPoint y * aForm byteWidth + (aPoint x // 8).
    aByte := aForm bitmap at: byteLoc + 1.
    val := (aByte bitAnd: (1 bitShift: 7 - (aPoint x \\ 8))).
    val = 0
      ifTrue: [^0]
      ifFalse: [^1]!
```

All in all, **displayChar** is merely a double loop that scans every part of a Rectangle surrounding the letter with a specific **asciiCode**. Variable **aBit** contains the logical value of the pixel at coordinate (*i*,*j*). To be more precise, **aBit** is either 0 or 1 but is always just one value. Since a character is represented by a matrix of pixels, it is quite natural to introduce a matrix to represent it within the program. Variable **matrix** keeps all bit values as true logical values, **false** and **true**, depending on the value of **aBit**. The last line in **displayChar** shows the ASCII value of the selected character (**displayOrdNum**) and draws it on the **pane** (method **redraw**).

```
download
    "Transfer matrix into active font."
    | aBit |
('standard' = self fontName)
    ifTrue: [ Menu message:
            'This font does not allow character downloading'.
            ^ self ].
('Russian' = self fontName)
    ifTrue: [ Menu message:
            'This font does not allow character downloading'.
            ^ self ].
('Greek' = self fontName)
    ifTrue: [ Menu message:
            'This font does not allow character downloading'.
            ^ self ].
```

```
('Cyrillic' = self fontName)
    ifTrue: [ Menu message:
        'This font does not allow character downloading'.
        ^ self ].
(asciiCode = nil)
    ifTrue: [ ^ self ].
newGlyphs := font glyphs.
1 to: charWidth do: [ :i |
    1 to: charHeight do: [ :j |
        (matrix at: i at: j) ifTrue: [ aBit := 1]
                              ifFalse:[ aBit := 0].
        newGlyphs at: ((asciiCode * charWidth) +
                (i - 1) @ (j - 1))
            put: aBit. ]. ].
font glyphs: newGlyphs.
self displayGlyphs2.!
```

Method **download** is the opposite of **displayChar**. First it refuses to alter standard Russian and Greek fonts and then uses the **at:put**: method from class **Form** to poke a pixel into a glyph called **newGlyphs**. **newGlyphs** is then assigned to the original **font**, which preserves font integrity. Finally, the complete font — and the changed letter within, of course — is displayed on **pane2** using method **displayGlyphs2**.

Other methods from the character menu are simple. **redraw** wipes the **pane** (**wipeForm**), displays its current state in **matrix** (**showBits**) and draws a coordinate maze (**drawMaze**) in order to simplify pixel poking with the mouse. Method **wipeAll** sets the complete **matrix** to black pixels (logical value **false**) and **redraws** it. Note the use of method **fill**: to set all **matrix** values at once — it is actually an **Array** method but is applicable to class **Matrix** through inheritance.

In method **reverse**, which puts black dots to white and vice versa, more or less the same effect had to be achieved with a direct **do**: loop.

```
redraw
self wipeForm;
    showBits;
    drawMaze.!

wipeAll
reverseTrue := true.
matrix fill: false.
self redraw.!

reverse
    " Reverse bits. "
1 to: matrix size do: [ :i | matrix at: i put: (matrix at: i) not ].
reverseTrue := reverseTrue not.
self redraw.!
```

6.21 DRAWING METHODS

The methods for drawing the enlarged character image are fairly low level. They are busy computing where the drawing pen should go. It was found that positioning points was much easier with the underlying grid. Methods **drawHorizontal:** and **drawVertical:** are obvious parts of method **drawMaze**, which simply embraces each of them with a loop.

```
drawHorizontal: y
    "Draw a horizontal at aPoint"
pen down.
reverseTrue ifTrue: [ pen white]
            ifFalse:[ pen black].
pen place: pane frame left @ y;
    goto: pane frame right @ y.!

drawVertical: x
    "Draw a vertical at x"
pen down.
reverseTrue ifTrue: [ pen white]
            ifFalse:[ pen black].
pen place: (x @ pane frame top);
    goto: (x @ pane frame bottom).!
drawMaze
    "Draw maze on the pane"
    | left right top bottom by c |
xRect := Array new: (charWidth + 1) .
yRect := Array new: (charHeight + 1).
left := pane frame left.
right := pane frame right.
by := right - left // charWidth.
c := 0.
left to: right by: by do: [ :x |
    c := c + 1.
    xRect at: c put: x.
    self drawVertical: x. ].
top := pane frame top.
bottom := pane frame bottom.
by := (bottom - top) abs // charHeight.
c := 0.
top to: bottom by: by do: [ :y |
    c := c + 1.
    yRect at: c put: y.
    self drawHorizontal: y].!
```

Once the grid is on the screen, the active points should be there too. Method **showBits** draws the complete **matrix**. Since the points that constitute the character image must be enlarged, variable **point** is declared as a Form. The defining Rectangle for such a **point** is computed in initialization routines and its coordinates are kept in arrays **xRect** and **yRect**. Local variable **rec** holds the current Rectangle and the **point** is painted white or black depending on the state of the corresponding **matrix** element. Finally, the current **point** is displayed with the usual **displayAt:** message.

```
showBits
    "Show complete matrix."
    | rec |
point := Form new
    width: ((xRect at: 2) - (xRect at: 3) + 1 ) abs
    height: ((yRect at: 2) - (yRect at: 3) + 1) abs.
1 to: (xRect size - 1) do: [ :i |
    1 to: (yRect size - 1 ) do: [ :j |
        rec := ((xRect at: i) @ (yRect at: j))
                    corner:
                ((xRect at: (i + 1)) @ (yRect at: (j + 1))).
        (matrix at: i at: j)
            ifTrue: [ point white ]
            ifFalse:[ point black ].
        point displayAt:
            ((1 + (xRect at: i)) @ (1 + (yRect at: j))).
        ].
    ].!
```

The rest of the methods in this group deal with the Form on which points are drawn. **refreshForm** and **showForm** merely help out the **wipeForm** method. Actually, a new Form, **form**, is created, painted white and drawn over the existing **pane** position.

```
refreshForm
form := Form new
    width: pane frame width
    height: pane frame height.
form white; displayAt: pane frame origin.!

showForm
formdisplayAt: pane frame origin.!

wipeForm
    self refreshForm.
    form white.
    self showForm.! !
```

6.22 FONT COMMANDS

These three methods directly correspond to options in method **menu3**. The fonts reside in global Smalltalk/V variable **ActiveFont**. It is a Dictionary, because it is by far the most convenient data structure for this purpose. There are two parallel arrays, one of strings (font names that the user sees in the **pane3** subpane), the other of Forms (glyphs), containing character images. **ActiveFont** has to be global because the data from the **FontDes** window must be shared with other windows (Pa, PaFreeDrawing and possibly others). Therefore, these three **menu3** options are nothing more than a communications link between the end-user and **ActiveFont**.

fontBlankAdd is a very straightforward piece of code, as is **fontDelete**. These are merely a couple of Prompters with some defensive code re standard font.

```
fontBlankAdd
    | prompt |
prompt := Prompter
    prompt: 'New font name ?'
    default: ''.
(prompt = 'standard')
    ifTrue: [ ^self ].
ActiveFont
    at: prompt
    put: self fontCreateBlank.!

fontDelete
    | fontName prompt |
fontName := self fontName.
(fontName = 'standard')
    ifTrue: [ ^ self ].
prompt := Prompter
    prompt: 'Confirm font deletion with YES ?'
    default: 'NO'.
(prompt = nil ) ifTrue: [ ^self ].
(prompt = 'standard')
    ifTrue: [ ^ self ].
(prompt = 'YES')
    ifTrue: [ ActiveFont removeKey: self fontName ].!

fontName
 ^ (ActiveFont keys asOrderedCollection)
    at: pane3 selection.!
```

fontCopy would also be simple if it didn't contain a new and very important message **copy:from:to:rule:** for copying a part of one Form to another. It first ensures that copying of the selected font is possible, then creates a new Form, **n**, with exactly the same proportions as the original font. Finally, it copies the first font into **n** and puts it into the **ActiveFont** dictionary.

```
fontCopy
    | prompt first second secondFont n m |
prompt := Prompter
    prompt: 'Copy to which font ?'
```

```
    default: ''.
(prompt = 'standard')
    ifTrue: [ ^self ].
(ActiveFont includesKey: prompt)
    ifFalse: [ ^self ].
first := self fontName.
second := prompt.
secondFont := (ActiveFont at: second).
n := Form new
    width: maxNoOfChars * charWidth
    height: charHeight; white.
m := (ActiveFont at: first) glyphs.
n copy: (0 @ 0 corner: m extent) from: m to: 0@0 rule: 1.
secondFont glyphs: n.
ActiveFont
    at: second
    put: secondFont.!
```

6.23 DISPLAYING THE FONT ON THE SCREEN

In this group of methods, message **copy:from:to:rule:** is our main tool because the current font is displayed on a GraphPane, **pane2**. The fact that **pane2** is a GraphPane forces us to do everything graphically, bit by bit if needed.

The first two methods are direct. **displayGlyphs2** only calls the **displayGlyphs2** method which does the real job. **displayOrdNum** puts the ASCII number of the enlarged character into the lower right corner of **pane2**.

```
displayGlyphs2
    "display current font on screen"
self displayGlyphs2: font glyphs.!

displayOrdNum
(asciiCode printPaddedTo: 3) displayAt:
    pane2 frame corner - (4 * charWidth @ 15).!
```



```
displayOrdNum
(asciiCode printPaddedTo: 3) displayAt:
    pane2 frame corner - (4 * charWidth @ 15).!
```


Here is the complete text of **displayGlyphs2:**. It is the heart of the **pane2** management.

```
displayGlyphs2: glyphs
    "display it on screen, all at once"
    | g h w g2 p |
    g := glyphs.
    w := charWidth. h := charHeight.
```

```
        chars := pane2 frame width // w - 1.
        rows := maxNoOfChars - 1 // chars + 1.
        1 to: rows do: [ :i |
            g2 := Form width: charWidth * chars height: g height.
            g2 copy: (((i - 1) * chars * w) @ 0 corner: g extent)
                                  from: g to: 0@0 rule: 1.
            g2 displayAt: (0 @ ((i - 1) * h + 2)
                                  + pane2 frame origin).
            ].
        mat := Matrix rows: rows columns: chars.
        matCharNum := Matrix rows: rows columns: chars.
        1 to: rows do: [ :i |
            1 to: chars do: [ :j |
                p := ((j - 1) * w
                          @
                     ((i - 1) * h + 2) + pane2 frame origin).
            mat at: i at: j
                put: (p extent: (charWidth @ charHeight)).
            matCharNum at: i at: j
                      put: ((i - 1) * chars + (j - 1)).
                ].
            ].
    self displayOrdNum.!
```

Let us now analyse this method piece by piece. The argument **g** is a glyph font, that is, a wide Form with character images in it. Variables **w** and **h** are dimensions of a single image within **g**. **chars** is the number of character images that will fit into the current width of **pane2**. **rows** counts how many rows will be needed for the complete character set. Pay attention to the coding:

```
rows := maxNoOfChars - 1 // chars + 1.
```

maxNoOfChars is constant (256 for a classical PC char set), defined in initialization routines. The above arithmetic expression is interpreted according to Smalltalk/V rules and the division operator // does *not* take precedence over addition or subtraction. For the PC character set this means a typical calculation like this:

256 − 1 = 255 // 45 = 5 + 1 = 6

that is, six rows if only, say, 45 characters fit into **pane2**. This manner of coding is quite common in Smalltalk/V. If you are in the least doubt, use parentheses!

Next comes a **do:** loop in which we first create a new Form **g2** wide enough to hold exactly one row of character images:

```
        g2 := Form width: charWidth * chars
                  height: g height.
```

The next statement copies input glyphs into **g2**:

```
g2 copy: (((i - 1) * chars * w) @ 0
        corner: g extent) from: g to: 0@0 rule: 1.
```

The first argument is a Rectangle — the amount which is to be copied into the receiver; argument for **from:** says from which Form to copy; argument for **to:** is the origin of the receiving Rectangle in the receiver; **rule:** defines the nature of interplay between the new and the old Rectangle.

Finally, **g2** is displayed:

```
g2 displayAt: (0 @ ((i - 1) * h + 2) +
        pane2 frame origin).
```

The product expression **((i − 1) ∗ h** + 2) lowers the next row.

The rest of the method serves only to save the coordinates of the displayed character images for later use. **mat** is a matrix of Rectangles which the images occupy while **matCharNum** is the ASCII number of the character. **mat** and **matCharNum** are again used in method **change2:**. (This method reacts when the left cursor button is activated in the **pane2** subpane.)

6.24 OTHER FONT COMMANDS

Other font commands use straightforward **Font** messages. The main message to create a new Font has a rather long name: **installFixedSize:charSize:startChar:endChar:basePoint:**. The only method that does not use it is **fontName**.

```
fontBlank
font := self fontCreateBlank.
ActiveFont at: 'blank' put: font.
self displayGlyphs2.!

fontCreateBlank
    blankGlyphs := Form new width: 256 * 8 height: 14; white.
    ^Font new
        installFixedSize: blankGlyphs
        charSize: (charWidth @ charHeight)
        startChar: 0
        endChar: 255
        basePoint: TextFont basePoint.!

fontCreateStandard
 ^Font new
        installFixedSize: SysFont glyphs
        charSize: (charWidth @ charHeight)
        startChar: 0
        endChar: 255
```

```
        basePoint: SysFont basePoint.!

fontStandard
font := self fontCreateStandard.
ActiveFont at: 'standard' put: font.
self displayGlyphs2.!

fontName
 ^ (ActiveFont keys asOrderedCollection)
     at: pane3 selection.!
```

6.25 INITIALIZATION

There are four initialization methods, one per subpane and one (**initializeConstants**) that initializes everything else. Methods that initialize GraphPanes must return a Form, a ListPane init method must return a collection of some kind while **initializeConstants** does not return anything, since it sets up the values of instance variables (global variables for the whole class).

```
initialize2: aPoint
form2 := Form new
      width: pane2 frame width
      height: pane2 frame height.
form2 white; displayAt: pane2 frame origin.
self displayGlyphs2.
 ^form2!

initialize3
 ^ActiveFont keys asOrderedCollection!

initialize: aRect
self initializeConstants.
form := Form new
      width: pane frame width
      height: pane frame height.
form white; displayAt: pane frame origin.
self showForm; drawMaze; wipeAll.
 ^form!
initializeConstants
      "ActiveFont := Dictionary new."
      maxNoOfChars := 256.
      charWidth := 8.
      charHeight := 14.
      label := ' Font design in size ',
            (charWidth printPaddedTo: 2) ,
            ' x ',
            (charHeight printPaddedTo: 2).
      pen := Pen new: Display.
```

```
    matrix := Matrix new: charWidth with: charHeight.
    matrix fill: reverseTrue. "true is white, false is black."
    reverseTrue := true.
    asciiCode := 33.
    newGlyphs := Form new width: maxNoOfChars * charWidth height:
                  charHeight; white.
    font := self fontCreateStandard.
    " ActiveFont := Dictionary new.
    ActiveFont at: 'standard' put: font. "
    CurrentFont := font.!
```

6.26 CHANGE COMMANDS

The last three methods represent changes in each subpane. As such, they are completely different.

The purpose of **change2:** is to discover over which character image the left mouse button was activated. The **change:** method in GraphPane receives a Point in which the button was pressed. So the question is how to discover the rectangle to which the Point belongs! There are several possible ways of finding out to which area a point belongs in a plane, but the **change2:** method I wrote uses the brute-force approach: first it memorizes (in **displayGlyphs2:**) the positions of rectangles, then checks each and every such position for the presence of the input Point. In reality, **change2:** first displays a white Form and draws a current set of characters. Then it loops over every character image (variable **rec**) and uses message **containsPoint:** to check for **aPoint**. If such a rectangle is found, the corresponding ASCII number goes into **asciiCode** and displays the enlarged character in **pane**. All in all, this is a fairly easy solution of a fairly difficult geometric problem. But don't try such solutions on slow computers!

```
change2: aPoint
    | rec code |
form2 white; displayAt: pane2 frame origin.
self displayGlyphs2: font glyphs.
    1 to: rows do: [ :i |
        1 to: chars do: [ :j |
            rec := mat at: i at: j. |
            (rec containsPoint: aPoint)
                ifTrue: [
                    code := matCharNum at: i at: j.
                    (code > 255)
                        ifTrue: [ ^ self ]
                        ifFalse:[ asciiCode := code.
                                ^self displayChar
                        ].
                ].
            ].
        ].!
```

Method **change3:** was very easy to write. Firstly all change methods for ListPanes must contain identical first two lines — the ones that use messages **changed:** and **restoreSelected:**. The rest usually does not exist, but in this case the last four lines merely set up instance variables and display character images in **pane2**.

```
change3: anInteger
pane3 changed: #initialize3;
    restoreSelected: anInteger.
font := ActiveFont at: self fontName.
CurrentFont := font.
choiceOfFont := self fontName.
self displayGlyphs2.!

change: aPoint
    | rec |
point := Form new "Take a typical rectangle."
    width: ((xRect at: 2) - (xRect at: 3) + 1 ) abs
    height: ((yRect at: 2) - (yRect at: 3) + 1) abs.
1 to: (xRect size - 1) do: [ :i |
    1 to: (yRect size - 1 ) do: [ :j |
        rec := ((xRect at: i) @ (yRect at: j))
            corner:
            ((xRect at: (i + 1)) @ (yRect at: (j + 1))).
        (rec containsPoint: aPoint)
            ifTrue: [
                (matrix at: i at: j)
                    ifTrue: [ matrix at: i at: j put: false.
                            point black.
                        ]
                    ifFalse:[ matrix at: i at: j put: true.
                            point white.
                        ].
                point displayAt:
                    ((1 + (xRect at: i)) @ (1 + (yRect at: j))). ].
        ].
    ].!
```

Method **change:** should reverse an enlarged pixel. One part of the problem is the same as in the **change2:** method — how to discover to which Rectangle the input parameter **aPoint** belongs. The solution is more or less the same as in the **change2:** method: organize two loops, find out the dimensions of the Rectangle that is an enlarged pixel (variable **rec** once again) and use **containsPoint:** to decide whether the aPoint is in or out. The only difference is that now variable **rec** does not receive its values from matrix **mat** but from two arrays of coordinates, **xRect** and **yRect**, that were previously computed in **drawMaze**. Finally, a point (variable **point**) in **pane** is a Form, either black or white. It suffices to send messages such as **point black** and **point white** to colour the form. Message **displayAt:** shows **point** on the screen.

```
change: aPoint
    | rec |
point := Form new "Create a typical rectangle."
    width: ((xRect at: 2) - (xRect at: 3) + 1 ) abs
    height: ((yRect at: 2) - (yRect at: 3) + 1) abs.
1 to: (xRect size - 1) do: [ :i |
    1 to: (yRect size - 1 ) do: [ :j |
        rec := ((xRect at: i) @ (yRect at: j))
            corner:
            ((xRect at: (i + 1)) @ (yRect at: (j + 1))).
        (rec containsPoint: aPoint)
            ifTrue: [
            ifTrue: [
                (matrix at: i at: j)
                    ifTrue: [ matrix at: i at: j put: false.
                              point black.
                    ]
                    ifFalse:[ matrix at: i at: j put: true.
                              point white.
                    ].
                point displayAt:
                ((1 + (xRect at: i)) (1 + (yRect at: j))). ]
        ].
    ].!
showAll: anInteger
    "Left mouse button pressed in some pane,
    show the complete row reversed."
pane3 changed: #initialize3;
    restoreSelected: anInteger.!
```

6.27 CONCLUSION AND ENHANCEMENTS FOR THE FONT DESIGNER WINDOW

This is a bare-bones font designer. One could easily express a desire for bells and whistles such as image rotation, slanting, translation, stronger printer support, easier keyboard redefinition, and so on. **FontDes** is wide open to changes; you have the code and it is up to you to implement your own enhancements.

6.28 CLASS PaStack — INTRODUCTION TO THE CALCULATOR WINDOW

PaStack is an internal data structure for the main subpane in window class **PaCalc**. More to the point, in **PaCalc** only one instance variable of type **PaStack** exists. I called it **paStack**. Class **PaCalc** handles the user interface (window, subpanes, etc.) and sends messages to **paStack**.

A note on inheritance: you do *not* have to use it! Earlier in this book a generic class *Stack* was introduced. It might be logical to incorporate all other stack types into it. Logical though it may be, I just didn't do it that way. Need I apologize, or rewrite already working code in class **PaStack**? No! This part of the book is about real-life programming with Smalltalk/V. First I wrote **PaStack** and months later pure **Stack** was developed. **PaStack** is made for BS; **Stack** is a textbook example. So I shall leave things as they are. The message to you is clear: oversights like this will continue to happen regardless of the language. There is no reason to feel guilty for 'not coding purely'.

PaStack begins just like all other classes.

```
Object subclass: #PaStack
    instanceVariableNames:
        'x y t lastX z radians '
    classVariableNames:
        'Y X T LastX Z '
    poolDictionaries: '' !

!PaStack class methods !

x
            "Answer the value of X."
        ^X! !
```

The original aim of this class was to export the result to **Pa**. Therefore, there is one class message, **x**, to do just that. Other class variables exist although they are not used. I give them only to illustrate how to transfer values of instance variables to class variables (see method **localsToGlobals**).

The essence of **PaStack** is maintaining a four-register stack. The registers contain only numbers, and sometimes act as a whole. That is, there are operations for each particular register and there are operations that affect the contents of all four registers at once. The registers are called x, y, z and t. We should think of them as four registers that are stacked one on top of the other. x is the lowest, y is above x, z is above y and t is above z. In the original RPN hand-held calculators, only the value in register x could be seen on the display. Therefore, most operations alter x. Actually, there is even a fifth register, called lastX. Its only function is to preserve the 'last' value of x. There are only four registers and the input value in x is often overriden by the final result. That is why the lastX register is also useful.

There is just one explicit operation on **lastX** — movement of its value to x. But as a side-effect, many operations automatically fill the x value into **lastX**.

A natural question to ask is why are there only four registers in the stack (and consequently in **PaStack**). Probably the first hand-held calculators could not contain more on the hardware level. And regardless of that, a four-register stack still serves its purpose to make numerical calculations easier. The method of 'making it easier' is radical, though. An RPN calculator (Fig. 6.7) calculates directly on the stack values, in the so-called Reverse Polish Notation (RPN, for short). It is a prefix notation. Instead of writing

$$2 + 3$$

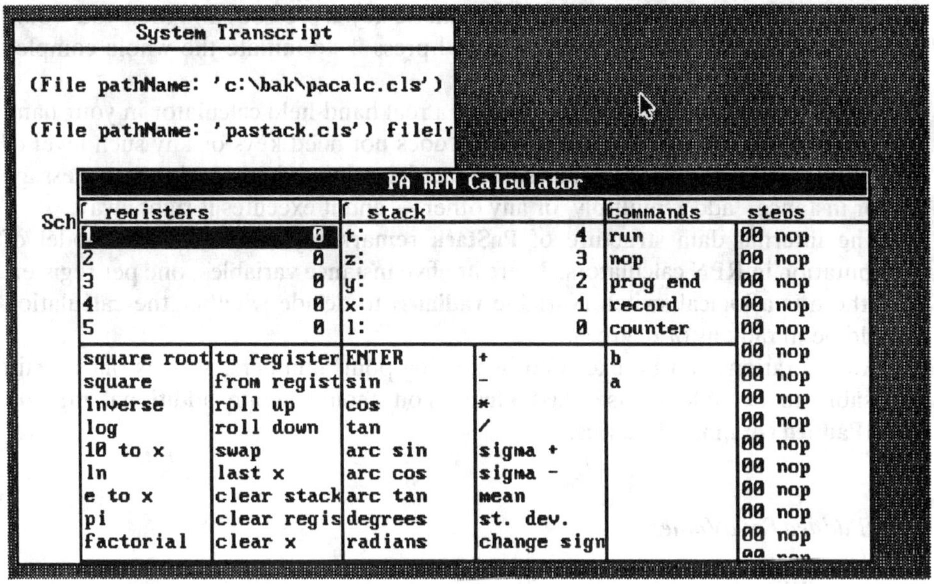

Fig. 6.7 — The RPN calculator.

which is called the infix notation because the adding operator is between the operands, in RPN one would write

+ 2 3

RPN is much better suited to computer logic. From left to right, it is quite easy to write a program that will scan the input string, recognize + for addition, and automatically know that the next two numbers are to be added. The operands (2 and 3 in this case) are deleted and the result, 5, is placed back instead of 2. Now we are only one step from the RPN stack: put 2 into x, 3 into y, devote a special key to addition and define the effect of that key as follows:

— take the number in x and add it to the number in y,
— delete both,
— place the result in x again.

Of course, there are side-effects. Addition affects lastX (which would have contained 2, the value of x before addition) and automatically rolls down the register contents. The values of x and y are destroyed, the value in z becomes the value of y, and the value of t becomes the value of z. The value of z remains unaltered.

How to initialize x and y? A special key, ENTER, solves the problem. Pressing ENTER puts the value of x into y and shifts the values in y and z to z and t respectively. The value in t is lost. So to put 3 into y you would first key 3 into x (that number is automatically shown when a numeric key is pressed) and then you would press ENTER. Then key in number 2 and press + to initiate the whole complex action described above.

So far I have talked in terms of having a real hand-held calculator in your hand and pressing the real keys. Class **PaStack** does not need keys or any such level of realism. It does not know how the user initiated the action; it is merely sent a message — for instance, 'add', 'multiply' or any other — and it executes it right away.

The internal data structure of **PaStack** remarkably resembles the model of computation in RPN calculators. There are five instance variables, one per register, and there is a logical switch (variable **radians**) to decide whether the calculation should be in radians or degrees.

All operations can be executed in floating-point numbers, so it is once again advisable to be able to use class **Float**. You should create additional method **printPaddedTo:** in it. Here it is:

```
printPaddedTo: aValue
    | s |
s := ReadWriteStream on: String new.
self printOn: s.
 ^ s contents!
```

With this method, the code in **PaStack** handles both integer and floating-point numbers in stack registers. It is precisely in cases like this that one comes to admire the idea of object-oriented programming!

There isn't much more to say about **PaStack**. It contains very straightforward code and the operations implemented are more or less the same as on the real calculator.

```
!PaStack methods !
abs
x := x abs.
lastX := x.!

add
x := x + y.
lastX := x.
self dropStack.!

arcCos
lastX := x.
radians
```

```
    ifTrue: [ x := x arcCos ]
    ifFalse:[ x := (x degreesToRadians arcCos) radiansToDegrees ].!

arcSin
lastX := x.
radians
    ifTrue: [ x := x arcSin ]
    ifFalse:[ x :=
        (x degreesToRadians arcSin) radiansToDegrees ].!

arcTan
lastX := x.
radians
    ifTrue: [ x := x arcTan ]
    ifFalse:[ x :=
        (x degreesToRadians arcTan) radiansToDegrees ].!

changeSign
x := x negated!

clearStack
x := 0.
y := 0.
z := 0.
t := 0.
lastX := 0.!

clearX
x := 0!

cos
lastX := x.
radians
    ifTrue: [ x := x cos ]
    ifFalse:[ x := (
        x degreesToRadians cos) radiansToDegrees ].!

degrees
radians := false!
divide
x = 0 ifTrue: [ ^ self ].
lastX := x.
x := y / x.
self dropStack.!

dropStack
y := z.
z := t.!

enter
t := z.
```

```
z := y.
y := x.!

eToX
x := 1 exp raisedTo: x.!
expX
lastX := x.
x := x exp!
factorial
x class = Float
    ifTrue: [ ^ self ].
lastX := x.
x := x factorial!

fromStack: aValue
aValue = 1 ifTrue: [^t].
aValue = 2 ifTrue: [^z].
aValue = 3 ifTrue: [^y].
aValue = 4 ifTrue: [^x].!

initialize
radians := true.
self clearStack.!

lastToX
x := lastX!
lastX

            "Answer the value of lastX."
    ^lastX!

ln
x > 0 ifFalse: [ ^ self ].
lastX := x.
x := x ln!

localsToGlobals
X := x.
Y := y.
Z := z.
T := t.
LastX := lastX.!

log
x > 0 ifFalse: [ ^ self ].
lastX := x.
x := x ln / 10 ln!

multiply
lastX := x.
x := x * y.
```

```
self dropStack.!

percent
lastX := x.
x := x * y / 100.
self dropStack.!

pi
x := Float pi!
radians
radians := true!

radians: aValue
        "Set the value of radians."
    radians := aValue!

reciprocal
x = 0 ifTrue: [ ^ self ].
lastX := x.
x := 1 / x!

rollDown
    | temp |
temp := x.
x := y.
y := z.
z := t.
t := temp.!

rollUp
    | temp |
temp := t.
t := z.
z := y.
y := x.
x := temp.!

sin
lastX := x.
radians
    ifTrue: [ x := x sin]
    ifFalse:[ x :=
            (x degreesToRadians sin) radiansToDegrees ].!

sqrtX
lastX := x.
x := x sqrt!

squaredX
lastX := x.
x := x * x!
```

```
subtract
lastX := x.
x := y − x.
self dropStack.

!swapXandY
    | temp |
temp := y.
y := x.
x := temp.!

t
 ^t!

t: aValue
t := aValue!

tan
lastX := x.
radians
    ifTrue: [ x := x tan ]
    ifFalse:[ x :=
            (x degreesToRadians tan) radiansToDegrees ].!

tenToX
x := 10 raisedTo: x.!

toDegrees
lastX := x.
x := x radiansToDegrees.
self degrees.!

toRadians
lastX := x.
x := x degreesToRadians.
self radians.!
toStack: aValue      | prompt |
aValue = 1 ifTrue: [prompt := self t].
aValue = 2 ifTrue: [prompt := self z].
aValue = 3 ifTrue: [prompt := self y].
aValue = 4 ifTrue: [prompt := self x].
 ^prompt!

toStack: aValue what: prompt
aValue = 1 ifTrue: [^t := prompt].
aValue = 2 ifTrue: [^z := prompt].
aValue = 3 ifTrue: [^y := prompt].
aValue = 4 ifTrue: [^x := prompt].!

x
 ^x!
```

```
x: aValue
x := aValue!

xRaisedToY
lastX := x.
x := x raisedTo: y.
self dropStack.!
y
 ^y!

y: aValue
y := aValue!

z
 ^z!
z: aValue
z := aValue! !
```

6.29 CLASS PaCalc — USER INTERFACE FOR THE RPN CALCULATOR

If you want the end-user to enjoy working with your program, be prepared to write long programs. **PaCalc** is about 780 lines long (not counting the code for **PaStack**). The thought of sitting down and writing 800 lines of program text is a bit daunting. But in Smalltalk/V it is really easier than in other languages. The **PaCalc** window consists of many subpanes, practically all of which are ListPanes. So after creating one such pane, I just copied the existing methods and cannibalized them into new subpanes. One of the things that I like about Smalltalk/V is that you don't really have to key in all those lines.

This is the last integral example in this book. **PaCalc** is a conglomerate of subpanes. For every subpane I just added new variables and methods. There are some forty-odd instance variables and more than 80 methods! But the internal scheme is recurrent, with just a couple of methods per subpane. In order to deal with that many identical subpanes I disciplined myself to begin all relevant methods with the same word. For example, the command subpane (the one with the commands in the calculators 'machine' language) has these methods: **commandPaneInit**, **commandPaneMenu**, **commandPaneShow**, **refreshCommand.** There are always two methods to correspond to mouse buttons, the third for the OrderedCollection which supplies the elements of the ListPane and the optional fourth methods is a 'refresh' method which updates the visual display of the ListPane.

The control subpane contains similar methods: **controlPaneInit**, **controlPaneMenu**, **controlPaneShow** and so on. Variable **controlPane** contains the control subpane and **commandPane** contains the command subpane. Actually, comprehending all this code is much easier than one could conclude from the sheer number of lines.

The **PaCalc** class definition is:

```
Object subclass: #PaCalc
    instanceVariableNames:
```

```
        'visible nop programEnd executing recordProgram
        programLength library libraryLength currentProgram
        libraryPane program programPane programCounter
        command commandPane dimension currentRegister
        noOption numWidth operations registers registerValues
        paStack stack keypad function shift control
        alternate topPane registerPane stackPane keyPane
        functionPane shiftPane controlPane alternatePane
        displayPane registerPaneName stackPaneName keyPaneName
        operationsPaneName'
    classVariableNames:
        'Ext Xvalue'
    poolDictionaries: '' !

!PaCalc class methods !

ext

 ^Ext!

libraryOfProgramsInitialize
LibraryOfPrograms = nil
    ifTrue: [ LibraryOfPrograms := Dictionary new.
              LibraryOfPrograms at: 'a' put: ''. ].!

xValue
^Xvalue! !
```

The class variables are **Xvalue** and **Ext**. Through **Xvalue** other windows can receive the result from **PaCalc**. **Ext** stands for file extension. It is not used as the program stands, but you can easily add the methods for I/O operations regarding source programs in **PaCalc** machine language.

Variable **LibraryOfPrograms** is not listed among class variables but its name begins with a capital. Ergo, it is a global Smalltalk/V variable! The idea was to offer a complete program in **Pa**, that is, to use **PaCalc** for developing a complete program and then to apply one such program whenever the input data in **Pa** were more complex than a simple number. This was not implemented in the final version of BS because I found a completely different way of offering the same functionality to the end-user.

The coding in method **libraryOfProgramsInitialize** is a usual way of saying: 'Make sure that it is a Dictionary but if it's not empty, leave it alone.'

6.30 OPENING AND INITIALIZATION METHODS

As usual, the **open** and **openOn:** methods come first:

```
open
self openOn: (50 @ 100 corner: 600 @ 340)!

openOn: aRectangle
```

```
| h s registerPaneHeight s2 s3 s4 s5 |
nop := '00 nop'.
programEnd := '99 end'.
executing := false.
recordProgram := false.
programLength := 100.
libraryLength := 10.
currentProgram := 1.
programCounter := 1.
noOption := 'nothing'.
numWidth := 6.
paStack := PaStack new.
paStack initialize.
paStack x: 1; y: 2; z: 3; t: 4.
dimension := 10.
registers := Array new: dimension.
registerValues:= Array new: dimension.
registerValues fill: 0.
currentRegister := 1.
s := 1/6.
s2 := 2 * s. s3 := 3 * s. s4 := 4 * s. s5 := 5 * s.
h := (1/15). "high end"
registerPaneHeight := 6 * h.
topPane := TopPane new.
topPane label: ' PA RPN Calculator';
        model: self.
topPane addSubpane:
     (registerPaneName := PaTextPane new
        model: self;
        name: #registerPaneNameInit; "initialize pane"
        framingRatio: (0 @ 0 corner: (s2) @ (h)) ).
topPane addSubpane:
   (stackPaneName := PaTextPane new
      model: self;
      name: #stackPaneNameInit; "initialize pane"
      framingRatio: (s2 @ 0 corner: (s4) @ (h)) ).
topPane addSubpane:
   (keyPaneName := PaTextPane new
      model: self;
      name: #keyPaneNameInit; "initialize pane"
      framingRatio: ((s4) @ 0 corner: (1) @ (h)) ).
topPane addSubpane:
     (registerPane := ListPane new
        change: #registerPaneShow:;
        menu: #registerPaneMenu;
        model: self;
        name: #registerPaneInit; "initialize pane"
```

```
            returnIndex: true; "specific to ListPanes"
            framingRatio: (0 @ h corner:
                        (s2) @ registerPaneHeight) ).
    topPane addSubpane:
      (stackPane := ListPane new
          change: #stackPaneShow:;
          menu: #stackPaneMenu;
          model: self;
          name: #stackPaneInit; "initialize pane"
          returnIndex: true; "specific to ListPanes"
          framingRatio: (s2 @ h corner:
                   (s4) @ registerPaneHeight ) ).
    topPane addSubpane:
        (commandPane := ListPane new
            change: #commandPaneShow:;
            menu: #commandPaneMenu;
            model: self;
            name: #commandPaneInit;
            returnIndex: true; "specific to ListPanes"
            framingRatio: (s4 @ h corner:
                      (s5 @ registerPaneHeight) )).
    topPane addSubpane:
        (libraryPane := ListPane new
             change: #libraryPaneShow:;
            menu: #libraryPaneMenu;
            model: self;
            name: #libraryPaneInit;
            returnIndex: true; "specific to ListPanes"
            framingRatio: (s4 @ registerPaneHeight corner:
                      (s5 @ 1) )).
    topPane addSubpane:
        (programPane := ListPane new
            change: #programPaneShow:;
            menu: #programPaneMenu;
            model: self;
            name: #programPaneInit;
            returnIndex: true; "specific to ListPanes"
            framingRatio: (s5 @ h corner: (1 @ 1) )).
    topPane addSubpane:
        (functionPane := ListPane new
            change: #functionPaneShow:;
            menu: #functionPaneMenu;
            model: self;
            name: #functionPaneInit;
            returnIndex: true; "specific to ListPanes"
            framingRatio: (0 @ registerPaneHeight corner:
                      (s @ 1) )).
```

```
    topPane addSubpane:
        (shiftPane := ListPane new
            change: #shiftPaneShow:;
            menu: #shiftPaneMenu;
            model: self;
            name: #shiftPaneInit;
            returnIndex: true; "specific to ListPanes"
            framingRatio: (s @ registerPaneHeight corner:
                    s2 @ 1) ).
    topPane addSubpane:
        (controlPane := ListPane new
            change: #controlPaneShow:;
            menu: #controlPaneMenu;
            model: self;
            name: #controlPaneInit;
            returnIndex: true; "specific to ListPanes"
            framingRatio: (s2 @ registerPaneHeight corner:
                    s3 @ 1) ).
    topPane addSubpane:
        (alternatePane := ListPane new
            change: #alternatePaneShow:;
            menu: #alternatePaneMenu;
            model: self;
            name: #alternatePaneInit;
            returnIndex: true; "specific to ListPanes"
            framingRatio: (s3 @ registerPaneHeight corner:
                    s4 @ 1) ).
    topPane reframe: aRectangle.
    self initializeAll.
    topPane dispatcher openWindow; scheduleWindow!
```

The first part of **openOn:** contains a lot of initialization code. In the end, it calls **initializeAll** to complete it:

```
initializeAll
self class libraryOfProgramsInitialize.
program := Array new: programLength.
program fill: nop.
command := Array new: 5.
command at: 1 put: 'run '.
command at: 2 put: 'nop'.
command at: 3 put: 'prog end'.
command at: 4 put: 'record '.
command at: 5 put: 'counter'.
self refreshRegisters: currentRegister.!
```

The trouble with writing about initialization routines is that they tend to be exposed out front. You write, rewrite and polish them throughout the whole process of class development.

Variable **s** in **openOn:** is the column width. Then variables **s2** to **s5** define the relative positions of the columns within the window. Variable **h** is the base for the vertical height of certain panes.

6.31 TextPanes IN PaCalc

A cursory look into **openOn:** shows three PaTextPanes (**registerPaneName**, **stackPaneName**, and **keyPaneName**). The **change:** and **menu:** methods for them are turned into comments and do not play any part in this window. The only existing method per text pane is **name:**. Here they are:

```
registerPaneNameInit
 ^' registers '!

stackPaneNameInit
 ^' stack '!

keyPaneNameInit
 ^'commands steps'!
```

They just set up a string to label the column that is below the string. The last method, **keyPaneNameInit**, labels two columns at once, one for commands to the programming environment (**commands**), the other for program steps (**steps**), i.e. the program that the user writes.

These three panes merely decorate the **PaCalc** window.

6.32 INTERACTIVE CALCULATOR COMMANDS

There are four panes from which you command the stack calculator. Each contains exactly nine operations. An operation is executed by clicking on one of the items in those lists. For example, if you want to add the numbers in the x and y registers you just click on option + from one of the panes. If you want to change the sign of the number in x, click over 'change sign'.

The names of these subpanes stem from the keys on the PC keyboard. Since there are four sets of operations, I imagined they were assigned to the function keys and combinations of function keys with **Alt**, **Ctrl** and **Shift**. Most programs use these combinations. Unfortunately, I do not know how to test for combinations of **Alt** and **Shift** with function keys so these shortcuts are not really implemented. This calculator is primarily mouse based.

All subpanes have ordinal numbers assigned to them. This idea was an afterthought. I introduced them in order to be able to record programs and later to replay them.

The normal Smalltalk/V convention uses the right mouse button to invoke a menu and then select from it. There is a good side and a bad side to this. A menu is on the screen only when you call it (the good side) but that is exactly why it can't contain

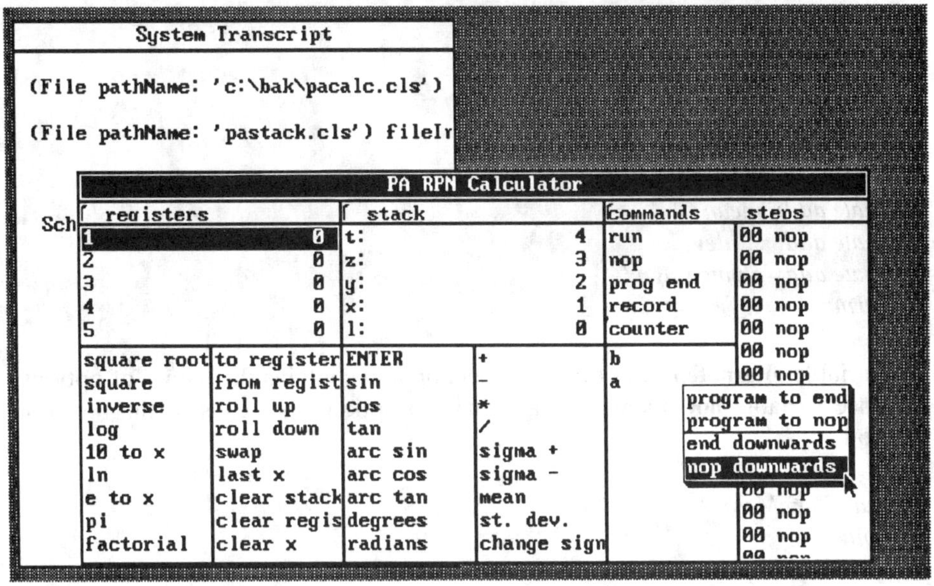

Fig. 6.8 — The RPN window — program menu.

more options than will fit on one screen height (that's the bad side). If you need more options, you can resort to more complicated forms of menus (there is a class for *hierarchical* menus in one of the Goodies packs), or you can invent something else. One such alternative solution is to have a constant screen-display of all available choices. It turns out that normal ListPanes fit the bill: an option is simply an item in the ListPane. As such, the menu options are always on the screen and it only remains to select one of them. It seemed more logical to select an item with the left mouse click. As far as programming is concerned, this means the method that you feed into the **change:** method while defining a subpane must interpret the option correctly and execute it immediately.

I coined special names for such methods. The method that corresponds to the left mouse button ends with **...PaneShow**. For example, if a subpane is called **alternate**, the action method will be **alternatePaneShow:**; for the subpane called **control**, the corresponding action method is **controlPaneShow:**, and so on. All methods with menus end with **...PaneMenu** (i.e. **alternatePaneMenu**), and all initializing methods end with **...PaneInit** (i.e. **alternatePaneInit**).

6.33 THE alternate SUBPANE

The **alternate** subpane contains arithmetic operation. Here are the options:

```
alternatePaneInit
alternate := OrderedCollection new.
alternate add: '+ '.
alternate add: '– '.
alternate add: '* '.
alternate add: '/ '.
alternate add: 'sigma + '.
alternate add: 'sigma – '.
alternate add: 'mean '.
alternate add: 'st. dev. '.
alternate add: 'change sign '.
 ^alternate!
```

Variable **alternate** is an OrderedCollection and contains the names of options. Instance variable **noOption** holds a string 'no option' and leads to the **nooption** method:

```
alternatePaneMenu
 ^Menu
    labels: noOption withCrs
    lines: #()
    selectors: #(nooption)!
```

The most important method is **alternatePaneShow:**. Its argument, **aValue**, is the ordinal number (between 1 and 9) of the calculator command that the user wants to execute. This method is simply a CASE statement in Pascal, but is coded here as a series of IFs because there is no explicit CASE in Smalltalk/V:

```
alternatePaneShow: aValue
( aValue between: 1 and: 9 ) ifFalse: [ ^self ].
CursorManager execute change.
self recordStep: (4 @ aValue).
aValue = 1 "+"
    ifTrue: [ paStack add ].
aValue = 2 "minus"
    ifTrue: [ paStack subtract ].
aValue = 3 "*"
    ifTrue: [ paStack multiply ].
aValue = 4 "/"
    ifTrue: [ paStack divide ].
aValue = 5 "sigma +"
    ifTrue: [ ^self sigmaPlus ].
aValue = 6 "sigma –"
    ifTrue: [ ^self sigmaMinus ].
aValue = 7 "arithmetic mean"
```

```
        ifTrue: [ ^self mean ].
aValue = 8 "standard deviation"
        ifTrue: [ ^self stDev ].
aValue = 9 "change sign"
        ifTrue: [ paStack changeSign ].
self refreshStack.
CursorManager normal change.!
```

The line

```
self recordStep: (4 @ aValue).
```

records the selected option. Number 4 is the code for this subpane and **aValue** is the selected option within it. Later, another routine will pick up these code pairs (Points), interpret them and achieve the effect of running a program in this window's machine language.

The message **refreshStack** updates the **stack** subpane (also a ListPane) and displays the changes on the stack. Some operations are more complex and that is why this and all other similar methods change the cursor shape while the operation is being executed.

The first four operations and the last (add, subtract, multiply, divide, change sign) are just messages to **paStack** (the instance variable for the **PaStack** class). The remaining four messages perform statistics on the data in the calculator's internal memory. These methods are explained together with other methods for the registers subpane.

6.34 THE shift SUBPANE

The commands in this subpane are related to memory and stack operations:

```
shiftPaneInit
shift := OrderedCollection new.
shift add: 'to register '.
shift add: 'from register '.
shift add: 'roll up '.
shift add: 'roll down '.
shift add: 'swap '.
shift add: 'last x '.
shift add: 'clear stack '.
shift add: 'clear registers '.
shift add: 'clear x '.
 ^shift!

shiftPaneMenu
 ^Menu
     labels: noOption withCrs
     lines: #()
```

```
selectors: #(nooption)!
```

The subpane number is 2. Several commands are messages directly to **paStack** (roll the stack up, roll it down, swap values in x and y, transfer the contents of lastX to x, clear the stack). The transfer of the x value to and from the selected memory location is in methods **xToRegisters** and **registersToX** (to be explained shortly).

```
shiftPaneShow: aValue | currentRegister |
( aValue between: 1 and: 9 ) ifFalse: [ ^self ].
CursorManager execute change.
self recordStep: (2 @ aValue).
aValue = 1 "from x to register"
   ifTrue: [ self xToRegisters ].
aValue = 2 "from register to x"
   ifTrue: [ self registersToX ].
aValue = 3 "roll the stack up"
   ifTrue: [ paStack rollUp ].
aValue = 4 "roll the stack down"
   ifTrue: [ paStack rollDown ].
aValue = 5 "swap x and y"
   ifTrue: [ paStack swapXandY ].
aValue = 6 "copy last x to x"
   ifTrue: [ paStack lastToX ].
aValue = 7 "clear stack"
   ifTrue: [ paStack clearStack ].
aValue = 8 "clear registers"
   ifTrue: [ self clearRegisters ].
aValue = 9 "clear x"
   ifTrue: [ paStack clearX ].
self refreshStack.
CursorManager normal change.!
```

6.35 THE control SUBPANE

In the conventional hand-held calculator, ENTER is the most important of all commands because it is the only way of sending the x register up the stack. (This implementation scores one better on that, allowing you to input all four register values directly.)

The rest of the **control** subpane concentrates on trigonometry. All messages are sent directly to **paStack**.

```
controlPaneInit
control := OrderedCollection new.
control add: 'ENTER '.
control add: 'sin '.
control add: 'cos '.
```

```
control add: 'tan '.
control add: 'arc sin '.
control add: 'arc cos '.
control add: 'arc tan '.
control add: 'degrees '.
control add: 'radians '.
 ^control!
controlPaneMenu
 ^Menu
     labels: noOption withCrs
     lines: #()
     selectors: #(nooption)!
controlPaneShow: aValue
( aValue between: 1 and: 9 ) ifFalse: [ ^self ].
CursorManager execute change.
self recordStep: (3 @ aValue).
aValue = 1 "ENTER"
     ifTrue: [ paStack enter ].
aValue = 2 "sin"
     ifTrue: [ paStack sin ].
aValue = 3 "cos "
     ifTrue: [ paStack cos ].
aValue = 4 "tan "
     ifTrue: [ paStack tan ].
aValue = 5 "arc sin "
     ifTrue: [ paStack arcSin ].
aValue = 6 "arc cos "
     ifTrue: [ paStack arcCos ].
aValue = 7 "arc tan "
     ifTrue: [ paStack arcTan ].
aValue = 8 "degrees "
     ifTrue: [ paStack degrees ].
aValue = 9 "radians "
     ifTrue: [ paStack radians ].
self refreshStack.
CursorManager normal change.
```

6.36 THE function SUBPANE

The **function** subpane has elementary mathematical functions. All of them are direct messages to **paStack**.

```
functionPaneInit
function := OrderedCollection new.
function add: 'square root '.
function add: 'square '.
```

```
function add: 'inverse '.
function add: 'log '.
function add: '10 to x '.
function add: 'ln '.
function add: 'e to x '.
function add: 'pi '.
function add: 'factorial '.
 ^function!

functionPaneMenu
 ^Menu
    labels: noOption withCrs
    lines: #()
    selectors: #(nooption)!
functionPaneShow: aValue
( aValue between: 1 and: 9 ) ifFalse: [ ^self ].
CursorManager execute change.
self recordStep: (1 @ aValue).
aValue = 1 "sqrt root"
    ifTrue: [ paStack sqrtX ].
aValue = 2 "square"
    ifTrue: [ paStack squaredX ].
aValue = 3 "inverse"
    ifTrue: [ paStack reciprocal ].
aValue = 4 "log"
    ifTrue: [ paStack log ].
aValue = 5
    ifTrue: [ paStack tenToX ].
aValue = 6
    ifTrue: [ paStack ln ].
aValue = 7
    ifTrue: [ paStack eToX ].
aValue = 8 "pi"
    ifTrue: [ paStack pi ].
aValue = 9 "factorial"
    ifTrue: [ paStack factorial ].
self refreshStack.
CursorManager normal change.
```

6.37 THE stack SUBPANE

The stack data have their internal representation in variable **paStack**. Since user communiuction is best handled through ListPanes, I introduced a ListPane-based representation of the four-register stack. Variable **stack** is an array of five elements (for stack and last x registers) and serves as an input collection to the ListPane.

```
stackPaneInit
```

```
    | s p1 p2 p3 p4 |
stack := Array new: 5.
p1 := paStack t.
s := self widen: 't:' with: (paStack t printPaddedTo: numWidth).
stack at: 1 put: s.
p2 := paStack z.
s := self widen: 'z:' with: (paStack z printPaddedTo: numWidth).
stack at: 2 put: s.
p3 := paStack y.
s := self widen: 'y:' with: (paStack y printPaddedTo: numWidth).
stack at: 3 put: s.
p4 := paStack x.
s := self widen: 'x:' with: (paStack x printPaddedTo: numWidth).
stack at: 4 put: s.
s := self widen: 'l:' with: (paStack lastX printPaddedTo: numWidth).
stack at: 5 put: s.
 ^stack!
stackPaneMenu
 ^Menu
    labels: noOption withCrs
    lines: #()
    selectors: #(nooption)!
```

The numerical data are in **paStack** and the corresponding strings are elements in **stack**. The conversion is best done through the **printPaddedTo:** message, but this would not be enough. Each item in the stack subpane is labelled with the appropriate register name. This means that the register value has to be on the right side of the stack subpane width. Method **widen:with:** widens the string (the first argument) with another string (the second argument). The widened string is assigned to the proper **stack** element and the ListPane shows it on the screen either automatically or when the **refreshStack** method is executed. Here are those auxiliary methods:

```
refreshStack
stackPane changed: #initPoints.
stackPane restoreSelected: 3.!
```

The third element in the pane is selected in order to always show the complete **stack** contents.

```
widen: s1 with: s2
    | w s f b |
f := SysFont width.
w := stackPane frame width.
s := w - (s1 size * f) - (s2 size * f).
b := ' '.
1 to: (s // (f + 1)) do: [ :i |
    b := b , ' '. ].
```

```
^s1 , b , s2!
```

The result of this method should be a string in which **s1** is on the extreme left and **s2** is on the extreme right edge of the pane width. The **widen:with:** method acts only on the **stackPane** width. First it computes the empty space width between input strings in points (**variable s**), then creates a new variable **b** with the appropriate number of blanks. Finally, it mixes **b** with input parameters, **s1** and **s2**.

The last method for **stack** pane allows direct setting of all four registers. It is enough to click with left mouse button on one of the registers and to answer its new value to the appearing Prompter.

The number assigned to this subpane is 0.

```
stackPaneShow: aValue | prompt |
(aValue between: 1 and: 4)
   ifFalse: [^ self ].
prompt := paStack fromStack: aValue.
prompt := Prompter prompt: 'Number ?'
      defaultExpression: (prompt printPaddedTo: numWidth).
prompt = nil ifTrue: [ ^ self ].
paStack toStack: aValue what: prompt.
self refreshStack;
      refreshCommand;
      recordStep: (0 @ aValue).!
```

6.38 THE registers SUBPANE

The data in this subpane are in numerical array **registerValues**. The string array which transmits them to the **registers** ListPane is **registers**. The method for widening the register's values is now **widen:with:forPane:** and is more general than **widen:-with:** itself. The number assigned to this subpane is 5.

```
registerPaneInit | s |
1 to: registers size do: [ :i |
      s := self widen: (i printPaddedTo: 0)
                  with: ((registerValues at: i) printPaddedTo: 0)
                  forPane: registerPane.
      registers at: i put: s. ].
 ^registers!

widen: s1 with: s2 forPane: pane
      | w s f b |
f := SysFont width.
w := pane frame width.
s := w − (s1 size * f) − (s2 size * f).
b := ''.
1 to: (s // (f + 1)) do: [ :i |
      b := b , ' '. ].
```

```
^s1 , b , s2!
registerPaneMenu
 ^Menu
     labels: noOption withCrs
     lines: #()
     selectors: #(nooption)!
refreshRegisters: aValue
registerPane changed: #initPoints.
registerPane restoreSelected: aValue.!

registerPaneShow: aValue
(aValue between: 1 and: registers size)
     ifFalse: [^ self ].
currentRegister := aValue.
self refreshRegisters: aValue;
     refreshCommand;
     recordStep: (5 @ aValue).!
```

currentRegister is the ordinal number of the selected "memory cell".

The relation between the stack and the registers is simple: you can transfer only the value in x to the selected memory location. (You select this location manually, by clicking on a ListPanc element in the **registers** subpane.) Method **xToRegisters** does this:

```
xToRegisters
registerValues at: currentRegister put: paStack x.
self refreshRegisters: currentRegister.! !
```

The inverse operation is to transfer from the selected register to x:

```
registersToX
paStack x: (registerValues at: currentRegister).
self refreshStack.!
```

Though there is no such option, you may consider adding these two methods for direct stack-to-memory correspondence:

```
recall: i
i between: 1 and: dimension
     ifTrue: [ registers at: i ]
     ifFalse:[ ^self ]!

store: i
i between: 1 and: dimension
     ifTrue: [ rregisters at: i put: paStack x.]
     ifFalse:[ ^self ]!
```

The simplest of the auxiliary methods for the **registers** subpane clears all registers, i.e. puts 0 into all memory locations and displays them:

```
clearRegisters
registerValues fill: 0.
self refreshRegisters: currentRegister.!
```

Methods **add:toRegister:** and **sub:toRegister:** take the current value of the selected register and add or subtract a number, y, in it:

```
add: y toRegister: i | s r |
r := registerValues at: i.
registerValues at: i put: (r + y).
s := self widen: (i printPaddedTo: 0)
            with: ((registerValues at: i) printPaddedTo: 0)
        forPane: registerPane.
registers at: i put: s.!

sub: y fromRegister: i | s |
registerValues at: i put: ((registerValues at: i) − y).
s := self widen: (i printPaddedTo: 0)
            with: ((registerValues at: i) printPaddedTo: 0)
        forPane: registerPane.
registers at: i put: s.!
```

These two methods form the basis of four complex arithmetic operations, symbolically denoted as **sigmaPlus**, **sigmaMinus**, **mean** and **stDev**. They are complex in the sense that they affect several registers at once, both from the stack and from the memory. **sigmaPlus** and **sigmaMinus** take the states of the x an y registers as input values, destroy them from the stack and display the ordinal number of the pair. These commands act on pairs of numbers — say, on points in a plane, or some otherwise measured data that are expressed as points.

sigmaPlus can be regarded as a kind of ENTER key for pairs of numbers. ENTER produces side-effects on the stack, while **sigmaPlus** alters not only the stack but specific registers as well. Exactly which registers are changed is an arbitrary decision and I chose the same ones as in a real hand-held RPN calculator. So the value of x is added to register No. 7, product x∗x goes to No. 6, x∗y to No. 5, y itself to No. 4 and 1 to No. 3. The new values are added to the previous states of those registers so after inputting a couple of pairs of numbers, register 7 contains their sum, and, for example, register 3 contains number 2 (there were just two pairs). Of course, all of this holds provided the corresponding registers were previously put to zero, perhaps by having previously executed the **clearRegisters** method.

```
sigmaPlus | x y x |
:= paStack x.
y := paStack y.
self add: x                          toRegister: 7.
```

```
self add: x squared                    toRegister: 6.
self add: (x * y)                      toRegister: 5.
self add: y                            toRegister: 4.
self add: 1                            toRegister: 3.
paStack x: (registerValues at: 3).
self refreshRegisters: currentRegister.
CursorManager normal change.!
```

sigmaMinus is identical in function to **sigmaPlus**, except that it subtracts from the current states in registers. This is useful for cancelling the mistakenly input pair of numbers from a previous **sigmaPlus**.

```
sigmaMinus | x y |
x := paStack x.
y := paStack y.
self sub: x                            fromRegister: 7.
self sub: x squared                    fromRegister: 6.
self sub: (x * y)                      fromRegister: 5.
self sub: y                            fromRegister: 4.
self sub: 1                            fromRegister: 3.
paStack x: (registerValues at: 3).
self refreshRegisters: currentRegister.
CursorManager normal change.!
```

Though **sigmaPlus** and **sigmaMinus** are best used for pairs, there is nothing to stop you from using them only on a series of numbers in x. There are specific operations for arrays of numbers. By far the most popular are computing the arithmetic mean and standard deviation of a series of numbers. You should key in those numbers and after each one execute **sigmaPlus**. Then you can execute methods **mean** and **stDev**, which expect their input data in certain registers. The **mean** uses registers 7 (the sum of x's) and 3 (the population size), while **stDev** needs values from other registers.

```
mean
paStack x: ((registerValues at: 7) / (registerValues at: 3)).
self refreshRegisters: currentRegister;
    refreshStack.
CursorManager normal change.!

stDev | r6 r7 r3 |
r6 := registerValues at: 6.
r7 := registerValues at: 7.
r3 := registerValues at: 3.
paStack x: ((r6
    - (r7 squared / r3))
    / (r3 - 1) ) sqrt .
self refreshRegisters: currentRegister;
```

```
refreshStack.
CursorManager normal change.!
```

6.39 THE command SUBPANE

The remaining subpanes in **PaCalc** are devoted to programming. The 'programming' in this context is limited to recording the items the user has selected. There is no looping, and nothing akin to an IF or a GOTO. These are easy enough to add.

The three subpanes for programming are **command**, **program** and **library**. **command** is nothing more than a menu from which you run an existing program, record a new one, put special codes into the program and set the program counter. The implementation of this menu is as before, through a ListPane menu whose items are options activated by left clicks. The methods are:

```
commandPaneInit
 ^command!
commandPaneMenu
 ^Menu
     labels: noOption withCrs
     lines: #()
     selectors: #(nooption)!
commandPaneShow: aValue
( aValue between: 1 and: 5 ) ifFalse: [ ^self ].
CursorManager execute change.
aValue = 1 "run"
     ifTrue: [ self run ].
aValue = 2 "nop"
     ifTrue: [ self noOperation ].
"aValue = 3 ifTrue: [ self backStep ]. "
aValue = 3 "program end"
     ifTrue: [ self programEndIntoProgram ].
aValue = 4 "record program"
     ifTrue: [ self recordProgramMethod ].
aValue = 5 "ask for program counter value"
     ifTrue: [ self setProgramCounter].
self refreshCommand.
CursorManager normal change.!

refreshCommand
commandPane changed: #initPoints.
commandPane restoreSelected: 1.!

refreshCommand: aValue
commandPane changed: #initPoints.
commandPane restoreSelected: aValue.!
```

Though it is only fourth in the menu list, the option **record** has to be selected to enable ‘programming’. From that moment on, all the selections and input values become program instructions as well and are displayed in the **program** subpane. That item is a switch saying ’record NO’ when turned off and ’record YES’ when catching user choices is turned on. Therefore, this method only sets that string and the value of a boolean variable **recordProgram**.

```
recordProgramMethod
recordProgram
    ifTrue: [ recordProgram := false.
            command at: 4 put: 'record NO'.
        ]
    ifFalse:[ recordProgram := true.
            command at: 4 put: 'record YES'.
        ].!
```

In all execution spots a suitable message to **self**, **recordStep:** has been placed. It is always executed and it further depends on the state of **recordProgram** whether command will be kept as a program instruction or not.

An interesting design decision is how to represent ‘instructions’. I chose the simplest strategy — show the user the internal program codes with the names of the options. Such a code (parameter **aPoint**) has two values:

x — the number of the subpane to which the instruction belongs and
y — the number of the executed instruction within that subpane.

Variable **xy** is a concatenation of those two numbers.

programCounter is an instruction number.

program is a collection of strings which contain the instruction code and name. The rest of this method is a simple CASE to find out where to take the instruction name from.

```
recordStep: aPoint | x y stVal all xy r |
recordProgram
    ifTrue: [
        x := aPoint x. y := aPoint y.
"put step code as first two string values"
        xy := (x printPaddedTo: 0) , (y printPaddedTo: 0), ' '.
        programCounter := programCounter + 1.
        self showProgramCounter.
        (x == 0) "stack values"
            ifTrue: [
                stVal := paStack fromStack: y.
                all := xy , (stVal printPaddedTo: 0).
                program at: programCounter put: all.
                ].
        (x = 1) ifTrue: [
                program at: programCounter put: (xy , (function at: y))].
```

```
        (x = 2) ifTrue: [
                program at: programCounter put: (xy , (shift at: y))].
        (x = 3) ifTrue: [
                program at: programCounter put: (xy , (control at: y))].
        (x = 4) ifTrue: [
                program at: programCounter put: (xy , (alternate at: y))].
        (x = 5) ifTrue: [
                r := currentRegister printPaddedTo: 0.
                program at: programCounter put: (xy ", r")].
    ].
self refreshProgram: programCounter.!
```

The **run** method is just the opposite. It takes **program**, decodes it (that is why in **recordStep:** variable **xy** was needed), and executes the instruction. Variable **executing** is **true** if the program is being executed and is **false** otherwise.

```
run    | vertical horizontal p p1 p2 c s old |
    "Run a program"
executing := true.
recordProgram := false.
c := programCounter.
programCounter to: program size do: [ :i |
    self refreshCommand.
    p := (program at: i). p1 := (p at: 1). p2 := (p at: 2).
    p = programEnd
        ifTrue: [ ^executing := false]
        ifFalse:[
            p = nop
                ifTrue: [ ]
                ifFalse:[
                    programCounter := i.
                    self showProgramCounter.
                    vertical := p1 digitValue.
                    horizontal := p2 digitValue.
                        vertical = 0
                            ifTrue: [ self stackExecute: horizontal ].
                        vertical = 1
                            ifTrue: [ self functionPaneShow: horizontal ].
                        vertical = 2
                            ifTrue: [ self shiftPaneShow: horizontal ].
                        vertical = 3
                            ifTrue: [ self controlPaneShow: horizontal ].
                        vertical = 4
                            ifTrue: [ self alternatePaneShow: horizontal ].
                        vertical = 5
                            ifTrue: [ self registerPaneShow: horizontal.
                                s := program at: i.
```

```
                        old := s at: 1.
                        s replaceFrom: 1 to: 1 with: ' ' startingAt: 1.
                        currentRegister := s trimBlanks asInteger.
                        s at: 1 put: old.
                        ].
                  ].
            ].
   ].
executing := false.
programCounter := c.
self refreshProgram; refreshCommand.!
```

Here is the only new routine that **run** needs:

```
stackExecute: aValue | s old1 old2 |
executing
   ifTrue: [
                        s := program at: programCounter.
                        old1 := s at: 1. old2 := s at: 2.
                        s replaceFrom: 1 to: 2 with: ' ' startingAt: 1.
                        paStack toStack: aValue what: s trimBlanks
                          asInteger.
                        self refreshStack.
                        s at: 1 put: old1. s at: 2 put: old2.
                        ].!
```

The 'execution' puts back the value that was captured in the stack register. So **stackExecute:** deletes the first two characters from the instruction in the **program** array, and hands it over to the stack. In this way the user can interactively set a stack register to some (constant) value and that value will be once again set into that same register during the program replay.

The remaining three options are actually for the **program** subpane. They are putting the 'no operation' symbol into the program, putting the program end symbol into the program and setting the program counter. The first two methods, **noOperation** and **programEndIntoProgram**, are straightforward. The third, **setProgramCounter**, raises a Prompter to ask for a new program counter value. That is important because the option **run** will execute the program from the current **programCounter** value. You can have a series of small programs in one program array and you can execute them at will. This option is an interactive GOTO statement.

```
showProgramCounter
command at: 5 put: ('counter: ', (programCounter printPaddedTo: 0)).
self refreshCommand.!

showProgramCounter: aValue
command at: 5 put: ('counter: ', (aValue printPaddedTo: 0)).
self refreshCommand.!

noOperation
```

```
programCounter := programCounter + 1.
program at: programCounter put: nop.
self refreshProgram; refreshCommand.!

programEndIntoProgram
programCounter := programCounter + 1.
program at: programCounter put: programEnd.
self refreshProgram; refreshCommand.!
setProgramCounter | prompt |
prompt := Prompter prompt: 'Program counter?'
          default: programCounter printString.
(prompt = nil)
     ifTrue: [ ^ self ].
(prompt asInteger between: 0 and: programLength)
     ifFalse: [ ^ self ].
programCounter := prompt asInteger.
command at: 5 put: ('counter: ', prompt).
self refreshCommand.
programCounter > 1 ifTrue: [
        self refreshProgram: programCounter. ].!
```

6.40 THE program SUBPANE

This subpane contains the recorded program steps. A standard group of ListPane routines supports it. The only additions are four menu commands. They put the symbols for program end or no operation into the complete program (**programToEnd** and **programToNop**, respectively) or only to its part below the current **programCounter** position (methods **programToEndFromPointer** and **programToNopFromPointer**, respectively). Those operations can be used to set an initial state of the complete program or of its parts. It is certainly advisable to set **program** to **programEnd** symbols before recording a brand new program.

```
refreshProgram: aValue
programPane changed: #initPoints.
programPane restoreSelected: aValue.!

refreshProgram
programPane changed: #initPoints.
programPane restoreSelected: 1.!

programPaneInit
 ^program!

programPaneMenu
 ^Menu
    labels: 'all to end\all to nop\end downwards
             \nop downwards' withCrs
    lines: #(2)
```

```
    selectors: #(programToEnd programToNop
            programToEndFromPointer programToNopFromPointer )!

programPaneShow: aValue
programCounter := aValue.
self showProgramCounter: aValue.
self refreshProgram: aValue.!
programStepWipeout
program at: programCounter put: nop.
self refreshProgram: programCounter.!

programToEnd
program fill: programEnd.
programCounter := 1.
self refreshProgram; refreshCommand.!

programToEndFromPointer
programCounter to: program size do: [ :i |
    program at: i put: programEnd].
self refreshProgram: programCounter; refreshCommand.!

programToNop
program fill: nop.
programCounter := 1.
self refreshProgram; refreshCommand.!

programToNopFromPointer
programCounter to: program size do: [ :i |
    program at: i put:nop].
self refreshProgram: programCounter; refreshCommand.!
```

6.41 THE library SUBPANE

Finally, you will have many programs and you will need a means of performing certain operations on programs as a whole. I devoted yet another ListPane to this cause. It lists existing programs. You select an item in this pane and the source is displayed in the **program** subpane. Click on **run** and the selected program will be executed.

This would be another standard ListPane if it were not for its data structure. A ListPane must have a collection suitable for holding (string) values that we can see in the subpane. Normally, that collection is an instance variable in a class but here it is a Smalltalk/V global variable, **LibraryOfPrograms**, which is declared as a Dictionary. Otherwise, it is all the same code as in most other subpanes in **PaCalc**.

There are two menu commands: create a new program and delete the program. To create a new program you tell the program name to the Prompter (see method **libraryStoreProgram**), and it is even easier to delete a program: just select 'delete' from the menu and the selected program disappears (see method **libraryWipeoutProgram**).

```
libraryPaneInit
 ^LibraryOfPrograms keys asArray!

libraryPaneMenu
 ^Menu
     labels: 'new program\delete' withCrs
     lines: #()
     selectors: #(libraryStoreProgram libraryWipeoutProgram)!

libraryPaneShow: aValue | array |
currentProgram := aValue.
(currentProgram between: 1 and: LibraryOfPrograms keys size)
     ifFalse: [ ^ self ].
CursorManager execute change.
array := LibraryOfPrograms keys asArray.
program := LibraryOfPrograms at: (array at: aValue).
self refreshProgram.
CursorManager normal change.!

libraryStoreProgram | prompt newProgram |
prompt := Prompter prompt: 'New program ?'
            default: ''.
newProgram := Array new: programLength.
newProgram fill: "programEnd" nop.
LibraryOfPrograms at: prompt put: newProgram.
self refreshLibrary: currentProgram.
self refreshProgram.!

libraryWipeoutProgram | array |
currentProgram = nil ifTrue: [ ^ self ].
array := LibraryOfPrograms keys asArray.
LibraryOfPrograms removeKey: (array at: currentProgram).
(currentProgram between: 1 and: array size)
     ifTrue: [
          self refeshLibrary: (currentProgram - 1).
               ].
self refreshProgram!

refreshLibrary
libraryPane changed: #initPoints.
libraryPane restoreSelected: 1.!
refreshLibrary: aValue
libraryPane changed: #initPoints.
libraryPane restoreSelected: aValue.!
```

Finally, a window like **PaCalc** can be used for many other user-oriented tasks. I found it convenient to write another window with a series of ListPanes for printer and general program parameters. It is a window in its own right, so the user can see and change program constants whenever needed, regardless of the states in other windows, and regardless of the state of the application as a whole.

6.42 HELP SYSTEM — THE PaHelpWindow

All serious programs should have some kind of help system. It is a rather tedious job for the programmer but is one of those chores that significantly raises the chances of the product's success. In other languages you would have both to write the help text and to invent special windows, menus, keyboards, editors, and the like. Well, Smalltalk/V lets you have all that interface automatically, thanks to windows and TextPanes. All you really have to do is to write the help text. Since you will probably write the user manual using a computer as a matter of course, nothing stands in the way of including that file directly into the **PaHelpWindow** (Fig. 6.9). The code is

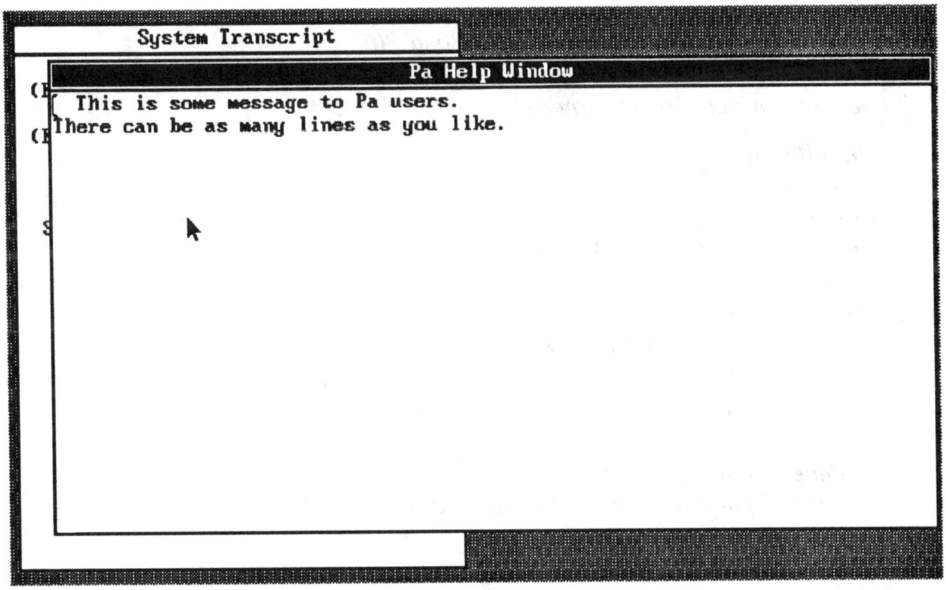

Fig. 6.9 — The **PaHelpWindow**.

simplicity itself. The new class has a **new** method, **open** and **openOn:** methods and — that's where you put the help text — in the **helpString** method. **openOn:** opens a text window, with just one subpane, of type **PaTextPane**. That's all there is to it, from the programming point of view!

Object subclass: #PaHelpWindow

```
    instanceVariableNames:
        'pane '
    classVariableNames: ''
    poolDictionaries: '' !

!PaHelpWindow class methods !

new
    ^super new open! !

!PaHelpWindow methods !

helpString
    | s |
s := ' This is some message to Pa users.
There can be as many lines as you like.
'.
 ^s!

open
    | origin corner |
origin := Display boundingBox origin + (30 @ 30).
corner := Display boundingBox corner - (2 @ 30).
self openOn: (origin corner: corner).!

openOn: aRectangle
    | topPane |
    topPane := TopPane new.
    topPane label: 'Pa Help Window';
        model: self.
    topPane addSubpane:
        (pane := PaTextPane new
            model: self;
            name: #helpString; "initialize pane"
            framingRatio: (0 @ 0 corner: (1) @ (1)) ).
    topPane reframe: aRectangle.
    topPane dispatcher openWindow scheduleWindow! !
```

Of course, the key to PaHelpWindow's operation is in an entirely different place — in class **PaTextPane**. It is a severely restricted version of a normal TextPane: the left and right mouse buttons do not function. In **openOn:**, the **menu:** and **change:** methods are left out and that is sufficient for this version of **PaHelpWindow**. Of course, you can always give menus to the user but you will, in all probability, also want to leave several options out. It does make sense to let the user search for a given word and it probably does not make sense to let the user write over help text. Or, you can completely leave out the usual TextPane options and replace them with the index of your help file. Or you may consider adding another subpane, of type ListPane, in which you will expose main help topics and then let the user click with the left mouse button on one of them and be transported immediately to that part of the text . . . .

Technically, to change the menu in **PaHelpWindow** you would have to visit classes **TextEditor** and **PaTextEditor** and change the initialization methods there.

Maybe you are so excited about all these possibilities for making life easier for your end-user that you are overlooking one important thing: thanks to Smalltalk/V we are immediately discussing the user interface.

6.43 CLASS PaPage — PRINTING Pa data

Methods in **PaPage** won't function until the following method is added to **Pane**:

```
font: aValue
curFont := aValue
```

Class **PaPage** exists only to print the **Pa** data. Method **print** from **Pa** starts printing:

```
print
    | paPage records |
paPage := PaPage new.
records := Array new: self size.
1 to: records size do: [ :i |
    records at: i put:
        ((paRecords at: 1), (paRecords at: 2),
        (paRecords at: 3), (paRecords at: 4))].
paPage rows: records;
        print.!
```

Here is the code for class **PaPage**. It is not long. Conceptually, it is page-oriented:

```
Object subclass: #PaPage
    instanceVariableNames:
        'rows printerStream recordCounter
        rowHeight rowWidth maxRows '
    classVariableNames: ''
    poolDictionaries:
        'CharacterConstants ' !

!PaPage class methods ! !

!PaPage methods !

createGraphicsLine
    | ro line li e |
recordCounter := recordCounter + 1.
ro := FontDes currentFont.
line := Form width: (ro charSize x * rowWidth)
                height: rowHeight.
recordCounter > maxRows
```

```
        ifTrue: [ ^ line white ].
li := rows at: recordCounter.
line black.
1 to: li size do: [ :i /
        e := li at: i.
        line copy: (e asciiValue * ro width @ 0
                                extent: (ro width @ ro height))
                        from: ro glyphs
                                to: ((i − 1) * (ro width) @ 0)
                        rule: 3 ].
recordCounter > maxRows
        ifTrue: [ line white. ]
        ifFalse:[ line reverse ].
  ^line!

print
CursorManager execute change.
recordCounter := 0.
maxRows := rows size.
printerStream := PrinterStream new.
rowHeight := 14. "in points"
rowWidth := 80. "in character widths"
[recordCounter > maxRows]
        whileFalse: [ self printPage ].
CursorManager normal change.!
printPage
        / halfPage line firstHalf hy ro /
"Generate first half of the page."
firstHalf := maxRows // 2.
ro := FontDes currentFont.
halfPage := Form new
        width: (ro charSize x * rowWidth)
        height: (firstHalf * rowHeight).
1 to: firstHalf do: [ :i /
        line := self createGraphicsLine.
        halfPage copy: line boundingBox
                from: line
                to: 0 @ ((i − 1) * rowHeight)
                rule: 3 ].
halfPage outputToPrinterUpright.
"Generate second half of the page."
halfPage white.
hy := 0.
firstHalf + 1 to: maxRows do: [ :iiii /
        line := self createGraphicsLine.
        hy := hy + 1.
        halfPage copy: line boundingBox
```

```
        from: line
        to: 0 @ ((hy - 1) * rowHeight) rule: 3.
    ].
halfPage outputToPrinterUpright.
printerStream nextPut: 12 asCharacter.!

rows: aValue
rows := aValue! !
```

The "main program" method is **print**. It sets values of all instance variables and treats the text as a series of pages. **recordCounter** is the current record printed, **maxRows** is the maximum number of rows to print, **rowHeight** is the character (font) height in points (pixels) while **rowWidth** is the number of characters per row. Please note that one measure is in pixels and the other is in characters. This difference does not seem to be significant.

The idea of **PaPage** is to print graphically. Instead of sending ASCII codes of letters to the printer and letting it decode what to print, **PaPage** directly prints character images in **CurrentFont**. It presupposes that the user has deliberately set the value of the active font using the lower right subpane of the **FontDes** window. It is convenient to build a narrow Form, wide enough to print across the page and keep character images of a line in it. There is a special method, **createGraphicsLine**, devoted to that task. There are two possible ways of printing this:

— print a line as soon as it is formed, or
— copy it properly into a bigger Form, that is, build a page in memory first and only then print it.

I prefer this latter approach because it facilitates mixing text and graphics. **printPage** implements it but in a convoluted manner. Memory requirements for a bit-image representation of a page exceed the 64K limit that the 80×86 family of processors imposes. So **printPage** prints two halves of a page. The message for printing is **outputToPrinterUpright** — that is all you need to print a Form! There is a similar message **outputToPrinter**, which prints in portrait mode.

The drawback of this two-part printing is that (at least on my dot-matrix printer) a small but visible white horizontal line is always left blank. It has something to do with the end of the printing a **Form** (see class **Form** for details).

After both halves are printed, the last line

```
printerStream nextPut: 12 asCharacter.
```

sends code 12 directly to the printer. That should unconditionally jump to the start of the next page. With a series of messages like this you can send any number of characters and/or printer codes to any printer.

Message **copy:from:to:rule:** is used for all large pixel movements from one Form to another. It also helps to create one particular line in method **createGraphicsLine**. Here is the crucial part:

```
1 to: li size do: [ :i |
    e := li at: i.
    line copy: (e asciiValue * ro width @ 0
                extent: (ro width @ ro height))
        from: ro glyphs
            to: ((i - 1) * (ro width) @ 0)
        rule: 3 ].
```

Variable **li** contains the row that is to be printed. **line** is the Form into which character images have to be placed. The above loop takes one character at a time (variable **e**), takes its ASCII value, and transfers it from the current **FontDes** font to the "one space to the right" in the Form that **line** is.

Instance variable **rows** is an array of rows to print. The calling sequence (for instance, from **print** in **Pa**) should prepare data so that **PaPage** gets an array of rows and nothing else. An even more flexible design would be to take out direct initialization of parameters from **print** and supply the client classes with methods to set them directly, from the outside. In that way **PaPage** can become a true post-processor for all other classes that need to print something in the current font.

6.44 FROM WINDOWS TO A FINISHED APPLICATION

Most users like to have a main program menu (Fig. 6.10), that calls all the windows that comprise the application. Of course, Smalltalk/V already has just such a menu, and you have used it all along. The question is: how to change it into a menu with your windows as options? The following story of three classes, **ScreenDispatcher**, **Dispatcher** and **DispatchManager**, is the inlikely answer. The relationships are:

— **ScreenDispatcher** hides the main program menu within its class method **initialize**,
— the place to invoke the main menu is in **Dispatcher'** method **processFunctionKey:**,
— the windows chain is actually a global variable **Scheduler**, the only instance of class **DispatchManager**.

This enables you to:

— change the text in the main menu,
— bypass the main menu and invoke any window you want by pressing one of the function keys,
— analyse existing windows and relate the new window in some way to them.

For instance, you can define the **F1** key to always invoke a help window. But if there already is one such window, you can decide not to create another window of the same kind, or you can create it but without overlapping with the existing windows of the same kind.

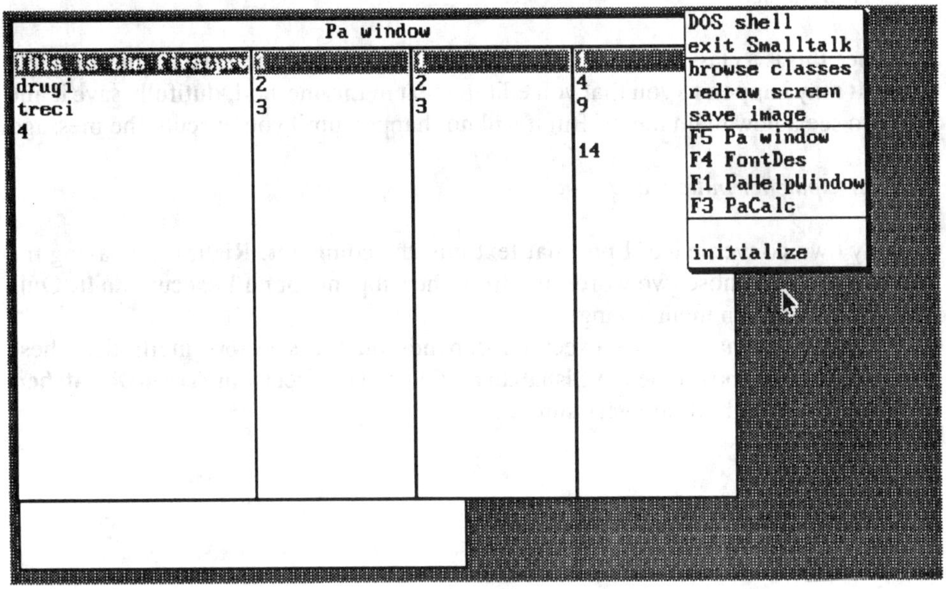

Fig. 6.10 — The main program menu.

There are minor hitches. From the user's standpoint, when the main menu is active, function keys (actually, all keys except those for menu manipulation) are inactive. As for the programmer, it will seem a bit strange to be forced to put all methods that directly correspond to options into one class higher (**Dispatcher**) than the class (**ScreenDispatcher**) that contains the menu from which options are executed. However, these are more curiosities than real obstacles.

Here is the code for the main menu — class method **initialize** in **ScreenDispatcher**:

```
initialize
    | aString sel |
        "Private - ScreenDispatcher initialize
        Initialize the system menu."
self setFontsToStandard.
aString := 'DOS shell\exit Smalltalk\browse classes
            \redraw screen\save image\F5 Pa window
            \F4 FontDes\F1 PaHelpWindow\F3 PaCalc
            \      \initialize' withCrs.
sel := #(dosMenu exit openClassBrowser redraw save
            openPa openFontDes openPaHelpWindow openPaCalc
            nothing schedulerInitialize ).
ScreenMenu := Menu
```

```
labels: aString
lines: #(2 5 9)
selectors: sel.!
```

Since this is a class method, it can be executed only as a message to the complete class. It may happen to you that you edit the text in this method, dutifully **save** it and hope to see a new main menu. But it will not happen until you execute the message

ScreenDispatcher initialize

For my own convenience, I put that text into the comment. Right after saving the method, I select those two words and from the subpane menu I execute **do it**. Only then does the main menu change.

Of course, what will be executed depends on the **selectors** methods. These methods are best positioned in **Dispatcher**, rather than directly in **ScreenDispatcher**. Usually, such methods are very simple:

```
openFontDes
FontDes new open3.!
openPa
Pa new open.!
openPaCalc
PaCalc new open.!
openPaFreeDrawing
PaFreeDrawing new open!
openPaHelpWindow
PaHelpWindow new open!
```

It goes without saying that all of these methods can be a great deal more complicated. For instance, they could ask existing windows for some information and then decide to appear in proper fashion on the screen. Or the new window has to ask for permission to appear at all!

Changing main menu options is easy. It is more complicated if you decide (as you always should, by the way) to give more capabilities to your end-user by activating the function keys. Which part of Smalltalk/V actually reads them? If you want the user to be able to activate the keys from any position regardless of the window situation, then the only choice is method **processFunctionKey:** directly in **Dispatcher**. Here is a variant of that method that will activate the windows as is denoted in the above **initialize** method of **ScreenDispatcher:**

```
processFunctionKey: aCharacter
        "Private – Process the keyboard function keys
        and mouse events represented by aCharacter."
    (MainMenuRequest == aCharacter)                "F7"
        ifTrue: [^ ScreenDispatcher  systemMenu
                    popUpAt: Cursor offset
                    for: Scheduler systemDispatcher].
```

```
(CreatePrintWindowFunction == aCharacter)        "F3"
    ifTrue: [ ^self openPaCalc ].
(DiskAccessRequest == aCharacter)                "F6"
    ifTrue: [ ^ Scheduler systemDispatcher
            openPaDiskBrowser].
(PrintParametersRequest == aCharacter)           "F8"
    ifTrue: [ ^ self printParameters ].
(CreateFontDesWindowFunction == aCharacter) "F4"
    ifTrue: [ ^self openFontDes].
(CreateHelpWindowFunction == aCharacter)         "F1"
    ifTrue: [ ^self openPaHelpWindow].
(CreateCalcWindowFunction == aCharacter)         "F5"
    ifTrue: [ ^self openPa].
aCharacter == SetLoc            ifTrue: [^self].
(Cursor cursorKey: aCharacter) isNil
    ifFalse: [^self].
aCharacter == SelectFunction
    ifTrue: [
        self select.
        ^self].
aCharacter == EndSelectFunction ifTrue: [^self].
aCharacter == CycleFunction ifTrue: [^self cycle].
aCharacter == PaneCycleFunction ifTrue: [^self cyclePane].

WindowMenuRequest == aCharacter
    ifTrue: [^pane topPane performMenu].
PaneMenuRequest == aCharacter
    ifTrue: [^pane performMenu].
ControlBreak == aCharacter
    ifTrue: [^self].
self doesNotHandle!
```

Only the first portion of the code is of interest here (the rest is standard Smalltalk/V). The comments on the right side denote the keys that will activate a particular-piece of code. The crucial question is how the link was made, and from where do names such as **CreatePrintWindowFunction**, **DiskAccessRequest**, and others come from. The solution is a dictionary pool called **FunctionKeys**. It is a dictionary, meaning that we can change it either directly or through some inspector or editor. Direct assignments are better and here they are:

```
"F1" FunctionKeys at: 'CreateHelpWindowFunction'
        put: 59 asCharacter.
"F5" FunctionKeys at: 'CreateCalcWindowFunction'
        put: 63 asCharacter.
"F3" FunctionKeys at: 'CreatePrintWindowFunction'
        put: 61 asCharacter.
"F4" FunctionKeys at: 'CreateFontDesWindowFunction'
```

```
        put: 62 asCharacter.
"F6" FunctionKeys at: 'DiskAccessRequest'
        put: 64 asCharacter.
"F7" FunctionKeys at: 'MainMenuRequest'
        put: 65 asCharacter.
"F8" FunctionKeys at: 'PrintParametersRequest'
        put: 66 asCharacter.
```

This series of statements must be executed at least once. **FunctionKeys** is a global Smalltalk/V variable and is persistent as such.

The above links the names that I have invented with scan codes for the PC keyboard. These codes are fixed, and regardless of the language, scan code 66 is for **F8** and 59 is for **F1**. In Smalltalk/V, it seems as if a symbolic name was given to a function key. For instance, according to the above statements, function key **F7** is called **MainMenuRequest**. In other words, pressing **F7** ought to, somehow, admin-

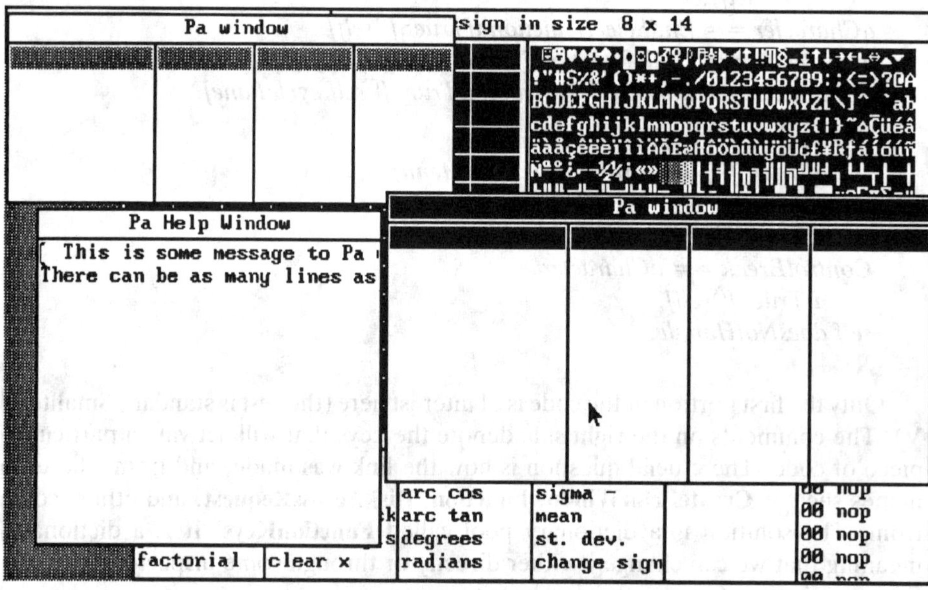

Fig. 6.11 — All windows for the Billings Schedule application.

ister the main menu. Once the key is recognized, it remains a purely technical matter of executing some code or calling a method. Indeed, keys **F3**, **F8**, **F4**, **F1** and **F5** create new windows by calling the methods that we have already seen. However, keys **F6** and **F7** are coded in an entirely different way. **F7**, the main menu request, should create the main menu. **ScreenDispatcher** contains variable **systemMenu**, which, of course, is a menu. But a menu has to be invoked, and that is done with the message **popUpAt:for:**. Now, the first argument for **popUpAt:for:** is easy to guess, since it is the physical position of the menu on screen. The second argument requires a dispatcher, preferably a dispatcher for the "whole screen". There is just one instance of **DispatchManager** in the system, the **Scheduler**. A look into **Dispatch-Manager** reveals that its dispatcher is **ScreenDispatcher** (in class variable **None**). Therefore, the argument of **for:** is **ScreenDispatcher** disguised as **Scheduler systemDispatcher**, as there is no other message in **Dispatcher** for that.

The code for **DiskAccessRequest**, **F6** function key, is

Scheduler systemDispatcher openPaDiskBrowser

which is a roundabout way of letting the **openPaDiskBrowser** method reside in **ScreenDispatcher** but be executed from the parent class, **Dispatcher**.

6.45 IDEAS FOR FURTHER USER INTERFACES

The messages to **Scheduler** let you learn what windows are active. You can even delete the active window (it is always the first in the **dispatchers** array) and set up another window, of different type or even of the same type with some changes. You might let your user change the interface completely by creating several windows that act upon the same global data but differ in menus, type of subpane and organization. Take menus, for example. They are a fairly good method of letting the user express a command to the system, but there are alternatives. Some users prefer icons over pop-menus that are Smalltalk/V's basic choice. Others may still prefer a fixed system of options in the window. Then there are pull-down menus and hierarchical menus, not to mention text input of commands... With the openness that the **Scheduler** gives you, by using a couple of OrderedCollection methods you can implement all these interfaces as different windows and leave it to the user to select the preferred choice. However, this is material for quite another book (that I will be happy to write if there is any interest).

PROBLEMS

6.1 Categorize your relationship with programming languages. What programming languages did you have to learn during your education? Have you ever learnt a language because it was part of an agreement with someone else? Is knowledge of a new language a precondition for what you want to do in the near future?

6.2 Discuss the term *automatically beautiful*. Write some Smalltalk/V code to emulate a standard user interface in some other commercial program of your liking. Would you prefer the Smalltalk/V graphical interface for all kinds of program? All kinds of machine? All kinds of user?

6.3 Does writing a couple of thousand lines of program frighten you? Would you rather use a program generator, a CASE tool or something entirely different instead of a programming language on its own?

6.4 Would you agree that the best feature of Smalltalk/V is its starting program design with the user interface? Does the prototyping approach work for you? Do you need Smalltalk/V in order to 'prototype first, program later'!?

6.5 Methods *doControl* in **PaListSelector** connect certain keyboard shortcuts with methods in **Pa**. Write the non-existing methods that are referenced in **PaListSelector**.

6.6 Add the missing options to the *duties* subpane menu in **Pa**.

6.7 Analyse method **asControl** and try to write **asAlternate**. Is there a need for a method such as **asShift**?

6.8 Analyse method **model** from **PaListSelector** and use it as a prototype for accessing the windows in **Scheduler**.

6.9 Class **Pa** treats subpanes as an array of panes. What are the merits of this style of coding?

6.10 **Pa** has four subpanes. How would you represent an additional three columns for quantity and price of human labour needed to develop a specific machine. Is opening another set of columns a meaningful alternative? How about treating both the text and the columnar data in a single PaListPane?

6.11 **Pa** and **PaRecords** make a great fuss of using an alien class, **PaField**, as their input device. Consider using a simple Prompter instead?

6.12 Invent a better syntax for search and replace operations. Try to imitate DOS rules (the usage of characters * and ?). Should the search and replace strings always be visible on the screen? If so, should they be part of a **Pa** window?

6.13 Consider variables **Scheduler** in Smalltalk/V as a whole, **paRecords in Pa**, **paStack** in **PaCalc**, and **field** in **PaRecords**. They are the only instances of some special class which does the main work for some other class. What are the benefits of this style of coding?

6.14 Smalltalk/V is easy to write programs with because it directs you to write one **open** method, one **openOn:** method, three further methods for user interface, and a host of auxiliary routines for these three methods. All of this has nothing to do with the object-orientedness of Smalltalk as such. Could the same approach to coding be equally beneficial to other languages?

6.15 Make a window for creation of Smalltalk/V windows.

6.16 Write the missing file operations in **Pa**. Use the existing methods from **PaRecords**.

6.17 Extend the main menu in **FontDes**. Add methods for the mathematical processing of character images. What are Bezier splines and how can you use them to represent letters?

6.18 Implement character sets longer than 256.

6.19 Implement non-proportional character sets.

6.20 Implement options that will take the character as its input and create bold and italic versions of the same letter.

6.21 Implement all these operations for fonts as a whole.

6.22 **FontDes** currently processes only one size of character. Change it to accept any character size.

6.23 Currently, you draw only by changing pixel by pixel. Implement more powerful commands, such as lines, arcs, rectangles, ...

6.24 What are the differences and similarities between **FontDes** and **BitEditor** classes?

6.25 On how many occasions have we found class **Matrix** of use in this book?

6.26 Write disk-based operations on fonts.

6.27 What are the differences between **PaStack** and **Stack**? Could they cooperate?

6.28 Admittedly, the interface for **PaCalc** was easy to write from the programmer's standpoint. Class **PaCalc** could look more like a true calculator. Implement such a window. You will have to omit ListPanes, except possibly for registers and the stack itself. You'll probably want a GraphPane with the various keys drawn: the numeric keys, the function keys, the programming keys, and so on. You can assign a single key to each operation or you can put several operations to a small number of keys and then switch their meanings with some special 'gold' and 'blue' system keys, for example.

6.29 After you've solved the previous problem, add a graph subpane to the calculator. It can graph the data, draw regression lines, etc. Invent new operations for that. Use the already existing code from this book.

6.30 Connect the numbers in the second and third subpanes of **Pa** with **PaCalc**. Enhance their menus with an option called 'program'.

6.31 Make accessing help data in **PaHelpWindow** easier. How about organizing an index? A table of contents?

6.32 Does it make sense to have several help windows on screen at once? Use knowledge about **Scheduler** to implement PaHelpWindows that will not overlap and that will not show the same part of the text.

6.33 Method **print** in **Pa** prepares for printing by converting four 'verticals' into an array of rows,where each row contains four elements. However, **PaPage** lacks the means of separating the rows of text. Introduce an instance variable **widths** to hold the number in which the rows should start. You can leave it to the user to set **widths** directly, or you can implement a clever scheme for columnar layout and printing.

6.34 Introduce class **FreeDrawing** into the main menu.

6.35 Enhance **PaPage** to incorporate drawings from **FreeDrawing** as headers and footers. This is made easy by the existence of the class variable **PictureDictionary** in **FreeDrawing**.

Index

ELLIS HORWOOD SERIES IN COMPUTERS AND THEIR APPLICATIONS

Series Editor: IAN CHIVERS, Senior Analyst, The Computer Centre, King's College, London, and formerly Senior Programmer and Analyst, Imperial College of Science and Technology, University of London

Narayanan, A. & Sharkey, N.E.	AN INTRODUCTION TO LISP
Parrington, N. & Roper, M.	UNDERSTANDING SOFTWARE TESTING
Paterson, A.	OFFICE SYSTEMS
Phillips, C. & Cornelius, B.J.	COMPUTATIONAL NUMERICAL METHODS
Rahtz, S.P.Q.	INFORMATION TECHNOLOGY IN THE HUMANITIES
Ramsden, E.	MICROCOMPUTERS IN EDUCATION 2
Rubin, T.	USER INTERFACE DESIGN FOR COMPUTER SYSTEMS
Rudd, A.S.	PRACTICAL USAGE OF ISPF DIALOG MANAGER
Rudd, A.S.	PRACTICAL USAGE OF REXX
Rudd, A.S.	IMPLEMENTING PRACTICAL DB2 APPLICATIONS
de Saram, H.	PROGRAMMING IN MICRO-PROLOG
Savic, D.	OBJECT-ORIENTED PROGRAMMING WITH SMALLTALK/V
Schirmer, C.	PROGRAMMING IN C FOR UNIX
Schofield, C.F.	OPTIMIZING FORTRAN PROGRAMS
Sharp, J.A.	DATA FLOW COMPUTING
Sherif, M.A.	DATABASE PROJECTS
Smith & Sage	EDUCATION AND THE INFORMATION SOCIETY
Smith, J.M & Stutely, R.	SGML
Späth, H.	CLUSTER ANALYSIS ALGORITHMS
Späth, H.	CLUSTER DISSECTION AND ANALYSIS
Stratford-Collins, P.	ADA
Teunissen, W.J. & van den Bos, J.	3D INTERACTIVE COMPUTER GRAPHICS
Tizzard, K.	C FOR PROFESSIONAL PROGRAMMERS
Turner, S.J.	AN INTRODUCTION TO COMPILER DESIGN
Tsuji, T.	OPTIMIZING SCHEMES FOR STRUCTURED PROGRAMMING LANGUAGE PROCESSORS
Wexler, J.	CONCURRENT PROGRAMMING IN OCCAM 2
Whiddett, R.J.	CONCURRENT PROGRAMMING FOR SOFTWARE ENGINEERS
Whiddett, R.J., Berry, R.E., Blair, G.S., Hurley, P.N., Nicol, P.J. & Muir, S.J.	UNIX
Xu, Duan-Zheng	COMPUTER ANALYSIS OF SEQUENTIAL MEDICAL TRIALS
Yannakoudakis, E.J. & Hutton, P.J.	SPEECH SYNTHESIS AND RECOGNITION SYSTEMS
Zech, R.	FORTH FOR THE PROFESSIONAL

Computer Communications and Networking

Currie, W.S.	LANS EXPLAINED
Deasington, R.J.	A PRACTICAL GUIDE TO COMPUTER COMMUNICATIONS AND NETWORKING, 2nd Edition
Deasington, R.J.	X.25 EXPLAINED, 2nd Edition
Henshall, J. & Shaw, S.	OSI EXPLAINED, 2nd Edition
Kauffels, F.-J.	PRACTICAL LANS ANALYSED
Kauffels, F.-J.	PRACTICAL NETWORKS ANALYSED
Kauffels, F.-J.	UNDERSTANDING DATA COMMUNICATIONS
Muftic, S.	SECURITY MECHANISMS FOR COMPUTER NETWORKS

